# Divine Economy

What has theology to do with economics? They are both sciences of human action but have traditionally been treated as very separate and isolated disciplines. *Divine Economy* is the first book to directly address the need for an active dialogue between the two.

D. Stephen Long traces three traditions in which attempts have been made to bring theology to bear on economic questions: the dominant twentieth-century tradition, which sought to give economics its independence through Weber's fact–value distinction; an emergent tradition based on the concept of liberation using a Marxist social analysis; and a residual tradition that draws on an ancient understanding of a functional economy. He concludes that the latter approach shows the greatest promise for a fruitful conversation between theology and economics because it refuses to subordinate or accommodate theological knowledge to autonomous socio-scientific research.

*Divine Economy* will be welcomed by all those with an interest in exploring how theology can inform economic debate.

**D. Stephen Long** is assistant professor of theology at Garrett-Evangelical Theological Seminary. He has previously published *Living the Discipline: United Methodist Theological Reflections on War, Civilization and Holiness* and *Tragedy, Tradition, Transformation: The Ethics of Paul Ramsey*.

**Radical Orthodoxy series**
Edited by John Milbank, Catherine Pickstock and
Graham Ward

Radical orthodoxy combines a sophisticated understanding of contemporary thought, modern and postmodern, with a theological perspective that looks back to the origins of the Church. It is the most talked-about development in contemporary theology.

**Radical Orthodoxy**
*John Milbank, Catherine Pickstock and Graham Ward*

**Divine Economy**
*D. Stephen Long*

**Cities of God**
*Graham Ward*

**Truth in Aquinas**
*John Milbank and Catherine Pickstock*

# Divine Economy

## Theology and the market

**D. Stephen Long**

Routledge
Taylor & Francis Group

LONDON AND NEW YORK

First published 2000 by Routledge
11 New Fetter Lane, London EC4P 4EE

Simultaneously published in the USA and Canada
by Routledge
29 West 35th Street, New York, NY 10001

Reprinted 2003

*Routledge is an imprint of the Taylor & Francis Group*

Typeset in Times by Taylor & Francis Books Ltd
Printed and bound in Great Britain by Biddles Ltd, Guildford and
King's Lynn

*British Library Cataloguing in Publication Data*
A catalogue record for this book is available from the British Library

*Library of Congress Cataloging in Publication Data*
A catalog record for this title has been requested

ISBN 0–415–22672–4 (hbk)
ISBN 0–415–22673–2 (pbk)

For Lindsey, Rebecca and Jonathan

# Contents

# Acknowledgments

The following work went with me through three institutional transitions. I began the research while working at Duke Divinity School, Duke University. The research transformed into writing while I worked for three years at St Joseph's University in Philadelphia. The work has come to completion at Garrett-Evangelical Theological Seminary in Evanston, Illinois. I owe a debt of gratitude to each of these institutions for their support of my family and me so that I could pursue this project. The project was conceived through many long runs with Stanley Hauerwas and Brett Webb Mitchell at Duke. I must thank them for the many conversations, and for letting me join 'the muddy runners club.' The work took shape in lectures and conversations at St Joseph's. I am particularly indebted to Paul Aspan, the chair of the theology department, and Nancy Fox, associate professor of economics at St Joseph's, and to the wonderful hospitality the Jesuits gave a Methodist theologian. They encouraged the project and allowed my teaching to be directly related to the research. Professor Fox and I team-taught a course that explored the differences between theology and economics. I learned a great deal from her and am grateful for her patient explanations to me of basic economic concepts.

Garrett-Evangelical welcomes new faculty by giving them a reduced teaching load during their first year. That reduced load meant I could complete this project in the midst of moving yet again across the United States and beginning a new teaching vocation. I am deeply grateful to Garrett for its excellent hospitality.

A number of people have read this manuscript, in part or entirely, and made significant contributions to it. Fritz Bauerschmidt, Dan Bell, Michael Budde, William T. Cavanaugh, Stanley Hauerwas, Kelly Johnson, David McCarthy, Rosemary Radford Ruether, and Linda Thomas gave me excellent criticism, most of which I have tried to incorporate within this final product. Of course, this is not intended to imply that they agree with everything that is present here: they do not, and for diverse reasons. Other persons were instrumental in helping me think through, in conversation, a number of the key issues. I owe a particular debt to the newly formed North

Shore Theology Society, with whose members I tried out several of these ideas – only to have to redo them. Thanks are due to Wes Avram, Michael Budde, David Cunningham, Mark MacIntosh and Kevin Vanhoozer. Michael Baxter, John Berkman, Julie Duncan, George Kalantzis, L. Edward Phillips, Philip Meadows and K. K. Yeo offered both intellectual advice and emotional support. I also wish to thank John Milbank, Catherine Pickstock, and Graham Ward for their support of this project.

Several parts of this manuscript appeared in an earlier form. The discussion of Bernard Dempsey's work had an earlier appearance in *Theological Studies* (1996), vol. 57, no. 4. My reading of Leo XIII and *Rerum Novarum* was presented in a series on *The Holy Family* published by St Joseph's Press. A briefer version of my interpretation of Alasdair MacIntyre appeared in the Villanova University journal *Peace and Justice*, vol. 9, no. 2. The discussion on law and virtue in Thomas was first published as "Christian Economy," in Nancey Murphy, Brad Kallenberger, and Mark Nation (eds) *Narrative, Virtue, and Practices*, © 1997 Trinity Press International. (reproduced by permission of Trinity Press International, Harrisburg, Pennsylvania). All those essays were early attempts to think through the larger project presented here.

My wife Ricka has been a constant source of support and joy. Her deep commitments to faith and economic justice persuaded me to leave the United States to work in a medical clinic in Honduras for one year before ever beginning my theological studies. There, in my work with her, a number of questions were raised, which I am only now beginning to answer. I am certain that in so far as those answers are adequate, their adequacy is due to the many gifts I have received – from all those named and from many others whom I simply cannot take the space to name. Of course, none of the above persons should be held culpable for the inadequacy of my attempts to formulate a faithful response to the question of how to relate theology and economics.

Finally, this book is dedicated to Ricka and my three children, Lindsey, Rebecca and Jonathan. Their daily care entrusted to us reminds us never to take lightly the issues explored in this text.

# Introduction

Let me begin with a confession. I am a theologian; I am no economist and I make no pretense to be one. In fact, when I became interested in the question of the relationship between theology and economics I structured my study of the discipline of economics according to a theological method. Christian theology can adequately be done only through the application of an historical method. It assumes an original revelation, given to the apostles, that we can designate, for want of a better description, 'the Christ event' (Karl Barth). This original event is given completely to and in history and then is diachronically passed on through its non-identical repetition in and through the church.

This does not assume that theology tries to uncover some original event 'behind' history through critical methods. It neither denies that the Word is present today; nor assumes that the past needs to be reconstructed to have access to the Word. It does privilege the apostolic witness, recognizing that the church produces this witness (although never through its own power alone), bears witness to it, and authorizes it. And thus theology is always situated in history, 'fleshing out' the apostolic witness, passing it on from generation to generation through hearing, speech, and practice. Such traditioning is no more passive than is tapping one's foot to a beautiful melody. As Barth put it, hearing itself is 'self-determination, act and decision.'[1] Theology critically assesses the historical performance of that passing on, but – and this is what makes theology so arduous and so suspect – all critical sources for evaluation will also be mediated through that historical performance itself. Theologians have no neutral, objective, and universal standpoint outside of the tradition from which to assess the performance of its transmission: we theologians are ourselves part of this performance.

For better or worse, when I began to study the relationship between theology and economics I applied these assumptions to the question under investigation. To try answering the question of how the disciplines of theology and economics are, and should, be related, I began by studying the economists' own original revolutionary event – Adam Smith – and then tracing the historical traditioning of that event through the philosophical liberals, the Anglican Christian political economists, the marginalist revolution, the Austrian school and the Keynesian revolution (forays into Marxism and socialist discourse were also necessary). I compared and contrasted these traditions of thought with the Christian tradition to identify the philosophical and theological narratives that rendered intelligible the discipline of economics.

As I talked with economists I was initially perplexed that many of them viewed such a procedure as suspect. Many appeared to treat the historical development of their own discipline as an irrelevance. In fact, few seemed to have read Smith's *The Wealth of Nations*, Ricardo's *The Principles of Political Economy*, or Malthus' influential *Essay on the Principle of Population*. It took some time to realize why my own interest in, and approach to, the study of this question is so markedly different from the economists'. Economists seem to be concerned with the facts present in the *now*. What occurred in the past is of mild interest: it is relevant to the extent that it helps us construct an ahistorical mathematical model appropriate to the present. The past is a storehouse of inert goods, usable only as we decide to appropriate them in the present. Perhaps my study on this topic has resulted in nothing more (or nothing less) than this observation. Economists do not envision their discipline as founded upon a dogmatic orthodoxy that must be preserved and developed by participating in an ongoing historical conversation; most theologians, at some level, do.

I now realize that my inability to 'get inside' economics as a discipline is in large part due to my self-conscious work as a theologian and my effort to maintain the priority of theology in assessing its relationship with economics. Such an effort restricts what I can accept of the dominant neo-classical economics because the priority of theology entails an acknowledgment of the significance of historical embeddedness – for itself, and for all the other disciplines. Like the rationality present in the incarnation and Christian redemption, economic rationality works not by abstracting from history but in and through its historical embodiment. The hypostatic union of the second person of the Trinity, wherein the divine and human natures constitute 'one person,' is the pattern by which creation itself is deemed reasonable from a Christian theological perspective. To have these two natures in one person is to find God in, not behind, the particularity of historical existence. To find God is, of course, from a theological perspective, to discover what *is* reasonable, what *is* true, good and beautiful. It is the end to which all other ends point. Because this end is entrusted to 'sacred doctrine,' theology has the task of evaluating the ends of all other discourses. That theology must evaluate the ends all other discourses serve cannot be maintained if economics is conceded a non-historical autonomous function. The concession of such a space renders economics impermeable by ends that are not intrinsic to its own autonomous method, an end such as 'utility.'

This is not to deny that theologians can derive a great deal of practical information from economists: we obviously can. But it is to deny that theologians can meet economists on their own methodological terms without sacrificing the content of theology, which is that the true end of creation is friendship with God.

When theologians sacrifice the priority of this end, either through the fact–value distinction or through a defense of the 'natural' that needs no theological coding and is thus self-evident, then too much is conceded to the economists' social science. Such concessions invariably result in abysmal theological pronouncements and the loss of theological content for the sake of a merely formal relevance. The pronouncements are 'abysmal' precisely because they lack historical embodiment. Theology becomes reduced to silence: its language is viewed as always radically inadequate, and therefore the ultimate word that can be said is nothing. God becomes the abyss that we cannot name rather than the splendor of luminosity through whom all things are seen and named.

Once God becomes the abyss the historical traditioning that makes Christianity what it is will be viewed merely as something to be overcome. A critical posture arises against all things historical, and this critical posture will be unable to offer any substantive critique of capitalism because it itself creates and relies upon such a culture. Not only will the market be liberated from any political or theological interference, but when theology itself adopts or accommodates this critical posture it liberates itself from its own history. Theology becomes reduced to a *meaningful evaluation* of facts, facts that bear little trace of a creation intelligible in terms of theology. A central theme of this book is that any theological acceptance of the fact–value, or is–ought, distinction will inevitably de-historicize and de-particularize theology, and render it to the margins of social, political, and economic discourse.

The fact–value distinction has become so determinative in the modern world that we seldom even recognize the many ways our politics, economics, even our theology assume and perpetuate this distinction. This distinction, however, did not occur because of some secular conspiracy against Christianity. It was produced within Christianity itself through the work of the theologians who created a two-tiered world where nature could be known without God. Such a self-evident nature gave rise to the modern fact–value distinction. It is now so embedded in our politics and economics that resistance to it can hardly even be recognized.

The facts presented by the television and the radio, by newspapers and on the Internet are assumed 'true,' or as 'true' as such facts can be, if they have been delivered by an appropriately objective method. This method resists beginning with any teleological understanding of what a good life is because such *values* are too wedded to particular histories to be of service in the construction of objective facts. Thus it is by prescinding from a premodern quest for a life that is good, true, and beautiful that the modern conception of 'fact' arises. Values can be discussed *after* the facts are presented. This form of rationality is being criticized from a number of diverse and conflicting sources. However, the socially formative power of a catholic or global market secures this fact–value distinction in ordinary everyday exchanges, such that these criticisms seem impotent to challenge the reality of living in a world where our 'values' have little relation to the 'facts.' This has arisen because all things can now be given a value and made subject to exchange. The *logoi* of formal equivalence and substitutability rule us. Let me give an example of how this occurs.

A popular textbook of introductory economics illustrates abstract equivalence and formal substitutability. First, 'opportunity costs' are explained: they are the costs incurred by someone for forsaking one choice in favor of another. Then a question is posed based on the following example: 'Mrs Harris spends an hour preparing a meal.' However, she is also a 'psychologist in private practice, and can obtain $50 per hour for her services.' Thus, we must ask: what are the opportunity costs involved in her preparing the family meal? This seems a harmless enough question. The situation is a nice way of explaining that for every action chosen, another opportunity is sacrificed. The *facts* seem incontestable. No matter what our *values* might be concerning family, work, religion, politics, etc., when Mrs. Harris makes dinner she foregoes the opportunity of generating $50.

But this description is misleading. While it appears to give us merely the facts, it gives us much more. It invites us to construe our lives, primarily our lives as family members, in terms of the activities of producers and consumers. The family meal loses all incommensurable status with other consumable objects. All such objects are placed before the individual and he or she is asked 'Which objects will you forego for the sake of the others? How long will you continue to exchange until you have sufficient $xs$ and adequate $ys$? How many $xs$ will you forego for the sake of how many $ys$?' The question assumes a form of rationality, known as 'marginalism,' that inevitably reduces all forms of life to 'utility' and 'interest.'

To pose the question this way assumes already the legitimacy of viewing all human action in terms of 'opportunity costs.' In fact, this putatively harmless example contains a complex metaphysics that assumes all human action and language takes place in a tragic world of scarcity. The ability to ask this question entails acquiescence to that metaphysics. Any action that I take will be inscribed in a world of lack wherein my choice is made possible only by the other options I choose against. Rather than viewing human action as arising out of a plenitude, this metaphysics assumes it is ensconced in scarcity. Death, violence, and antagonism become the source and end of such a metaphysics.

What could not be substituted into the calculation of opportunity costs? Let us suppose that Mrs Harris engages in sexual intercourse with her husband. And let us suppose that he could hire a prostitute at fifty percent of the opportunity costs incurred for the time they spend together. Although our *values* might be shocked by such a calculation, the economic *facts* are clear. It costs this couple $25 per hour for sexual intercourse. If he utilized the services of a prostitute and she worked the hour, the economic index of productivity would increase by $75.

These so-called *facts* are no more settled than the *values* one putatively chooses. For the principle of formal substitutability treats all human action as if it were a disconnected or isolated event. The fact of the matter is not that Mrs. Harris' husband saved the family $25 and increased productivity by $75. The fact is that he committed adultery and thus denied God's purposes for marriage. This *fact* has much more concrete or empirical reality than the putative economic facts mentioned. We can point to the concrete historical embodiment of something called 'adultery' much more readily than something called 'opportunity cost.' Yet in a social reality determined primarily by marginalist rationality, the latter is called a 'fact' and the former a 'value.'

My argument throughout this book seeks to move theology beyond the marginalist revolution and its understanding of rationality. I seek to do this by presenting and discussing the strengths and weaknesses of three 'traditions,' or twentieth-century strategies, that relate theology to economics. The three strategies I examine structure the three parts of this work – the dominant, emergent, and residual traditions. Each designation is intended to imply a relationship of theology to the marginalist rationality that orders, and arises from, modern political and economic formations. The dominant tradition is most consistent with marginalism. The emergent tradition is at odds with it, but still seems to maintain some of its vestiges. The residual tradition is in opposition to it.

The theological themes emphasized in the dominant tradition are most consistent with marginalism and the fact–value distinction. The theologians I will present as constituting this dominant tradition are not usually so placed together in a tradition. In fact, they are seldom allies on specific political and church policies: significant differences exist among Michael Novak, Max Stackhouse, Philip Wogaman, Dennis McCann, and Ronald Preston. I place them together in a tradition not because they give us similar public policies on economic matters, but because the theological themes they select to make theology relevant to economics are so similar. They also hold in common an inability to incorporate more specific confessional themes into their strategy to relate theology and economics. That these shared themes do not result in similar political and economic prescriptions interests me less than do the shared themes themselves. For I will argue that it is precisely in their formal and abstract nature that these theological themes do not give us a substantive alternative to marginalism.

The emergent tradition represents a break with the dominant tradition in its rejection of capitalism. 'Liberation' theology emerges out of the liberalism, or neo-liberalism, nascent in the dominant tradition. These liberation theologies represent an important protest against the dominant tradition in that they recover the voices of marginalized and oppressed peoples. James Cone recovers the witness of the black church. Gustavo

Gutiérrez and Jon Sobrino show us the significance of the poor and dispossessed in Latin America. Rosemary Radford Ruether draws upon the household and the corporate power of women as an alternative form of cultural and economic production. These theologians tell us that capitalism has been the source of pain and oppression, not liberation, for these peoples. They can point to the blood of martyrs to make their case. Their theology arises from the beauty of a severe holiness that eschews sentimental piety. However, the category of 'liberation' within which this theology is emerging also bears unmistakable continuities with the dominant tradition and the emancipatory discourses of modernity. Both seem to employ an *analogia libertatis* as the decisive site where God can be recognized. In human striving for freedom, we gain access to knowledge of God.

The third tradition is so *residual* within contemporary theology that a Jesuit economist and a philosopher have to be called upon to present it here. Alasdair MacIntyre's recovery of the tradition of virtue opens the space for this residual tradition. In some sense, this tradition is not a strategy to make theology relevant to economics. Instead, it shows how modern economic arrangements work against the cultivation of virtue. MacIntyre taps into a more ancient understanding of the economy, called the 'functional economy,' preserved primarily among Roman Catholics. Bernard Dempsey, a Jesuit economist, sought to maintain this more ancient understanding in the twentieth century. The Anglo-Catholic theologian, John Milbank, presents an explicitly theological development of both MacIntyre's recovery of virtue and a Catholic notion of economy, understood in terms of 'complex space.' His theology gives a central role to theological themes, which the dominant tradition incorporated into its strategy with difficulty – a central role for Christology and ecclesiology.

This work is fundamentally a comparison of theology with economics as theoretical disciplines. I do not deny that theory and practice are inseparable. Thus, I attempt to make references throughout to the concrete practices such theories assume and reproduce. Nevertheless, the fundamental question this work raises deals with the relationships between the discourses assumed and perpetuated by the modern discipline of economics and those present in contemporary theology. Because both subject matters are internally contested, such comparisons are exceedingly complex to make. Little agreement exists as to what constitutes theology, and how a good theology is to be discriminated from a poor one. Although economists seem more committed to basic principles than are theologians, the application of those principles does not find universal agreement among economists. When the disciplines themselves are internally fragmented, how can they be brought into conversation? The answer to that question can only be found in the doing of it. This book is offered as one way in which to begin a conversation without our options having to be *either* capitalist *or* socialist, *either* liberal *or* conservative. It asks what the *logos* of the incarnation has to do with the *logoi* that constitute modern economics.

# Part I

# The dominant tradition

Market values

# 1 Introduction to Part I

What has theology to do with the economy? Given the standpoint of the average economics textbook, the answer from the economists' perspective is obvious: nothing. Theology might have relevance for the cultural values that undergird the economic system, but actual economic practice is best served when theology keeps to its own proper sphere. Premodern theological efforts to speak a decisive word on economic practice are described by both economists and many theologians as misguided, irrational, and authoritarian.

What has the economy to do with theology? Despite the economists' neglect of theology, a number of theologians work on the relationship between theology and economics. In so doing, they have maintained the ancient tradition that faith and economic matters are inextricably linked. This is a considerable achievement because it works against the historical development of modern economics. As a discipline, economics has increasingly developed an anti-humanistic mode. Political economists first freed economics from theology at the end of the eighteenth century with Adam Smith's revolution. Economists then freed economics from political theory in the nineteenth century. In the twentieth century economics has become an increasingly abstract – mathematical – science. That theologians continue to make claims on it runs counter to long-standing trends. All of us who care about both faith and economics are in their debt because the gravest temptation we face is that the rending asunder between them will one day be complete. No one will remember to ask 'What has Jerusalem to do with Wall Street?' The ancient tradition will disappear.

The term 'tradition' is, as Raymond Williams noted, 'a particularly difficult word.'[1] Although it once designated 'surrender or betrayal' it now signifies the activity of passing something along in history. This is both active and passive.[2] Without the passivity of reception, nothing can be handed down. At the same time, once this knowledge is received it will inevitably reflect the situation of the inheritor. Thus tradition results from human activity, an intentional (and unintentional) shaping of received knowledge. And this can be 'radically selective.' Certain things will be emphasized and others neglected.[3]

In twentieth-century Christian theology, a number of theologians find doctrines of creation, anthropology and original sin as particularly relevant in relating theology and economics. Part I examines the work of five such theologians. They represent different ecclesial traditions and political positions. They would not agree on public policy questions. Nevertheless, despite their differences on a number of issues, they answer the question of how we are to relate theology to economics by selecting similar, if not identical, theological themes. I have identified this group of theologians as 'the dominant tradition.'

By 'dominant tradition,' is meant that human selection which 'seizes the ruling definition of the social.'[4] In other words, what counts as 'social' is self-referential. Members of those institutions, movements and formations that currently constitute the 'social' define it so that what counts as 'social' fits with those ruling definitions. Then, by definition, what doesn't fit cannot be social. It can have only the status of the sectarian, utopian, irrational, personal or private. Max Weber demonstrated that with the rise of capitalism theological forays into economics were increasingly viewed as irrational remainders that described those things for which the mathematical facts could not account.[5] If Weber was correct about the role of theology in the modern world then all theologians are reduced to the same status before the science of economics; we are all transgressors on the economists' terrain. Nevertheless, some theologians transgress that landscape less than do others.

The theologians examined in Part I, Michael Novak, Max Stackhouse, Dennis McCann, Ronald Preston, and Philip Wogaman, do not represent a decisive transgression against capitalist orthodoxy. They differ in their economic prescriptions – ranging from a defense of the classic liberal economy (Michael Novak) to Keynesian models of welfare capitalism (Preston and Wogaman) to somewhere in between (Stackhouse and McCann) – but the theological themes they select, and the economic prescriptions they offer, fitted well with ruling social–economic ideas in the late twentieth century. None of these theologians represents a position that could be characterized as radical, counter-cultural, or revolutionary. They may suggest important reforms of capitalism and capitalist institutions but, on the whole, their work fits comfortably with the dominance of global capitalism and the culture that makes it possible and is produced by it.

That their theological selections occur within a framework that seeks relevance to the public order is not surprising: they do not find that public order – democratic capitalism – a threat to Christian theology. Therefore they can easily pose the question: How can we construct a Christian social ethic that will 'bear on economic life in our increasingly global era?'[6] What is of interest is the theology that takes shape once this becomes the central question theology answers. Novak draws primarily on an anthropology that emphasizes liberty. Stackhouse and McCann emphasize the need for capitalism to remain grounded in a religious metaphysical moral foundation that stresses the freedom of the person to transcend his or her historical particularity. Ronald Preston draws upon the contributions of the social sciences and theology's need to be relevant to them. He likewise finds a theological entrance to the economists' landscape through an anthropology of liberty, as does Philip Wogaman.

Consistent with this anthropological focus is the strong dependence of all five theologians on the doctrine of original sin. All five find Reinhold Niebuhr's work to be the source for this understanding of the doctrine. However, they all neglect to note the similarity between Niebuhr's account of original sin and the Stoic doctrine of unintended consequences, which so deeply influenced Adam Smith's metaphysical moral vision. These theologians also develop a critical posture against the premodern theological tradition. Novak and Stackhouse work from a critical hermeneutics of suspicion that resonates well with Nietzsche's understanding that modern morality arises from resentment. For instance, Novak once stated that 'claims on the part of groups to represent "conscience," "morality," and "principle" must be exposed for what they are: disguises for naked power and raw interest.'[7] Stackhouse likewise conceives of an adversarial culture of elites that cloak their powerlessness behind outmoded moral and theological principles. Such suspicion is also directed against the Christian tradition itself. That one finds this critical suspicion present in something described as 'the dominant tradition' may at first seem surprising. To modern ears the term 'dominant tradition' conjures up images of hierarchy, authoritarianism, and dogmatism. How can a dominant tradition be based on critical suspicion rather than on the very thing I am arguing for – a dogmatic orthodoxy? The answer is found in the particular anthropological vision of liberty that holds the dominant tradition together. As the market itself had to be 'liberated' from outside interference, so an anthropology relevant to it must also be based on freedom from undue interference, a freedom that promotes critical suspicion. Critical suspicion represents little if any threat to a tradition formed by the culture that makes the global capitalist market possible; less still when we recognize that this critical suspicion is related to the work of Max Weber as developed by the theologians in this tradition.

Weber is central not only for the development of the social sciences on which the dominant tradition draws, but for the specific fact–value distinction by which this tradition makes theology relevant to economics. Weber provides the basic strategy to relate theology to economics. This is accomplished by accepting the fact–value distinction and by arguing that theology's role is to give the *facts* a meaningful critique through the *value* that theology offers.

Part I of this work examines this dominant tradition by developing the common theological themes that bind these theologians together. First I develop and consider critically their common strategy for relating theology to economics. Second I argue that the foundational theological theme they employ is an anthropology which assumes the human person is free to choose and through her or his choices gives value to things in the world. This does not deny the possibility of a metaphysical order to which those values must be subordinated, whether it is called natural law or common grace, but it does assume a metaphysical order that does not challenge the heart of this anthropology. In fact it is through this anthropology that we know God's work in the world; an *analogia libertatis* is at the heart of the dominant tradition's theology. This liberty is limited only by the constraints of original sin. Human freedom to intend the good does not guarantee the good because of the unintended consequences of our free human action. This anthropology of liberty does not aim toward a substantive good Christologically determined, but it functions best when in service to the *useful*. Third I show how the Weberian strategy and the dominance of the theological anthropology result in a subordination of Christology and ecclesiology to a doctrine of creation. It is this third point that renders the first two so problematic.

# 2    The Weberian strategy

## Theology's importance as value, ethos, or spirit

Michael Novak's inheritance from Weber is obvious from the titles of his books – *The Spirit of Democratic Capitalism* and *The Catholic Ethic and the Spirit of Capitalism*.[1] Although he critiques Weber for not recognizing that the Catholic rather than the Protestant ethic contributes to capitalism's possibility, he finds Weber's work indispensable for his identification of 'spirit' as the decisive element in understanding economics. Novak writes:

> What needs to be explained is not private ownership or the means of production, the existence of markets, and profit or accumulation.... What Weber set out to explain is something quite different.... To put it simply, Weber detected something new, a novel *Geist* or spirit or cultural inspiration, some new complex of social attitudes and habits.[2]

For Novak, this spirit is Catholicism, rightly understood. Weber's work allows theology to be relevant to economics because of the dialectical relationship between facts and values. The market is a semi-autonomous sphere that operates on the basis of its own facticity. However, it also operates within a cultural system that sustains it. Yet that cultural system is not produced by the market itself; the market needs cultural values that come from outside it. It needs the 'spirit' that Roman Catholic theology offers.[3]

Novak divides the democratic capitalist system into three distinct yet related systems. First is the market economy; second is political democracy; and third is the moral–cultural system that must be 'pluralistic and liberal.'[4] For Novak, these three systems work together. You cannot have one without the other. Both the political and economic system are 'nourished' by the cultural liberal–pluralist system. But how theology is supposed to contribute to the operation of these three systems is not clear: much of Novak's work argues that the church has failed to understand its own congruity with the cultural system. He emphasizes that congruity by locating it in the 'liberty' at the heart of Christian theology. The essence of the spirit of democratic capitalism is the creation of 'a non-coercive society as an arena of liberty within which individuals and peoples are called to realize through democratic methods the vocations to which they believe they are called.'[5] And although other cultural systems can provide this, Catholicism, rightly understood, *guarantees* it. Thus the central theological connection with economics is for Novak an *analogia libertatis*. But this analogy functions univocally. Where the spirit of liberty is, there is the Lord. Theology and economics are related through an analogous underlying liberty, a liberty capitalism requires and one that Catholic theology, rightly understood, can provide.

## I    Novak's Catholicism and capitalism, rightly understood

The key here is Catholicism *rightly understood*, for Novak acknowledges that the resistance to capitalism in some countries and cultures results from their Catholicism. Novak's argument that Catholicism is both necessary for, and a detriment to, capitalism can be confusing. His appeal to Catholicism is to a re-formed Catholicism similar to that which he extolled in an early work praising Vatican II, *The Open Church*. Novak is a reformer. His purpose is to develop a social ethic that can preserve liberty and human dignity. What makes his work controversial is that he finds capitalist institutions necessary for political liberty, and political liberty necessary for capitalist institutions. The role of the church and of theology must then, *a priori*, fit with that 'liberty.'

Catholicism, rightly understood, is consistent with the cultural system necessary for capitalism. But this cultural system is not merely the sum of individuals' intentions. Novak shares with Weber (along with Stoic philosophy, Adam Smith and Reinhold Niebuhr) a doctrine of unintended consequences.[6] For Novak this doctrine functions to show how a sound political economy will be concerned more with consequences than intentions and yet nevertheless produce the best form of political life.[7] A 'virtuous self-interest' results in a maximization of liberty.

Although the doctrine of unintended consequences is indebted to Weber, he used this doctrine in a way radically different from Novak's. For Weber, the virtues of abstinence and self-abnegation led to an 'iron cage': where 'the Puritan wanted to work in a calling; we are forced to do so.'[8] The unintended consequences for Weber were not increased liberty but constraint: 'More and more the material fate of the masses depends upon the steady and correct functioning of the increasingly bureaucratic organization of private capitalism. The idea of eliminating these organizations becomes more and more utopian.'[9] Novak does not refute Weber's charge. He does not challenge Weber's realism that finds capitalism inevitable despite human intentions. Novak agrees with Weber's unintended consequences. He notes: 'We are all capitalist now, even the pope. Both traditionalist and socialist methods have failed; for the whole world there is now only one form of economics.'[10] This statement seems homologous to Weber's iron cage, with one important difference: Novak denies that the all-encompassing power of the market is an iron cage resulting from bureaucratic rationality. Instead it is based on 'insight and practical wisdom,' and therefore he finds it liberating even though it is a spirit that arises despite substantive human intentions.[11] Yet Novak then suggests that the market economy, political democracy, and the moral–cultural system share 'one fundamental reality: choice.'[12] But if we are all now capitalists, even the Pope, despite our intentions, how can this be a matter of choice? I am not suggesting that Novak finds capitalism to be an inexorable historical necessity. His work argues that the political and cultural systems must preserve capitalism, for it cannot preserve itself. The contradiction in his strategy to relate theology to economics is the contradiction between a doctrine of unintended consequences and a morality of choice.

Novak's use of Weber, coupled with his strategy for theology's relevance, results in an irresolvable contradiction. On the one hand we are told that capitalism needs theology because of the anthropology it provides, where the person is free to act on the basis of his or her choices. And on the other hand we are told that we have no choice. We are all now capitalists. At this point in his argument, Novak's 'spirit' contradicts itself, and we discover that the 'new complex of social attitudes and habits' Weber identified cannot be so easily appropriated for theological purposes. If these attitudes arise from the unintended consequences of our actions, then they cannot be based on our moral capacity for free, intentional, human action unless that free, intentional, human action is purely formal. In other words, the spirit that is produced from our choices is not the freedom for any particular good: it is not a freedom for that which is beautiful, true and holy. Instead, it is the freedom itself, the formal ability to choose, that produces this spirit. This spirit is the human creature's ability to give 'value' to the world irrespective of any intrinsic beauty, goodness, or truth embodied in the objects chosen.

Novak does critique Weber for only acknowledging two systems – the cultural and the economic. Here he seeks to 'go beyond' Weber by connecting the two systems with a third – the system of political liberty. This is necessary because Weber failed to see that capitalism is destroyed when the state encroaches on the market.[13] Here Novak appeals to Joseph Schumpeter as someone who helps us go beyond Weber by acknowledging the need for political liberty.[14]

Novak reads Schumpeter as showing us that the success of capitalism 'in the political order and in the economic order undermine it in the cultural order.'[15] Schumpeter certainly acknowledged that the social institutions that undergird capitalism are constantly threatened by it and will eventually be undermined. But how Novak uses this argument does not fit well with Schumpeter's own use. For Novak, democratic capitalism is not a threat to itself. Instead, an adversarial class of elite moralists has claimed the high ground against the weaker and oppressed business class. (As we shall see, this idea of a business class oppressed by misguided theologians and moralists is also a common theme with Stackhouse and McCann for which they call theologians to repent.) Novak puts it this way:

> The relative weakness of the business class in the field of ideas and symbols as compared with the massive strength of the new class in precisely these areas has significantly altered the power relationship between the two elites. In the sphere of culture, to put it bluntly, the business elite has taken a beating.[16]

How has this oppression of the business class by the cultural elite occurred? Primarily through the latter's dominance as the 'communicators of culture.'[17]

## II   The adversarial elitist conspiracy: *ressentiment*

Novak never explains how this adversarial class of elitists has dominated communication networks. But the claim that it has needs explanation. Communication networks in the United States are inseparable from business – they *are* business. AT&T, IBM, SAS, Microsoft, Hollywood, Rupert Murdoch, Ted Turner, etc. – are these corporations and people behind the elitist conspiracy against business? That notion that some class intentionally opposed to the free market dominates communication networks reveals a weakness in Novak's argument. His three systems allow the capitalist market to be free from blame for the consumer culture that it produces and which produces it. As Michael Budde has suggested, Novak's ability to move between the three systems, finding fault with the cultural and the political but not the economic, is like a shell game that avoids the obvious: capitalist economics and a consumer culture go hand in hand.[18]

That there is an adversarial class opposed to business interests remains a consistent theme throughout Novak's work, but the constitution of that class changes dramatically. In an early work, Novak claimed that the genius of capitalism was found in its pragmatic empiricism. At the level of theory, he suggested, capitalism cannot be adequately defended: 'The theoreticians of our system do make it sound more crass in theory than it actually is in practice.'[19] Thus the adversarial class has the advantage because Adam Smith, Ayn Rand, and Milton Friedman's theorizing of capitalism does not capture its essence. But the genius of capitalism is that it is 'heedless of theory.'[20] Of course, this makes Novak's defense impenetrable. For he can turn back any criticism with his statement: 'The world of action is not the same as the world of faith or vision or theory or ideal.'[21] In fact, Novak's work is geared toward providing politicians, business persons, and cultural communicators with the discourses of power appropriate to the destruction of capitalism's cultural detractors, particularly its theological detractors. Thus Novak suggests:

To change the structure of the game the corporate executive needs to find the moral weakness of the new class. The weakness is its own affluence.... If the game concerns morality, the moralists will win. If the game concerns costs, the business man will win.[22]

Some fifteen years later we find an 'adversarial culture' still at work in Novak's theorizing, but now it is the culture of *pragmatism*: the adversary is Richard Rorty's 'cheerful nihilism,' which eschews truth-claims for 'pragmatic social preference.' But this sounds quite similar to the essence of capitalism that Novak defended in 1979. Now, Novak argues, the 'conception of unalienable rights on which the American experiment rests is intelligible only in terms of truth, nature and nature's God.' Where before the genius of capitalism was its basis in pragmatism and its heedlessness of any foundational theory, now its genius resides in its foundations in the natural law.

Although the constitution of the adversarial class shifts in Novak's thinking, the reason why they conspire to oppress the business class remains constant: they envy them. The cultural elite – academics and artists – resents the fact that corporate managers get paid more than they do. The cultural elite undermines capitalism because of the latter's success.

Novak is here consistent with Weber, to a point. Both accept Nietzsche's theory of *ressentiment*.[23] Moral arguments are nothing but disguises to cloak a group's powerlessness, allowing it to seek revenge while clothing its desire for power with the language of morality. Yet Novak has lost an important nuance in both Weber and Schumpeter. For Novak, the cultural system is separate from the market system. For both Weber and Schumpeter the market system encroaches on and constitutes the cultural. They cannot be kept separate. The market creates a culture that then destroys theological traditions, and (for Schumpeter) even the market itself. The market system is threatened because the culture is thoroughly capitalist. But for Novak the market system is threatened because the culture is insufficiently capitalist. He writes: 'Democratic capitalism is more likely to perish through its loss of its indispensable ideas and morals than through weaknesses in its political system or its economic system. In its moral–cultural system lies its weakest link.'[24] He cites Schumpeter as an ally for this idea, but in so doing misses Schumpeter's critique. The 'loss of its indispensable ideas' is not capitalism's undoing. Rather, capitalism's indispensable ideas are its own undoing. Schumpeter wrote: 'Bourgeois society has been cast in a purely economic mold ... success is identified with business success.' And he suggested that 'capitalism creates a critical frame of mind, which after having destroyed the moral authority of so many other institutions, in the end turns against its own.'[25] Schumpeter agreed with Marx that this moral authority was destroyed first in the family, whereas for Novak socialism destroys the family by teaching 'free love.'[26] And Schumpeter suggested that capitalism is undermined by its own cultural system because the conformity of factory discipline destroys human culture. This is not the vibrant pluralism Novak finds in capitalism.[27]

Schumpeter cannot be the ally Novak sees him to be. The very thing Novak proposes as the solution to the problem of capitalism's destruction Schumpeter identified as the problem. In fact, Schumpeter is more sympathetic to the scholastic critique of capitalism than Novak or any theologian working within the dominant tradition. As Schumpeter observed:

> Capitalist practice turns the unit of money into a tool of rational cost–profit calculations, of which the towering monument is double-entry bookkeeping. Without going into this, we will notice that, primarily a product of the evolution of economic rationality, the cost–profit calculus in turn reacts upon that rationality; by crystallizing and defining numerically, it powerfully propels the logic of enterprise. And thus defined and quantified for the economic sector, this type of logic or attitude or method then starts upon its conqueror's career subjugating – rationalizing – man's tools and philosophies, his medical practice, his picture of the cosmos, his outlook on life, everything in fact including his concepts of beauty and justice and his spiritual ambitions. In this respect it is highly significant that modern mathematico-experimental science developed, in the fifteenth, sixteenth and seventeenth centuries, not only with the social process usually referred to as the Rise of Capitalism, but also outside of the fortress of scholastic thought and in the face of its contemptuous hostility.... By cursing it all, scholastic professors in the Italian universities showed more sense than we give them credit for. The trouble was not with individual unorthodox propositions. Any decent schoolman could be trusted to twist his texts so as to fit the Copernican system. But those professors quite rightly sensed the spirit behind such exploits – the spirit of rationalist individualism, the spirit generated by rising capitalism.[28]

For Schumpeter capitalism will not collapse because of some adversarial culture that resents others' success and so sublimates that resistance by creating cultural values that undermine it. Capitalism will collapse because of the cultural system it creates. Capitalism generates a formal spirit of critique where the good, the true and the beautiful no longer are honored; only the useful remains – and that is determined solely by the critical spirit of the accountant's cost–benefit calculation. Such a constant 'critical frame of mind' is antithetical to the theological tradition.

Can this 'spirit' identified by Weber and Schumpeter be appropriated by Novak to make theology relevant to economics? Only if Weber and Schumpeter were wrong in describing capitalism. Novak truncates their work even while using it for theological purposes. He evidently finds them wrong in their identification of the spirit of capitalism as Protestant rather than Catholic. Yet he finds them helpful in the formal identification of a 'spirit' to the market system.[29] But Novak separates this formal claim from the material content both Weber and Schumpeter gave to it. The result is the bland claim that for Weber 'spirit' impacts social formations without any serious investigation into the content of that spirit that Weber so ingeniously developed. Nevertheless, Novak adopts two central arguments in Weber that are dangerous for theology. First he adopts the distinction between facts and values. The free market is based on fact; theology provides values that help it operate freely. These values are called 'spirit' and are a formal liberty. Second, moral opposition to the fact of the free market is fundamentally *ressentiment*. In making this argument Novak tips his hand in favor of a critical posture against the moral and theological traditions – the critical posture that Schumpeter argued is the culture created by capitalism. Moral theology is placed under suspicion by a formal liberty.

## III  The formal spirit of liberty and J. S. Mill as a Thomist

The formal nature of Novak's 'spirit' is also demonstrated in his discussion of the third system, the political system. A political system of liberty needs to be in place, and for Novak was in fact in place, for capitalism to flourish. Novak finds the seeds for this institution in the work of John Stuart Mill, which he argues was later adopted by Catholic social thought. 'The liberal institutions which Catholic social thought has come increasingly to appreciate owe much of their development to Anglo-American liberals, of whom Mill is an early prototype.'[30] Novak even writes: 'Had J. S. Mill been a Catholic, his thought would perhaps have inspired the popes and theologians more than it did.'[31] This is a claim that should surprise the popes, the theologians, and Mill himself. It implies congruity between Catholic social thinking and Mill's advocacy of liberal institutions. It is an unwarranted claim.

The liberal institutions Mill supported sought to establish an unqualified freedom of speech. In *On Liberty* he maintained that truth could be known only through an unqualified freedom to speak. How can this view of liberty fit with the consistent Vatican teaching that true freedom must be bound by truth? Mill lived out his conviction by distributing literature on the necessity of limiting population expansion. He went to jail for his convictions.[32] The centrality of birth control in economic liberalism, from Adam Smith through Ricardo, Mill, and even among today's economists, does seem to conflict with Catholic social thinking. How can Novak reconcile the contradictory elements of these two traditions?

Novak argues that Mill corrected Malthus' population principle by Mill's better understanding of wealth production; he suggests that Mill thought the central issue with respect to poverty was not population but production. Here Novak is simply wrong. Mill's economics was as indebted to Malthus as had been the Christian political economy of the eighteenth century. Both took Malthus' principle as sacrosanct even as they developed it in different directions: the philosophical radicals used it for the prospect of human perfectibility, whereas the Christian political economists used it against that prospect. But for both the production of wealth was inextricably associated with the necessary natural laws of the market disciplining reproduction within the family. In his *Autobiography*, Mill stated:

> Malthus's population principle was quite as much a banner, and point of union, among us as any opinion specially belonging to Bentham. This great doctrine, originally brought forward as an argument against the indefinite improvability of human affairs, we took up with ardent zeal in the contrary sense, as indicating the sole means of realizing that improvability by securing full employment at high wages to the whole laboring population through a voluntary restriction of the increase of their numbers.[33]

Not only wealth production but population limitation is key in Mill's political economics. Without voluntary birth control, wealth production is not possible. This is not an auxiliary argument among the classical liberal economists: it is central to their thinking.

Novak also states, in opposition to R. H. Tawney's critique of Mill, that the 'acquisitive instinct' which Tawney pillories in Mill is actually an instinct for 'self-sacrifice and creativity.'[34] Why Novak sees Mill as arguing for this 'self-sacrifice' is unclear to me. Certainly Mill did think that the capitalist class was composed of 'creative' people whose 'better minds' were necessary for the education of lesser minds.[35] But Mill was not especially laudatory toward capitalism. He viewed it as a 'necessary stage' as humanity progressed toward the 'stationary state' where unlimited production could not continue. As a good utilitarian, Mill argued:

> I cannot, therefore, regard the stationary state of capital and wealth with the unaffected aversion so generally manifested towards it by political economists of the old school. I am inclined to believe that it would be, on the whole, a very considerable improvement on our present condition. I confess I am not charmed with the ideal of life held out by those who think that the normal state of human beings is that of struggling to get on; that the trampling, crushing, elbowing, and treading on each other's heels which forms the existing type of social life, are the most desirable lot of humankind, or anything but the disagreeable symptoms of one of the phases of industrial progress. It may be a necessary stage in the progress of civilization.... But the best state for human nature is that in which, while no one is poor, no one desires to be richer.[36]

Capitalism is a necessary evil as humanity progresses toward the stationary state. Still Novak does find in Mill the central principle he celebrates in the market economy: the principle of liberty. Mill and papal teaching are compatible because of Novak's *analogia libertatis*. Both Mill and the popes supposedly teach that only an anthropology grounded in freedom can secure the necessary political and cultural conditions for the preservation of a free market.

Novak is viewed by Wogaman and Preston as a 'neoconservative'[37] and as an 'ex-liberal.'[38] But such dismissive critiques are deserved only in part. Not since Adam Smith has 'the natural system of perfect liberty' been as passionately defended as it is with Michael Novak. He is a consistent liberal. Some years ago Robert Paul Wolff argued that a fracture occurs among American intellectuals and their commitment to liberalism, particularly as they are the inheritors of Mill's work. Most 'liberals invoke the authority of *On Liberty*,' while conservatives draw upon *The Principles of Political Economy*. Wolff shows how this leads to 'conceptual chaos' in American politics.[39] Novak is an exception to this rule. He is a consistent, and self-proclaimed, neo-liberal who draws on both sides of Mill.[40] He is a willing inheritor of Mill's liberalism and views it in continuity with the Thomistic Catholic tradition.[41]

Through his use of Weber, Mill, Adam Smith, and, as we will see below, Thomas Jefferson, Novak embraces the modern spirit. He finds this spirit consistent with Thomistic theological themes. The Continental tradition of liberalism, the Anglo-American tradition, and the Thomistic inheritance are wrapped together into a single tradition that provides the basis for the 'spirit' of democratic capitalism. They are bound together through the underlying conception of *liberty*. His work is eclectic, but the fundamental strategy he employs to relate theology to economics is Weberian. Novak identifies a 'spirit,' and argues that this spirit is both necessary for, and dependent on, capitalist economics. This 'spirit,' however, is nothing more than the formal ability to choose designated as 'freedom.' This freedom is the ability of human creatures to give 'value' to objects in the world and to have those values contribute to a 'spirit' that lacks material content. This freedom is theology's central contribution to economics.

## IV  Max Stackhouse: religious metaphysical–moral foundations

Like Novak, Max Stackhouse finds Weber's work compatible with a Christian theological ethic.[42] Unlike Novak, Stackhouse rejects the utilitarianism of J. S. Mill, which he finds also in Adam Smith. Stackhouse's inheritance is less the Anglo-American tradition of liberalism than it is its Continental version. He is not as eclectic as Novak, but more consistently develops the Weberian inheritance. He finds Weber superior to both Marx and Adam Smith because Weber's fact–value split allows theology (the value side) and the social sciences (the fact side) to interpenetrate, without either side losing its distinctiveness. No theologian here examined is more indebted to a sociological method for relating theology to economics.

Stackhouse employs a method similar to that of Ernst Troeltsch. For Troeltsch, the essence of Christianity is discovered by grasping 'the decisive and driving religious idea and power out of the complex whole which is the reconstruction and interrelation of facts into a causally comprehensible historical picture.'[43] Following Weber's notion of charismatic authority, Troeltsch found historical movements to be grounded in an 'original idea.'[44] These original ideas then get developed into historical events. The task of the social ethicist is to look at the past history, conceptualize it in terms of a formal essence and then act in the present with a view to realizing that essence in the future.[45] Likewise, Stackhouse essentializes Christianity into individual dignity and universal rights by distilling four 'significant developments' from the history of the early church.

The first development is the idea of a universal moral law. Second, this moral law is capable of being fulfilled because we can act in history in such a way that we are freed from the 'unnecessary burdens' of our past. Third, individuals were 'brought under the protection' of the universal moral law through 'dignity and respect.' Fourth, this occurred by the creation of a new universal community not subject to the particularities of clan, tribe, family, etc. This abstract sediment becomes the necessary religio-moral ethos the church contributes to political economy and to the family.[46]

The condition for this ethos is the *idea* of creed. The distinctive feature the church offers is that it 'provides a space for bonding around a creed.' [47] The content of that creed does not seem to be as important as is the 'social space' that allows for a non-coercive association based on free consent.[48] This is the transcendental condition for universal human rights.[49]

Weber's usefulness for Stackhouse's project is obvious. His method makes theology relevant to economics in a non-particular way that allows for Stackhouse the vocation of a 'public theologian.' He can have both the 'facts' of modern economic science and the 'values' of Calvinist theology. He can suggest, for example: 'So the "rationalization" of modern economic life must be understood, at least in part, by reference to its religious heritage.'[50] The religious heritage of covenant and bonding around a creed provides the possibility of social co-operation such as is found in the modern corporation. No substantive historical connections are necessary because the influence of the religious heritage is not primarily material: it is a formal, albeit natural and providential, development. That it is natural and providential can be seen in Stackhouse's argument that history has a natural flow in which we can see the 'wreckage of civilizations that opposed independent cities with their independent households, schools, businesses and religions.'[51] God has given 'providential networks for our well being' in 'covenanted communities' such as the family and the corporation.[52] (The church itself plays a surprisingly small role in this providential schema. Its task seems to be to generate these other spaces for social bonding.) To reject these communities is to live against the foundational moral order God has established.

For Stackhouse theology has a direct role in providing the necessary values for the economic system. These values are grounded in a religious metaphysical–moral foundation that implies that they cannot merely be produced through human will. As he puts it, 'we do not entirely create the normative principles under which we must live.'[53] Although this foundation is similar to Roman Catholic natural law, it is not quite the same. For, as a Reformed Protestant, Stackhouse denies that the biological order alone can give us an ethics, and he affirms that a natural law ethic renders irrelevant the biblical witness.[54] Rather than describing this foundation as 'natural law,' he calls it *common grace*. Thus he states: 'The Protestant traditions hold that there is an onto-theological order that everyone almost knows.'[55] This order that everyone 'almost' knows is based on the overarching value of covenant: it is 'the covenantal heritage' where persons band together through their wills into covenants for the common good.

The value of covenanting together for the common good is so central to Stackhouse's narrative that he cites Henry VIII's break with Rome over the 'reinterpretation of the sacrament of marriage' as an important moment in bringing marriage in concert with its religious foundations. Stackhouse offers the following recasting of marriage according to this event:

> Henry VIII required an heir in a system in which primogeniture was the least violent means of succession in a predemocratic era still tied to gene-pool identity. He needed a divorce to marry a wife who might give him a son, and the Roman authorities would not allow the divorce because of their theory of the sacrament [of marriage]. To fulfill his vocation in society, he felt he had to break with Rome. These challenges to the authority of the church brought with them a search for a new normative definition of marriage.[56]

That new pattern of marriage would not finally arrive until after the Reformation, when covenant becomes the religious foundation for not only marriage but the state and the corporation. This is the central value religion contributes to economics.

Although Stackhouse clearly has a philosophical–ontological realism against which political, economic, and family life should be measured, the 'value' emanating from that realism is the capacity of persons to covenant together through the binding of their wills. What purpose this binding serves is not well articulated. Given his citation of Henry VIII, it obviously does not serve the purpose of fidelity, except the fidelity to do one's vocation in the public order, which is also based on the binding of the will through a doctrine of political right.

Like Novak, Stackhouse argues that the religious moral foundational values cannot be produced by the economic system itself, although it depends on them. Once the values are lost, a 'secular utilitarian calculus' will prevail. This utilitarianism is opposed to the 'liberal–Puritan synthesis' which, along with the conciliar Catholicism of the Council of Constance, and the ecumenical Christianity of the old Federal Council of Churches (particularly with its social creed), best embodied Christianity's essence.

Although the liberal–Puritan synthesis 'forms the deepest ethic of American life,' Stackhouse believes this tradition has been usurped by a 'utilitarian and pragmatic liberal ideology.'[57] Thus Stackhouse (unlike Novak) finds Adam Smith, J. S. Mill, and the utilitarian tradition to be a cultural threat. Adam Smith, he suggests, 'spelled out the utilitarian logic of how a market economy worked.' In so doing, he replaced the liberal–Puritan concept of 'vocation' with that of 'gain,' and thus theological foundations were rendered private.[58] In an argument similar to Novak's, Stackhouse suggests that the liberal–Puritan synthesis confronts an adversarial culture where 'the systems have lost their consciousness of a theological dependency; they run by a utilitarian secular calculus.'[59] That adversarial culture is different from Novak's because Stackhouse finds self-interest a threat to faith. Novak is more willing to see the utilitarians as allies and is less indebted than Stackhouse to a Kantian ethic of disinterestedness.

But, like Novak, Stackhouse calls on Weber as an ally against the adversarial culture, and here Stackhouse finds Weber helpful. He provides theologians with the tools necessary to combat this utilitarian logic. According to Stackhouse, 'Weber has demonstrated that modern social realities cannot be understood without detailed knowledge of the metaphysical–moral visions that, along with other factors, brought into existence the modern ethos on which our political and economic systems depend.'[60] A public theology developed 'beyond the privileged insights of our confessional communities' will preserve this metaphysical–moral vision and save economic life from a purely 'utilitarian secular calculus.'[61] Why we must be saved from this purely utilitarian secular calculus is not immediately clear. As we shall see, Stackhouse does not seem to think that capitalism and its corporate culture pose fundamental problems to Christianity. What seems to drive his work is not so much an articulation of that from which public theology will save us as the assumption that theology must be public and non-confessional in order for it to save us. Stackhouse is explicit that theology must now be done post-confessionally. And Weber, unlike Smith and Marx, points us in this direction. That is why Weber should be embraced and Smith and Marx eschewed.

Stackhouse has accused the Protestant theologian Jürgen Moltmann and the Latin-American liberation theologian Juan Luis Segundo of 'misinterpreting' what is at stake in the debate between Weber, Smith, and Marx. But he himself has given a puzzling reading of this debate.[62] Weber's work is necessary, he suggests, because it discloses how a religio-moral foundation generates and sustains social formations. But the center of this argument will not hold. That center makes religion, now in the form of

Calvinist theology, central to capitalism. But, like Novak, Stackhouse ignores the heart of Weber's argument. The 'rationalization of modern economic life' may have been produced as the unintended consequence of a Calvinist ethic, but nowhere does Weber suggest that the continuation of modern economic life presupposes this religious heritage. Weber does not demonstrate that modern social realities are dependent on the metaphysical–moral visions that undergird them. If anything, his work demonstrates the opposite tendency. While it is true that Weber argued consistently that the 'inner-worldly asceticism of Puritanism first produced a capitalist ethics,' he also quickly adds that this was 'unintentional.'[63] Far from Calvinist theology being necessary for the ongoing practice of capitalism, Weber argued that the depersonalization of the capitalist system turns against faith and destroys it. And, of course, Weber thought true religion required a *sacrificium intellectum* that renders this religious–metaphysical vision at best irrational.[64]

Stackhouse reads Smith as a proto-Marxist who viewed economic relations solely in terms of the 'laws of economic development.' But this is a misreading of Smith, for he, much more so than Weber, articulated a metaphysical–moral vision for capitalist economics. This particularly is the case if *The Wealth of Nations* is not read in opposition to *The Moral Sentiments*. In the latter, Smith stated that the 'general rules of morality' are based on the 'laws of the Deity.' And, quite in keeping with *The Wealth of Nations*, he wrote:

> The divine being contrived and conducted the immense machine of the universe so as at all times to produce the greatest quantity of happiness.... [By] acting according to the dictates of our moral faculties, we necessarily pursue the most effectual means for promoting the happiness of mankind, and may therefore be said, in some sense, to co-operate with the Deity, and to advance as far as in our power the plan of Providence.[65]

To claim that Adam Smith had no religious–metaphysical–moral vision at the base of his economics and that Weber makes one necessary is mistaken. This mistake arises because of the religio-moral–metaphysical vision to which Stackhouse is indebted. It renders suspect all self-interest in favor of a sacrificially disinterested morality. This fits better with Weber's work than it does with Smith's.[66]

Stackhouse inherits from the Continental liberal tradition the foundational principle that ethics is fundamentally about obligation and therefore disinterestedness. 'What is ethics?' he asks with Dennis McCann, and they answer: 'Ethics is about how we *ought* to live.'[67] That '*ought*' finds its most definitive expression in the idea of a cosmopolitan society wherein people act on the basis of universal right and claim no special privilege for their particularity.[68] Ethics begins by asking 'What ought I to do?' And the answer is that I must act in such a way that the maxim of my action can be the basis for universal right. This results in suspicion of self-interestedness, a political theory of rights, and a desire for a non-particular public theology.

The suspicion of self-interestedness contributes to Stackhouse's discontent with Adam Smith. Universal human rights assume a disinterestedness that overcomes our particular loyalties as we journey toward a cosmopolitan state. If all we have are confessional communities then, as Stackhouse notes, 'we would undercut all truth claims about human rights.'[69] Universal human rights and democratic cosmopolitan structures grow out of the 'law of love.'[70] Following Reinhold Niebuhr, the law of love is disinterested. Rights then are the necessary features of a universal human nature that is known through common grace. In arguing for universal human rights on the basis of a disinterested love, Stackhouse ignores and/or dismisses the positions taken by Alasdair MacIntyre and John Milbank.

MacIntyre has suggested that among the 'consequences of the failure of the Enlightenment project' was the reconceiving of morality by finding something in the human person *qua* human person upon which morality could be grounded. Two attempts were crucial: Mill sought to create a new *telos* where happiness was to be understood solely in terms of the increase of pleasure or the diminishment of pain; and Kant discovered in practical reason a universal basis for rights. Stackhouse rejects Mill's utilitarianism, but affirms Kant's doctrine of political right, an attempt MacIntyre has argued was bound to fail. MacIntyre argues that both attempts are 'moral fictions' because both 'purport to provide us with an objective and impersonal criterion, but they do not.' Yet he also sees a necessary connection between these two efforts. Rights and utility provide useful moral fictions because the former is the basis for modern politics and the latter for modern economics. For MacIntyre the fictive character of rights and utility in the modern era does not lead to a substantive moral vision; instead it leads to an incessant protest, a critical posture against any conception of the good.

> But protest is now almost entirely the negative phenomenon that characteristically occurs as a reaction to the alleged invasion of someone's *rights* in the name of someone else's *utility*. The self-assertive shrillness of protest arises because the facts of incommensurability ensure that protestors can never win an *argument*; the indignant self-righteousness of protest arises because the facts of incommensurability ensure equally that the protestors can never lose an argument either. Hence the *utterance* of protest is characteristically addressed to those who already share the protestor's premises. The effects of incommensurability ensure that protestors rarely have anyone else to talk to but themselves. This is not to say that protest cannot be effective; it is to say that it cannot be *rationally* effective and that its dominant modes of expression give evidence of a certain conscious awareness of this.[71]

Stackhouse dismisses MacIntyre's critique. He still holds forth the neo-Kantian promise of a cosmopolitan state where all particular loyalties are overcome in a non-confessional public theology based on universal right. He simply ignores arguments suggesting that our postmodern problematic is precisely that this project has been achieved and that it ended in nihilism. Stackhouse continues to assume its viability, finding all other ethical alternatives to be utopian.

Milbank, like MacIntyre, finds fault with the politics of right. He has argued that the Kantian trajectory tends to be more 'metaphysically dogmatic' than medieval theology precisely because it assumes 'direct cognitive access in practical reason to what the immaterial and atemporal is like.' This metaphysical knowledge of God occurs without any necessary historical traditioning and then posits 'abstract, negative right as the foundation of human society, as opposed to any positive conception of a common "good" as a collective goal.'[72] Precisely because knowledge of God is had without any sense of history or tradition, the public realm can be based on an abstract negative right. Stackhouse cannot take such criticism seriously for he assumes both such metaphysical knowledge and such a basis for political society, while arguing that theology must be 'post-confessional.' That this leads Stackhouse to assert (and confess) the need for a non-confessional public theology is not at all surprising. Kantian ethics assumes a relationship between a metaphysically dogmatic knowledge of God and a politics of right. The latter is based on the former. This knowledge of God is secure and certain against all confessional particularities. Therefore Kantian ethics dogmatically requires that all confessional particularities must ultimately be overcome.

Stackhouse's cosmopolitan social ethics produces a self-sacrificial morality. This allows our actions and our gifts to others to be alienated, with no expectation of return. We should do our duty because it is our duty within a providential ordering characterized by family, market, and state. We serve these institutions irrespective of their contribution to our own happiness, blessedness, and joy. This certainly fits with Kant's account of obedience, which allows us to argue as much as we want, as long as we obey; but it does not fit with the Thomistic account. Aquinas viewed our natural inclinations as one way in which we participate in God's eternal law, and the sign of a truly moral action thus would be that it gives our will rest and makes us happy.[73] The argument that Christian moral action should be disinterested was a eighteenth-century innovation. Adam Smith's appeal to self-interest is clearly preferable to the Continental liberal tradition of disinterestedness.

Smith introduced the idea of *self-interest as a dynamic economic law*. This has tempted many contemporary theologians to find fault with him. If the gospel is about disinterested love, how can we live in an economic system based on self-interest? Yet the gospel is not about disinterested love, and thus it is not self-interest that is objectionable in Smith. It is his Stoicism.

Adam Smith's famous phrase is often considered to be a problem for Christian ethics because of its explicit endorsement of self-interest. Smith wrote:

> It is not from the benevolence of the butcher, the brewer, or the baker, that we expect our dinner, but from their regard to their own interest. We address ourselves, not to their humanity but to their self-love and never talk to them of their own necessities but of their advantages.

The first sentence of this famous passage is unobjectionable. I should expect the baker to have a primary interest in her sustenance and the sustenance of her own family. I should hope for the baker's happiness. To expect her to feed me at the expense of her own life and the life of her family would be vicious.

The problem is found in the second sentence. It is Smith's prohibition to speak of 'their necessities' in favor of speaking only of their 'advantages.' Here Smith juxtaposes an antagonistic either–or rooted in scarcity: *either* the baker's interest *or* mine. I must not let the baker know of my needs, but persuade her that it is in her own best interest to enter into an exchange with me. We are antagonists who are each seeking our own advantage under conditions of scarcity.[74] This antagonism grounded in lack is an intrinsic feature of his free-market system (as well as of both Christian and political realism). It makes necessary class warfare and deceit through pitting our interests each against the other's because we fear scarcity. It requires also that exchanges occur through the manipulation of each other's will.

This antagonism is grounded in Smith's Stoical sympathy. For Smith, the essence of morality is 'sympathy,' which is a 'fellow-feeling.' However, this fellow-feeling is not for others in their sorrow but in their joy. Smith wrote: 'Nature, it seems, when she loaded us with our own sorrows, thought they were enough, and therefore did not command us to take any further share in those of others, than what was necessary to prompt us to relieve them'[75] Expressions of grief and sorrow, and the desire for charity, become contemptible attitudes. True fellow-feeling occurs when I rejoice in the baker's good fortune. If I speak of my own needs then I ask the baker for a contemptible form of fellow-feeling and deny nature's implantation of moral sentiments. The result is an aesthetic contempt toward the poor and toward suffering.[76] From the perspective of Christian theology, Smith's Stoicism is a grave threat. For if God assumes human suffering in Christ, then Smith's Stoical aestheticism trains us in contemptuous attitudes toward God. We must turn our eyes away from the cross for it lacks dignity.

How would this reading of Smith alter Stackhouse's critique? It shifts the theological concern with utilitarianism away from the problem of self-interest to the problem of abstract value. We need not fear the self-interestedness of the utilitarian calculus. Novak's 'virtuous self-interest' is better fitting with traditional Christian theology than is Stackhouse's

Kantian inheritance of 'disinterestedness.' The problem with utilitarianism is not that it makes us self-interested. The problem is its abstractness: it can give a value unit to everything, never assuming the incommensurability of things. And here Stackhouse's appeal to Weber does not overcome the key problem with utilitarianism but rather accentuates it. Weber's ideal-types result from the establishment of relative values based on the principles of abstract equivalence. As John Milbank explains it, 'this regulation only works because of the acceptance of a not self-evidently "rational" (though not necessarily irrational) circumstance which measures all commodities on a single scale, and makes their "value" equal merely their formal substitutability.'[77] This formal equivalence becomes Novak's 'spirit' and Stackhouse's 'ethos,' and allows them to see formal continuities that deny the conflict and lack of commensurability obtaining between the church and other institutions. It prevents Novak and Stackhouse from setting forth a political and economic life based on a substantive theological account of what is good, true and beautiful. Stackhouse does seek to preserve the family against the encroachment of the market, but even though he recognizes the threat the market poses, he nevertheless defines the family as a unit which 'accumulates not only material capital but also social and moral capital.'[78] The formal nature of the ethos he identifies constantly becomes filled with the content of the dominating social institution.

## V   Ronald Preston and the ambiguous contribution of theology to economics

Ronald Preston, like Novak and Stackhouse, draws upon a firm fact–value split as a theological entrée into economics. However, unlike Stackhouse he does not so much emphasize that theological values should provide a metaphysical foundation for economics as chide theologians for lacking a substantive engagement with the empirical realities of economics while simultaneously offering abundant pronouncements. He agrees with Novak, McCann, and Stackhouse that theologians have neglected the empirical realities of modern science.

Preston was a student of R. H. Tawney at the London School of Economics. One of Tawney's statements had a particular influence on Preston's work: 'The social teachings of the Church had ceased to count because the Church ceased to think.'[79] Preston often cites this statement, and it forms the background for his central concern that if the church is not more rigorously attuned to the modern world it will be increasingly marginalized. Precisely because Preston believes that the church matters on economic issues, he prods theologians to be more rigorous in their study and application of economics.

Weber's influence also is decisive for Preston. Like Stackhouse, Preston argues that Weber shows the reasonableness of the Calvinist tradition. He recognizes that Tawney had 'important reservations' about Weber's thesis, but Preston sides with Tawney against Samuelson, who argued that the Calvinist–Puritan influence was marginal in the development of capitalism.[80] Preston sets this reasonable Calvinist tradition against an unreasonable traditional Catholic authoritarianism.[81]

Tawney argued that the Catholic church became irrelevant to economics because it could not relinquish its commitment to the usury proscription. Economic formations had advanced far beyond the supposedly static-state models of Aristotle and Thomas, but that model was rigidified in the scholastic era. Thus, the church fell behind because it could not understand that the world constantly changes and that intellectual reflection must negotiate those changes. Theological values must be moored to the modern facts. The church had little critical capacity with which to engage capitalism because it had no idea of what actually was going on. When finally the church caught up, it then 'capitulated uncritically' to the rise of capitalism.

Preston agrees with Tawney's analysis of usury. He describes the medieval church's position as 'a clear example of the failure of social theology to come to grips with a new situation that required a re-examination of traditional presuppositions.'[82] In fact, he finds Catholic moral theology still bound by this inability to engage modernity.[83] He argues that Calvinist theology is superior because of its recognition, then and now, of the need to engage the 'new commercial society.'[84]

The Weberian strategy is clearest in Preston when he explains the role of the Christian theologian in economic matters. Theologians cannot simply rely upon 'Biblical studies, Church history, systematic theology or any of the classical theological disciplines.' These disciplines provide only a 'basic stance or orientation.' And then this basic orientation must 'come to grips with the empirical data.'[85] Only this can prevent theologians from becoming irrelevant once again by the mere repetition of out-dated principles. But this falsely assumes that theology deals with some non-empirical data where the social sciences deal with the empirical data. This concedes to the social sciences the facts in respect of which theological values have a merely evaluative function.

Preston finds many current theologians perpetuating the same problems faced by the medieval theologians. Both Jürgen Moltmann and Douglas Meeks do this by assuming that the doctrine of the Trinity provides adequate resources for a theological economics. Although the Trinity may have some relevance for economics, Preston writes that one first 'has to be sure that one understands the market and the economic trends of one's own time, if the precise role of the market and the framework needed around it are to be thought out.'[86] This is also his main charge against V. A. Demant, F. D. Maurice, the British Christian Socialists, the Club of Rome, the Christendom Group, and the liberation theologians. He writes constantly about theologians' need to come to grips with 'the empirical data.'[87]

Because Preston brings this charge against other theologians with such regularity, should we not expect him to explain to us 'the precise role of the market?' But nowhere does he do this. Nor does he give us many assessments of empirical data. In fact, the few economic readings he has given turn out to be erroneous. In 1979 he stated: 'But if one asks, Are the [command economies] collapsing? The answer must be "No".'[88] A decade later the 'empirical' data proved him wrong. Had Preston not so confidently asserted what engagement with the empirical data could produce, had he not insisted that the precise role of the market could be explained, his inability to extrapolate from the empirical data to future results would be forgivable. No social scientist predicted the collapse of the command economies. But that is precisely the point. No necessary causal explanatory scheme exists that allows social scientists to predict the future based on law-like generalizations for extrapolating from the empirical data. Such explanations do not exist. While theologians should not ignore trends, continuities, and regularities in human action, neither should they assume that such 'empirical data' can provide a basis for theological engagement with economics. Such a Weberian strategy has itself failed; it is irrelevant.

## VI    Philip Wogaman's theological economics: the facts and values of Christian economics

Philip Wogaman, at first glance, appears to offer a non-Weberian strategy to relate theology and economics. He argues that economics must not be autonomous and separate from theology. In fact, he critiques the scientific rationality of both Marxism and capitalism. This appears to be a criticism of the fact–value distinction, where the former is conceded to the social scientist and the latter given over to the theologian. But this is not Wogaman's point. Instead he suggests that neither Marxism nor capitalism exists on 'a scientific foundation needing no support from moral values.'[89] Wogaman does not move us beyond the fact–value split: he argues still that two components are present in any economic analysis – the *facts* of the social sciences and the moral and theological *values*. Despite the difference between his economic prescriptions and those of Novak, Stackhouse, and McCann, Wogaman remains indebted to the same Weberian strategy.

Wogaman is a systematic thinker, drawing upon an ethics of obligation. He is heir to the Kantian tradition in that he begins with a firm distinction between moral will and moral intelligence.[90] Two 'objective reference points,' he suggests, form the foci around which theological economics works: 'the faith tradition and the factual world.'[91] That faith and facts already constitute different foci reveals to us that faith occupies some space such as Kant's noumenal realm or Weber's irrational remainder. Theology is relevant to economics because it provides the values which economics should serve.

Like Stackhouse and Preston, Wogaman essentializes Christianity into certain values. Those values are:

- the goodness of created existence;
- the value of individual life;
- the unity of the human family in God; and
- the equality of persons in God.[92]

Beginning with these presumed values, the facts are then interrogated. The purpose of Wogaman's work is to give us not so much concrete wisdom as a method that can be used to connect theology with economics.

Like Preston, Wogaman works from a Christian standpoint that begins with the assumption that Christian theology should not cause offense within our pluralist societies. This is because 'Christian values are not the exclusive possession of Christians.'[93] The significant theological values are not a scandal to non-Christians. They are values such as the 'transcendence of God' that can be 'taken seriously by non-Christians as well as by those who are already committed in some way to Christian faith.'[94] The 'values' are not embodied in particular historical communities, but are found in some metaphysical realm beyond those communities. As Stackhouse and McCann suggest, these values are post-confessional. And although Wogaman is clear that 'the essential nature of God is revealed in Jesus Christ,' this does not pose a problem for the trans-cultural nature of a Christian economic ethics because 'that nature is one of pure unbounded love for each of us.'[95] Christian values can be brought to bear on economic realities without offense because those values can be validated by reasons other than Christian theology.[96]

That Christian theological claims contain a fullness that exceeds the Christian community and makes demands on others is undoubtedly true, otherwise it would be sectarian. That Christian theology is consistent with nature is likewise a common and necessary theological claim. But Wogaman's economic ethics pays a heavy theological price for its universal and trans-cultural values, because the content of Wogaman's significant 'Christian values' lacks any Christian particularity. For only those values that can already be universalized are accepted as the relevant 'values.' A formal universality determines what constitutes Christian content.

Wogaman sets out the significant Christian value presumptions on a number of different occasions. In his 1977 publication *The Great Economic Debate* he defines them thus:

1   The doctrine of creation shows that material well-being is necessary as a basis for human fulfillment.
2   The basic unity of the human family is in mutual love.

3   Each individual human being is valuable and therefore we should be committed to individual freedom and the opportunity for individual creative development and expression.
4   Human rights should be based on equality.
5   Human sinfulness is universal.[97]

These five values contain no intrinsic relationship to Christianity.

In his 1986 publication *Economics and Ethics*, Wogaman has expanded these presumptions to six:

1   The material world is good because God created it to reflect good purposes.
2   Grace is prior to works. If justice is patterned in accordance with the priority of grace then economic goods should be produced and distributed in such a way as to enhance human well-being, self-acceptance, and communal fellow-feeling without asking first whether people have deserved what they receive.
3   We presume in favor of the well-being of our physical existence and of social relationships.
4   We are invited, through grace, into the vocation of creative activity.
5   The theological perspective of stewardship does not permit us to treat those socially defined property rights as absolute or as derived from some natural order of things.
6   Original sin demonstrates our tendency toward self-centeredness, such that we do well not to separate the world into good people and bad people.[98]

These two sets of presumptions show how consistent Wogaman's system has been and why his work fits within the dominant tradition. For instance, Novak also enumerates six 'liberal benchmarks,' which he states express the 'logic of Catholic thought.' They are:

1   the dignity of the human person;
2   the interdependence of all people;
3   the economic development of all nations;
4   an institution of human rights;
5   a communitarian personality; and
6   the vocation of each human being to become a co-creator with God.[99]

These six characteristics match up almost identically with the basic Christian values Wogaman enumerates. Both of them stress the dignity of the individual as well as the interdependence of all people. This is developed from a communitarian personality that is to be respected through the assertion of human rights. For both, the central vocation of the human person is to participate with God in creation for the purpose of material well-being. The decisive theological value is the human liberty to be productive. However, any connection between these theological values and Christian particularity is, at best, tenuous.

# 3    An anthropology of liberty constrained by original sin

## Theology as *analogia libertatis*

The dominant strategy of relating theology to ethics through Weber's fact–value distinction and the assumption that what theology contributes is found in the 'value' part of that distinction leads theologians in the dominant tradition to emphasize anthropology as the decisive theological theme. This chapter explains that anthropology of liberty. As noted above, the Weberian strategy used by theologians assumes a metaphysics where the atemporal and transcendent is known outside of historical particularities. It is discovered by its relationship to the human creature's freedom. Thus, I shall argue, a consistent theme in the dominant tradition is that knowledge of God relevant to economic matters is mediated via an *analogia libertatis*, an analogy from our freedom to God's freedom.

## I    Novak on liberty and co-creation

Novak has gone through a number of changes in his thinking, yet this theme has remained constant, 'Liberty is our culture's most cherished value.'[1] Although the majority of theologians working in economics stress that economics should serve the interest of human liberty, Novak's commitment to freedom and his uncompromising explication of it are unparalleled. Yet this consistent theme of liberty produces some irresolvable contradictions and results in some curious theology.

Michael Novak began his theological career as a self-professed 'radical.' One of his early books, *A Theology for Radical Politics* (1969), was critical of America and its economic system. Novak referred to America as 'an idol' and argued that Christians 'must be critical of America.'[2] He castigated the 'consumer's freedom' it extolled and he argued for a revolution, quoting Stokely Carmichael and Malcolm X. 'The "system" of American life,' he wrote, 'as it has been perceived by young people is racist, counterrevolutionary and militarist.'[3] Novak even countenanced the possibility of violent rebellion: 'Against armed ranks of policemen, a grenade is more serious and effective than calling names.'[4] And he argued that the traditions of the church in 'its language and its methods are in fact, too narrow and parochial.' Christians must learn to speak in a new secular way without their speech 'fitting into older molds.' Jesus himself is not that useful for the revolution because 'not all men are attracted to him, not all admire him in every respect.' Thus, the new revolution should return to nature and the doctrine of creation: 'Christians do not need more Christianity but less; Christians need a greater openness to nature.'[5] To do so we must pronounce the death of the Christian God who has repressed us, especially in our sexuality: 'For many of the young no human experience is more full of awe, joy, and holiness than sexual intercourse. It is from this experience, for many, that religious language becomes meaningful again.' Can this be the same Michael Novak who dedicated his 1993 publication *The Catholic Ethic and the Spirit of Capitalism* to John Paul II and argued that America can no longer be considered a 'racist country'? The answer is yes. But Novak's apparent transformation can be deceiving. His 'radical theology' changes very little. His theology is a consistent and passionate defense of liberalism and modernity undertaken by drawing upon the doctrine of creation. Indeed significant changes have occurred in his work. But these changes take place within an underlying consensus that can be marked by the following three themes:

1    Explicit Christological language can be relevant but not determinative for an economic and political order. Something more universal is necessary to bind people together. Christology can be transformed into secular language without altering its content.
2    The modern revolutionary spirit with its commitment to liberty marks a significant advance to which the church can accommodate itself because this spirit represents a sentiment already present in the church, even if the church is slow to recognize it.
3    The doctrine of creation, and the recognition of the human person as a co-creator with God through producing wealth, are at the heart of a Catholic social ethic, rightly understood.

Within these continuities are also found interesting contradictions. What constitutes the universal in the first continuity shifts from nature and the beauty of creation in *A Theology for Radical Politics* to Thomistic natural law in *The Spirit of Democratic Capitalism* and *The Catholic Ethic*. The American Revolution remains a watershed moment for Novak, but his early work finds America sliding into a counter-revolutionary spirit which is marked by the lack of equality of opportunity for African Americans. Novak's later work places the blame for this lack of equality on the welfare state, population increase, and an other-worldly black culture. The centrality and importance of the American Revolution remains consistent, but the counter-revolutionary movement that threatens it shifts. In the early Novak, the counter-revolutionaries, or 'the adversary culture,' were the 'old left,' and the 'capitalist order.' In the later Novak, the counter-revolutionaries are the socialists. Curiously, the means the adversary culture employs remain the same – the university, the church and the media. The most substantive change after his *Theology for Radical Politics* is that he realizes liberalism is best, or perhaps only, preserved via capitalism. And the Catholicism he sees produced by John Paul II supports that preservation.

Novak consistently argues for a liberal–pluralist democratic society and for individuals to have the freedom to create themselves, or at least be co-creators of their own destiny. The consistency of this point of view can be seen in the following passages that span nearly the entirety of his work over the past quarter of a century.

> At a certain point, you decide who you are; you create yourself.... Genuine community exists for the sake of the development of as many free, self-defining persons as it can possibly generate.
>
> (*A Theology for Radical Politics*, 1969, pp. 36–7)

> The world as Adam faced it after the Garden of Eden left humankind in misery and hunger for millennia. Now that the secrets of sustained material progress have been decoded, the responsibility for reducing misery and hunger is no longer God's but ours.
>
> (*The Spirit of Democratic Capitalism*, 1982, p. 28)

> The human person acts in a self-planned, creative, intelligent way. He makes his own decisions about himself. This is the radical theology Pope John Paul II propounds.
>
> (*Freedom With Justice*, 1984, p. 161)

> Social justice means the freedom to choose one's own destiny, the right to the pursuit of happiness: the right to choose the meaning of life, so declaring one's own identity before God and humankind.
>
> (Ibid., p. 209)

> It is distinctive of Judaism and Christianity among the world's great religions that they teach us that each human being is a creator.... Who would have expected that in ordinary sand is hidden silicon and that in a single chip of silicon no bigger than a fingernail millions of bits of information could be stored.... Spirit and matter ever more closely interpenetrate. The old boundaries are collapsing. The bases of production – and, above all, the bases of human communication – are being transformed before our very eyes. This earth is being re-created new.
>
> (*Will It Liberate?* 1986, p. 78)

> God gave us a vocation to wonder at His creation and to bring it to its latent perfection, so far as in us lies.
>
> (*The Catholic Ethic and the Spirit of Capitalism*, 1993, p. 204)

The foundation on which Novak relates faith to the economy is an anthropology in which God has created us, and a world, such that we are at liberty to fashion it and ourselves into something better.

This emphasis on co-creation certainly has precedents in the theological tradition. In the third part of this work we shall see that John Milbank also emphasizes co-creation in his Christological poetics, but he invokes it to argue for a Christian socialism. However, for Novak this co-creation is fundamentally an anthropological claim that finds analogies in the work of Weber, Smith, Mill, and Jefferson. Novak also argues that this liberty is consistent with Catholic moral theology because of its continuity with Thomas Aquinas. Here his argument is stretched beyond its breaking point.[6]

For Thomas, only our participation in God's over-abundant goodness allowed for this co-creative power; his is a theological claim. That this co-creation was a participation in God meant abiding by certain substantive principles of the natural law that would direct our actions toward virtuous ends, principles such as the usury proscription, the just wage and the universal destination of all our goods which placed limitations upon private ownership. And these principles require the virtues for their intelligibility, not only the virtues of justice and prudence, but even more importantly the theological virtue of charity. Novak neglects, or explicitly rejects, these substantive principles and seldom develops these virtues. In fact, as we shall see, he argues that capitalism entails virtues that the church has not yet emphasized. His appeal to 'natural law' is an appeal to human nature's free creativity. Thus our co-creative power becomes unbounded – except for the bonds of original sin.

## II   The limitations imposed by original sin

Although, for Novak, we are at liberty to fashion our world, we are bound by original sin such that perverse consequences can result from our best intentions. Otherwise we might be tempted to think that our co-creative powers would make socialism possible. The doctrine of sin limits our creativity in that we cannot control the consequences of our actions. And God has established the world thus. 'Just as God did not make the world perfect, but shot through with contingency, failure, error, evil and malice, so the Catholic Church has seen God's governance as Providence, as Prudence.'[7] To claim that God did not create the world perfect appears heretical and inconsistent with the teaching of the Catholic Church.[8] It leads to the idea that 'all human acts are tinged with irony and tragedy' because the consequences of our actions are unforeseeable. The best intention of communal sharing can result in tyranny, while conceding the inevitability of sin can lead to plentitude and prosperity. We are called to participate as co-creators, but we do so mindful of an imperfect creation and an original sin that requires prudence to negotiate the tragic reality in which morally good deeds do not correlate with morally good consequences. Novak has conceded too much to Smith, particularly to his Stoicism.[9] God refused to create a perfect world, but instead left it to our freedom to bring the imperfect creation to the highest perfection possible. Therefore, those social formations that allow for this freedom to create and produce are the closest analogies we have to how God works. In our liberty to produce we discover God.

## III   Dennis McCann: Niebuhrian realism over liberation utopianism

Novak emphasizes an anthropology of liberty within the constraints of an imperfect creation. God creates an imperfect world so that we can make it better, but our making it better must be analogous to God's activity. Like God, we cannot make this world perfect. This reflects Novak's appropriation of Niebuhrian realism.[10] It is this that sets him in opposition to much of Latin American liberation theology. Stackhouse and McCann follow suit.

Stackhouse finds liberation theology to be misguided, insufficiently scientific and dependent on a neo-fundamentalist reading of Scripture. He states that '[liberationists] are on the fringes of serious political and economic thought,' which for Stackhouse seems to be a decisive argument against a theological position.[11] McCann, however, has carefully explained his differences with liberation theologians. He finds their work a 'sincere but confused protest,' wanting in comparison to Reinhold Niebuhr's 'paradoxical vision of the Hidden God.'[12] Central to the dominant tradition is this reliance on Reinhold Niebuhr's theology.

This appropriation of Reinhold Niebuhr's theology by the dominant tradition poses limitations for a *theological* engagement with economics because Niebuhr himself was not a theologian. Niebuhr understood himself primarily as a social ethicist and was unconcerned with the development of Christian theological doctrine. In fact, most of his theology simply assumed the work of Paul Tillich. Niebuhr does not need much from theology other than, as Charles C. Brown noted, 'a transcendence that critiques all finitude.' And this is precisely what Tillich's 'Protestant prinicple' provided.[13] The protest of the Reformers does not assume a specific end in which the unity of the church could actually be envisioned. Instead, the protest itself becomes the end. More specific Christian theological themes were simply not necessary, and Niebuhr either did not adhere to them or thought they were unnecessary for his ethics. As Gary Dorrien notes:

> Niebuhr did not believe in the historicity of Christ's resurrection, but his writings failed to offer any alternative account of Christianity's Easter faith. Neither did his writings develop a theology of the Trinity or the incarnation, or even use trinitarian or incarnational language. He did not develop a theology of the Holy Spirit or the church. The great

Christian themes of regeneration, sanctification, and the church as the body of Christ thus had little place in his work. Except as a transcendent ideal that stands in judgment over history, Niebuhr gave even less sanction to the doctrine of the kingdom.[14]

Whether or not Niebuhr has given us a Christian theology even implicitly in his ethics, or merely a Stoic doctrine of creation, remains an open question. Yet what the dominant tradition culls from Niebuhr is an anthropology mired in a tragic created order ruled by a doctrine of unintended consequence termed 'original sin.'

McCann's argument for Niebuhr's superiority to the liberation theologians shows the beginnings of a clear line of thought that led him to find in capitalism a new form of Christian mission. The key themes present are a metaphysical anthropology mired in a tragic scarcity. Like Novak and Stackhouse, McCann argues for the superiority of Christian realism by drawing, first, on an anthropology that views human nature as a paradox of sin and grace, and, second, on the ubiquitous presence of original sin. The result is an epistemological humility about what good can be actually accomplished in this life, culminating in an insistence on a politics of negative right against any substantive notion of the true, the good, or the beautiful. This epistemological humility serves as the legitimation for democratic capitalism.

Because of its 'humble recognition of limit,' McCann finds Niebuhr's anthropology superior to that found in liberation theology. Niebuhr's anthropology results in anti-utopian democratic structures that are non-revolutionary. McCann states: 'Democracy works because it institutionalizes the conflicts of interest inherent in human nature.'[15] Christian realism does not believe a revolution can bring about 'once and for all promises of revolutionary change.' Niebuhrian realism makes epistemological humility fundamental to its practical theology so that it denies the possibility of creating a society based on the good, the true and the beautiful. The best we can do is concede people human rights where their antagonistic human natures do not finally destroy each other. This then privileges democratic capitalism whose defenders seldom argue for its truth or beauty: they readily admit it is not a perfect society. It is only the best of all the alternatives.

As Christian realism is socially superior to liberation theology because it argues for limited political and economic objectives, so it is theologically superior because it makes limited truth-claims for God. God's activity is 'never known with certainty' for Christian realism, but 'his abiding truth may be recognized in moments of prayerful transcendence shaped imaginatively by Christian myth.'[16] But McCann's argument contradicts itself. His 'realism' claims superiority over liberation theology because the realist knows with certainty what cannot be known about God. The liberation theologians transgress the limits of our knowledge of God. But who established this boundary in the first place? How does McCann know what can not be known about God? His 'uncertainty' rests on the implied premiss of a certainty as to what can and can not be known about God. McCann's 'realist' practical theology is just one more version of an idealist epistemology wherein we are certain of that about which we can have no certainty. It is only because McCann 'knows' what can not be known about God that he is able to accuse the liberation theologians of transgressing the limits to human knowledge of God.

McCann objects to liberation theologians such as Gustavo Gutiérrez because they feel compelled, in order for their work to be persuasive, to make historical truth-claims for their reading of Scripture. And such readings reveal the naivety of their arguments and their lack of engagement with modern science.[17] For Christian realism, the mytho-poetics of Scripture gives us only the most general truth-claims, nothing so substantive as a specific politics. For McCann, Niebuhr's mytho-poetics gives us a general wisdom about human events, but nothing too specific such as one finds in the liberation theologians. But here McCann has misread the Latin American liberation theologians, for we shall see that both Gutiérrez and Sobrino deny that either theology or scripture gives us a specific politics. They are similar to McCann in claiming that theology and scripture provide basic values or a fundamental orientation in liberation theology, but theology and scripture alone cannot provide a social ethic. For that, sociology is necessary.

McCann accuses liberation theologians of too much and too little. They claim too much when they suggest they know how God is working in the world. They violate a humble recognition of limits. At the same time, they claim too little in that, while seeking to be orthodox in their theology (something McCann admits is not necessary for Christian realism), this orthodoxy cannot be squared with the Marxist dialectical vision that liberation theology employs. McCann finds no possible distinction between the process of conscientization used by liberation theologians, drawing on the work of the Marxist educator Paulo Freire, and Feuerbachian humanism. Therefore, he thinks it inevitable that liberation theologians will not be able to sustain their orthodoxy. Those liberation theologians who no longer make pretense to orthodoxy represent for him the true trajectory of liberation theology, whereas others, such as Gutiérrez, are sincere but misguided. He asks of Gutiérrez: 'In what way can salvation-history promote the emergence of "man" as a "Subject" when God and his Son, Christ the Liberator, are the principal or ultimate Subjects in the process of liberation?'[18] In so asking, he seems to assume Weber's principle that a grace-infused life is in conflict with the moral life. He does not seem to countenance the possibility that both the priority of God as Subject *and* the human person as subject are possible. He lacks a profound theological *poesis*.

McCann, unlike Novak, does not pretend to base his economics on orthodox Christianity. Instead, he explicitly argues for 'an irreducible plurality of Christian religious visions.'[19] Although Novak does argue for an 'historical orthodoxy,' he also invokes pluralism as central to his economic ethics. Capitalism fits well this irreducible plurality of religious visions because its dependence upon the formal and substitutable nature of value precludes it from any substantive truth-claims. We should not be surprised that all the ethicists working in the dominant tradition make references to, and celebrate, pluralism. This is consistent with their theological compatibility with capitalism. The 'logic of the simulacrum' defines capitalist culture.[20] Ever-intensifying, yet disconnected, images play upon and constitute our perceptual reality such that the norm has become plurality and difference. Reebok, Nike, the Democratic and Republican Conventions, Coca-Cola, all these social formations seek now to present their image in terms of an ever-expanding plurality. What has become odd and unintelligible is not a plurality of vision but single-mindedness and unity. Any ethics that seeks relevance to capitalist culture must advocate pluralism. And, as should be expected, we will discover that those theologians like Jon Sobrino who seek to liberate theology from capitalism recognize that they cannot advocate pluralism.

McCann also argues for the superiority of Christian realism because it offers a universal ethic, whereas liberation theology has produced only sectarian base communities. At first glance, McCann's insistence on a universal ethic and a 'plurality of visions' might appear contrary. But this combination of universal and plural makes perfectly good sense and fits well with his embrace of a global market. It operates precisely through difference based on an assumed commensurability of one cultural value with another. Thus, a universality of pluralities defines capitalism's cultural logic. Any community that makes a claim for incommensurability would be *a priori* viewed as sectarian. This is unacceptable for McCann because, as he argues, a truly catholic (i.e. global) ethics cannot be sectarian. Notice that *catholic* no longer functions as a mark characterizing the particular community of the church. 'Catholic' now means non-particular. Curiously, although McCann blames liberation theologians for abandoning a truly catholic ethics, he feels little compunction in making his own ethics dependent on the views of the Protestant theologian who wrote: 'The Catholic doctrine of the Church is in fact a constant temptation to demonic pretensions, since it claims for an institution, established in time and history, universal and absolute validity.'[21] McCann's notion of catholicity fits Niebuhr's anti-Catholic ecclesiology.

Although all the members of the dominant tradition utilize Niebuhrian realism, with its two theological foci of anthropology and sin, no one has developed it more thoroughly and carefully than has McCann. This has led him to argue for democratic capitalism as the social context that makes best sense of Niebuhr's theology. However, McCann's use of Niebuhr trades on an abstraction. Scripture as mytho-poetics is too flexible to be of any substantive use in a theological ethics. Such an understanding of scripture serves merely to keep it from direct application. But that is precisely McCann's point. For then a metaphysical anthropology must do all the work. But this anthropology does not adjudicate economic considerations. In some sense, this anthropology insures that theology will not be embodied in any particular history. 'All politics and all economics,' McCann and Stackhouse suggest, 'must be conducted under the context-transcending principles of truth, justice and love.'[22] The keyword in that phrase is 'context-transcending.' For these virtues are best exemplified in a cosmo-politan ethics that makes no confessional claims. So he suggests, along with Stackhouse, that the theology of the future will 'reach beyond confessional particularities' and develop a 'cosmopolitan social ethics.'[23]

# 4  The subordination of Christology and ecclesiology to the doctrine of creation

That theologians select anthropology and an *analogia libertatis* as a strategy to make theology relevant to economics is not a problem *per se*. The theological problem that occurs in the dominant tradition is that other more substantive theological themes such as Christology and ecclesiology are subordinated to this overarching *analogia libertatis*.

## I    Novak's Christological limitation

A weakness in Novak's development of the doctrine of creation is to be found in his Christological reflections. As already mentioned, the radical Novak found Christology too particular for a universal morality. The later Novak does not set the particularity of Christ against the possibility of a universal morality but finds Christ present in a secular universal morality.

Because the center of Novak's thinking is that perfect system of liberty set forth by Adam Smith, he does not seek to impose his theological convictions on the pluralist public square. This does not imply that Jesus is irrelevant for economics. But who Jesus is and what he has done no longer depends either on the church or on the particular language used about him. Novak first articulated this in his *A Theology for Radical Politics*:

> The 'good news' of Jesus has been spread abroad, has been appropri-ated in countless ways in the scientific, social and political life of the world, and in many diverse ways in the personal lives of men. There are by now few men who have not been touched by the sources of life and value that Jesus sowed in history. To be sure, these realities are no longer always called by Christian names or expressed in theological concepts. They have taken on secular forms.[1]

Twenty-five years later, in 'A New Vision of Man: How Christianity has Changed Political Economy,' Novak revisits this theme. He notes that 'Jesus revolutionized the political economy of the ancient world.' And, he argues, 'that revolution still profoundly affects the world today' and was best exemplified in the American Revolution.[2]

As in his *Radical Politics*, he notes here that these 'lessons may be, and have been, secularized.' But he departs from that earlier work in now suggesting that those lessons cannot be secularized 'without losing their center, their coherence, and their long-term persuasive power.'[3] This seems to imply that the political and economic revolution he sees exemplified in democratic capitalism must be explicitly connected to Christology. Novak has consistently denied this and denies it here. One need not profess Christianity to participate in this revolution, for it is accessible to 'secular thinkers.' As evidence of the revolutionary impulse of Jesus he quotes the 'modern progressivism' of Richard Rorty and Bertrand Russell. But what does he mean by saying that Russell and Rorty (as well as Thomas Jefferson) represent secular thinkers who have appropriated Christology without losing its center? What then is Novak's Christological center?

We discover Novak's Christological center in his explication of the revolutionary lessons taught by Jesus and embodied in America. First, there is one God, Creator of us all, who freely willed to create. This teaching of Jesus has three corollaries for us as economic agents. We are to 'be intelligent,' to 'trust liberty,' and to 'understand that history has a beginning and an end.' As an example of how this revolutionary teaching impacted America Novak quotes Jefferson, who said: 'The God who gave us life gave us liberty.' But this insistence on God granting us liberty cannot constitute any 'Christological center.' Jesus is not necessary as 'the center,' either of this ethic or for its 'coherence' and 'long-term persuasive power.' Furthermore, these teachings seem unrelated to any Christological themes in the Christian or the Catholic tradition. In explaining the Christological center, Novak has developed a theology that fits much better with Benjamin Franklin and Thomas Jefferson; they become the theologians who provide resources for his 'Christological center.' Christology plays no substantive role in this 'Christological center.' Novak assumes the liberty espoused by Franklin and Jefferson to be consistent with the freedom Jesus presents, but nowhere does he argue for this. Is there an adequate basis for this assertion? Jefferson himself had to cut-and-paste the gospel narratives to make Jesus fit his account of liberty. Has Novak not done the same? The liberty let loose at the American Revolution defines Novak's Christology. Christology does not, however, give to liberty any particular form.

Novak never successfully shows how Christianity or Catholicism is necessary for capitalism. In fact, he often demonstrates the opposite. The problem with Latin America, he argues, is that it is Catholic. 'If Latin Americans shared the ethos, the virtues and the institutions of the Japanese, they would assuredly be among the economic leaders of the world.'[4] In fact, a number of non-Christian cultural ethics lend themselves well as a support for capitalism. Then certainly experience shows that Jesus is not necessary for the 'coherence and long-term persuasive power' of a cultural ethos that will sustain capitalism.

Likewise Novak argues that the Christianity stemming from the black church contributes to African American poverty. 'Most blacks' he writes, 'are in fact disciplined, ambitious, hardworking, and conscientious in seizing opportunity.' Yet the emotional nature of black Protestantism does not so much plan for tomorrow: it is too focused on 'surcease from the day's woes.'[5] Thus 'it is a form of Calvinism different from others, and may have different economic and political effects.' It has created a welfare mentality that is a form of slavery foisted upon African Americans by the socialist vision of the adversarial class, buttressed by an overly emotional, passionate, and otherworldly Protestant theology.

Because the cultural system of a people is so central to Novak's defense of capitalism, and because that cultural system is a function of choice, Novak suggests that 'minorities' possessing 'spiritual qualities' amenable to capitalism 'typically demonstrate economic advancement even in the midst of majority populations still suffering considerable poverty.'[6] Because people choose their cultural ethos, '[w]hat people cannot do is choose one ethos and then complain of the disadvantages within which it constrains them.'[7] Novak feels no compulsion to discuss how history could shape and necessitate a culture, a history such as slavery. Because Christian theology's central contribution is this anthropology of choice, particular histories are not subjected to analysis.[8]

For the African American community to participate in the advantages of the capitalist revolution, Novak argues, its culture must change. What are these cultural and moral values that must be adopted? They seem to be discipline and the observance of regular hours. Once again, the central 'theologian' he draws upon is Benjamin Franklin. But as John C. Cort and Alasdair MacIntyre have argued, Benjamin Franklin's account of the virtues has, at best, a tenuous relation to the Christian tradition, and is in fact more indebted to utilitarianism than Christian truth.[9] Franklin's insistence on discipline and regularity arises from his understanding of time and money, which is directly set against the majority Christian tradition. It is based on his assumption that 'time is money ... credit is money ... money can beget money, and its offspring can beget more.'[10] Likewise MacIntyre notes that the ends served by the virtues in Franklin's work are not the ends of Thomas Aquinas. Franklin's virtues do not direct our activities to friendship with God. As MacIntyre puts it, for Franklin, the

end to which the cultivation of the virtues ministers is happiness, but happiness understood as success, prosperity in Philadelphia and ultimately in heaven. The virtues are to be useful and Franklin's account continuously stresses utility as a criterion in individual cases: 'Make no expence but to do good to others or yourself; i.e. waste nothing', 'Speak not but what may benefit others or yourself. Avoid trifling conversation', 'Rarely use venery but for health or offspring.'[11]

Discipline and the observance of regular hours make sense only as virtues in terms of some end. Novak's end, like Franklin's, seems to be utility. He has proven Schumpeter's point. A kind of factory discipline becomes the dominating 'value' people must embody if efficiency and utility are our ends.

Novak argues that Catholicism and Christianity are both necessary for capitalism and at the same time impediments to it. What he has actually demonstrated is that no intrinsic connection exists between Jesus, Christianity, Catholicism and capitalism. In fact, Novak even raises the question: 'Are the traditional Christian virtues sufficient as a base for democratic living, or do some new virtues need also to be learned?'[12] Novak tells us that Jesus 'is the teacher of many lessons indispensable for the working of the free society,'[13] and at the same time Novak shows us that this free society can work just as well without Jesus. In fact Novak argues that a Confucian culture is more amenable to capitalism than are some Christian cultures.[14] This contradiction in his role for Christology and capitalism arises because he subordinates Christology to a doctrine of creation, in which creation is identified as rightly ordered without any Christological knowledge.

For Novak, creation is prior to Christology. Jesus does not bring the Kingdom: it is already here in every culture through creation and mediated by an *analogia libertatis*. We do not learn anything from Jesus about economics that cannot be learned from nature and found in a number of diverse cultures. Instead, Jesus reveals the 'structure of human life,' which lets us know that by his suffering and death the 'forces of evil and oppression were stronger than He. The liberation He came to bring does not liberate us from the structures of oppression, from evil forces of this world.'[15] Jesus does not bring a new creation. He reveals only the structures within which we must work, a structure marred by tragic irony as well as by creation's latent possibilities. Once this doctrine of creation gains priority over Christology, then ecclesiology loses its preeminence – another consistent theme of Novak's is an anti-triumphalistic ecclesiology.

Novak offers a sober and critical ecclesiology. He argues that liberalism was necessary because individuals needed to be defended against the church and the state.[16] He finds pre-modern Catholicism deficient in its appreciation of the rise of capitalism, and he finds post-Vatican II Catholicism equally deficient. The former treated wealth as if it 'were limited and static.' In fact, he argues, Catholic bishops still view 'credit as usury and scorn profit.' Thus they have not advanced beyond the static Thomistic teaching on the economy. Novak questions whether the United States could have developed as it did had it been mired in the medieval teachings of the Catholic church.[17]

Although Vatican II is a step forward in its embrace of the modern world, its 'fatal flaw' is that it has consistently ignored the most important symbol of modern liberalism, 'liberty.'[18] Novak does appeal to the encyclical teaching for support of capitalism, and especially the encyclicals of John Paul II, and he rejects the interpretation of those encyclicals as a 'third way,' which is neither communism nor capitalism. He recognizes Catholic efforts to find a 'middle way' as utopian.[19] He argues that Catholic countries have terrible records in creating democracies and notes that this is a sign of some 'missing insight' in Catholic teaching.[20] Although 'Pope John Paul II has begun to make a difference,' Novak insists that Catholic tradition still 'has some new things' to learn from 'American democratic capitalism.'[21] This is because democratic capitalism *is* the so-called 'third way' of the papal teachings.

Novak's work begins from the assumption that the church must be made relevant to modernity. This assumption was present in his 1962 publication *The Open Church: Vatican II, Act II, A Brilliant Report of the Struggle to Open the Church to the Modern World*. That book continued a theme from *Radical Politics* – that the church has become irrelevant to modern life because of its commitment to 'nonhistorical orthodoxy,' the medieval system of theology that asserted propositions about God without making those propositions 'relevant to the historical realities of the present.'[22] Twenty years later Novak repeated this theme in his *Confessions of a Catholic*.[23] 'Nonhistorical orthodoxy' continues as a modern heresy. He gives as an example the 'dreadful simplifications' in the Second Vatican II document, *Gaudium et Spes*: 'One reads in these passages intimations of a world entirely reasonable and without sin: a world without war. This is not a Christian experience.'[24] What Novak finds so objectionable is the bishops' claim: 'It is our clear duty, then, to strain every muscle as we work for the time when all war can be completely outlawed by international consent.' Although the bishops' statement may have a utopian ring to it, the basis for this claim comes a few paragraphs earlier, where they wrote:

> That earthly peace which arises from love of neighbor symbolizes and results from the peace of Christ which radiates from God the Father. For by the cross the incarnate son, the prince of peace reconciled all men with God. By thus restoring all men to the unity of one people and one body, he slew hatred in his own flesh; and, after being lifted on high by his resurrection, he poured forth the spirit of love into the hearts of men. For this reason, all Christians are urgently summoned to do in love what the truth requires (Eph. 4:15), and to join with all true peacemakers in pleading for peace and bringing it about.[25]

How can the assumption that the 'peace of Christ' might actually be incarnate among persons in their political relationships be viewed as heresy? Would not an orthodox understanding of the incarnation lend support to such a hope?

Novak sees the bishops' call to embody Christ's peace as the heresy of nonhistorical orthodoxy and then gives an example of 'historical ortho- doxy.' He explains that the creedal affirmation 'through him all things were made' reveals the unique particularity of all things. Novak defines orthodoxy in terms of our ability to imitate God in using liberty creatively:

> In part each of us discovering our uniqueness, we are also called to improvise and to invent, to use our liberty to its fullest to find unexpected resources in ourselves, not to hide from insecurities and to bury our talents safely, but to be a new voice, in this way imitating the Creator.[26]

If this is orthodoxy, what constitutes 'heresy'? For Novak, heresy arises when we think this liberty can be employed to achieve a perfect political order. Not even the Creator was able to overcome evil's historical resistance in this world. Orthodoxy and heresy now function as modalities related to the need for human beings to express a creative liberty within the limitations of the political orders in which they express this liberty. Both orthodoxy and heresy lose any decisive relationship to Christology: they now function as statements about the freedom of the human will and its analogical likeness to God's will. But this subordinates the church to the market and privileges a formal liberty as the decisive site of God's action in the world, independent of any ecclesial presence.

Novak is also highly critical of the guidance given the church by the US bishops. He calls their pastoral on the economy a form of fundamentalism that seeks to apply pre-capitalist biblical texts to modern capitalist realities. The bishops fail to see how the bible was mediated through history, particularly through Thomas Jefferson who viewed the United States as a 'second Israel.'[27]

Novak constantly reiterates that the United States is a new creation founded on biblical principles. Jefferson and the American founders captured the basic 'biblical' idea of 'liberty' and 'equality.' Jesus teaches us 'equality as uniqueness,' but Jefferson and the American founders brought that idea to fruition. They also gave this insight institutional form through their insistence on 'inalienable rights.' And they developed the biblical insight that history changes; progress can be made. So they stated, 'When in the course of human events ...'. The doctrine of creation that Novak sees at the heart of Christianity, and by which he interprets Christology, is best exemplified in the American Revolution: 'The Americans were aware of creating something "new": a new world, a new order, a new science of politics. As children of the Creator, they felt no taboo against originality; on the contrary, they thought it their vocation.'[28] But nowhere does he develop the central ecclesiological insight that Jesus' gathering of the twelve and the institution of the church is the restoration of Israel and the establishment of a new creation that is primarily signified and embodied in the historical church.[29] Novak does not develop an ecclesiology grounded in the historical and visible church. Instead, he draws upon America as the embodiment of that new creation. He does not find troubling the American claim on the ecclesiological statement of *e pluribus unum*. For the oneness and catholicity of Jesus' teaching are best preserved not through the church and the fundamentalist US bishops, but through democratic capitalism.

Novak's Weberian strategy to relate theology to economics takes as its foundational theological element an anthropology that views the human person as creative through his or her choices, a creativity bound only by a marred and tragic creation. Although the human person is to be creative, he or she cannot create outside of a context that will produce unintended consequences such that striving for virtue is more dangerous than forming society on the basis of formal yet conflicting interests. Novak utilizes Niebuhrian realism to support this theme. Any adequate ecclesiology must be made relevant to this historical reality; Novak calls this 'historical orthodoxy.' But the result is that both Christology and ecclesiology are de-particularized and their usage in a social ethic is constrained by an anthropology based upon a doctrine of unintended consequences. Although Novak will defend the results of the ecumenical councils, his orthodox Christology does not have a direct bearing upon his social ethic. It is appealed to only as evidence for his own theological metanarrative grounded in creation and an *analogia libertatis*.

## II   The formal substitutability of the Church in Stackhouse's cosmopolitan ethics

Stackhouse does not deny the central role of revelation for Christian theology. He states that 'revelation, understood as a gift of God, grasped by faith is an indispensable ground of theological thought.' But he does suggest that criteria outside that revelation must determine its truthfulness: for it to be reasonable it must be assessed to determine whether it is 'more or less compatible with the most universal human understanding of holiness, justice, truth and creativity.' This assumes a criterion of justice and truth more universal than revelation itself. It also privileges the social scientist's understanding of reality, and leads him to suggest that public theology 'in this view is properly understood to be the philosophically and socially informed attempt to interpret what could be true about God and God's relationship to humanity, society and the world ...'[30] Neither the gospel nor Christian theology is 'socially informed' in and of itself. For theology to be socially informed, it must draw upon the work of philosophers and social scientists, and allow them to provide the conditions for the truth that can be said about God. The result is that Stackhouse's public theology delivers theology over into the hands of the philosophers and social scientists. It is not surprising that a formal universality becomes the means by which the church and the corporation are rendered nearly substitutable, one for the other.

In his *Creeds, Society, and Human Rights*, the principle of abstract equivalence is the basis for Stackhouse's discussion of 'creeds.' Their value is not their substantive content, but the formal social space that provides the possibility for non-coercive voluntary associations. The idea of a creed has a formal substitutability such that its particular content is not as important as the value of the social space it opens up. Therefore, once Stackhouse is convinced that the corporation is not based on a self-interested greed and not in violation of the obligation for disinterestedness, the corporation and the church constitute a formal substitutability.[31] He writes:

> The Church established in practice and later in law, the notion that it was possible to form collective identities that were 'non-natural' in origin and that were dedicated to the transformation of every aspect of life .... [This] set the precedent for disciplined use of economic resources by an organized group independent of familial or imperial control.[32]

Stackhouse's ecclesiology provides legitimation for transnational corporations as significant theological actors analogous to the church. Similar to its status in Novak's thinking, the corporation here becomes a form of grace whereby God transforms the world. Weber's methodology misleads Stackhouse such that he can speak of the *persona ficta* of the corporation in terms comparable to the *corpus mysticum*.

Max Stackhouse has found an ally in the Catholic theologian Dennis McCann. Together they have called on theologians to repent for the contempt they have expressed toward capitalism and toward corporations. Instead of contempt, theologians must help Christians 'learn to love [corporations] as we have learned to love our churches.'[33] McCann also perceives a theological conspiracy against the business community, and argues that this results from Christian ethicists' fascination with socialism.

Stackhouse and McCann accept the argument that modern science is necessary to discern what God is doing in the world. They argue against utopian thinking and for a scientific approach to Christian ethics. Although this argument has some formal similarities with Marx and Engel's famous call for a 'scientific socialism,' Stackhouse and McCann do not find socialism an acceptable 'modern science.' Herein lies their problem with contemporary Christian ethicists. They have naively adopted socialism, but in so doing have failed to adopt modern science. Stackhouse and McCann write:

> Many contemporary forms of theology – fideist, fundamentalist and liberationist – are so alienated from modern science, technology, culture and especially business that they cannot discern where, in the midst of these sectors of our contemporary life, God is accomplishing something new.[34]

Rather than these confessional forms of theology, they argue for a post-confessional theology that will develop its social ethic consistently with those social sciences that have demonstrated the scientific reasonableness of capitalism. Curiously, the very theologians whom McCann and Stackhouse find most naïve – the liberation theologians – also speak of the need for a socio-analytic mediation, based on social science, of empirical social facts to theology. They do not differ on the need for theology to adopt the methods of the modern social sciences in order to make relevant pronouncements on the market. They differ only over which of the social sciences is to be adopted. For Stackhouse and McCann, socialism is no longer viable as a social science.

Dennis McCann joined Max Stackhouse in announcing the death of socialism after the collapse of the Berlin Wall. They have announced that 'no one thinks anymore that the route to social justice and prosperity necessarily lies in the political control of the marketplace and the means of production.'[35] This is reported as a 'fact,' although a great many people still think that political control of the marketplace will lead to social justice, and they are not all communists. In fact, only the most ardent of libertarians would argue against some political controls for the economy. What McCann and Stackhouse mean by an economy free from political control is never clearly set forth.

Despite the similarities between their theological economics and that of Novak's, they try to distance themselves from the 'libertarian neoconservative' position by asserting that questions of social justice are 'a necessary part of modern economics.' This is a weak critique of the neoconservatives. Who among them argues that social justice has no place in economics? Novak certainly does not make that argument. He argues that true social justice depends on the kind of freedom the capitalist market requires. McCann and Stackhouse seem to argue something quite similar. Their difference with Novak is difficult to ascertain.

Because they emphasize that the economy must not be controlled politically, Stackhouse and McCann seem hard pressed to explain how social justice will impact modern economics. If, as they state, no reasonable person would accept political control of the market, how can justice be exercised? How is justice to be enforced against a thoroughly non-political economy? How does a non-political market fit with their claim that we must all now be 'reformed capitalists' who use 'law, politics, education and especially theology and ethics to constrain the temptations to exploitation and greed everywhere?' ('A Postcommunist Manifesto,' p. 950).

Their appeal for Christian theologians to repent and learn to love the corporation raises a host of questions, the first of which is: have they named our sin adequately? Is it true that Christian tradition, and theological ethicists, hold the corporation in contempt? No argument is produced to explain how theologians and clergy have done this. This rather serious charge is brought merely as an assertion. No theologian in the Christian tradition that I have read has argued that buying and selling, and forming associations for that purpose, are contemptible. They have provided guidelines by which these practices can be engaged in while also caring for souls. They acknowledge that 'storing up treasures on earth' can be damaging to one's soul. And this has led to conflicts between the church and certain merchant families who did not find that these guidelines made their lives easier. But can holding forth moral guidelines grounded in the theological tradition be construed as contempt for corporations? That question is important, because if McCann and Stackhouse are correct about this contempt, it surely shows the hypocritical nature of Christian ethicists. But if they are incorrect, then they have mistaken proper moral guidance for mere contempt, and in so doing delegitimize appropriate moral guidance and inordinately legitimize and elevate corporations.

Is this contempt to be found in the ancient Christian tradition? Many biblical teachings focus on economic issues. Luke Timothy Johnson has characterized the biblical teaching in terms of three patterns – complete renunciation of worldly goods, almsgiving from one's own possessions, and common ownership. All three patterns are found in scripture, although Johnson argues that complete renunciation has inordinately dominated Christian theology and so he calls for a recovery of the neglected tradition of almsgiving.[36] This may be true, but that some are called to complete renunciation is clear in scripture. This complete renunciation of earthly goods could certainly be viewed as teaching contempt for business, but this contempt is based not so much on a disdain for business *per se* as on the assumption that the material goods of this world can distract one from the church's mission. An ascetic contempt for worldly possessions is certainly present in scripture and Christian tradition, but to call Christians and theologians to repent for this would be to challenge the centrality and urgency of the ecclesial mission. Surely this is not the contempt for business for which Stackhouse and McCann call theologians to repent?

As the church's teachings on economics developed, there was a growing emphasis on common ownership and care for the poor. The *Didache* teaches that 'the Father wants his own gifts to be universally shared.' Yet it also warns those who receive gifts from others that they must do so only on the basis of true need. The *Didache* teaches that 'the ones who look for profit have no pity for the poor, and do not exert themselves for the oppressed.'[37] This leads to the way of death. This teaching may be an example of the church's contempt for business: a life lived for the sake of gaining profit is viewed with suspicion.

If this is what McCann and Stackhouse object to, then a number of the church fathers could be considered as teaching contempt for business. For instance, Tertullian asks 'is trade adapted for a servant of God?' And he answered the question primarily in the negative, for three reasons: it lends itself to mendacity, covetousness and idolatry. Idolatry pertains specifically to trade in goods produced for idolatrous worship. Such businesses were not to be open to Christians. Yet even Tertullian stated: 'Let none contend that, in this way, exception may be taken to all trades.'[38] Likewise, Irenaeus, Origen, and Clement of Alexandria made reference to the story of the rich young ruler, and all found his sin to be covetousness. Like Tertullian, they identified covetousness as a vice that threatened those who engaged in trade. It is remedied by the virtue of charity through the social practice of almsgiving. Still, the early church fathers did not treat business *per se* contemptuously; nor did they issue a call for scientific socialism. They treated covetousness, mendacity and inhospitality to the poor contemptuously.

Justo Gonzalez argues that the attitudes toward sharing one's possessions changed after the Constantinian shift.[39] But this shift in attitude was not an intensification of contempt for trade. Rather it was an accommodation to it. The threat to faith has seldom been contempt for business and its fruits; the threat has rather been an insufficient contempt for what has been laid before the church.

Aquinas addressed the question whether the business trade was licit for Christians, and he responded that although Jesus ejected traders from the temple and that '*negotiando*' is forbidden to the clerics, nevertheless the problem with trading is not the craft itself, but the vices of the person engaged in the craft. He concluded: '*Ergo negotiari secundum se non est illicitum.*' Yet he stipulated that trading could not have gain as its only end, but should be directed to a virtuous end. Four such ends were allowed: sustaining one's household; helping the poor; the good of the '*publicam utilitatem*'; and gain as a due payment for labor.[40] Is this an example of contempt for business? Because McCann and Stackhouse argue that the only end business should serve is wealth production, they profoundly disagree with Thomas' economic ethic. But his is surely not an example of contempt for business.

Is then Stackhouse and McCann's charge of contempt warranted? Or is it a misplaced criticism of the church's appropriate moral guidance toward the necessary practice of business? The Christian tradition is not riddled with contempt for business; but perhaps this contempt is not to be found in the ancient or medieval tradition. Perhaps it is only a modern creation in the endorsement of socialism by Christian ethicists. A number of Christian ethicists do argue explicitly for socialism. Although, as we shall see, both Gutiérrez and Milbank argue that Christian theology demands a socialist order, neither of them argues that participation in daily economic exchanges is contemptible. In fact, Milbank recognizes that a Christian anthropology acknowledges the 'exchangist' character of our dealings, not only with one another but actually with God. Because this exchange is so central to our lives, Milbank denies that a disinterested, self-sacrificial, ethic is Christian. His call for a Christian socialism is not based on contempt for business, but on the necessity of exchange.

Nevertheless, Christian theologians should not deny that much of our theological economics has issued in a call for common ownership that has seldom been embodied in either the life of the church or in the lives of the theologians issuing the call. As Luke Timothy Johnson has argued, we have been preoccupied with common ownership by drawing upon Acts 2 and 4, passages that resemble more Plato's *Republic* than Jesus' New Creation. Christian theologians have too easily invoked common ownership as a sign of the Kingdom and ignored its tyrannical temptation. Plato himself recognized that to create such a society we must first rid ourselves of all our history by removing everyone over ten years of age.[41] Such a proposal has been tried often enough for it to cause us a theological pause. If Stackhouse and McCann simply seek to point this out to us, they have done us a service. But they seem to want something more, and this is what is theologically troubling. They want us to develop a 'non-confessional theology' that will serve the interests of their cosmopolitan ethic.

What is a non-confessional theology? Is it a theology without specific articles of faith? Surely neither Stackhouse or McCann would suggest that theology can be done without doctrine and dogma. They seem to be suggesting that the theology selected for their cosmopolitan ethic should be sufficiently broad as to be appropriable by persons outside the church, particularly non-Christians in the corporate world. It will have the same contours as the notion of 'value'; sufficiently non-particular that persons will be able to substitute ethical commitments from one community to another. This non-confessional theology has the same shape as the formal, but contentless, character of global capitalism. It recognizes 'value,' but not substantive and particular goods. The possibility that they may be correct in naming our theological future is alarming. The idea that this ethic is new is unwarranted. It has been around at least since Kant's *Perpetual Peace*. Theologians of an earlier day recognized this ethic as a threat. Public theologians today embrace it.

McCann and Stackhouse delegitimize an appropriate theological guidance and introduce an innovative 'orthodoxy.' It is grounded in the assumption that salvation might be mediated through corporations. So they write that 'working to serve people's needs in the marketplace may be a holy vocation in and for the salvation of the world.'[42] Economic exchanges are a necessary feature of human living and flourishing; that cannot be denied. But McCann and Stackhouse approach defining the global market as a salvific institution. This is evident when they speak of a new missionization where the church's mission is to teach people in poor countries 'how to form corporations and manage them.'

The economic prescriptions they offer show the outlines of their innovative orthodoxy. First, they argue that 'creating wealth is the whole point of economic activity.'[43] This is an odd view of human labor. It refuses the more modest claim that wealth production is an important part of economic activity, along with such other considerations as the cultivation of virtue, as we will find was argued by St Thomas and by the Jesuit economist Bernard Dempsey. It fails to recognize wealth production as an infravalent end that must also be positioned in terms of humanity's final end – friendship with God. Instead, McCann and Stackhouse propose that the 'whole' of economic activity has one purpose – the creation of wealth. So now considerations such as the location of corporations must become subservient to the creation of wealth. A 'failure to move' a corporation to a more efficient area is deemed 'a misplaced patriotism.'

Not only does a supernatural and theological end no longer circumscribe the end of wealth production, but the notion of mission within Christian theology is reformed. It is now to be defined by 'capitalization.' They state: 'Enhancing the capacity for capitalization in responsible corporations is as much the new name for mission as development is the new name for peace.' They conclude that the modern business corporation is to be a 'worldly ecclesia.' They do qualify this confession to the corporation with the contradictory claim: 'Corporations can become idols, in short, when we think that they can bring salvation to human life.'[44] But this qualification is too little, too late. They already bore witness to the formal substitutability of the church and the corporation.

McCann and Stackhouse have called theologians to confess a sin for which they are not guilty, and they have failed to identify sin where it actually exists. In fact, the problem in theological economics is not some tradition of contempt on the part of theologians toward the practice of business. It is the economists who have treated the church's teachings contemptuously – a contempt which has a long history.[45] The results of the economists' contempt toward all things theological is evident in contemporary conflicts between the church and the corporation. For instance, the Briggs and Stratton Corporation moved 2,000 unionized jobs from Milwaukee to the south. A number of the officials involved in this decision were Roman Catholic. When the *National Catholic Reporter* questioned Briggs and Stratton for their layoffs, the corporation filed a $30 million suit against the NCR for 'invasion of privacy.' The response of an official of Briggs and Stratton was that one's 'religious upbringing' has 'nothing to do with basic economic decisions.'[46] McCann and Stackhouse would want to argue that a religio-moral metaphysics does have relevance for 'basic economic decisions.' But this metaphysics would not seem to add anything to the official decisions already made by Briggs and Stratton. Their theology is relevant and public, but sacrifices traditional teachings for that relevance and publicity.

## III   Ecclesiology implicitly subordinated to the state: Preston's ambiguity

Preston writes both for and against the church. He acknowledges the emergence of pluralist societies and the consequent loss of Christendom. This poses a new problematic for the church because it maintains institutional structures with residues of Christendom in a changing social context where those structures are no longer relevant. He does not seek to restore Christendom, but he wants the church to have a public role, and he concludes that any theological contributions relevant to the public realm cannot be distinctively Christian. 'It is dangerous always to be wanting to say or stand for something that is so distinctively Christian that no one else is likely to see the force of it.'[47] This is dangerous, because Christian social ethics should build a common society in a pluralist world without reproducing Christendom. Such a common society will recognize the fact of pluralism and thus curtail any ethics grounded in a particular community, any *Sittlichkeit* ethics.

In arguing that the new role for the church is to contribute to a common morality and do so in such a way that it does not demand any distinctively Christian practice, Preston throws off the mantle of his mentor R. H. Tawney. Tawney called for the church to begin a discipline that refused to compromise with 'the idolatry of wealth which is the practical religion of capitalist societies.'[48] Like the liberation theologians, Tawney found idolatry to be a threat capitalism poses to faith. Thus, he called for a disciplined and distinctive Christianity. But Preston finds this both impossible and unwise. It is impossible because the church no longer has the ability to discipline its members. It is unwise because it smacks of a sectarian interest, which would be appropriate only if 'the Church were a tiny minority in an overwhelmingly pagan situation.' Instead the task of the church is to hold society together by the creation of 'fellow-feeling and cooperation.'[49] Its main contribution is the production of 'disinterested good will.'[50]

This is an odd claim. First, Preston acknowledges a post-Christendom reality where society is pluralistic. He even draws upon Alasdair MacIntyre's argument that modern society is more than pluralist: it is fragmented. Yet Preston goes on to argue that 'the first political task of the Church is to strengthen the sense of a common morality in the community, the moral virtues or basic human decencies that Adam Smith presupposed.'[51] But if post-Christendom society is pluralist, and this is a good thing, why do we need a common morality? What kind of 'pluralism' is based on an underlying commonality? The answer is, once again, that pluralism which fits well with the idea of a capitalist economic structure. What is exchanged can be as diverse as possible, but the way it is exchanged, the underlying structure that makes the exchange possible, is monistic. It must be held together. Once Christian theology accepts this as the empirical reality that it must accommodate, then theologians find themselves in the odd situation of arguing that the distinctiveness of Christian ethics is that it provides a common morality for a pluralist society, one that lacks any Christian distinctiveness.

Preston's first concern is to preserve the soundness of the church's witness to modern economics. To do so he selects two theological themes, Christian anthropology and the doctrine of original sin. This anthropology views the human person as a freely acting agent, intended for communal living.[52] Typical of all the members of the dominant tradition, Preston finds the norms for ethics to be grounded in some aspect of human nature as it is.

An anthropology becomes the theological foundation for discussing economics. And this requires the development of the doctrine of creation in such a way that it is either separate from, or related only indirectly to, specific Christological themes.[53] For instance, like Novak, Stackhouse and Wogaman, Preston identifies certain basic principles that are derived from his Christian anthropology:

- the basic equality of all human beings
- a concern for the poor and unprivileged
- the participation of people in decision-making
- the state as an institution under God.[54]

These four principles are related. The only way to insure the first three is for Christians to be more supportive of the state. Christians, argues Preston, have been too suspicious of the state and have failed to understand its necessary role in economics. For economics demonstrates that markets do not work best when they are unregulated and free.[55] In fact, Preston goes as far as to argue: 'The state's cohesion is threatened if citizens are allowed on any scale to be exempted from government requirements on the grounds of disagreement with particular government policies.'[56] Does Preston intend to sound as extreme as he sounds here? Wouldn't this make the honorable tradition of civil disobedience immoral? The list of Christians who have been heralded for standing up against particular government policies is rather long. A few of them are held in sacred memory, such as Tertullian, Athanasius, Ambrose, Thomas à Becket, Thomas Moore, Dorothy Day, Martin Luther King, Oscar Romero. Surely their actions *did* threaten the state's cohesion? Preston's position suggests that we side with the government against these witnesses.

The *analogia libertatis* employed by Novak to keep the state from interfering in the economic order is employed by Preston to advocate state intervention. The state plays a central role for Preston's relationship between theology and economics because it insures liberty. This is based on three propositions. First, the science of economics has persuasively demonstrated that Keynes was correct: government intervention can be the engine behind capitalism. Second, the state is an order of creation, a sphere of sovereignty, that is given to all and thus does not depend upon particular Christian claims; it seems to be more catholic than the church. The state as a sphere of sovereignty should be supported by Christians. It allows them to participate in the public realm within pluralist societies without introducing partisan theological arguments. Third, the doctrine of original sin reveals the need for the presence of a strong state. Both Novak and Preston defend particular institutional formations because of their reading of the doctrine of original sin. For Novak it requires an unfettered market; for Preston it requires one fettered by the state. The decisive issue between them appears to be which social scientist should be believed? Preston finds Keynes compelling. Novak believes the economists have not adequately theorized the genius of the free-market system, but classical liberalism represents its greatest possibility. However, that the democratic modern state is ordained by God and rendered necessary because of original sin fits well with the positions of Novak, Stackhouse, McCann, Wogaman, and Preston. They all claim this Niebuhrian legacy.

Preston finds Reinhold Niebuhr's doctrine of original sin to be foundational for an economic ethics. Although Christology has direct relevance only within the church, the doctrine of original sin has universal relevance. That Christology is problematic because too particular, but original sin is not because it can be universalized seems to be a peculiar argument among theologians in the dominant tradition; one constantly asserted but never defended. Like Niebuhr's ironism (and Adam Smith's Stoicism), the doctrine of original sin prevents statecraft from assuming a posture of virtue. 'Sin in its subtlest forms will feed on virtues and achievement and is likely to corrupt them. So an earthly utopian economic order is ruled out. There will always be trade-offs.'[57] The essence of Jesus' teaching is the proclamation of the Kingdom of God. The essence of that proclamation is disinterested love.[58] However, all our actions are tinged with self-interest. This self-interest must be transcended. It is transcended through the 'prophetic' critique of any social order that claims it can overcome self-interest. Christian theology contributes to economics the recognition that the good, the true and the beautiful can never be embodied in a particular historical tradition. It contributes 'the Protestant principle.' And this is the contribution Christology makes to theological reflections on economics.

For Preston, Jesus' teaching on the Kingdom of God is 'always transcending any particular expression.'[59] This Christology has direct relevance for our pluralist societies because these 'basic doctrines of the Christian faith' are connected to 'fundamental human experience.' They 'take to a deeper level through Jesus Christ fundamental human experiences in everyday living.' They can be drawn upon even when their 'deeper significance in Christian terms is not known or not accepted.'[60] Why? They are about personal freedom and the need to transcend our self-interest to create fellow-feeling. The result is that Christians should support the welfare state because it provides best for this 'fundamental human experience.' The welfare state has 'enlarged freedom of choice for most people,' and it 'has opened a way of bearing one another's burdens which the philosophy of individualism could only leave to the fateful whim of private charity.'[61]

The Christology in Preston's selection of theological themes functions in a way that is consistent with the central capitalist cultural value identified by Schumpeter – a constant critical frame of mind. Jesus brings critique, not a new social order. Preston rejects as false apocalyptic thinking the claim made by Tawney and others that Jesus inaugurates a new social order.[62] Preston even mentions his deep discontent that this apocalypticism has found its way back into the life of the present Episcopal church when in the eucharistic liturgy the people pray: 'Christ will come again.' He contrasts this apocalypticism with an appropriate eschatology. An appropriate eschatology emphasizes that Christians must seek to be obedient today 'within the perspective of the future that can be readily foreseen.'[63] What is meant by readily foreseen? Is this an unwarranted appeal to a particularist Christology on Preston's behalf? No, because what we can readily foresee is not determined Christologically. Instead, an appropriate eschatology suggests: 'The call is for joyful obedience today; the materials for decision come from the empirical data of the day.'[64] Rather than a Christological emphasis, our reading of the times is to be based on the 'empirical data' that allow us to act in the present in ways consistent with Preston's four principles, already elucidated.

What does Preston's Christian anthropology provide? A Christian anthropology supports a form of capitalism because it provides those necessary moral values which capitalism itself cannot generate. Here we find a strong continuity between Preston and Novak. Preston writes: 'The [radical Right] theorists do recognize what has by no means always been recognized, that the free market economy which it advocates pre-supposes moral values which it does not generate itself.'[65] What moral values does Christianity offer? Respect for property and law, individual initiative and creativity.[66]

Does Christianity, finally, offer anything distinctive in Preston's economic ethics? Could we not find a number of philosophies and religions that would provide a similar anthropology and corresponding moral values? That Christianity does not contribute anything distinctively *Christian* to the economy is not a critique of Preston, but a restatement of his position. The economy belongs to all people. People live in pluralist societies. The task of the Christian theologian is to distill those teachings that have universal significance (fundamental human experience) and contribute those teachings to the common good.

Several problems emerge with Preston's strategy. First, it makes Christian ethics dependent on the state. The state appears more universal than the church because the state establishes the boundaries within which pluralist societies function. The church becomes one such society and is then implicitly subordinated to the state. Second, it finds the relevance of Christian theology to be its understanding of sin and its anthropology. This anthropology is not wrong: it is indiscriminate. Nearly every theologian working on economics appeals to it either as a critique of, or a defense for, the capitalist order. The *analogia libertatis* does no work that could discriminate among the various economic prescriptions set forth by the theologians within the dominant tradition. The anthropology itself is irrelevant without fitting it with a larger theological whole. What is troubling within the dominant tradition is that this anthropology carries so much of the burden in relating theology to economics. It has too large a role to play.

The central role of the doctrine of original sin is also quite puzzling. Why do theologians who are concerned about imposing specific Christian doctrines on a pluralist public feel no crisis of conscience in imposing the Christian doctrine of original sin as a legitimation of the state? Is original sin somehow less particular to Christianity? Why do such theologians find relevance in the negative aspects of Christianity – the inevitability of sin – and not in its positive aspects – that all are redeemed in Christ? The central reason for this may very well be that the doctrine of original sin is so readily relevant to a capitalist economic order.

As we noticed earlier, Preston, like Tawney, sought relevance for the church and for theology in the public sphere. Both worried that theological commitment to traditional teaching had rendered the church voiceless in the modern era. But Preston's own position is quite consistent with neo-scholastic theology. It likewise sought to develop morality on the basis of a doctrine of pure nature where the moral life could be set forth fundamentally through reason and nature alone, separate from the specificities of sacred doctrine. When Pius XII defended fortress scholasticism against the integralism of the *nouvelle theologie*, he insisted that although sacred doctrine was 'morally necessary,' nevertheless 'human reason by its own nature, force and light can arrive at a true and certain knowledge of the one personal God …' Pius XII worried that the return by moral theologians to sacred scripture 'diminished the value of human reason.'[67] Neo-scholastic theology was committed to a strong nature–supernature distinction. The French Jesuit theologian Henri de Lubac attempted to overcome this distinction and integrate what had been rendered asunder – nature and supernature. He argued that the neo-scholastic emphasis on a doctrine of pure nature 'leads to a being sufficient to himself and wishing to be so; it leads to a natural morality pure and simple, which must tend to be a morality without religion.'[68]

Preston's reliance on the social sciences perpetuates that rigid nature/supernature distinction. It likewise allows for a nature untouched by the supernatural or by sacred doctrine. This natural reality is present to human creatures through reason alone, and reason alone can present it to us. But this fails to consider that 'nature' is not self-evident to reason, that it always requires human 'implements' for its presentation. Social sciences are such implements, and implements presume the context within which they can function. It is not surprising that Preston, utilizing the science of economics as that which presents empirical reality to the Christian theologian for consideration, finds some form of capitalism inevitable. As a discipline, economics cannot work without the presumption of the context of capitalism. As Robert Heilbronner has argued, 'the disinterested motives of economics' are 'intrinsically embedded in capitalism and to some degree thereby becomes its self-justifying voice, even when it is quite oblivious of serving that purpose.'[69] The implements we use to discover 'empirical reality' may, in fact, presuppose the very discovery we seek to unearth.

Has Preston merely selected one particular tradition, the tradition of liberalism with its institutionalization in the state, over that of Christianity with its institutionalization through the church? Is he seeking converts to the state without the critical awareness that this is the logical outcome of his analysis? If this is true then it poses a serious problem for theological economics. If the science of economics presupposes the tradition of liberalism with its institutionalization in the modern nation–state, then we find the disagreements between theologians like Preston and the neo-conservatives to be nothing but disagreements within a common tradition. Preston cannot accept that the New Right is grounded in the same tradition as he is, the tradition of liberalism. So he mentions that 'the liberal tradition [*sic.*] of the New Right denigrates politics by assuming that removing state power removes domination.' Preston denies that Novak and the New Right are true inheritors of his own liberal tradition (which he seems to deny is a tradition altogether). Yet here Preston is wrong. As I argued earlier, no one is a more consistent Millian liberal than is Michael Novak.

Distinguishing Preston's work from Novak's is difficult to do. Both view modernity as a great step forward. Both consistently argue against the church's medieval teachings on the economy. They draw on a similar anthropology and suggest that the Christian doctrine of the person is the decisive contribution of Christian theology to economics. This anthropology states that we are made in the image of God to be creative intelligent individuals, living within communities, and imitating God through the productive capacity grounded in our freedom. For Novak, we are 'co-creators' with God. For Preston, 'wealth-creation is a vocation, a response to a God-given possibility.'[70] Both appeal to Reinhold Niebuhr for support, and both view democratic forms of government as the best possible form of life and a necessary defense against tyranny because of the doctrine of original sin. The key difference between them is whether democratic *capitalism* creates possessive individuals (Preston's charge) or democratic *socialism* destroys Christian personalism (Novak's charge).

Novak has defended capitalism against the central charge brought against it by theologians like Preston, namely that it produces a 'possessive individualism,' and thus violates a disinterested ethic of obligation. Here Novak's work is compelling. Since Adam Smith, capitalism has not been based on a possessive accumulation. That would be hoarding, the very thing Smith and most spokespersons for the market despise. Capitalism is based on the practice of individuals allowing their property to be at the disposal of others, particularly corporations. The money by which I purchased my house, my automobile and my college education came from the capital of so many others that I could not even begin to discover its manifold sources. Likewise, my pension plan, mutual fund and savings account are assisting others in their (hopefully) productive enterprises.

Far from creating a possessive individualism, capitalism creates structures of interdependence and connectedness that are so universal and deeply entrenched that we cannot even name all the various purposes our investment serves and those which serve us. It creates a *catholic* economy. Capitalism is creating exactly what McCann and Stackhouse see as the future for theology – a cosmopolitan social ethic. In fact, depending on the market, my individual possessions can change from day to day with little to no control on my part, or with little connection to my actual labor.

If the distinctive Christian contribution to economics is an anthropology according to which we discover God at work in the world through an *analogia libertatis*, and if the only substantive critique of capitalism is that it creates *possessive* individuals, then Novak's work is by far the most persuasive. Far from creating possessive individuals, capitalism creates global networks of interdependence that we are incapable even of naming. My labor and my possessions are rent asunder. The problem with capitalism is not that it creates possessive individuals but that it fragments and destroys identity, and produces a false catholicity seemingly unable to rest until it has consumed all our identity without reserve. Preston's conclusion differs from Novak's – Preston wants a welfare capitalism, Novak a capitalism unfettered by the state. But they argue from within a common tradition. And both of them elevate the role of some institution (Novak the market, Preston the state) over that of the church in the divine economy.

## IV  Grace without the New law of the Gospel: Wogaman's subordination of Christology to liberty

A Christian anthropology that views 'man's personhood' as capable of choosing between good and evil constitutes both the beginning and the end of Wogaman's economic ethics. He writes: 'The fulfillment of his potentialities as a unique person requires respect for his individuality and his freedom.' Likewise he speaks of 'the inherent dignity and value of the individual human person. Wogaman speaks of this anthropology in terms of the individual as 'a social being,' a term similar to Novak's 'communitarian personalism'; in fact, both cite Walter Muelder, the Boston Personalist, to explain this anthropology.[71] Where we find such a 'personhood' being advanced in the world, we find God at work. Again the metanarrative relating theology and economics depends on an *analogia libertatis*.

For Wogaman, as for Novak, creation, anthropology, and original sin remain paramount, and the doctrine of grace is emphasized as the context within which human creativity occurs. But for Wogaman the basic idea of grace is unconditional acceptance. Wogaman sets grace decisively over and against works and the law.[72] Thus he opposes the idea that income necessarily should be based on one's actual labor. Yet this grace-apart-from-works implies also that we are to act from motives of 'responsible freedom' and not from 'religious laws,' which are 'essentially negative.' He states: 'Christ has set us free from religious laws.'[73] This freedom is also a freedom from any historical and temporal claims an institution might make to represent the good.

Like McCann, Wogaman argues for epistemological humility. We do not have access to a determinative good. Any reliance upon such a good can result only in self-righteousness, and this remains the gravest threat to social and political life. This means that all social formations will be infected with sin, and thus any sound political economy will recognize this fact. This Niebuhrian theme sounds consistently throughout Wogaman's work:

> Among contemporary theologians the interpretation of original sin as a universal tendency of men to put themselves first has found general acceptance.

> Sin continues to infect the whole human enterprise.

> Theology has much to say about sin, about the brokenness of human life, about the tragic necessity to participate in unjust, evil structures and institutions while seeking to bend them toward something better.[74]

Wogaman, like Preston, McCann, Stackhouse and Novak, uses this doctrine as a critique of Marxism.

Wogaman gives a mixed response to Marxism. While Novak argues its inconsistency with Christian values, in that it denies human creativity, Wogaman believes Marxism to be consistent with those values because it allows the human creature to be self-creating. One of the two, it seems, is confused about how Marxism fits with their common Christian anthropology. But Wogaman finds Marxism inconsistent with Christian values because it does not 'make continuing provision for the sinfulness in human life.'[75] Here Wogaman agrees completely with Novak. Yet Wogaman also uses the doctrine of original sin as a critique of *laissez-faire* capitalism. It 'liberates the human spirit from undesirable constraints of the natural world,' but this liberty is often for trivial products.[76] Moreover, the free market does not insure that equality will be preserved. Thus, some governmental interference is necessary. Here Wogaman believes Novak has missed something.

For Wogaman, the economic order must be 'fully accountable to the political order,' and the political order 'must be democratic.'[77] By *democratic* is meant not only majority rule but a majority rule that allows minority dissent:

> The important question is whether or not the outcomes are a fair representation of majority views and whether those who are in opposition are free to express their opposition through speech and press and organized political action.[78]

Because the doctrine of original sin is about a universal tendency toward unfairness, the economic order must be subordinated to the political order. Original sin functions in Wogaman's work as it did in Preston's: it provides a central role for the state. It must interfere with the market only in so far as it provides the conditions for fairness and freedom upon which the market should work. The state must exercise this limited interference because of humanity's propensity toward sin. Novak reversed this argument. The state must not interfere with the market because of humanity's propensity toward sin. Novak agrees with Wogaman that sin is this universal tendency toward unfairness, but argues that this unfairness is rather intensified than checked by state interference. The market insures freedom and fairness better than would state intervention. Therefore, the doctrine of original sin requires the separation of state and market.

Which of the two is correct? The contradictory results produced, given the similarities in the theology of each, leave us wondering: what does theology matter? What work does it actually do?

# 5 Conclusion to Part I

The dominant tradition is indebted to Weberian sociology and Niebuhrian realism. It views pluralist western democracies as the best possible form of organized socio-political life. And this makes confessional Christian language problematic in the public realm. This dominant tradition finds many aspects of modernity worth embracing, although it is critical of the premodern medieval church and the postmodern 'balkanization' of politics. Because modernity is embraced while postmodernity is eschewed, some within the dominant tradition find a conspiracy occurring against the wisdom of modernity. In particular, Novak and Stackhouse find an 'adversary culture' of elites who have derailed modernity into postmodernity. They find postmodernity to be less extension and intensification of modernity than a well-intentioned, yet misguided, effort to undo modernity's gains.[1] The vociferousness of their attack against post-liberal and liberation theologians has to be understood in light of their admirable concern that the public role of theology has been compromised by a self-righteous privatization of theological discourse.

All of these ethicists are 'public theologians' who are concerned not only with relating faith and economics but with securing for theology a 'public' role in promoting the common good. Perhaps this is a utopian desire, which does not take into account what Weber demonstrated – that from the perspective of modernity theology can be left only the irrational remainder. Still, their intention is to maintain a tradition of religious participation in political economy. Whether they have given us sufficient means to do this remains an important question.

This dominant tradition finds Marxism suspect, and all its members disagree, to variable extents, with the liberation theologians. The theologians of the dominant tradition share a cluster of theological themes that they find relevant to economistic thinking: in particular, an anthropology, the doctrine of creation, and the doctrine of original sin. But they have difficulty with the direct relevance to economics of explicitly Christological themes and strong ecclesiologies. They find scripture relevant for its general values but not determinative in its specifics.

Weber's work is utilized in this dominant tradition because it supposedly allows for 'spirit' to be a causal factor in political economics. Whereas for Marxism the driving force behind history is historical materialism, but for Weber it is ideas. These ideas constitute a 'spirit,' which then forms the basis for the possibility of practical action. Exactly what this 'spirit' consists in is difficult to say. Weber himself acknowledged the difficulty of the term, suggesting that it is 'a complex of elements associated in historical reality which we unite into a conceptual whole from the standpoint of their cultural significance.'[2] This is related to his typological method. The sociologist examines history from a value-neutral perspective, and asks: 'What motives determined and lead the individual members and participants in this socialistic community to behave in such a way that the community came into being in the first place and that it continues to exist?'[3] Weber began with the individual as the basic element that contributed to 'the spirit of ...'. For the individual is 'the upper limit and sole carrier of meaningful conduct.'[4] Individuals are not manifestations of a spirit working above them, nor the products of material production; they are rather the key contributors to meaningful action, and they contribute to it in predictable and general ways that can be typologized.

Weber typed human action in terms of a continuum of rationality that correlates ideas and interests.[5] The more rational form of social action is where ideas and interest mesh as they would with a calculative rationality based on 'marginal utility'; that is to say where individuals choose on the basis of 'the extra satisfaction gained by a consumer from a small increment in the consumption of a commodity.'[6] Weber described less rational forms of action in terms of 'value,' 'affect,' or 'tradition.' Traditional forms of action are, of course, those done for the sake of tradition. Value-rationality would be social action based on the natural law or a categorical imperative. By 'rational' Weber did not mean reasonable in terms of a moral good – as a sociologist he refrained from questions about which form of rationality more approximated the good – he meant nothing more than the 'interpretive grasp of meaning' of an individual's actions. Thus the 'more' rational understanding of human action occurs when there is congruence between one's ideas and one's interest. But this is unsatisfactory.

Despite his efforts to provide a *value-neutral* description of social phenomena, Weber has slipped in a morally normative account of human action, i.e. that action which can be more readily understood occurs when an individual acts on the basis of marginal utility. Therefore, in rational – versus traditional or affectual – human action, people will act based on a calculation by which they give value to things for want-satisfaction. Weber recognized that such human action would be an 'ideal type,' and that other considerations were almost always present.[7] Still, this ideal type became the norm by which human action was categorized.

Within the dominant theological tradition, the common anthropology selected as relevant for economics fits well with Weber's rationality of human action. The human person is viewed as one who freely chooses based on possibilities set before her or him. This freedom constitutes the *imago dei*. In these choices, the human person gives meaning to the world and creates the world anew. The freedom underlying this anthropology is an empty freedom – the freedom to create, never the creation itself. The content of those productions, or the objects to which this freedom directs us, plays no central role in this *analogia libertatis*. It is the bare freedom to give value to the world that matters, not the content of any particular object that freedom should serve. The important question is whether the dominant tradition develops this anthropology simply because of the pressures exerted from material forces let loose from the political and economic transformations that characterize modernity. Or is this anthropology congruent with the church's ancient tradition? In other words, is this anthropology the inevitable result of a moral theology that first seeks to be relevant to the dominant social order when that order is defined by capitalism? That question can be answered only by placing this emphasis on anthropology within the larger grammar of faith to see its effects on theology as a whole. We saw how that anthropology subordinated Christology and ecclesiology to its understanding rather than allowing our understanding of human nature to arise from Christ and his church. It is this narrative performance of theology that renders the dominant tradition's anthropology suspect. It invites a pure formality of freedom that cannot embody the specific content of the Christian tradition, but can see that content only as something to be overcome in order to be relevant to global capitalism. This fits well Weber's understanding of rationality.

The standpoint from which Weber viewed things was clearly that the more reasonable form of economic rationality occurs when it remains 'formal' rather than 'substantive.' By 'formal' he meant that economic action which takes place on the basis of 'quantitative calculation or accounting.' By 'substantive' he meant that which takes place 'under some criterion of ultimate values.'[8] Yet what warrants this standpoint? Why should we view the world this way? Why should this be the grid through which we observe the Middle Ages, the Indian Brahmas, the Chinese Literati? Because Weber's standpoint was supposedly value-neutral, Weberians would have to dismiss such questions. But only when human action can be defined in amoral (or pre-moral) terms can Weber's sociology maintain its claim for neutrality. And from a theological perspective, this is precisely the problem. What makes human action human is its inextricable relationship with morality. Morality is not about subjective values, but the ends for which humans should act. To even attempt to define human action in the same terms as the growth of a sycamore tree or the breeding patterns of a fruitfly is already to see it as less than human. Insofar as Weber's sociology examined human economic action, it was and is inescapably moral. And as a morality it contains within itself implicit ends for human action. That makes it 'theological,' even if those ends are now anti-theological.

The acceptance of Weber's approach by the theologians of the dominant tradition poses significant problems. Perhaps the major problem is Weber's understanding of theology. Deeply indebted to Kantian thinking, he distinguished the grace-infused life from the moral life. Thus he suggested:

> Every type of actual dispensation of grace by a person, regardless of whether his authority derives from personal charismatic gifts or his official status within an institution, has the net effect of weakening the demands of morality upon the individual just as does ritualism.[9]

He posited this antinomy between infused grace, ritual and the moral life because he was convinced that morality requires 'the necessity of developing an individual pattern of life based on ethical foundations.'[10] Those ethical foundations must transcend all particular forms of life and be capable of universalization. They will be bound by duty alone. They will be characterized by disinterestedness.

Traditional Christian theology has never set an infused grace against the exercise of the moral life. It viewed them as compatible. A Weberian ethic requires their separation. In so doing, it allows theologians to speak of the moral life in separation from the theological life. We can still use natural law, spheres of sovereignty, or individual rights, or any other ethic that easily allows of disinterestedness and universalizability. But the evangelical law, the theological virtues, the infused powers of the sacraments, or the end of humanity as happiness in the vision of God cannot be used. These particular substantive confessions pose problems for Weberian rationality. They likewise pose problems for the theologians of the dominant tradition. And they pose problems because of the assumption of *pluralism*.

All the dominant theologians work with a concern that theology does not impose its particularity on the public square. Thus some of them will assert that theology must now be *post-confessional*. Their concern is important. If an ethics grounded in a confessional theology entails violence and arrogance toward other cultures and peoples, then it is unacceptable and contemptible. Their desire for peace in a pluralist world leads these theologians to speak of a post-confessional theology. However, if they have defined our present reality inaccurately, if 'pluralism' does not describe the increasing homogeneity of a catholic market, then confessionalism may not be the problem. Perhaps the inescapable unity of our daily practices in service to a global reality has become our 'confession.' Then the only way to maintain some sense of diversity is through an alternative confession, with its different practices.

A second problem for a theological usage of Weber's work is that his account of charismatic authority was based on the formal impact of the leader's influence rather than on the truthfulness of the message. The substance of the message was not his concern, only its formal effectiveness. Technically, Weberian sociology cannot differentiate between Jesus and

Hitler. Both were charismatic figures. Both were effective in promoting a social movement. But theology cannot dissociate the substance of the message from its formal effectiveness. A sign of the dominance of Weber's rationality will be that formal and universal claims will gain ascendance while substantive truth-claims will be neglected. Only as they fit within the formal and universal rationality are they still permitted. Stackhouse's defense of 'creeds' as formal social spaces, Wogaman's constant invocation of 'grace' as a de-particularized, antinomian, formal acceptance, Novak's use of creation and Preston's translation of Christology into 'fundamental human experience' are all consistent with Weber's formal rationality.

Third, Weber posed a false antinomy between *traditional* authority and *rational* authority. He defined the pure type of traditional authority as when 'legitimacy is claimed for it and believed in by virtue of the sanctity of age-old rules and powers.'[11] This is not a helpful definition because of the vagueness surrounding 'age-old.' How much time must elapse before something is called 'age-old'? What type of authority could not be accused of this, given that all forms of authority must be exercised at a precise moment and therefore can only be always already bounded by time? However, once this distinction is operative, certain forms of authority can be described as *rational* over and against *traditional* because the former seem to escape the contingent character of time-boundedness. Then we become blind to the fact that all rational authority is inseparable from tradition. Weberian sociology itself now becomes a traditional form of authority, which is dangerous precisely because it cannot be recognized as such.

The real difference between Weber's traditional and legal forms of authority is focused on a personal versus an impersonal exercise of authority. In *legal* authority people obey the 'impersonal order' and not a person. This may be an adequate description of modernity, but does it deserve the status of 'more reasonable' given to it by Weber? The result of this impersonal account of authority is that obedience to abstract ideas mediated through individuals becomes acceptable, but obedience to a person because of his or her role within a community, such as a bishop, a priest or a saint, is viewed as unacceptable. The indictment against any economic ethics grounded in an ecclesial authority then becomes obvious. The result is that forms of rationality grounded in an institution's tradition are easily dismissed. We see evidence of this in the neglect of, and contempt for, the premodern church's teachings on economics within the dominant tradition. The problem with this neglect and contempt is that they are based on the assumption that these teachings are viewed as necessarily wrong because they are fostered through tradition rather than the rational authority of modern social science. But this objection would not hold if the distinction between rational and traditional authority were false.

A fourth problem is that Weber reduces religion to the irrational. He takes too literally Kant's claim, 'I have therefore found it necessary to deny knowledge to make room for faith.' Religion may be respectable, but for

Weber it requires a *sacrificium intellectum*. For this reason, the optimism of the theologians in the dominant tradition that through Weber's sociology we can make theology relevant to modern economics seems unwarranted. We cannot look to Weber for a faith seeking understanding.

A fifth problem with the use of Weber is the illegitimate way some theologians actually use his ideas. For instance, his work is often cited as evidence for the historical causality of religious ideas. This was not what Weber showed. His argument suggested that ascetic Protestantism resulted in unintended consequences that then turned upon it and were set against the viability of any religious ethic. Weber masterfully shows us how theological ethics is rendered superfluous in modern economic arrangements. The dominant tradition neglects this central Weberian insight.

Finally, does Weber's work itself provide a new form of legitimate domination? Does it necessitate the idea of a value-neutral description of social actions that must first be presented by the social scientists (particularly by economists) and only after that presentation may theologians and moralists do with them what they will?[12] If that is the case, then such domination exerts pressure on theologians to provide an account of theology that will fit this social perspective. It would require that theology be relevant at a distance, that it fit with the anti-humanistic anthropology of the social sciences, and that it recognize the errors of the traditional authority exercised by the church. This is precisely what we found in the dominant tradition.

The effort to make Christian theology relevant to economics by way of a Weberian strategy results in serious theological problems. These efforts result in a rationality based on marginal efficiency, the principle of abstract equivalence and the fact–value distinction. The theology selected to fit within this rationality creates a common tradition despite the fact that the economic prescriptions of each theologian defend a different kind of capitalism. The result is a theology that is relevant to capitalist economics. But the lingering question is whether that relevance has been purchased at the expense of the theological tradition.

The difficulty in the comparisons between the theologians in the dominant tradition is that they use a similar theology to arrive at different economic prescriptions. An anthropology is identified as Christian, which both lends itself to and requires democratic political structures. The doctrine of creation is selected to emphasize humanity's creative potential. The affirmation that creation is good is used for the purpose of defining the vocation of the human person as a co-participant in the production of wealth. An *analogia libertatis* identifies God's work in the world. But this analogous work of liberty assumes a problematic doctrine of God. Liberty itself becomes more foundational in defining the relationship between God and creation than is that relationship itself. In other words, the theologians of the dominant tradition implicitly violate Anselm's great theological insight that God is that than which nothing greater can be conceived. The liberty by which they identify God's work becomes a metanarrative greater than God's own disclosure in Jesus Christ. This results in a doctrine of God in which God can be conceived in terms only of utter simplicity and formal power. This nominalist doctrine of God leads to antinomian tendencies where human freedom, like God's, is unbounded by anything true, good or beautiful. The logical conclusion is that particular themes within Christian theology are either construed as problematic or are overlooked altogether. Thus, nowhere in the dominant tradition do we find a discussion of the *telos* of human nature as defined by the particularity of Jesus of Nazareth or an emphasis on the historical character of redemption in and through Jesus' particularity. Instead, human nature as it is, both in its sinfulness and in its potential creativity, grounds this theological economics. This is not surprising. Theological defenders of capitalism can be trapped only within the modern.

Alasdair MacIntyre has explained how the modernist project developed as an effort to justify morality by neglecting any teleological rendering of the human person. Instead of understanding the moral life as a project of becoming that which human nature should be, morality was justified in terms of something identifiable in human nature *per se*. The dominant ways of doing this were through the autonomous use of reason or via a free choice grounded in the pursuit of pleasure or the diminishment of pain, termed 'utility.' Human nature as it is becomes the given of morality rather than its project. But MacIntyre has shown us how this has failed.[13] The theological 'performance' present in the dominant tradition lends support to MacIntyre's thesis. For what we discover is a theology that seems not to matter, and thus a theology that has failed. Similar theological themes are selected as basic principles and applied to economics with different prescriptive results. But these different results arise within the context of the already present major political options in modernity. The key variation within this tradition is the degree to which the market or the state is to be conceded the leading role in preserving liberty, but the entire theological drama is subordinated to modernity's overarching narrative quest for liberty. These theologians seem undeterred in their confidence about that modernist project despite its historical performance in the twentieth century and the countless indictments brought against it, beginning with Nietzsche's prescience as to what this century would bring.[14] They herald liberty as if the 'advent of nihilism' is yet to come.

A decisive theological criticism that can be made against this tradition is its inability to sustain the centrality of a particular reading of Christology and ecclesiology. The place of the church as a significant theological actor within the divine–human drama is diminished, and either the corporation or the state becomes elevated to the status of main character. The church receives, at best, a bit-part. This is evident particularly in the transvaluation of *catholicity* as defining the church to defining instead either an epistemology or the market process itself, without the recognition of any sense of loss.

Nowhere do we find an argument for the catholicity of the church grounded in the evangelical law distributed at baptism. Instead, *catholic* has become either the principle of universalization or the global reality of the current market system. Then, only those doctrines that can be universalized are selected as theologically relevant for economics – creation, anthropology and sin easily fill the bill. Some form of capitalism is conceded as necessary because it allows for co-creativity, the freedom of the human person along with the tragedy of original sin.[15]

That humans can cooperate as they would need to within a socialist order is viewed as an impossibility because of the lingering effects of sin. This gives the doctrine of sin too important a role in theology. It becomes the rational basis for political and economic life rather than that against which Christianity is set. Curiously, even though all these theologians were concerned to maintain pluralism, and either translated into secular terms, or neglected altogether, too distinctive Christian themes, they felt no such similar compunction toward the unique Christian doctrine of 'sin.' Why does this particular theological theme get selected and universalized while themes grounded in Christ's particularity are no longer admissible? It is because sin, like 'value,' remains formal and abstract: it loses any distinctive Christological determination. It functions as merely a critique of any effort to create a better society. It functions precisely as the critical frame of mind Schumpeter identified to be the core capitalist value. Sin and evil are not viewed as privation from a basic ontic good, as they were for Thomas and Augustine. Thus, sin is no longer dependent upon a prior account of that which is good. It does not need Christology for its own intelligibility. Sin becomes intelligible apart from goodness. Then the argument always reduces to the same statement: 'Democracy and capitalism are the worst forms of government and economic systems, except for all the alternatives.' Democracy and capitalism win by default. They are garments of skin given us because of sin. Thus, one part of Augustine's political theology is selected – that secular government results from sin, and the other part neglected – that secular government should be divinely ordered.[16] Secular rulers (including corporate executives) are now free from theological interference except for that theology which can be universalized for a cosmopolitan social ethics. The result is already painfully clear. The secular rulers of Briggs and Stratton seem puzzled that church people would question their practices.

The similarity in theological themes likewise stems from a shared understanding of what constitutes *rationality*. The center of the tradition focuses on an anthropology for which to choose freely to enter into relationships with others constitutes the *imago dei*. Human volition becomes the basis for reasonable political and economic exchanges. Although not identical with it, this anthropology fits well the marginalist rationality that provides the basis for capitalism as 'scientific' social organization. Marginalist rationality assumes that goods are not intrinsic to forms of life, and therefore it does not question whether certain goods might be incommensurable. For marginalist rationality all goods are subject to the overarching law of value. All goods are potential objects of human choice, and thus through a person's choices, she or he gives value to that which is. These choices can then be indexed and regularities observed. These regularities are subject to change, but through statistical methods we can chart and negotiate the changes. We may not approve of these choices, but they reflect the 'facts' of economic life, the empirical realities. Morality cannot alter this facticity. Instead, it gives values that the moralists hope will bring people to make different choices. If the task of theology is to be relevant to modern economics, then it must adopt this posture. The result is an emphasis on an anthropology that does not conflict with the economists' science.

What we have witnessed above all in the dominant tradition is that a defense of capitalism seems to carry with it an inability to articulate orthodox theological themes. This is not surprising, for at least three reasons. First, capitalism requires the denial of tradition. Second, the free-market economy arose as an alternative to the social charity embedded in the Catholic church, which was viewed as a threat to the liberty of the market. Third, the capitalist alternative to the Catholic church was based on a natural theology that, though this is seldom recognized today, remains as the suppressed theological premiss within which capitalist economic analysis operates.

As Schumpeter noted, the culture of capitalism requires a constant and continuous critique of all things traditional. Capitalist defenders must position capitalism against the 'deformed irrationality' of a previous age. They assume a complete rupture with what went before, and thus see capitalism as the always new and improving. It demands a critical posture toward the past and an ever-revolving call for the new and improved. Such a cultural logic cannot sustain orthodox Christian claims because they arise from a contingent history, which can then be expressed only through human participation and transmission in that history that calls for a faithful obedience toward that transmission. Theologians in the dominant tradition either explicitly reject any concern to sustain such claims or they fail in the execution of such a concern. This is not accidental: it is intrinsic to the position.

The free market first sought freedom not from the state but from the Catholic church. This is clear in Adam Smith's writings and it is a narrative economic historians share. When Adam Smith published *The Wealth of Nations*, he stated that the church of Rome posed the greatest threat to the civil order, liberty, and happiness of humankind that the free market could guarantee. To secure a free market, the church's charity must first be contained so that it would not 'disturb the state.'[17] The market's apologetes freed it first from the church. This does not imply that these two institutions must remain in opposition. But they undoubtedly embody counter traditions and histories. Before the opposition can be remedied a forthright discussion of those differences and a recognition of these competing histories are necessary. The selection of theological themes present in the dominant tradition does not lend itself to such a forthright discussion and potential conflict between theology and economics. Instead they result in a harmonious relationship between the church and the global capitalist market, overlooking their tumultuous and conflictual histories.

Although capitalism is presented often as a natural reality subject to objective scientific investigation, it has a history. This history includes moral and theological themes that originally scripted it. The doctrine of unintended consequences found in Smith, Weber, and Niebuhr (and repeated in contemporary economics textbooks and introductions to Christian ethics) continues to reflect those moral and theological themes, even though they are no longer recognized as such. Why is it the case that aiming for the good results in economic disaster but aiming for the *useful* produces an unintended good? Smith was clear that this required a doctrine of providence. That doctrine of providence was then replaced by nature, that was in turn replaced by human desiring, willing and preferring. Nevertheless, the science of economics is the inheritor of natural theology. This has become a suppressed premiss within capitalist economics that is seldom recognized and never defended, yet its natural theology assumes some entity – god, nature, the regularity of human desire and choice, the laws of the market – that insures a proper eschatological end to self-directed *useful* human action. That this is the *suppressed* theological premiss within economics results in a complete lack of questioning as to the moral and/or theological legitimacy of this foundational doctrine. Any theological engagement with capitalist economics must question whether this natural theology is dispensable to its structure and whether it results in theological incompatibilities in respect of a Christian theology seeking to subordinate the useful to theological themes that are more than natural alone – that are also supernatural.

Where the theologians of the dominant tradition essentially differ is in the degree to which they acknowledge either a completely unencumbered market capitalism or a state-regulated one to be the better means of securing democratic liberties. Wogaman and Preston are willing to argue for a democratic socialism, a 'socialism' that appears similar to Keynesianism. Neither Wogaman nor Preston gives us a detailed analysis of how, or why, workers should own the means of production. They may not be as critical of Marx as are the tirading Novak, Stackhouse, and McCann, but they are sufficiently critical that their democratic socialism resembles the current status of the Democratic Party in the United States, or the Labour Party in the United Kingdom.

In the dominant tradition Marx is either pilloried (Novak, Stackhouse) or dismissed as failing to be sufficiently cognizant of the Christian doctrine of sin (a very odd argument to be employed by theologians calling us to respect pluralism). A recurrent criticism is that Marxism fails as a social science. Because the social sciences remain so central to the dominant tradition, this failure is decisive. The failure stems from the common argument that Marx's labor theory of value is wrong as a scientific claim. If Marx was wrong about this, then his central notion of the expropriation of surplus value by the owners of the means of production will not hold. He is wrong because of the marginalist theory of utility. The additional numbers of laborers necessary for the production of commodities rises initially, but eventually a saturation point is reached at which the continuing rise in number of laborers does not increase but rather diminishes the value of the product. Hence the conclusion, labor does not produce the value of a commodity when all other factors of production are held constant. If Marxism is held to be a social science and nothing more, this critique is potent. In fact it finds support in Engels' essay 'Socialism: Utopian and Scientific.' However, as we shall see Marxism might still offer insights that can be theologically appropriated, if we deny it its *scientific* character. Although the liberation theologians point us in this direction, they remain indebted to a version of Marxism as a social science that makes them susceptible to this critique.

Although there are a number of good criticisms of Marx's labor theory of value – in particular its claim to be generated from social science alone – Novak's critique is tendentious. He finds the labor theory of value wrong because it assumes labor to be the basic element of value when in fact it is *intellect*. For instance, he argues that the labor theory of value is wrong because two farmers working side by side will create different productive values. A farmer with inferior implements can through wit and intelligence, and actually less labor time, create greater value. This is an odd criticism of Marx's labor theory of value. If a criticism of the theory is that equal labor does not result in equal value, then the same criticism surely must apply to Novak's 'creative theory of value.' It is equally preposterous to assume that superior wit and intelligence create greater value in a capitalist society. Novak himself has suggested that capitalism is one part lottery.[18]

For all of these theologians the Thomistic tradition is to be criticized for misunderstanding money. Thomas falsely considered the economy to be 'static' and money to be sterile. For Novak, this is also the central problem with Marx. Here he repeats the arguments of marginalist economics that narrates Marx's economics in terms of a dogmatic tradition stemming from Aristotle and extending through Thomas. This tradition is viewed as irrational and dogmatically authoritarian. Yet, that money is sterile is not *prima facie* an unreasonable argument. Sheep, people, pear-trees, blueberry-bushes, corn-plants – all these reproduce because God endowed them in nature with the capacity for reproduction. Money has no genitalia. It cannot reproduce on its own. Who could deny this claim? Theologians and economists who understand wealth production better than Marx–Aquinas–Aristotle want to convince us that money is not sterile: it reproduces.

Obviously money is sterile. Anyone who tells us otherwise is using language in a veiled way: they mean something other than what they say. I think what they mean to say is that wealth is not a zero-sum game. Fair enough. I don't think Marx, Aquinas, or Aristotle would have disagreed. Through human labor – in all its facets including intelligence, risk, inventiveness and contingent circumstances – money can be employed in productive ventures and a profit result. I can buy two sheep, and – if they are a male and female – I might receive the profit of a third. I can buy farm land and plant it, and receive a profit. I can invest in some enterprise, and that money might yield a profit. But the *money* has not reproduced, because money simply cannot do that. What has happened is that through potentialities present in creation, including contingent circumstances too numerous to ever be totally accounted for, that investment created the conditions whereby profit was generated.

This may not exactly be the labor theory of value, but Tawney was correct – Marx was closer to the Christian tradition on this one than were the liberals. The dominant tradition, however, seems embarrassed by the medieval teachings on usury. St Thomas had argued that 'to take usury for money lent is unjust in itself, because this is to sell what does not exist, and this inevitably leads to inequality which is contrary to justice.'[19] It leads to inequality and opposes true virtue because it sells what doesn't exist for commodification: i.e. it sells the *use* of a commodity rather than the commodity itself, and in so doing it sells time. And it denies the reality that in Thomas' time had been taught since Aristotle's: money does not fructify. Thomas did allow for the possibility of a '*societas*,' a joint-venture by which both creditors and lenders could share in profit making. But the heart of the Thomistic teaching is not merely these proscriptions: his is not an ethics of obligation preoccupied with providing precepts for what is permitted and what denied. The heart of his teaching is neither the usury proscription nor the permission of receiving interest for losses incurred in a joint-enterprise. For Thomas the heart of the matter is that law should direct human actions to virtuous ends. The heart of his teaching was that our economic activity should be able to be directed to those virtues that assist us in our ultimate end – friendship with God. That is why the medieval teachings are important. They seek to direct our lives in all their physical embodiment to that single end and to uphold charity as necessary for our journey.

Such an end does not seem to orientate theological economics in the dominant tradition. We are never told whether capitalism can be directed to this ultimate end.[20] Instead, we are constantly caught up in the need to develop a new and relevant ethics for the 'global era.' Thus, Stackhouse and McCann call for the 'reconstruction of Christian Ethics as it bears on economic life in our increasingly global era. Reconstruction is necessary because much of the analysis used by theologians and pastors to think about economic life in the past few decades is socially and theologically suspect.'[21] The theologians of the dominant tradition argue for a new global ethics because other theologians do not understand how markets operate.[22] Of course, there is some truth to the claim that theologians will be better equipped to consider economic matters if they understand how their subject works. Still, this concern can translate into an acceptance of the economist (or business executive) as the gatekeeper to sound theological pronouncements on economics. Scripture and church tradition will then be filtered through the 'empirical' study of economics. But only an ethics that maintains a formal and substitutable character can be so easily deconstructed and reconstructed. And this is the profound problem with the dominant tradition. The theology selected for economic relevance is not wrong. Who could deny a place for creation, original sin, and a viable Christian anthropology in any theological economics? But the order of these selections truncates theology's narrative wholeness such that more distinctive themes which might resist being incorporated into a global economic ethic are dismissed, neglected, or forgotten. The problem with this theological economics is that it is so *easily* used, so *readily* relevant. It will not create martyrs. It will only legitimize the dominant social practices of the ruling powers, even when it seeks to reform them with religio-moral values.

What provides the formal and substitutable character of this dominant ethic is the idea of 'value.' Both the Anglo-American tradition of utilitarianism and the Kantian tradition make 'value' the center of moral considerations. 'Value' allows human actions to be discussed in ahistorical, non-narrated, terms. It is disinterested. It occupies a formal social space without requiring particular truth-claims. And it renders the dominant tradition too receptive to the 'facts' of the economists.

Christian moral theology has a rich tradition of reflection on economic matters, particularly in its insistence on the theological virtues of charity, faith, and hope as completing the natural virtues of justice and prudence, and as rendering intelligible the church's rules about usury, a just wage, buying and selling, avoiding greed, mendacity and covetousness. These themes are neglected within the dominant tradition because of its preoccupation to bring the church in line with modern developments. The result is a formal theology in service to the modernist project. What becomes central to theological economics is some version of a relatively autonomous economics supported by easily-dispensed-with theological doctrines. In the final analysis, the similar theologies but different economic prescriptions within the dominant tradition prove that the theology itself matters very little. It is relevant and useful, but it lacks concrete historical specificity. The economics *supported* by these theological doctrines actually does not need them. Instead, by hitching its wagon to the increasingly powerful discipline of economics (and business management) theology seeks to maintain its own legitimacy and sustainability. This apologetic strategy is bound to fail. It fails to develop a theological economics out of the richness of theology, and instead produces a reactive ethic based on a perceived need to make theology relevant to a reality defined by global capitalism. The result is that theological pronouncements will begin to take their shape from the reality of that to which they must react. The language of pluralism, inclusivity, individual freedom, growth and heterogeneity is the language of the market. Likewise, economics has established the parameters for a new theological 'orthodoxy.' This has particularly infected the Protestant churches, but now it appears that Catholicism, with its long-standing antimodernist tradition, is succumbing as well.[23] Theology does not matter to the economy, and this results not from the lack of theological work in this area, but because of it.

Rather than shift our theological ethics to be relevant to a global ethics, we should realize that the philosophy producing and sustaining it is a species of nihilism. It assumes that the only meaning, i.e. 'value,' in the world is that which arises through human will. As the great economist Alfred Marshall put it in 1890, 'The desire to put mankind in the saddle is the mainspring of most economic study.'[24] It is what Nietzsche called 'incomplete nihilism,' in that rather than forsaking the 'values' once attributed to God they become the values attributed to humanity. Heidegger explained it this way:

> Incomplete nihilism does indeed replace the former values with others but it still posits the latter always in the old position of authority.... Creativity, previously the unique property of the biblical god, becomes the distinctive mark of human activity. Human activity finally passes over into business enterprise.[25]

The shared anthropology developed by this tradition of theologians embodies well this incomplete nihilism. As Novak put it: 'The world as Adam faced it after the Garden of Eden left humankind in misery and hunger for millennia. Now that the secrets of sustained material progress have been decoded, the responsibility for reducing misery and hunger is no longer God's but ours.' That Novak cannot see that this is a species of atheism is confusing.[26] That Marshall realized it was is telling. That a theological ethic should be relevant to such a 'science' is its undoing.

Yet, as Raymond Williams pointed out, 'no dominant culture ever in reality includes or exhausts all human practice, human energy and human intention.' Thus the dominant tradition always must position itself against both residual forms of tradition (such as the early and medieval church's rules on economic matters and the virtue tradition) and emergent forms of tradition (such as liberation theology, post-liberal theology, and 'sectarian' Christian base communities). By showing the selectivity of the dominant tradition, I hope to show how what we have forgotten in the Christian tradition may have more to teach us than what has been remembered and passed on within this modern theological tradition. To remember against the present is itself, of course, a passing on, a traditioning. And I am convinced that ancient theological terms can stand in their own right as reasonable criticisms of economic relations. Thus this traditioning can be independent of an autonomous social science that works outside any theological gaze. A theological rendering of economics is possible.[27]

Such an argument will have to wait until the third part of this work. Before that effort at recovering a theological memory, I explore another possible alternative to the dominant tradition – the tradition of theology that has now emerged out of the concept of *liberation*.

The theological economics of the dominant tradition has kept alive the important question of the relationship between theology and economics. But they have not given us a theology sufficient to avoid the all-encroaching power of the economists' worldview. The role of the church is overshadowed either by the market or the state. We must look elsewhere.

# Part II
# The emergent tradition

The protest of the *oikos* and the *polis*

# 6   Introduction to Part II

The possibility of an emergent tradition already suggests limits to the scope of any dominant tradition. It can never thoroughly encompass theory and practice because tradition is a process of intentional and unintentional selection. This necessarily excludes certain possibilities, which can become alternative sites to the dominant tradition even though they are often relegated by it to a private, personal, irrelevant, utopian, sectarian or out-moded realm.[1] Such alternative sites can be viable as tradition, however, only if we recognize that tradition is something more than the accumulation of positive desposits chosen by unencumbered free agents. Tradition assumes something more than a collection of free individuals who stand outside history and select and use the past for their present purposes.[2] Otherwise we merely repeat the economic marginalist's account of human agency where free unencumbered choice gives values to things in the world. An autonomous human freedom cannot provide the basis for tradition because tradition is an inheritance and gift. As gift it always includes more than can be selected: abundance is present. Because Christian theology assumes that the gift arises from God made flesh, the gift is inexhaustible.

Some theologians have sought to discover alternative sites – both heretical and orthodox – and have combined them with Marxist social theory or other forms of critical discourse. Because these emergent traditions find engagement with Marxism and/or other critical traditions fruitful for theological reflection, they deny the claim that ideas themselves can construct a theological alternative to the dominant tradition. They do not follow in Weber's 'spirit.' Instead, the critical engagement between a particular historical social location and the theological tradition results in the creation of new theological meanings out of residual possibilities.[3]

This emergent theology has become known as 'liberation theology.' The number of theologians working in this field at present is so vast that no survey of its scope is possible. The theologians examined in Part II are selected because they initiated various traditions of liberation theology, all of which are forms of protest against traditional theology: James Cone's *A Black Theology of Liberation* appeared in 1970; Gustavo Gutiérrez's *A Theology of Liberation* in 1971; Rosemary Radford Ruether's *Liberation*

*Theology: Human Hope Confronts Christian History and American Power* in 1972; and I have included Jon Sobrino because his theological development of Latin-American liberation theology represents what I believe to be the best response to liberation theology's thoughtful critics.

These theologians oppose the notion of theological compatibility between Christianity and capitalism, and all argue for some version of socialism, although this is more strongly set forward by Gutiérrez and Sobrino than it is by Ruether and Cone. Their opposition to capitalism has produced the selection of some similar theological themes. In particular, eschatology plays a more central role than it did in the dominant tradition. Whereas Preston opposed the recovery of the statement 'Christ will come again' in the Anglican Eucharistic prayer as a form of false apocalypticism, the members of the emergent tradition emphasize eschatology for a political theology. This is an interesting development. An eschatological focus has often been associated with an other-worldliness and a non-reflective sense of need that eschewed politics and alienated people from the historical conditions of their poverty. Such an argument is found in Marx, who recognized that eschatology was a form of consolation to working people and thus an expression of their alienation. But it was Troeltsch who argued that this 'other-worldly' Christianity lacked political and social significance. His historical interpretations of this apolitical eschatology had tremendous influence on twentieth-century theological ethics.

Troeltsch argued that Christianity was not a *political* but a *religious* movement that thus appealed to the

> lower classes which do the really creative work, forming communities on a genuine religious basis. They alone unite imagination and simplicity of feeling with a non-reflective habit of mind, a primitive energy, and an urgent sense of need. On such a foundation alone is it possible to build up an unconditional authoritative faith in a Divine Revelation with simplicity of surrender and unshaken certainty.[4]

This simple faith originated because the essence of Jesus' teaching was his proclamation of the Kingdom of God as a 'purely religious idea.' Troeltsch's sentimentalized poor are those most capable of forming a community based purely on a religious idea rather than a social or political one. Unlike the rich and powerful, the poor are prone to an other-worldliness. Jesus' other-worldly teaching attracted the poor and persuaded the early Christians to be unconcerned about the world and social problems. For these considerations, 'belong to the world and will perish with the world.'[5] While these romantic but simple peasants gave Christianity its abiding creative power, it was a power that lacked social and political engagement. So Troeltsch asserted that only as this simple faith 'fuses' with intellectual culture could it endure and become a social ethic. To be social, Christianity must fuse with some other, non-eschatological, culture.

The incorporation of eschatology into a political theology within the emergent tradition contains an implicit critique of Troeltsch's correlation between the poor and an other-worldly religious eschatology. Some version of this incorporation is present in the work of each of these liberation theologians. Yet this incorporation does not seem to have arisen as an intentional or explicit form of opposition to Troeltsch's theological ethics. In fact, as we shall see, the centrality of the Kingdom of God in liberation theology maintains some continuity not only with the work of Troeltsch but with major currents in late-nineteenth- and early-twentieth-century theology that reduced eschatology to ethics. This makes the incorporation of eschatology into a political theology all the more interesting: it seems to arise because of the emergent tradition's different social location – for Gutiérrez, Sobrino and Ruether it arises as they incorporate the perspective of the poor, for Cone the perspective of the black church.

This incorporation of eschatology into a political theology finds an ally in the Mennonite theologian John Howard Yoder. He presented an explicit challenge to Troeltsch's de-politicized eschatology, and his work has much in common with that of the theologians in the emergent tradition. Cone cites his work as an example of a politically engaged Christology,[6] and Ruether's earliest liberation theology develops similar Anabaptist eschatological themes.[7] As early as 1954 Yoder argued that an understanding of eschatology was necessary to make sense of the Anabaptists' non-violent political struggles; this position was further developed in his 1972 *The Politics of Jesus*. In his 1971 *The Original Revolution*, he explained the role of eschatology as 'a hope which, defying present frustration, defines a present position in terms of the yet unseen goal which gives it meaning.'[8] This definition also illuminates how eschatology functions within the theology of the emergent tradition.

The compatibility of this eschatology and Marxism should be obvious. Utopia in Marxist critical social theory has a function similar to that of eschatology in liberation theology.[9] Some philosophers find Marx's work dependent upon a secularized Christian eschatology.[10] Whether this is an adequate interpretation of Marx is irrelevant to understanding the theologians of the emergent tradition; for they do not adopt Marx's utopia, but posit in its place the reign of God. This is another central theme shared in this tradition: the kingdom of God as political critique. God's reign, often identified as a reign of life, is contrasted with contemporary political economy, often identified as a reign of death. Among the Latin American liberation theologians, the former is characterized by plenitude, the latter by scarcity.

The connection of this reign to other theological themes, such as ecclesiology and Christology, differs among the various theologians. Ruether and Cone establish a loose relationship between God's reign and Christology, while Gutiérrez and Sobrino present a tighter relationship. Nevertheless, all these theologians use the theme of God's Kingdom as a means to relativize the role of ecclesiology in the economy of salvation. This is because all four theologians find that the category of 'liberation' characterizes God's reign most decisively.

The emergent tradition's theologians differ on the extent to which Marxism is used to make theology relevant to economics. Gutiérrez advocates for a Marxist social analysis more than does Ruether and Cone. Ruether has consistently maintained a critical distance from it even though she incorporates it, along with feminist, ecological, and neo-pagan resources, into her theology. Cone was initially suspicious of socialism because he found the economic and political plight of blacks in socialist countries not markedly advanced over that of African Americans in the United States. But, through the influence of Cornel West, he has increasingly recognized the need for such an analysis alongside a cultural analysis that arises from the particular perspective of both the black church and other radical black movements. More than anything else these theologians appear to share a formal method. Gustavo Gutiérrez defined it as 'critical reflection on praxis.' What distinguishes their work from each other is which historical praxis provides the material content for this formal method. The critical appropriation of Marxism, the selection of eschatology and the reign of God, which is conceived primarily as liberation, and a method centered on praxis are the key themes that unite these theologians within a shared tradition as they relate theology to the economy.

The discussion in Part II begins with an analysis of the Marxist strategy to relate theology to economics. This argument will suggest that in so far as the use of Marxism recovers the significance of a contingent, historical, and political base for economic facts, it offers a genuine emergent strategy out of the dominant tradition. It makes possible and necessary a historical narration of economic practice in a theological economics. Theologians must not forget the importance of original accumulation, the conditions of daily labor that make theological production possible, the history of slavery and the conquest. However, in so far as liberation theologians incorporate Marxism merely to suggest that all theological production is limited and constrained by its social conditions, then the original gift that makes theology possible has been reduced to a theologically unwarranted materialism. The result is that theological production is assumed to be finite and limited. But this can only be the result because such a 'limitation' presumes knowledge of a greater unlimited whole. This implicit un-limited whole does not move us beyond a modernist metaphysics of identity. The identification of our freedom with God's freedom becomes a more secure foundation for theological reflection than themes such as ecclesiology and Christology. Therefore, after discussing the Marxist strategy, I will argue that the eschatological impulse in liberation theology subordinates ecclesiology to the Kingdom of God in such a way that the visible church becomes a problem for God's liberating activity rather than a source of it.

The result is an inability to move beyond a metaphysics of identification where all theological production is rendered as a lack. This understanding of the historical scarcity of theological production results in an inability to distinguish between orthodoxy and heresy.

# 7 Marxism as a theological strategy to relate theology to economics

None of the theologians in the emergent tradition has a strong version of historical materialism according to which 'the mode of production in material life determines the general characteristics of the social, political and spiritual processes of life.' Such a strong version can be found in the Marxist Louis Althusser who suggested that religious practices such as prayer were an 'ideological intervention' where religious people learn to say, Amen, i.e. – so be it – to the 'reproduction of the relations of production.'[1] This is because the church functions primarily as a 'religious ideological State apparatus' (RISA),[2] which is distinct from a (repressive) State apparatus yet in service to it through means not explicitly violent. The church as a RISA 'always-already' constructs subjects such that

> the subjects 'work', they 'work by themselves' in the vast majority of cases, with the exception of the 'bad subjects' who on occasion provoke the intervention of one of the detachments of the (repressive) state apparatus. But the vast majority of (good) subjects work all right 'all by themselves', i.e. by ideology.... They are inserted into practices governed by the rituals of the ISAs. They 'recognize' the existing state of affairs, that 'it really is true that it is so and not otherwise', and that they must be obedient to God, to their conscience, to the priest, to de Gaulle, to the boss, to the engineer, that thou shalt 'love thy neighbour as thyself', etc. Their concrete, material behaviour is simply the inscription in the life of the admirable words of the prayer: 'Amen – So be it.'[3]

Althusser argued that we are all subjects constituted by ideology through practices. There is no way out until a change in the material modes of production occurs. Theology cannot escape this fate any more than could Althusser himself.

Such a strong version of historical materialism leaves little room for a theological alternative to any dominating tradition. Critical reflection on practice will be of little use; for practice itself is possible only within ideology.[4] Although theologians in the emergent traditions would take seriously the church's role in the construction of religious ideology in service to the state apparatus, only with difficulty could they accept a version of Marxism such as Althusser's and remain the theologians they are.[5] Just as theologians in the dominant tradition would deny accommodating theology to Weber, theologians in the emergent tradition would deny accommodating theology to Marx. More than any explicit use of Marx, what binds these theologians together is their rejection of capitalism as an appropriate practice for Christians. Nevertheless, any use of Marx must recognize that Marxism represents a strategy made possible by the emancipatory discourses let loose in modernity. Although these theologians are critical of capitalism, they have not always provided us with a careful analysis of its historical rise and cultural production. This has left them open to the dominant tradition's criticism that capitalism is as much about liberty as is liberation theology. Can the category *liberation* be employed as a criticism of the rise of capitalism or will it inevitably be incorporated into the dominant metanarrative of freedom that defines modernity?

Liberation theologians have not adequately dealt with the fact that capitalism itself developed as a tradition of liberation – liberation from the ancient regime, from the church and from interference by the state (even though the market needs the external coercive structure of the state). We cannot avoid the suspicion that liberation theologians within an emergent tradition who find Marxism significant for their project do share something in common with theologians within the dominant tradition. For, as Louis Dupré reminds us, 'Marx's critique remains within the parameters of a culture conceived as a process of self-directed transformation.'[6] The language of 'self-directed transformation' is unmistakably present in these liberation theologians.

It could be that both the theologians in the dominant tradition and those of the emergent tradition share a common conception of culture and nature where freedom is understood to be an exercise of autonomous human making in the construction of one's social and political future. If such a culture is shared by these theologians then what would appear to be radically different alternatives between the dominant and emergent traditions would be but significant variations within a common theme; one established by a modernist metanarrative of liberty as self-directed transformation. Present within this modernist project is the encouragement and toleration of protest as a sign that no single account of the good, the true, or the beautiful has been allowed to dominate political and economic life. Instead protest insures that political being remains defined by rights. A negative conception of rights tolerates incessant protests as a sign of its superiority to any political life based on a substantive good. Only in so far as liberation theology has produced martyrs whose protests were not accommodated within this notion of political society can they escape the charge that protest itself only further entrenches the modernist project. In fact, the power of liberation theology is that it has arisen from the deaths of holy persons.

# I   Dialectical materialism or a dialectic of martyrdom?

James Cone's liberation theology arose out of the deaths of holy persons –
Dr King and Malcolm X.[7] In the 1989 Preface to his book *Black Theology
and Black Power*, first published in 1969, Cone stated: 'It was the challenging and angry voice of Malcolm X that shook me out of my theological
complacency.'[8] Malcolm X's angry voice proclaimed the inadequacy both of
the Christian church and of democratic capitalism as responses to the
historical legacy of racism in America. Cone does not capitulate to X's
denunciation of Christianity; in fact he argues that X himself had to draw
on Christian biblical themes to appeal to the African American community.[9]
Nevertheless, Cone recognized that theologians must respond to X's critique
for the sake of Christianity itself.

Cone's theology does not develop economics *per se*, yet black theology is
unintelligible without an account of its emergence out of a particular
economic history. Resisting that history, suggests Cone, is as important for
contemporary black theology as it was for nineteenth-century slaves. He
argues that

> the literal color of Jesus is irrelevant. What is primary is that blacks
> must refuse to let whites define what is appropriate for the black com-
> munity. Just as white slaveholders in the nineteenth century said that
> questioning slavery was an invasion of their property rights, so today
> they use the same line of reasoning in reference to black self-
> determination.

This economic history of a people whose primary relationship to others was
a matter of property rights makes Cone more than merely suspicious of
associating Christianity with capitalism. In fact, he argues, such an
association is a 'denial of the lordship of Christ.'[10]

Insofar as holiness and particular histories may be conceded a role in the
relationship of theology to economics, Cone's theology is relevant to
economic considerations. But we will not find in Cone an autonomous
social science at work. We do not find any discussion of the most efficient
means to allocate scant resources; little credence is given to the social
sciences – Marxist or marginalist. In fact, Cone suggests that the
'sociologist's tools' have the consequences of 'tucking theology into an
insignificant corner.'[11] Rather than sociological analysis by means of socio-
analytic mediation, Cone's social analysis proceeds by introducing us to the
blues, spirituals and the historic experiences of the black church and the
Black Power Movement.

Jon Sobrino's theology also reveals a lack of engagement with the social
sciences. Rather than rely on the social sciences, the heart and the persuasive
power of Sobrino's work is the holiness of martyrdom. The holiness of the
church he suggests, is discovered when it is persecuted and produces
martyrs. This gives Sobrino's theology, like Cone's, a profundity that makes

it difficult to subject to critique. His theological reflections stem from the reality of the holiness of martyrdom – of 'the disappeared' in El Salvador, of the priests, the nuns, and their co-workers, of Archbishop Romero, and of his fellow Jesuits and friends at Central American University. Sobrino tells of his personal experience with this reality of death and its implications for his theology:

> If we do not forget those who are being crucified today, it will be more difficult to forget the crucified Jesus. But if we keep him in mind, of necessity we must ask about God. And, although the formulation, like all formulations, is limited, and is open to questioning, I think there is no substitute for calling this God 'the crucified God.' Allow me to say this with a very personal experience. On 16 November 1989, when the Jesuits of the Central American University were murdered outside their house, the body of Juan Ramón Moreno was dragged inside the residence into one of the rooms, mine. In the movement one book from the bookcase in the room fell on to the floor and became soaked in Juan Ramón's blood. That book was *The Crucified God*. It is a symbol, of course, but it expresses God's real participation in the passion of the world.[12]

Sobrino's work seeks to explain this moment of holiness in the church in El Salvador, where something occurred which had not occurred since the assassination of Thomas à Becket in his cathedral on December 29, 1170. After a period of eight centuries, once again government authorities found it necessary for reasons of national security to kill an archbishop as he presided at the Mass. This time it was Archbishop Oscar Romero on March 24, 1980. Such an incident has profound theological implications for the relationship between theology and economics. For it was the defenders of capitalism who deemed it necessary to protect the people from their own archbishop.

Sobrino does not see the martyrdom of Romero as merely a misguided effort on the part of some over-zealous government leaders: it is instead a representation of the death of Christ. When a voice speaks out against the structures of power and domination and for the voiceless then those forces respond as they know best – with an aggressive assertion of power. The death of the priest Rutilio Grande for his controversial pastoral ministry at Aguilares, suggests Sobrino, sparked a transformation within Romero from a pliant servant to the established powers to a 'voice for the voiceless.' This conversion was based on a simple proposition: 'if Rutilio had died as Jesus died, if he had shown that greatest of all love, the love required to lay down one's very life for others – was this not because his life and mission had been like the life and mission of Jesus?'[13] This simple proposition is an empirical fact more secure than the principles of scarcity, substitution, and marginal utility that form the foundation for economic analysis. And this basic principle of martyrdom conflicts with the principles of economic scarcity. Love that gives all is more true, good, and beautiful than an economic system that assumes the all is insufficient and must be struggled for through an antagonistic competition for scarce resources. To understand the relationship between theology and economics, we need not engage with mathematical models for the most efficient distribution of scant resources; instead we need to ask who killed Romero and for what interest?

The fact that both Cone and Sobrino eschew the use of sociological tools in relating theology to economics does not result in a loss of social analysis. Both the history of the black church and the martyrdoms in El Salvador are inextricably connected with socio-economic questions, especially survival under an unjust regime. For these liberation theologians, theology cannot adequately be related to economics without remembering that the original accumulation of capital in the United States was associated largely with the social practice of slavery and the conquest of the Americas. Such a history precludes persons from the dominant forms of cultural production, so that listening to its alternative modes gives us a different social analysis. For Cone the social institution that is privileged for the purposes of social analysis is neither the *polis* nor the *agora*; it is the black church.[14] Sobrino had learned from his friend and colleague Ignacio Ellacuria, martyred in 1989, that the true church will be constituted by the poor. While both employ Marxist analysis at points in their theology, neither make Marxism central: that position is occupied by the daily suffering and death inflicted upon the poor and oppressed.

Although neither Cone nor Sobrino employ sociological tools, liberation theology has not emerged from the formal method we saw present in the dominant tradition that concedes an independent role to the social sciences. Latin American liberation theology in particular argues for an autonomous employment of the social sciences, even though the theologians themselves seldom do this work. This raises the question that what fundamentally separates theologians within the emergent traditions from those within the dominant tradition is not theology *per se*; for they seem to share a similar social and political *telos* – liberty. Perhaps what distinguishes their work is the different and/or incommensurable social analyses used as the means to that common end. If this is the case, then perhaps theology itself does not matter in either of these traditions; instead the key distinguishing factor between these traditions is not any theological theme, but rather their diverse social analysis. Do the theological themes selected by these theologians matter?

## II    Marxism or marginalism, does theology matter?

Perhaps what fundamentally separates the various forms of liberation theology from the dominant tradition is not a unique theological undertaking at all, but merely a socio-scientific debate about the appropriate means to assess economic realities – Marxism or marginalism? Liberation theologians share the assumption that capitalism fundamentally exploits workers and the poor. They find compelling Marx's analysis of production. Thus theology should help liberate the poor from capitalist exploitation. The dominant tradition, however, finds Marx's theology of exploitation less than compelling. Although they likewise think the poor should be liberated from their bondage, socialism will not provide such liberation; for the problem of poverty is not capitalism *per se*, but the incomplete nature of the capitalist revolution. If this were the decisive difference between these two traditions, then the theology each selects would be of secondary importance. We have theology in service to different socio-economic analyses.

A comparison of the work of Gutiérrez with that of Novak can help us determine whether their theology matters. Novak finds persuasive the marginalist interpretation of production whereas Gutiérrez still holds to some version of Marxist exploitation theory. The difference between them is whether capitalism exploits workers for the profit of capitalists or whether the market is merely a neutral technological instrument that efficiently and rationally produces and distributes on the basis of people's utility prefer- ences and creative powers. If this is the key difference, then the debate between them participates in a history of economic debate that began in the mid-nineteenth century. Perhaps that debate has subsided now because the marginalists have so thoroughly won. Nevertheless, the work of liberation theologians keeps this debate alive precisely because most of liberation theology explicitly or implicitly assumes the correctness of the Marxist analysis. If that social analysis is wrong, the theology of liberation might remain intact, but it would not be relevant to capitalist society. Gutiérrez might feel the need to join Novak, as have other ex-socialists, in finding capitalism to be better suited to the purpose of allowing each to enjoy the fruits of his or her own labor.

Although both Novak and Gutiérrez insist on liberty, the crucial differ- ence between them is over that from which we need to be liberated. Novak would certainly concur with Gutiérrez's claim: 'Theological analysis (and not social or philosophical analysis) leads to the position that only liberation from sin gets to the very source of social injustice and other forms of human oppression and reconciles us with God.'[15] But where they disagree is over what constitutes the sin from which theological analysis calls for liberation.[16] This difference becomes clearer through a comparison of what Novak and Gutiérrez have to say on 'liberty.' Gutiérrez identifies 'three reciprocally interpenetrating levels of meaning' of liberation – the biblical, the historical and the social–political. At the biblical level, they would agree: both Novak and Gutiérrez recognize that 'Christ the Savior liberates from sin, which is the ultimate root of all disruption of friendship and of all injustice and oppression.' At the historical level, they also agree. Novak could hardly object to Gutiérrez's statement: 'Humankind is seen as assuming conscious responsibility for its own destiny.' But at the economic–

social–political level, the agreement is qualified. Gutiérrez states: 'Liberation expresses the aspirations of oppressed peoples and social classes, emphasizing the conflictual aspect of the economic, social and political process which puts them at odds with wealthy nations and oppressive classes.'[17] That liberation expresses the aspirations of the oppressed does not conflict with Novak's analysis, but that this oppression arises through oppression of the poor by the wealthy separates Gutiérrez from Novak. For Novak, poverty is not the result of social, economic and political conditions perpetuated by the 'first' world against the poor. Instead, the poverty present in the 'third' world is the result of an incomplete liberation from mercantilism to democratic capitalism. This decisive difference between them reflects the different sides they take on the Marxist–marginalist debate.

Where Novak stands on this side of the debate is obvious: 'The "labor theory of value" was an intellectual error of monstrous proportions' because 'creative ideas, not labor, are the greatest sources of wealth.'[18] Novak here shows his indebtedness not only to Schumpeter but to the marginalist school of economics; his opposition to the labor theory of value presupposes the marginalist position. This position denies that value is produced through labor alone, and thus finds the Marxist theory untenable.

William Stanley Jevons (1835–82) of England, Carl Menger (1840–1921) of Austria, and Léon Walras of Switzerland are all considered to have originated marginalism simultaneously without knowledge of each other's work. Jevons stated that 'value depends entirely upon utility.'[19] That is to say, the value of a commodity is not determined at all by the labor used to produce it. Its value is measured solely by its want-satisfying performance in a free market. Individual preferences determine a commodity's value. Jevons considered this to be a 'natural law,' and he overtly set this theory of value against what he perceived to be Ricardo's labor theory of value. Jevons recognized that the 'utility' of a commodity could not be measured through scientific tools and that interpersonal comparisons of utility were impossible. However, he thought that an individual's utility preference could be measured through the marginal utility of different goods for an individual. He referred to 'marginal utility' as 'final utility,' and it represented 'the degree of utility of the last addition, or the next possible addition of a very small, or infinitely small, quantity to the existing stock.'[20]

Carl Menger likewise argued that utility determines value. His work became the basis for the Austrian School of Economics whose representatives included persons such as Friedrich von Wieser and Eugene Böhm-Bawerk. Von Wieser formulated the opportunity cost principle while Böhm-Bawerk is often heralded as 'the man who answered Marx' on the basis of marginalist principles. A core marginalist principle is that rent and interest are not 'unearned income,' as classical economists suggested. They wrongly suggested this, according to the marginalists, because they postulated that labor was the true source of value. Once utility was put forth as the true source of value, then rent and interest were viewed as necessary reimbursements for the delayed satisfaction of needs, or as payment for creative ideas or for facilitating optimal utility exchanges. Marginalists insist that owners of land and property have an inherent right to interest. They were at the forefront of interest theory and they were central in arguing that the medieval church was irrational precisely because of its prohibition of interest through the usury proscription.[21] This unnecessarily limited the utility of capital employment and prohibited the production of wealth. Like the majority of classical, neo-classical and marginalist economists, the economic historian Brue sets the rise of the 'rational' free market against the irrationality of the Catholic Church. He states: 'Because the Reformation struck a powerful blow at authority, it loosened the hold of tradition on people's mind. Because it called into question ideas that had long held sway, it strengthened the temper of rationalism.' This blow at (Catholic) authority and tradition let loose the rationalism of the marginalist revolution – a rationality similar to Weber's where what counts as rational is based on a congruence between one's interest and one's actions.

Another important marginalist principle is that individuals make 'rational' decisions based on 'balancing present against future needs.' Even though marginalists recognize that value is based on demand, and that 'demand depends on marginal utility, which is a subjective, psychological phenomenon,' economic historians still credit marginalists with making economics a 'more exact social science.'[22] They did so by recognizing that utility rather than labor alone is the basis for value. This allows for a scientific analysis of value through supply and demand curves.[23]

Marginalists often trace the errors of the Marxist labor theory of value back through David Ricardo and Adam Smith, and, as I will show, with Eugen Böhm-Bawerk, even back to Aquinas and Aristotle. David Ricardo's rent-differential theory, however, is also recognized as an early, albeit inchoate, version of marginalism.

Since Adam Smith's *Wealth of Nations*, classic political economy viewed labor, land and capital as the component parts of wealth production through wages, rent and profit. People were remunerated either for services rendered, products created, or, in the case of capitalists, for their abstinence from consumption while allowing others to use their capital for productive enterprises. Thus early in classic liberalism labor was viewed as at least one necessary component of wealth production.[24] Smith did not advocate a labor theory of value, as would Ricardo after him, but he was 'the first to analyze systematically the emerging capitalist society in terms of the fundamental class division between capitalist landowners and wage-laborers.' Central to this analysis was the assumption that 'wages cannot be increased by the Poor Laws, by charity or by trade unions.'[25] The *natural* system of liberty he put forward assumed that only the free interaction of these three component parts could produce wealth. All other interference worked against the 'nature' of the thing.

Smith did suggest that 'labour is the real measure of the exchangeable value of all commodities.' But this does not imply that labor alone gives commodities their value. Instead it assumes that through the division of labor people are no longer able to provide 'the necessaries, conveniencies, and amusements of human life' through their own labor. Someone cannot be pinmaker, brewer, butcher, baker and coat manufacturer all at the same time. Instead each person does one thing well, and the wealth he or she accrues for doing that one thing then purchases 'the necessaries, conveniencies, and amusements of human life' which are provided by other people's labor. This is why Smith suggests that 'labour is the real measure of the exchangeable value of all commodities.' And by 'labor' he meant two distinct things. First, he meant 'the toil and trouble of acquiring': the value of a commodity depends on the extent of effort one person exerts to acquire it and wealth is the accumulation of a capacity for such exertion; wealth is 'a power of purchasing; a certain command over all the labour, or over all the produce of labour which is then in the market.' Second, he meant the time and effort spent in the production of some commodity. In this respect Smith argued that labor value is difficult to estimate. The most accurate measure of a commodity's value is not labor *per se*, but a commodity's proportionate exchange 'adjusted by the higgling and bargaining of the market ... which though not exact, is sufficient for carrying on the business of common life.'[26] In his attempt to determine this value more precisely, Smith argued that 'corn rents' were the best approximation to a commodity's value.

David Ricardo picked up where Smith ended and argued against allowing some commodity like corn to be the means of value comparison.[27] He began his *Principles of Political Economy* with this claim:

> The value of a commodity, or the quantity of any other commodity for which it will exchange, depends on the relative quantity of labour which is necessary for its production, and not on the greater or less compensation which is paid for that labour.[28]

Ricardo did not argue that the value of every commodity is dependent only on the labor necessary to produce it. He recognized that some things are valuable because of their scarcity, but considered these to be few in comparison to the commodities that do receive their value through labor.

Ricardo's position is best described as the *objectified* labor theory of value because of his rent-differential theory. This theory suggests that a commodity's value is 'determined by the amount of labour embodied in the product of the marginal piece of land.'[29] For Ricardo this is how the value not only of agricultural commodities but of all commodities is determined:

> The exchangeable value of all commodities, whether they be manufactured, or the produce of the mines, or the produce of land, is always regulated, not by the less quantity of labour that will suffice for their

production under circumstances highly favorable, and exclusively enjoyed by those who have no peculiar facilities of production; but by those who have no such facilities; by those who continue to produce them under the most unfavorable circumstances; meaning – by the most unfavorable circumstances, the most unfavorable under which the quantity of produce required, renders it necessary to carry on the production.

In other words, Ricardo's labor theory of value assumes that the value of commodities gravitates toward the amount of labor necessary in the least productive enterprise. It is the limitation of these 'natural' conditions that sets the basis for his labor theory of value.

Marx's labor theory of value differs from Ricardo's at precisely this point. For Marx, value is not determined by an objectified labor arising from natural conditions of marginal disutility. Marx's labor theory of value results not from the 'nature' of exchanges, but from the alienation of a person from his or her labor because of particular social and political conditions.

Through his effort to find the 'equivalent form of value' in commodity exchange, Marx claimed to discover that the law of value was of central importance to an appropriate analysis of capitalism.[30] A commodity is 'an object outside of us, a thing that by its properties satisfies human wants of some sort or another.'[31] For Marx, like Smith and Ricardo, a commodity has both a use value and an exchange value. The use value is its utility and is independent of the 'amount of labour required to appropriate its useful qualities.' This is because use values are limited by their physical properties and their ability to be consumed.[32] In so defining a commodity, Marx agrees to an extent with the marginalist analysis that locates value in the marginal utility of products, although marginalism makes no connection between a thing's physical properties and its use. For Marx, utility is based not simply on subjective desire but on the properties a commodity possesses. However, Marx goes on to discuss another form of value, *exchange value*. It is here that critics, such as Böhm-Bawerk, find his analysis problematic. For Marx, exchange value 'presents itself as a quantitative relation, as the proportion in which values in use of one sort are exchanged for those of another sort, a relation constantly changing with time and place.'[33] Here a commodity has a 'great many' values, for wheat can be exchanged for so much silk or gold or stockings, etc. Yet when any two commodities are exchanged there must be a form of equivalence that allows the exchange to take place. As Marx puts it, $x$ quarters of corn $= y$ pounds of iron. And for this equivalence, all that matters is the quantity of the commodity that can be exchanged, not the quality of the commodity, which would be a function of its use value. In other words, whether the commodity is corn, iron, or something else is irrelevant to the possibility of exchange. Marx wants to know what it is, then, that makes this equivalence possible, and he says: 'If then we leave out of consideration the use-value of commodities, they have only one common property left, that of being products of labour.'[34]

It is at this point in Marx's argument that Böhm-Bawerk took exception to his analysis. He is credited with answering Marx because, as Brue notes, marginalists demonstrated that 'under competitive circumstances, the pay received by workers would be equal to their contribution to the value of the output'; thus 'the marginalists helped counter the marxian call for revolution by the proletariat.'[35] Böhm-Bawerk denied that capitalism exploits the labor of workers through surplus value. He questioned Marx's analysis thus:

> Only one quality? Do not goods possessing exchange value have other qualities in common? For example, are they not rare in relation to the demand for them? Or are they not the object of supply and demand? Or are they not privately owned? Or are they not 'products of nature'?... Now my question is, why the principle of value cannot just as well be contained in one of these common qualities, as in the quality of being a product of labor. For Marx has not offered a ghost of a positive reason to support the latter.[36]

This passage helps illustrate Böhm-Bawerk's criticism of the labor theory of value. For he has no objection to the moral principle that a worker should receive the entire product of his labor.[37] But he faults the socialists for failing to understand the scientific principles by which markets work, such that time produces great differences in valuations between present and future goods. Thus, he argues, the socialists err by seeking to give the worker 'the entire future value of his product now.'[38]

Böhm-Bawerk's argument is that through the division of labor, the production of a good employs different tasks over a period of time. Someone producing the nuts and bolts that hold an automobile together cannot expect to be paid for the value of her contribution to the completed product until that product is complete and available for purchase. But this takes time, and 'present goods have a higher value than future goods of the same kind and quality.'[39] Thus if a finished product commands $10,000 in future value, then the value of that product should be completely distributed to the workers who produced it but with varying valuations based on their temporal proximity to the finished product. And this is not a social convention, argues Böhm-Bawerk, but a natural reality, 'We humans live out our lives in a temporal world, that our Today with its needs and cares comes before our Tomorrow.'[40] This is 'a law which owes its existence to no social or governmental institution but directly to human nature and to the nature of things.' In fact, the state can grossly disturb this nature of things because it is an institution based on social convention, and need not 'take such strict account of the temporal difference in the giving and receiving of goods.'[41] But, of course, if workers waited for the finished product before they were reimbursed, they would not be able to provide for their daily needs. Thus capitalists provide wages to sustain workers until the finished product can be sold.

Because of the 'nature' of time, capital contributes to wealth production, and this is neither injustice nor exploitation:

> In this system the full value of the product of labor is not distributed as wages, but only a lesser sum, though at an earlier point in time. But the worker suffers no unjust curtailment in his claim to the full amount of what he produces, provided one condition is fulfilled, and that condition provides as follows. The total sum of wages distributed in installments must not fall short of the ultimate price of the final product by a greater amount than is necessary to bridge the gap representing the prevailing difference in the valuation of the present and future goods.[42]

Another way Böhm-Bawerk puts this is to say that 'the total wages must not be exceeded by the price of the final product to a greater degree than is represented by the prevailing interest rate.' If the prevailing interest rate is 8 percent and the finished product is valued at $10,000, then the total wages given in installments must be no less than $9,200.

In this scenario, wages are a kind of intratemporal trade. A capitalist provides wages to workers foregoing present consumption for the purpose of production. The interest the capitalist makes on her investment is merely the difference in the relative price of future and present goods. So capitalist and worker provide services each to the other for the purposes of production.

But this is precisely where Marx's analysis is useful for theology. For the exchange value of a commodity is not based on 'objectified labor,' as it was with Ricardo and surprisingly enough with Böhm-Bawerk as well, who sees the labor relationship situated within an unchangeable natural reality. It is not solely that the value of the product results from the labor alone in some easily computed mathematical form. Rather, for Marx, the exchange value is based on 'abstract labor.' As an intratemporal trade, the worker's labor and the capitalist's future-valued commodity are treated as equivalences by abstracting from the social and political conditions that make such intratemporal trades possible. Labor power becomes the equivalent form of value, not in any natural sense but because of the specific political and social relations in capitalist society whereby, as Marx put it, the

> exchange of commodities of itself implies no other relations of dependence than those which *result from its own nature*. On this assumption, labour-power can appear upon the market as a commodity, only if, and so far as, its possessor, the individual whose labour-power it is, offers it for sale, or sells it, as a commodity. In order that he may be able to do this he must have it at his disposal, must be the untrammelled owner of his capacity for labour, i.e. of his person. He and the owner of money meet in the market and deal with each other as on the basis of equal

rights, with this difference alone, that one is buyer, the other seller; both, therefore equal in the eyes of the law. The continuance of this relation demands that the owner of the labour-power should sell it only for a definite period, for if he were to sell it rump and stump, once for all he would be selling himself, converting himself from a free man into a slave, from an owner of a commodity into a commodity.[43]

Marx's analysis of capitalism is not an analysis of the economic relation as a natural phenomenon; it is an analysis of the social conditions that make such relations possible which then appear 'natural.' Of course, the mathematics of Böhm-Bawerk will be credible. Given the stipulation that each person is an equivalent abstract individual seeking his or her best interest in conditions of scarcity, then the mathematics will always work: $x$ number of laborers meet $y$ capitalists and engage in an intratemporal trade of their own free will to produce $z$. The symbols $x$, $y$ and $z$ name not social relations but individual components of a neutral market mechanism allocating scant resources under temporal restrictions. As social scientists, the marginalists are much more compelling than are the Marxists. But this is because all they are really saying is that the *actual* is the *rational*. What *is* exists by the rational choice of individual agents. The order that exists is natural and reasonable in so far as it comports with the rational choices of abstract individuals, and of course it does – unless there has been undue interference with the market. Economists must always assume this to be the *a priori* natural order of things. This is why they need not study politics, philosophy, theology or history, even the history of their own discipline.

The abstract nature of Böhm-Bawerk's scientific analysis leads him to find Marx's position too much like theology. In fact, he dismisses Marx's position as *fideistic* – akin to a 'profession of faith.' So, he suggests, 'Marx believed in his thesis as a fanatic believes in dogma.' And this was supposedly because the labor theory of value 'stood under the aegis of those celebrated authorities, Adam Smith and David Ricardo.' For Böhm-Bawerk, Marx was foolishly wedded to tradition. Böhm-Bawerk questioned how a 'scientifically trained man' could hold to such a position.[44] Thus he dismissed Marx's theory because it smacked of theology.[45] Here we find the significance of the debate between these two schools of thought. In so far as both are arguing about neutral, scientific, economic data, the marginalists will always be more compelling than the Marxists. Their mathematics works. Scientific Marxism has not been equally successful. But such a scientific Marxism concedes too much of Marx's insight to the social scientists. Marx did not privilege economics as an independent object for observation by a technical science: economics is always already situated within a social and political order embodied in a particular history.[46] No analysis can be adequate that fails to recognize this. In this respect, Böhm-Bawerk was correct, much, I am sure, to Marx's own protestations.[47]

Marxism is more like theology than economics in as much as both Marxist and theologian assume that, if they are to be intelligible, their intellectual discourses must be situated within contingent social and historical practices.[48] Because of the incarnation and the necessity of Jesus' life for redemption, theology requires the recognition of its own historical contingency. As I endeavor to show in discussing Leo XIII's analysis of the relationship between theology and economics, it is the contingent, yet necessary, labor of Joseph and Mary that makes Jesus possible. Of course, this then requires that even their labor, Mary's in particular, also flows from his grace. (A doctrine such as the immaculate conception becomes necessary to tell the story well.) The usefulness for theology of the Marxist analysis is found in its recognition of the historical and contingent practices that all economics assumes. These practices need not be read as 'natural' alone, but themselves become subject to historical contingency. Theologians need not reduce all of life to Marx's materialism, but this is not because theology abstracts from, or denies, the material. The hypostatic union, which seeks to describe the unity of divine and human in the second person of the Trinity, frees theology to embrace the material without in any way losing God.

Marx's theological usefulness stems less from his socio-scientific analysis than from the priority he gives to the socio-historical political conditions that make certain exchanges seem natural. Marginalist economic analysis (which is finally the only kind of economic analysis there is today) takes a particular moment, abstracts from its social–historical context and sets it up as a natural exchange based on a necessary underlying reality. It then becomes designated 'natural,' and never political, historical, or social.

How does all this answer the question of whether the difference between Novak and Gutiérrez, or between dominant and emergent traditions, is nothing but a debate within the social sciences, with a little theology tacked on to distinct socio-scientific positions? It suggests that this debate itself has moved us beyond the social sciences with the realization that they alone are incapable of a sufficient analysis of *economic* considerations. Theologians do not *need* Marx; but, in so far as Marx demonstrated the contingent social and political realities behind a supposedly self-interpreting 'natural' from which the science of economics abstracts, Marx can be of *help* to theology. Economics, like theology, does not rest in some factual world of natural necessity; it is, like theology, a science of contingent human action.

An illustration will reveal how economic considerations assume, without critique, an underlying political context, which itself makes the analysis possible but is not subject to critique. Baumol and Blinder put forward a common economic argument against any price regulations 'by decree.' Such regulations, they state, always result in certain consequences:

1  A persistent shortage develops.
2  An illegal or 'black' market often arises to supply the commodity.

3   The prices charged on illegal markets are almost certainly higher than those that would prevail in free markets.
4   A substantial portion of the price falls into the hands of the illicit supplier instead of going to those who produce the good or perform the service.
5   Investment in the industry generally dries up.

Baumol and Blinder do not argue that such inevitable consequences depend on underlying political and social conditions that could, or should, be changed. They do not present their analysis as a series of contingent social and political results. Instead, they present those results as the natural consequences of 'battling the invisible hand,' a peculiarity found in 'lawmakers and rulers ... from Rome to Pennsylvania.'[49] In other words, these economists cannot ask the question whether price regulations might work otherwise in a polity that is different from one in which landlords are assumed (or formed) to act on the basis of those regulations' marginal utility. They assume the political and social context of capitalist society to do economic analysis. In so far as capitalism could recognize the contingent character of its own analysis, it would be subject to political, moral, and theological investigation. But once this contingent practice is designated as 'natural' then politics, morality and theology must be made relevant to the facts of this natural order; no investigation is possible. The *facts* are certain; theology is relegated to the adjudication of *values*.

## III   Slavery, capitalism, and resistance

Cone's black theology also challenges the 'naturalness' of capitalism from the perspective of a particular history. His book *The Spirituals and the Blues* draws on the resources of the cultural production open to slaves – the spirituals – to elucidate a theology of resistance to the commodification of black humanity. Cone writes: 'The slave songs reveal the social consciousness of blacks who refused to accept white limitations placed on their lives.'[50] The historical reality of slavery, and the resistance present within the black church, provide the resources by which Cone condemns capitalism and suggests the need for alternative economic configurations.

At what point the history of slavery fits within the rise of capitalism is controversial. From the economists' perspective, slavery is irrational because it precludes an individual from freely entering into labor agreements, thus rendering the slave incapable of maximizing his or her own utility. One's interests cannot be correlated with one's actions, so that in terms of marginalist rationality slavery is 'irrational.' Even Marx suggested that the rise of capitalism opposed slavery because workers must commodify their labor power, though not themselves, as a pre-condition for capitalist exchange; otherwise the social conditions whereby workers and owners meet as abstract individuals cannot be set in place.[51] Marginalism would not work under conditions of slavery: it would not appear 'natural.' In fact, in Marxist analysis one of the conditions for the rise of capitalism is the bourgeois revolution, against either the feudal or the seigniorial class, for the control of state power. Slavery is often associated with the latter.

Eugene Genovese has shown how certain intellectual defenses of the American slavocracy – a seigniorial form of production – recognized the incompatibility of their own social institution and that of capitalism. Such a defense is found in the work of the Southern slavocrat George Fitzhugh. 'Fitzhugh's greatest achievement,' suggests Genovese, 'lay in the negative insight that slavery as a system of society ... was incompatible with capitalism and that the two could not long exist.'[52] But this does not lead Genovese to argue for capitalism. In fact, he finds Fitzhugh capable of recognizing certain bald truths that liberal capitalists failed to recognize about themselves. Fitzhugh recognized that 'the only income possibly resulting from capital is the result of the property which capital bestows on its owners in the labor of other people.'[53] In other words, Fitzhugh recognized that the profit from slavery and the profit from capitalism bore some resemblance. Both treated laborers primarily as commodities. That certain Southern planters and their defenders understood the slavocracy as anti-liberal and anti-bourgeois does not result in an either–or choice: slavery, or capitalism with its attendant liberal freedoms. In fact, as Genovese reminds us, it was not, finally, the superiority of liberal capitalism that destroyed the Southern slavocracy: it was General Sherman. 'We should not forget that our liberal, confident, tolerant and good-natured bourgeoisie, when for once confronted with a determined and powerful internal foe, forgot its commitment to reason altogether and reached for its revolver.'[54]

James Oakes finds Genovese's argument to be overstated. George Fitzhugh, suggests Oakes, is not a representative defender of the slave-holding class. Rather than embodying an anti-capitalist paternalism, the slave-holding class was motivated by market interests compatible with capitalist society. Little conflict was present between the paternalistic defense of slavery and a commitment to market capitalism. Thus Oakes argues that the American Revolution for rights and individual freedoms was consistent with the American appetite for slave-holding. 'A political movement taken up in defense of property rights was no threat to slaveholders.'[55]

The differences between Oakes and Genovese should not be overstated. Neither denies that a seigniorial paternalism was present in the slavocracy. Neither denies that this paternalism existed within the context of an alternative social formation, an emerging market capitalism. Genovese emphasizes that certain defenders of the slavocracy recognized the incompatibility of seigniorialism and capitalism. Oakes finds such a recognition the exception, not the norm. Neither would defend seigniorial paternalism or capitalism as a social configuration capable of freeing African Americans from bondage.

In fact, early economic analysis by Adam Smith did not present a challenge to slavery based on that analysis alone.[56] Adam Smith's appeal to 'perfect liberty' for commodities did not lead to a condemnation of slavery. Using a slave in North America as an example of the 'natural' market price for labor at its most elemental level, Smith argued that the highest level of productivity owners could expect from their laborers was double the cost of their maintenance.[57] This was the highest expectation of profit based on the lowest possible costs of production. Here we see, early on in the development of economic analysis, the pernicious effect of positive–normative or fact–value distinctions. The 'natural' fact is that a slave represented the cheapest possible form of labor.[58] The economists' tools merely unearth the economic facts of a situation irrespective of its underlying socio-political formation. Thus they appear to have universal applicability, but at the expense of any substantive social, moral, or theological analysis. The latter is relegated to the question of *value*, and a bifurcation occurs between the economic analysis of the *fact* that will produce the greatest utility and the *values* that depend on questions of what is good, true, and beautiful. But the latter, like questions of utility, are already reduced to individual preferences. Thus what the economists' tools 'unearth' is also what they assume – the most efficient form of economic life will result from little to no regulation of individual preferences as that which determines a commodity's value. How can this assumption possibly offer any opposition to slavery? It does so only in so far as it assumes *a priori* that no one would ever 'choose' to be a slave.

This is not to suggest that economists are of one mind on the causal relationship of economics and politics. While an economist like Mansfield argues that the economists' sociological tools can work in any social setting, others like Hayek claim that the unfettered competitiveness of capitalism will ensure political freedom. On the one hand, Mansfield suggests that the economists' tools can explain how 'rational' choices occur even under authoritarian regimes. Hayek, on the other hand, suggests that capitalism, once unfettered from the state, will bring political liberty. That is to say, once the economic choices have become 'rational,' political freedom follows. He saw in capitalism the single source of resistance to slavery. Without capitalism we are 'on the road to serfdom,' because the individual freedom produced by capitalism prevents 'serfdom' and enslavement.[59] His intertwining of free-market economics and liberal politics also contains a moral–theological component that at best can be called 'relativism' and at worst 'nihilism.'

Hayek argued that the freedom which economic competition insures has necessary analogues in both morality and religion; thus morality and religion should be conceived non-teleologically. He insisted that no 'single end' of a 'complete ethical code' exists; and just as no command economy should be imposed on people, neither should a single morality, particularly no single *telos* of what constitutes a good life for which all people should strive. Instead, 'we are constantly choosing between different values without a social code prescribing how we ought to choose.' This constitutes freedom in economics, morality, and theology. Hayek recognized that morality within capitalism 'tended to become merely limits circumscribing the sphere within which the individual could behave as he liked.' And he linked this morality with economics. Just as there is no common moral *telos*, neither should there be an economics based on a common good; for the 'liberty' that capitalism produces is based on the notion that 'the individual should be allowed, within defined limits, to follow their own values and preferences rather than somebody else's. The individual is the ultimate judge of his ends.'[60] For Hayek, this is the genius of Christianity as well. It, too, produces a 'basic individualism' so that individuals are freed to 'shape their own life' with the 'recognition of their own views and tastes as supreme.' True religion, morality, and economics assume an individual who makes decisions based on preference; all three are based on individual preferences, otherwise known as 'values.'[61]

Hayek and his heirs, such as Milton Friedman, also recognize that this individual freedom requires strong governments capable of employing force to ensure the market's liberty. As Friedman states in his Introduction to Hayek's *Road to Serfdom*, 'socialists must be persuaded or defeated if they and we are to remain free men.'[62] Thus the free market is necessary for political liberty, and a strong and violent political structure that insures individual freedom is necessary for the free market.[63]

Does this 'freedom' for individual values proffered by capitalism rule out the possibility of slavery? The marginalist revolution assumes that rational individuals will seek to increase their utility and decrease their disutility. Could slavery be a 'rational' choice? The ex-slave Ezra Adams seemed to think so. He stated:

> De slaves on our plantation didn't stop workin' for old marster, even when dey was told dat dey was free. Us didn't want no more freedom than us was gittin' on our plantation already. Us knowed too well dat us was well took care of, wid pleny of vittles to eat and tight log and board houses to live in.[64]

If the 'scientific' basis for economics is that individuals act to increase their utility and/or decrease their disutility, then how could Mr Adams' statement not be construed as 'rational'? He chooses 'more vittles' over 'more freedom.' Other individuals held merely different preferences. Morality, like liberal politics, theology, and free-market economics should not impose some single moral code on Mr Adams' value preferences. Indeed others, such as the ex-slave Stephen McCray, will hold different values. He stated:

> The coon said to the dog: 'Why is it you're so fat and I am so poor, and we is both animals?' The dog said: 'I lay round Master's house and let him kick me and he gives me a piece of bread right on.' Said the coon to

the dog: 'Better then that I stay poor.' Them's my sentiment. I'm lak the coon; I don't believe in 'buse.[65]

But capitalist economic analysis cannot make a moral distinction between the rationality of Ezra Adams and that of Stephen McCray. Otherwise it would require the very thing to which Hayek objected – the importation of a common *telos*. But if that is the case, how does capitalism prevent serfdom? It doesn't and won't. And the above illustration shows that utility is in fact nothing but a fiction. It does not have the ability to discriminate between the forms of life that Adams and McCray 'choose.' It loses the ability to argue that McCray's life is better because it is good and true.

Because his theology arises from the particular historical tradition of the black church, Cone's theology is implicitly suspicious of sociological analyses such as are found in Hayek. Capitalism did not provide some inevitable road out of serfdom for African Americans. Capitalism was the problem, not the solution. The history of African Americans in the United States has undeniably demonstrated that their serfdom, during slavery, Jim Crow, and under the insecurity of wage-slavery in the present, was not because capitalism was not yet triumphant, but because it was.

Despite opposition to capitalism by Southern defenders of the slavocracy such as Fitzhugh, slavery and the rise of capitalism were linked. As Peter Parish has noted:

> Slavery owed its very existence in North America to the rise of capital-ism in Europe, and yet it provided the foundation for a distinctive Southern social and economic order which lived uneasily with full-blown nineteenth century capitalism – or, indeed, in the opinion of Eugene Genovese and others, was basically incompatible with it.[66]

But Parish doesn't bring out the cultural codes present in the contradictory nature of the Southern slavocracy as it is found in Genovese's work.[67] The slavocracy was in conflict with capitalism, but this conflict was also a contradiction present in the slavocracy itself – the contradiction between its defense as paternalistic and its reality as a mode of production. As Genovese stated it:

> Slavery as a mode of production creates a market for labor, much as capitalism creates a market for labour-power.... Ancient slave society could not, however, remove the limits to commercial expansion – could not raise the marketplace to the center of society as well as the economy – for its capitalization of labor established the firmest of those limits. The modern bourgeoisie, on the other hand, arose and throve on its ability to transform labour-power into a commodity and thereby revo-lutionize every feature of thought and feeling in accordance with the fundamental change in social relations.[68]

The marketplace was not the center of ancient slave society precisely because persons could not be falsely treated as equal 'individuals' who met simply to exchange commodities such as labour-power and wages. They could not have imagined the reduction of politics, morality, and religion to 'values.' Slaves were not considered to be 'individuals,' because such a category did not yet exist. The individual as a value-preferring isolated entity must first be in place before the market can expand into every aspect of our lives and create its catholic hold. Thus, for Genovese, the myth of paternalism was a necessary feature of the slavocracy that limited the triumph of the market. However, the Southern slavocracy also existed within that time when the market transformed all of society, and its notion of the individual was taking center stage. What his analysis reveals is not only the uneasy alliance between the slavocracy and capitalism, but how the latter could develop an impulse from the former. First, capitalist social relations reduce us to 'individuals.' Then the market becomes the social center. These two forces remove the myth that any paternalistic care is owed to those individuals who meet us in the neutral market place and exchange equal 'commodities' – labor-power for work opportunities. The market for human labor remains central, as it was in the slavocracy, but now as a market for labor-power. Now individuals who freely enter into exchanges of their own making are not even entitled to a modicum of shelter, clothing, health, and food.

Although the rise of capitalism was not a decisive break with the slave-holding past, the slavocracy and capitalism existed in tension, one with the other, and resulted in legal and social practices that 'exposed the hybrid nature of the regime' and revealed the contradiction between 'economic interest' and the 'paternalism' present within it.[69] This does not mean that the paternalism was feigned; rather, Genovese shows, the paternalism and the bourgeois revolution produced contradictions that prevented the complete habituation of the paternalism by the slaves themselves:

> As the masters saw, the working out of the legal system drove the slaves deeper into an acceptance of paternalism. As the masters did not see, it did not drive them into an acceptance of slavery as such. On the contrary, the contradictions in the dual system and in the slave law per se, which had developed in the first place because of the slaves' assertion of their humanity, constantly reminded the slaves of the fundamental injustice to which they were being subjected.[70]

Genovese's argument that the dual nature of the slavocracy resulted in resistance through the slave's 'assertion of their humanity' finds parallels and confirmation in the black theology of James Cone (which had as its predecessor the work of W. E. B. Dubois). In fact, this willful assertion of humanity against nihilistic forces represents the heart of Cone's work. It is much more central to him even than an analysis of the relationships between slavery, racism, and capitalism. To understand the relationship between theology and economics in America, we must become acquainted with the history of black survival, an historical reality that can be made intelligible only in the light of a profound theological affirmation of God's presence with, in, and for an oppressed people. This history rather than social analysis, be it Marxist or marginalist, of the facts is the key to a true understanding of the relationship between theology and economics.

What makes the work of some of the liberation theologians more compelling than what is produced by those in the dominant tradition is that it prompts us to question the contingent social and political practices that give economic 'facts' their formal rational appeal. But it does this only in part. Like Marx, liberation theologians still seek a 'scientific' social analysis. Thus what makes the liberation theologians still too similar to theologians in the dominant tradition (and therefore insufficiently 'emergent') is their residual accommodation to the social sciences as that which presents to theology what is 'natural.' This nature may already be 'graced,' but it does not need theological analysis to identify it as such. In fact, a 'nature' already oriented to grace, discovered and analyzed based on an independent socio-scientific analysis, continues to marginalize the role of theological analaysis. Theology remains excluded to the margins. It gets to pronounce only value judgments on a nature known without theological descriptions.

## IV   Rosemary Radford Ruether: the wickedness of capitalism and the protest of the *oikos*

Rosemary Radford Ruether's theology embodies both the emergent possibilities and the residual accommodation to the modern conception of the natural, found in the emergent tradition, which excludes specific theological language to the margins of social and political analysis. On the one hand, she acknowledges what the dominant tradition does not seem to countenance: capitalism has a history of exploitation, and that history must be narrated. On the other hand, she seems to find the resources within this modern history for its healing and correction. Secularity poses no significant problem to the Christian gospel, but in fact preserves the essence of the gospel against its repression by the church's tradition.

Ruether finds capitalism wicked because it has arisen out of imperialism and because it is marked by male aggressiveness, dominance and ecological destructiveness. She states that 'Western industrialization related to the rest of the world in the form of colonialism or neocolonialism,' and she identifies 'the revolt of the non-Western world' against western industrialization as a significant theological event. In her early work, this revolt 'marks the demand for the fruits of modern knowledge in an autonomous and dignified way, rather than in a chattel relationship to Western superiority.'[71] These two themes – that capitalism has a history of exploitation based on an unjust original accumulation, and that modern knowledge is potentially liberating despite this history[72] – reflect Marx's conception of capitalism as a necessary historical phase through which humanity must pass. Nevertheless, she is more critical of Marxism than are the Latin American liberation theologians; she finds Marxism helpful as an emancipatory discourse along with other such discourses in modernity, including liberalism.

Ruether's relationship to modernity is ambiguous.[73] She recognizes therein a destructive will to power and at the same time she makes concessions to it, to science in particular, as a potential source of emancipatory praxis. Modernity's destructiveness resides in the evil of its ecological posture. To counter this posture she turns to a humanistic Marxism. Drawing upon Marcuse, she states: 'the real crux of Marx's argument lies not merely in the physical but in the spiritual or human impoverishment of the subjective essence of man by the servitude of the person to the thing.'[74] But in her early work she challenged this human impoverishment by advocating the 'mastering' of the technological relationship: 'Rapid technological advance' puts 'men in a new relationship to the earth and to each other and *if this new relationship is not properly mastered*, it will bring the annihilation of man in overpopulation, pollution, national rivalry and destructive wars.'[75] Such an argument rings with less hope than did Marx himself; indeed, it sounds more in tune with the somber political–economic tones of Malthus.

This early ecological concern of Ruether is related also to her selection of eschatology as a central theme with which to relate theology to political and economic concerns. We are headed for an apocalypse brought on by human misappropriation of creation. Although she does not hold men entirely responsible for the impending apocalypse, male domination has set us on this course. We find in Ruether, as in the thinking of theologians of the dominant tradition, a conspiracy of elites. She states:

> The roots of this evil lie, as we have suggested, in patterns of domination, whereby male elites in power deny their interdependency with women, exploiting human labor and the biotic community around them.[76]

Yet, even though we find a conspiracy of elites, liberation will not result merely from their demise. Ruether never argues for a politics based on a violent contest of power. This makes her eco-theology somewhat resistant to the charge that John Milbank has made against eco-theology in general: that it is a crypto-fascism set forth as a modern natural theology.

For Ruether, liberation will not arise from a merely socialist revolution. In fact, rather than looking to the proletariat, she looks to the household – particularly the historical structure of women's labor – as a critical basis from which to resist capitalism. And, unlike Wogaman and Preston's appeal to social democracy, Ruether's vision does not look to the state and its bureaucratic institutions to solve our ills. In the divine–human drama the state for her seldom appears as a major actor. She notes that 'the economic structure of industrial capitalism is one of pervasive, structural discrimination against women.' She argues that 'state-sponsored day cares [and] low cost contraceptions and abortions' represent 'a significant advantage for women in socialist societies in contrast to capitalist societies.' Nevertheless, she affirms (in a way oddly consistent with Catholic social teaching, given what she has just stated) the home as a locus of resistance against both the capitalist and the socialist state.[77] 'If collectivism means state control, then an abolition of the home would be the total alienation of one's life to institutions external to one's own control and governed by a managerial elite.'[78] Ruether recognizes the fascist threat that is represented by such a totalization of one's life by the state. In opposition to this she argues for a residual tradition of women's work in the domestic sphere as a possible pattern for emancipatory practice against both capitalism and socialism. We need to take 'back to communalized households work functions that have been taken over by capitalist or state party managers [because] the work functions of women in the home appear as the remnants of a pre-industrial world of home-based economy.'[79]

Here we find the strength of Ruether's work: she reminds theologians of the productivity of the household and that the very conditions – the leisure to read and write – that have made possible the production of theology have been inextricably connected with a denial of that power to women: 'The domination of women through most of human history has depended on the freeing of males for cultural control by filling women's days with most of the tasks of domestic production and reproduction.'[80]

Ruether, it should be noted, is not arguing that the family is a source of liberation for women. I do not intend to equate *the household* with *the family*. The family has often been a source of oppression for women. That is undeniable. The phrase 'the protest of the household' is meant to indicate women's resistance to patriarchal oppression by their discovery of alternative forms of cooperative power against the patriarchal family's efforts to divide and conquer this source of strength. By *household* is intended that cooperative economy where women have worked outside the constraints of male dominance. But Ruether raises the protest of the household not only against the family but against the church itself. She has examined theology from the perspective of the household, asking whether its mode of production has a place in theology. For instance, in her analysis of the church fathers, she finds evidence of the influence of St Macrina on the work of her brothers Gregory of Nyssa and Basil the Great. Such evidence is productive of a theology less patriarchal than that of Augustine or Aquinas. In the latter's thinking the role of the household, far from being necessary, seems to disappear altogether, for Ruether.[81] It is as if neither man had any connection to a household and its production of daily sustenance for them to do theology. Ruether teaches us to ask: where is the *oikos* in the production of theology?

Ruether is not an advocate of that liberal feminism which grants women simply access to the public male realm. Her argument is more akin to Engels', that capitalism is riddled with the contradiction between socialized production and capitalistic appropriation. He argued that this conflict 'exists, in fact, objectively, outside us and independently of the will and actions even of the men who have brought it on.'[82] Likewise for Ruether: women's labor functions as an objective sign of capitalism's contradiction. It is also a source of resistance: for this domination gives women access to knowledge of social production and reproduction denied to male elites. Ruether's work can best be understood as the protest of the *oikos*, not only against the state but against the church itself.

This account of women's labor does not remain confined within the household. Even the production of theology is challenged by it. This is a significant achievement; it calls for a new form of theological production that resists a sharp division of labor. This could make possible an understanding of theology more intimately connected to historical material communities.[83] To this extent, Ruether's work points beyond the dominant tradition.

While Ruether does raise the question of the relationship between theology and the household, she does not then connect theological production more intimately with traditional ecclesiology. The historical performance of the church in the subjugation of women's labor to male cultural production renders traditional ecclesiology too suspect. This leaves her suspicious of orthodoxy and tending toward those heretics defeated by the anti-heresiologists. Marcion, Montanus, and Valentinus become theologians of a non-hierarchical radical eschatology that made space for women's prophetic, unmediated, spirit-filled leadership.[84] This original Christian movement, quashed by orthodoxy, awaits recovery. In fact, as we shall see, this original movement finds itself preserved better in the rise of a secular order than in the church itself. This positive evaluation of the secular leads her to reevaluate the distinction between orthodox Christian theology and heresy, but it does so because the essence of the gospel is still understood as *liberty*. Ruether continues to work within the context of modern emancipatory discourses, and thus in her work, like the dominant tradition, God's activity in the world is known through an *analogia libertatis*.

## V    Gustavo Gutiérrez: the protest of the poor and modern freedoms

Although the similarities should not be overstated, both the dominant and emergent traditions rely on an *analogia libertatis* to identify God's action in the world. Do they differ in their account of liberty? Novak, Stackhouse and Wogaman find deep continuities between modern freedoms (particularly the American Revolution) and the theological tradition whereas Gutiérrez argues that liberation is not an extension of modern freedoms.[85] But this is not Gutiérrez's only word on modern freedoms; in fact his position toward them is ambivalent.

Gutiérrez, like Novak, has a criticism of the Second Vatican Council's document *Gaudium et Spes*. Both of them suggest that it lacks *realism*. Novak found in it an example of his 'non-historical orthodoxy' because it did not take into account human propensity for sinfulness, which made both capitalism and warfare necessary. In *The Power of the Poor in History* Gutiérrez also finds in it an unwarranted avoidance of the conflict inherent in modernity, and especially in capitalism, which should warrant consideration for socialism:

> With moderation and reserve, the great demands of modernity are accepted.... There is no serious criticism of the implications of the monopolistic domination of the popular classes, especially the poor, by capitalism. The council is concerned with something else. The moment has arrived for dialogue with the modern world. The fact that this society, far from being a harmonious whole, is shot through with confrontations between social classes is not a circumstance falling in the council's direct line of sight.

Here Gutiérrez distances himself from modernity, its attendant freedoms and the church's accommodation to these freedoms. Yet on other occasions his language suggests continuities between liberation theology and the 'gains' of modernity over and against the church's tradition. He narrates the nineteenth-century Catholic church's rejections of modern freedoms as a 'sad story' and notes that in the twentieth century necessary distinctions were made to allow for the 'mistakes' that led to the rejection of those freedoms. The result of these mistakes is the realization that 'Much of what we now criticize in modern society is due to the fact that we Christians could not be lucidly involved in its construction, attentive to what is valid in its demands, and able to share our own message.'[86] Here he seems to argue not that liberation is opposed to the church's accommodation to modern freedoms, but that those freedoms have not yet gone far enough. Unlike the dominant tradition, Gutiérrez argues that modern society suffers because basic Christian principles were given no room in its construction: it is not yet sufficiently free.[87] Many of modernity's faults result from Christian intransigence toward, or exclusion from, participation in the construction of the civil and political order. Gutiérrez does not see this exclusion from the construction of modernity as a theological gain; nor does it constitute a site of resistance to modernity's corrosive tendencies. Instead, this theological exclusion needs to be rectified by the production of a theology that will assist in the development of a new society, a truly liberated one.

Gutiérrez does not find the Catholic church's opposition to modernity a source of political resistance, even though, as Novak has taught us, modern freedoms and capitalism are inextricably connected. Gutiérrez does note an ironic twist in the frequency with which liberation theologians are indicted for challenging the 'modern liberties' that the popes once rejected.[88] Nevertheless his work displays an aloofness to preoccupation with modernity. This seems to be the result of a concern different from those found in much of modern and postmodern theology: a concern he characterizes as the Latin American question of life or death – as distinct from, for example, the North American quandary of belief or doubt.

Gutiérrez does recognize that modern theology's responses to the secular critique of religion and the call for 'man's release from his self-incurred tutelage' were inextricably connected with 'the bourgeois unbeliever.' Modern theology, he consistently argues, mistakenly takes this bourgeois unbeliever too seriously and seeks to address his needs. 'Liberal theology' utilized the 'historical and critical methods' which amounted to a 'capitulation' to modernity – 'as if the rational and the modern could ever become the criterion of what is authentically Christian!'[89] He seeks to develop theology without any explicit worry for this 'bourgeois unbeliever.'

This is not to say that he refuses to engage with modern theologians. He draws on European Catholic theologians such as de Lubac, Blondel, Rahner, and Chenu. And he finds the Protestant theologians Barth, Bultmann, Bonhoeffer and Tillich 'a brilliant group of thinkers' because of their resistance to the modern spirit. By resisting it they produced a fruitful theological turn. He acknowledges that Barth and Bonhoeffer were much more successful at this than Tillich and Bultmann. This contains a certain paradox, because Barth,

> the theologian of God's transcendence, unlike Bultmann, pays little attention to the hearer of the word. And yet he is sensitive to the situation of exploitation in which these broad segments of humanity live.... The one who starts with heaven is sensitive to those who live in the hell of this earth; whereas the one who begins with earth is blind to the situation of exploitation upon which this earth is built. Many will find this paradoxical, but the paradox is only apparent... For an authentic, deep sense of God is not only not opposed to a sensitivity to the poor and their social world, but is ultimately lived only in those persons and that world.[90]

This is a more careful interpretation of Barth than is found in Ruether and Cone, both of whom critique Barth for his inability to engage the social world. Gutiérrez recognizes that the language Barth uses about God does not finally reject analogical speech about this world, and that his profound sense of the *wholly other* God also leads to a theological intimacy with this world because redemption and creation cannot be decisively separated.[91] This also says something about Gutiérrez's own method. Although, as I will argue, he finally finds in Rahner rather than Barth an opening for liberation theology,[92] Gutiérrez also recognizes that liberation theology need not begin with 'the hearer of the word.'

Gutiérrez is first and foremost a theologian. Although he argues that theology should be responsive to the social sciences (something Barth would never have done), Gutiérrez seldom actually employs them. He condemns capitalism for theological reasons, not on socio-scientific grounds.

## VI    Sobrino's dialectic: the crucifixion, Marxism, and geography

Sobrino's argument against capitalism, like Gutiérrez's, is not finally based on socio-scientific analysis. Instead, it is grounded in the historical reality of the crucifixion and its representatives. Because of those who have died in El Salvador, the conditions under which they died, and the similarity between their deaths and that of Christ, capitalism has been revealed to be on the side of those principalities and powers opposed to the reign of God. Rather than perpetuating 'the history of humankind is the history of class struggle' narrative, Sobrino offers the meta-narrative of the history of humankind as the history of the crucified who await resurrection.

This historical dialectic leads Sobrino to find traditional Christologies unacceptable because they avoid the Jesus who involved himself with 'prophetic denunciations.'[93] So central is this dialectical emphasis to Christian practice for Sobrino that he boldly states that if Mother Teresa's 'works of mercy' do not bring conflict then 'they cannot be compared to the miracles of Jesus.'[94] Suspicious readers might find in such statements an indication that Sobrino has allowed a Marxist dialectic to become the lens through which he develops his Christology. Perhaps so, but remarkably little attention is devoted to any explication of Marxism in Sobrino's theology. Claims such as 'We gain access to Jesus only through a specific kind of praxis which the gospels describe as the "following of Jesus" or "discipleship" ' have a formal resemblance to Marxist thought in that know-ledge arises from praxis, and not praxis from knowledge. But to make of such claims anything more than a formal resemblance would certainly exaggerate Marx's influence: the substance of praxis in Sobrino is the *following of Jesus*, which was certainly not on Marx's horizon as a source of proletariat revolution. In fact, Sobrino's later work suggests that liberation theology has distanced itself from Marx because Marxism gives an insufficient role to the poor as 'agents of history.'[95]

There is some resemblance between Marx's fetishism of commodities and Sobrino's 'theologal–idolatric' structure in that the 'economic configura-tions of society' become 'natural' and are then imbued with the sacred, and thus become idols. A superstructure of 'military, political, cultural, juridical, intellectual and often religious' elements then protects these idols.[96] And Sobrino, like the early Gutiérrez, uses dependency theory as a link between the 'affluence' of wealthier societies and 'the wretched poverty of the rest of the world.'[97] The extent to which Marxism provides the basis for liberation theology's use of dependency theory is certainly questionable. Neither Marx nor Engels viewed the global expansion of capitalism as a moral problem. As Robert Gilpin points out, Marx argued that 'no social system is displaced by another until it exhausts the productive potential inherent in it.' Thus both he and Engels 'regarded the global extension of the market system, even through violent means, to be a step forward for humanity.'[98] Development, then, seems to be prerequisite to the emergence of a higher form of economic production.

Dependency theory is less indebted to Marx than it is to Lenin. Lenin's analysis of imperialism argued that the under-consumption of capital in the periphery led to the constant expansion of capital to new regions, making those regions dependent upon the core and resulting in a systematic exploitation of the periphery by the core.[99] The extent to which this analysis is persuasive has been increasingly challenged, such that former dependency theorists have themselves abandoned the theory.[100] Gutiérrez as well seems to have abandoned it.

The collapse of dependency theory without the collapse of liberation theology suggests two possibilities. First, that the collapse of liberation theology is imminent because one of its pillars, a socio-scientific analysis of poverty grounded in dependency theory, has been knocked down.[101] We have not yet witnessed the demolition of liberation theology, but it is inevitable. Perhaps liberation theology continues to stand for some reason extrinsic to its own logic; some vested interest of publishing companies; or maybe the consumptive patterns of North American intellectuals are perpetuating this theology long after its foundational pillars have collapsed. Second, that liberation theology continues to stand despite the collapse of dependency theory because it is, at heart, independent of an autonomous socio-scientific analysis. In fact, perhaps those who find it defeated because of this failure of dependency theory betray their own indebtedness to a sociological analysis that stands over and against theology. However, as long as Sobrino, like Gutiérrez, makes such claims as that 'the social sciences analyze the concrete misery of the real world,'[102] the fact of the collapse of the socio-scientific analysis liberation theologians originally used, conceded an autonomous space to, and often still assume, cannot be dismissed as simply extrinsic to their theology.

Nevertheless, Sobrino's theology cannot be dismissed as unduly influenced by Marxism, and this is not always to his advantage; for *geography* functions more than does *class* as the category he employs for theological social analysis. He does not differentiate theology solely on the basis of class. He gives us no analysis of the relationship between the owners of capital and the proletariat and of their relationship to the production of theological works. Instead he differentiates theology on the basis of geography and culture. It is either European or Latin American. These two geographical theologies may correlate roughly to class divisions, but when

Sobrino notes the contrast between them a key distinction seems to be their respective approaches to reality rather than their access to capital and power. Latin American theology 'approaches reality as it is,' but European theology 'approaches reality through the mediation of thought' – through philosophy, theology, and culture. European theology is concerned with 'explaining the truth of the faith and clarifying its meaning when it is obscured,' whereas liberation theology is concerned with 'liberating the real world from its wretched state.' European theology addresses the issues raised by the 'first Enlightenment,' initiated by Kant, which seeks 'liberation of reason from all authority' and thus is concerned with 'rationality.' In contrast, liberation theology addresses concerns issuing from the 'second Enlightenment,' initiated by Marx, and is concerned with 'a liberation from the misery of the real world' – with transformation. The key difference between the two theologies, suggests Sobrino, has to do with the seriousness with which liberation theology takes Marx's 'Thesis XI' on Feuerbach.[103] Sobrino suggests that it 'is the paradigm for the liberative aspect of theological understanding.'[104] But this distinction between some 'first' and 'second Enlightenment' is merely asserted and never explained. This kind of analysis does not convincingly move theology beyond its confinement to the emancipatory discourses let loose at the rise of modernity.

## VII   James Cone's black theology: Marx, class, and limitations

Cone admits to a blindness regarding the 'problem of classism' in his early work.[105] He states the reason for this early blindness in his 1986 Preface to *A Black Theology of Liberation*, originally published in 1970: 'My strong negative reaction to the racism of many white socialists in the United States distorted my vision and prevented me from analyzing racism in relation to capitalism.'[106] Despite this admission, we still do not find in Cone's work a close analysis of racism in relationship to capitalism. He does follow the traditions of Malcolm X and King in recognizing that they 'turned toward economic issues during their later lives.'[107] In fact, Cone's *Martin and Malcolm and America* is the closest he comes to analyzing this relationship between racism and capitalism. But even there we do not encounter a thorough analysis. Nevertheless, Cone does offer a constructive theology that incorporates economic considerations within both his soteriology and eschatology. In his early work he stated:

> Christianity is essentially a religion of liberation. The function of theology is that of analyzing the meaning of that liberation for the oppressed so they can know that their struggle for political, social and economic justice is consistent with the gospel of Jesus Christ. Any message that is not related to the liberation of the poor in society is not Christ's mes-

sage. In a society where persons are oppressed because they are black, Christian theology must become black theology.[108]

And this led him to use Marx for the project of black theology.

Cone suggests that Marx is useful because he recognized that one's social location determines consciousness. A difference between white and black theology in America must exist because these two communities represent different social locations.[109] Theology must pose the question: 'What is the connection between dominant material relations and the ruling theological ideas in a given society?' Cone asks this interesting question, but a direct answer is not provided. Instead, he addresses the issue by suggesting that a 'serious encounter with Marx will make theologians confess their limitations, their inability to say anything about God which is not at the same time a statement about the social contexts of their own existence.'[110] But why is it a 'limitation' to assume that theological speech is always located within a social context? Isn't the genius of black theology precisely that blackness in America provides a critical insight which has a fullness that must flow out beyond, but nevertheless from within and through, the borders of the black church itself? If God has visited our social existence and assumed flesh, how can the fact that theological speech will always be limited to a particular social location lead to the inevitability of lack? For Cone, Marxism imposes 'limitations' on theology because it recognizes its socially productive character. The result is that traditional Christian theological themes will be subordinated to an overarching metaphysical liberty; for the latter must be known with certainty in order that we can now recognize that our specific theological expressions are always partial. If the greater emancipatory whole cannot be recognized, we wouldn't know that what we have is partial. This common theme in liberation theology will result in necessary ecclesiological and Christological limitations and finally fail to offer a significant alternative to the metaphysics of scarcity that capitalism assumes. It results in a critical posture against tradition, based on the security of a metaphysical liberty independent of historical theological themes. The reign of God will be recognized in spite of the church and not because of it, and this is because that reign is secured by a metaphysics that identifies our liberty with God's.

# 8    The subordination of theology to metaphysics

## Eschatology, ecclesiology, and the reign of God

### I    Historical liberation – liberation from the historical

In Ruether's work, tradition functions primarily as something to be overcome or used for some present purpose by free agents who stand outside of historical traditions. Notice her description of method in *Gaia and God*: 'I also sift through the legacy of the Christian and Western cultural heritage to find usable ideas that might nourish a healed relationship to each other and to the earth.' The same expression was used ten years earlier to define her position in respect of the past in her *Disputed Questions: On Being a Christian*, where she stated that 'in light of new cultural demands, one might have to look again at some apparently closed questions from one's past to see what is usable.' This ability to sift through a historical past to discover ideas on the basis of their present usefulness assumes that the agent herself is somehow separate from that historical past and can pick and choose concepts from tradition based on the criterion of usefulness. It assumes that the historical past is somehow 'closed' like sealed documents in the dusty recesses of a library. Thus tradition functions as an inert storehouse of ideas activated through human will.

Ruether has good reasons for her suspicion of the tradition, particularly in her concerns about Christian anti-Semitism and patriarchy. And this free appropriation of the past for its usefulness leads her to move beyond traditional historical boundaries, incorporating elements from other traditions into Christianity that were hitherto deemed antithetical. She utilizes pagan resources to supplement Christianity. But behind her utilization of both Christian and pagan sources lies the unencumbered modern subject. Her method suggests that this subject is free from history, constituted by some noumenal freedom, where she can survey the whole and choose what is useful. Useful for what? For what is emancipatory, liberating, freeing. And this is known without historical mediation. She states: 'Liberation is ... the resurrection of autonomy and self-esteem.'[1] Does this account of liberation give us a substantive good capable of historical embodiment? Or is it a mere formal principle, one more modern effort to construct an impersonal, objective, and universal ethic? That it is the latter is suggested by the fact that this liberation can be identified primarily by what it opposes.

Whatever opposes liberation is sin. As with theologians of the dominant tradition, sin has a key role to play in Ruether's theological drama. Yet this doctrine of sin is identifiable separately from any substantive good. This seems to hypostasize sin itself and overturn the ancient tradition in which sin is understood as a privation, and thus as 'nothing.' For Ruether sin no longer requires the good for its own 'intelligibility.' Sin is not a privation from a good that must be known prior to evil and thus it lacks the possibility of Christological determination. Instead, sin becomes a formal category identifiable by the denial of mutual reciprocity in human relationships. 'Sin, as that sort of evil for which we must hold ourselves accountable, lies in distortion of relationships, the absolutizing of the rights to live and power of one side of a relation against the other parts with which it is, in fact, interdependent.'[2] One might object here that freedom is itself the good against which sin is measured, but such an objection is not compelling, for freedom itself can never be a substantive good. In fact, when freedom alone is forced into the role of a substantive good, the result is an embrace of death. The above description of sin hints at this when it speaks of evil as 'absolutizing the right to live.' Ruether's criticism of capitalist society does not avoid the inevitable consequence of the modernist project that capitalism requires as a condition for its possibility – an embrace of death. Because life cannot be without historical particularity, and freedom assumes emancipation from historical particularity, death must finally be the emancipatory discourse.

The formal character of Ruether's doctrine of sin does gain content when she identifies sin with patriarchy. We are to be liberated from the wickedness of male power, from a patriarchy that subjugates women, minority traditions, and the environment to its incessant striving for power. Yet her concern is to oppose this subjugating power by summoning us to flee into 'critical freedom.'[3] As I argued in my analysis of the dominant tradition, however, 'critical freedom' is consistent with the cultural logic behind the subjugating power of capitalism. Thus even though she identifies the problem of an all-consuming power incapable of directing us toward good, Ruether does not give us a substantive alternative.

Capitalism's all-consuming subjugating power is based on a contentless criticism of all other forms of life. An alternative to such a power can be discovered only by, first, locating this contentless criticism within a particular history with its concomitant social institutions and, second, by countering it with substantive goods from an alternative history embodied implicitly or explicitly in oppositional social institutions. Otherwise, criticisms of the dominant tradition will be characterized by their reaction against it. Despite her acknowledgment of a temptation toward the development of a 'revenge theology,' Ruether's work doesn't seem to provide a substantive alternative to a theology wedded to a reactive moralism. Her liberation theology recognizes what it opposes, but no clearly defined substantive alternative is indicated. Liberation remains too formal. The flight to 'critical freedom' cannot sustain a community.

The formal character of this liberation arises from her commitment to the modernist project of creating a new and cosmopolitan humanity. The purely formal nature of such a community cannot posit substantive historical goods that would accomplish anything more than criticism: it can lead only to an unending protest and continual self-criticism and judgment. And it is here in Ruether's work that we see the residual effects of the dominant tradition. She does not yet seem free of the so-called 'Protestant principle' – that twentieth-century creation of Protestant theologians, which brilliantly allowed them to maintain their political position of power in capitalist society by refusing to settle on any substantive good. This principle perpetuated a constant deferral of the good through the reduction of 'humility' to an epistemological method. All goodness is subject to perpetual criticism except the instrument through which this criticism itself occurs. The result is an unending protest always in search of a cosmopolitan society that can be approached only asymptotically. But since the cosmopolis does not exist, this project functions only as a regulative ideal. This in itself does not constitute a problem – regulative ideals can be politically useful, whether they be the dominant tradition's cosmopolitanism, Marxist utopianism, or the emergent tradition's reign of God. But as a source of criticism and unending protest, this regulative ideal turns against all *Sittlichkeit* ethics and renders them relative and partial, and incapable of expressing through their particularity an 'authentic universalism.'

For Ruether, the universal cannot be mediated through an historical particular. The universal exists beyond all historical particulars subordinating them to itself. Otherwise, she fears, universalism can become a form of 'imperialism.' She contrasts an imperial universalism with a 'true universalism,' and suggests that the latter 'must be able to embrace existing human pluralism, rather than try to fit every people into the mold of religion and culture generated from one historical experience.'[4] This true pluralism recognizes that there 'is no final perspective on salvation available through the identity of only one people, although each people's revelatory point of reference expresses the universal in different contexts.'[5] But how could one know this? This statement is intelligible only if the agent herself has access to the universal in a way not open to any faith-community that maintains its historical particularity. But such a position is inherently contradictory. It assumes an absolute judgment that it must at the same time eschew. And it then imposes this judgment upon all historical faiths. They must not view themselves as the chosen people through whom God mediates salvation, but they are a manifestation of a more profound and yet unnamable universal phenomenon that we can call 'God,' 'Allah,' 'Yahweh'.[6]

This particular account of God assumes knowledge of God that is separate from its historical and material mediations, and which thus implicitly subordinates those mediations to something more basic – *being* itself. This is a characteristic feature of much modern theology. Ironically, in its effort to appreciate diversity this modern theology collapses all difference into an overarching sameness – into being *qua* being. How this works can be readily seen in the most definitive performance of this modern theological understanding: the work of Paul Tillich. His use of symbol, and his effort to correlate Christian theology with existentialist philosophy, readily reduced the divine mystery to a metaphysics of being that was more secure than traditional theological language itself. The result is that theological language becomes something that must be denied and rendered void, even when it is affirmed.

Theology, for Tillich, is an 'answering theology.' It allows philosophy to raise the question of being, a question that philosophy itself cannot answer. Theology's role is to answer the question philosophy poses about being.[7] But theology's role remains purely formal; it is reduced to providing the 'meaning' for the question that philosophy raises – why do I exist? Being itself is prior to any theological expression of it. And the entirety of theology is reduced to being's dialectical relationship with itself. Being is estranged and then reconciled through a dialectical movement where all that is not being is called into question. Tillich's theology allows a philosophy of being – and of being as struggle, as an antagonistic conflict between essence and existence – to get the better of his theology. Because we already know being as our ultimate ground, particular theological language is rendered preliminary, as is all social, political and economic language. The result is an understanding of God solely in terms of power, an inability to make sense of the Trinity, the reduction of faith to a voluntarist conception of courage, and the loss of Christological particularity.[8]

For Tillich, 'God must be called the infinite power of being which resists the threat of non-being,' or God is called 'being itself' or 'the infinite ground of courage.' Because God is this unitary power of being, Tillich cannot make sense of the Christian doctrine of the Trinity. He asks: 'How can ultimate concern be expressed in more than one divine hypostasis?' For him, the doctrine of the Trinity does not allow us to pray well because it does not direct our mind to the unity of an ultimate concern – to being itself. And thus he calls for a 'radical revision of the trinitarian doctrine.' Likewise he denies that faith is concerned with assent to intellectual propositions. Instead it is 'the courage to be.' The result is Tillich's need to sacrifice the particularities of Christian theology to this philosophy of being. So he writes that 'Jesus of Nazareth is the medium of the final salvation because he sacrifices himself completely to Jesus as the Christ.'[9] Of course, such an antagonistic philosophy of being results in the loss not only of all theological particularity but of any theological rendering of the political, the social, or the economic.[10]

Tillich's theology contrasts theology's object as an 'ultimate concern' to any 'preliminary concern,' such as the embodiment of the sacred in the social through such disciplines as aesthetics, science, medicine, politics, and economics.

> The object of theology is what concerns us ultimately. Only those propositions are theological which deal with their object in so far as it can become a matter of ultimate concern for us. The negative meaning of this proposition is obvious. Theology should never leave the situation of ultimate concern and try to play a role within the arena of preliminary concerns. Theology cannot and should not give judgments about the aesthetic value of an artistic creation, about the scientific value of a physical theory or a historical conjecture, about the best methods of medical healing or social reconstruction, about the solution of political or international conflicts.[11]

Because he knows being, first and foremost, philosophically, and because he finds theology secure in its unique ability to give the answer – the meaning – to philosophy's question of being, Tillich renders theology *a*social and *a*historical.[12] He liberates theology from the social and the social from theology.

The subordination of theology to a metaphysics of being (now understood primarily as *liberty*) is a feature regularly encountered in the writings of theologians within the emergent tradition. Ruether's confidence that each historical manifestation of revelation is a partial manifestation of some greater whole assumes this metaphysics. Tillich's work directly influenced James Cone. Cone makes Tillich's work more historical by connecting it with the history of the black church; but when Cone suggests that Jesus is 'an important revelatory event among many,' the question arises: how does he know this? What revelatory event other than Jesus is so secure that a theologian can find in Jesus a manifestation of that more foundational revelatory event? Tillich's philosophy of being easily provides the answer. If I already know God as the ground of my being, through my being *qua* being, and I recognize that my liberty is the categorical realization of that being, then I can bypass historical theological language and ecclesial production for a more immediate access to God, based on this more secure metaphysical foundation.

Gutiérrez and Sobrino are not indebted to Tillich directly, but their insistence on finding true liberating faith outside the historical community of the church is indebted to a reading of Rahner's theology that resembles Tillich's. A similar understanding of transcendent being seems to arise from Ruether's 'classicist' education that recognized theological language as a secondary articulation upon a prior experience of a 'theophany of encounter with the numinous.' There is a universal religious pattern to all faiths, which begins with a theophany that then is instituted in a cult and finally reproduced in story. This allows her to assert: 'Although the underlying reality of the divine may be one, the appearances of the divine are necessarily many and distinct according to the different configurations of site, community and historical moment.'[13] Into this classical metaphysics Ruether fits Christology. The result is an epistemological humility about Christological pronouncements: Jesus is 'the name *only for us.*'

This classicist framework resembles the antique religiosity of the Roman Empire that Hans Urs von Balthasar described as a 'pagan ethic' because it neglected a universality centered on Christ for one more pluralistic and syncretistic.[14] Such an imperial religiosity appears homologous with the dominant understanding of religion within liberal society (which also takes place under the sign of the eagle). It seems consistent with Kant's religion within the limits of reason alone, and it reproduces his private–public split where confessional language is private, the domain of the 'divine,' but the 'scholar' has access to a more fundamental universal experience. This understanding of being is also the logic of the dominant tradition. Because being is secure in an abstraction from historical communities, rather than in and through them, emancipatory discourses often resemble modernity's quest for the cosmopolis. This quest is then given a theological shape using eschatology as a source of critique of all things historical.

## II   Radical eschatology, or the quest for *cosmopolis*?

The significant theological difference between Ruether's work and that of theologians of the dominant tradition is that where the latter often begin with creation she begins with eschatology. In her early work, *The Radical Kingdom: The Western Experience of Messianic Hope* (1970), Ruether established a goal that she has consistently maintained: it is to 'demonstrate an identity between Christianity and an élan toward a new order in history.'[15] In fact, in a way similar to Novak's she has argued for certain 'parallels' between 'theological patterns' and 'secular social theory.'[16] She even suggests that, with secularization, 'Some fundamental substance of the gospel was rescued from its domestication in the ecclesiastical institution and reinserted into the stream of historical experience.'[17] This 'fundamental substance' is an apocalyptic desire for a new humanity where people are freed from oppression and poverty.

Just as Novak found secular parallels to the gospel in the philosophies of Jefferson, Bertrand Russell and Richard Rorty, Ruether finds parallels in various Enlightenment, utopian and socialist discourses. She identifies three distinct patterns that relate Christianity to a secular order – patterns of 'apocalyptic crisis,' of 'an inward journey,' and of a 'Great Master Plan.' Each of these patterns is prompted by a need for redemption from poverty and oppression, but it is the apocalyptic crisis pattern that is potentially productive of a social ethic, because it contains within itself a recognition and a consciousness of social oppression.[18] This pattern has the seeds of a social ethic more clearly than does either the 'inward journey' of mendicant asceticism or the utopianism of 'an elite, redeemed community where the new age can be glimpsed, but the present world is abandoned to fester.'[19] The Great Master Plan does let loose an evolutionary process through which the 'revolutionary message of the Gospel' has the potential to become a 'social revolution,' but this can occur only 'where the dispensation of the historical church and the society it had founded had been relativized, thus releasing again the idea of a genuinely new event occurring in future history.'[20] This 'new event' is the possibility of a 'new humanity' based on an authentic universality.

Ruether finds the church, as did Troeltsch, compromising an original apocalyptic revolution. But unlike Troeltsch she does not read this as a necessary capitulation to the inevitable for the sake of the church's longevity. Instead, all of her work, in some sense, is an effort to recover that original revolution, and it cannot be recovered through orthodox Christianity precisely because orthodoxy is the problem to be overcome. Thus another consistent theme in her work is a suspicion of traditional orthodox themes in Christianity, particularly in Christology. We must look to the heretics to recover the original apocalyptic message because of the conspiracy of the male elites to subjugate all difference under their controlling master plan (the central culprit here is St Augustine). This includes challenging 'the finality of the revelation through Christ.'

The Montanists and the Donatists, with their Third Age of the Spirit, become a basis from which Christianity can be made once again a 'future-oriented, social, revolutionary message.' They have this potential because their 'doctrine of the Third Age restored the revolutionary expectation that was lost in the Augustinian domestication of the messianic age into the already accomplished era of the church.'[21] For this social revolution to occur, not only must the established historical church be 'relativized' but society must be secularized. Only then does the 'historical expectation reenter Western history in a social revolutionary form as a movement that sets itself in opposition to the established church and Christian society.' And this secularization 'rescues' the gospel from 'its domestication in the ecclesiastical institution.'[22]

How does secularization rescue the gospel from the church? It does so by recovering a transcendent future orientation based on the promise of an apocalyptic new humanity that has been lost with Augustine's account of the church as an already redeemed historical community grounded in God's eternity. We can recover this promise because it was kept alive by an 'apocalyptic church that was carried along in an underground stream through the Middle Ages.' It re-surfaced in the Anabaptists, who 'recovered the primitive apocalyptic view of the church as a transcendental community that leaps ahead of this present world in anticipation of the future age to come.' Then in the eighteenth century there

> gradually emerged a new secular version of the doctrine of the millennium that was to be brought about within history and on the earth by

the immanent workings of the forces of history.... [In] the new secular tradition of the Enlightenment we can find the birth of a future hope that aimed at the ultimate perfection of mankind on earth.

Ruether views this as a marked advance, because the secular view, unlike the Augustinian, 'restores the doctrine of transcendence in its dynamic relationship to history; it views transcendence as a future possibility rather than as an eternity unrelated to history.' Thus secularism 'restored the patristic conception of salvation that we find in Origen and Irenaeus.'[23]

In *The Radical Kingdom* are several themes that have subsequently put in regular reappearances in Ruether's work. First and most important, we find here an assumption of human perfectibility. This decisively separates her work from the dominant tradition which, following Malthus and Niebuhr, argues that human imperfectibility makes capitalism necessary. For Ruether, the doctrine of sin does not determine political and economic possibilities. Her work offers more hope for human cooperation than the dominant tradition allows.

Second, the 'fundamental substance' of the gospel is a transcendent universal that is dynamically related to history both as critique and as future possibility. But this theme resonates both with Kant's 'religion' and Niebuhrian 'realism.' Ruether's early work draws explicitly on these themes. The heart of the gospel remains a 'flight into critical freedom' or a 'prophetic faith.' But this second point places limits on the first one – limits that show up in her apocalyptic approach to ecological issues.

Third, this meta-narrative of a universal new humanity becomes the ordering discourse that establishes the role for all other theological themes, especially incarnation, redemption, creation, and for Christology and ecclesiology.

Fourth, this universality leads to a loss of particularity: in fact, sin becomes defined as whatever threatens this universality. This ultimately leads inexorably to its conclusion – death as a source of hope.

Ruether finds in Kant's *Religion Within the Limits of Reason Alone* one of the seeds for the new humanity. The statement she selects as 'setting the tone for the Christian socialist and Social Gospel tradition' is from Kant's *Religion*: 'the gradual transition of ecclesiastical faith to the universal religion of reason, and so to a (divine) ethical state on earth, has become general and has gained somewhere a public foothold, even though the actual establishment of this state is still infinitely removed from us.' This statement seems similar to Ruether's own definition of Christianity's role in the social revolution.[24] Its task is to point to the new humanity, and to accomplish this it must free itself from the church. Ruether explains this in the concluding comments to her *Liberation Theology*, demonstrating the relationship between her eschatological starting-point for theology and the expectation of the 'birth of a planetary humanity':[25]

Messianism puts an end to any static societal integral of heaven and earth; society and its transcendent possibilities, and places heaven (transcendence) ahead of man as the source of constant exoduses to new possibilities. History is opened up as the arena of the infinite. To teach men to live humanly, repentantly and yet joyfully with this historical tension is the task of a Christian theology of revolution in that modern revolutionary world to which Christianity itself has given birth. In order to find a new human society which can live in this radically *historical* manner, man must do nothing less than give birth to a new humanity which can resist the age-old temptation to dogmatize and eternalize his human historical works and yet not make of the Revolution a Moloch which devours each present generation for the sake of that future 'new man' who is never here, but always 'on the way.'[26]

To live humanly and historically is to live in such a way that we recognize the always partial and limited character of all historical works as we asymptotically await the future historical work – the new humanity – which is always a transcendent reality. But each historical work is not to be reduced to a mere phase on the way to the future historical work. As we shall see, Ruether's work here has some resonances with that of John Milbank and his recovery of a 'radical orthodoxy,' except for the significant difference that her openness to the arena of the infinite does not need specific human theological language as does Milbank's. In fact, it mitigates against such language, finding in the secular something essential to the Gospel. Her revolutionary theology is an 'historical' openness to the future possibilities of a new humanity constantly deferred, whose point is to qualify the significance of any historical expression of that transcendence. This eschatology points us away from ecclesiology and toward an unending protest against all historical claims to embody the transcendent. In so doing, it loses the hypostatic union of the second person of the Trinity. As I will argue, Christology and ecclesiology are thereby vastly diminished in their social and historical significance. Before exploring that loss more thoroughly, I will argue that a similar movement is present in both Gutiérrez and Sobrino.

## III   Ecclesiology and the supernatural existential

Whereas Ruether's critical freedom relativizes the historical church because transcendent reality eludes its grasp, Gutiérrez's theology relativizes ecclesiology by means of Rahner's supernatural existential. While the theology of Gutiérrez must be viewed in the context primarily of the perspective of the poor of Latin America, it can also be rightly understood only in the context of ongoing debates within Roman Catholic theology on the relationship between nature and grace.[27] It stands in the tradition of the efforts by the *nouvelle theologie* and the Rahnerians to integrate faith and reason, grace and nature. Gutiérrez, like Rahner, seeks to integrate grace and nature, avoiding the extrinsicism of the scholastic notions of grace and the immanentism Pius XII accused Henri de Lubac of propagating. Rahner's supernatural existential avoided these two positions by suggesting that human creatures do have a real 'potency' for the 'Love which is God himself.' This potency is constitutive of human nature, although it is not yet supernatural. This potency is not just the 'non-repugnance' of nature to grace, but an existential orientation toward it. However, this potency is also 'freely given.' It is not something owed to the human creature *by virtue of* her human nature. It is 'unexacted' and thus also 'supernatural.' Because the reception of God's love is gift, i.e. it is grace, we then know the difference between this grace and the nature that is 'left over.' Nature becomes a 'remainder concept' known only after grace is discovered.[28] But this grace is always already present in human nature such that no nature *qua* nature is present. Not all persons might recognize their supernatural existential, but it is a constitutive feature of being: it is the transcendental horizon of being.

Rahner calls this transcendental experience of God the 'dark abyss of the wilderness.' It makes possible our thoughts and actions, but it is never given purely in its transcendence. It is always also associated with the categorical, with our connection to the world, the things of the world, including other people. Much as we know nature only from the perspective of grace, we know the transcendental only from the categorical. Nevertheless, Rahner is clear that the transcendental is 'always present, and it should not be confused with the objectifying, although necessary, reflection upon man's transcendental orientation towards mystery.' This allows Rahner to argue that with the categorical 'we are only making explicit for ourselves what we already know implicitly about ourselves in the depths of our personal self-realization.'[29] Rahner insisted that this did not result in the relativization of either ecclesiology or Christology. God as the abyss was his attempt to find in creation the possibility for, and the preapprehension of, God. In some sense, Rahner's work is an effort to explain how God became human against Kant's strictures on such thoughts. Rahner clearly opposes Kant's limits on what can be known when he states that 'there is always question of a noetic hylemorphism, to which there corresponds an ontological hylemorphism in the objects, in the sense of a thoroughgoing determination of knowing by being.'[30] Unlike Kant, Rahner does not pose God as a necessary postulate of our practical reason because of the moral necessity of human freedom. For Rahner, God is known neither by negation (*remotio*) alone nor by comparison (*comparatio*) alone, but through the 'way of eminence' (*excessus*) that makes possible negation and comparison. The first two do not exhaust the *excessus*, but assume it as a non-thematized background.

Rahner translates Thomas' *excessus* as *Vorgriff*: it is the 'pre-grasped' or the transcendental horizon of being. He then asks what this *Vorgriff* is. It is one of two possibilities: either it is 'the imagination of infinite space and time' or it is God.[31] Rahner asserts it is the latter. He cannot imagine the possibility of the former, because that would be to imagine the possibility of nihilism. That Rahner could not imagine the possibility of nihilism says something about his theological commitments, about his certainty that the God incarnate in Jesus is also the God who makes possible being, and all thought and action. But Rahner did not seem to contemplate the possibility that theology would drift into an acceptance of the imagination of the infinite as wholly mystery as an alternative to the Triune God. He did not seem to contemplate the possibility that theology could be threatened by its own secularity as it comes to fruition in a nihilism where the dark abyss we call 'God' is now merely affirmed as the dark abyss. Rahner then leaves ajar the door to the embrace of a nihilistic secular as the site of the truly theological over against the church. Elizabeth Johnson, developing the work of Rahner, borders on this embrace of the secular when she writes:

> The indifference of secular culture coupled with the ambiguity of history creates an ambience in which even for believers the experience of divine absence is often a characteristic of faith itself.... According to Karl Rahner's analysis, this 'burning experience of agnosticism' may be a positive thing, if human beings know that the meaning of their existence is shrouded in darkness but nevertheless trust the mystery surrounding it which is called God.[32]

Embracing the darkness and affirming the void become the epitome of faith.

Gutiérrez does not call upon us to affirm the void and the secular as God, but he draws upon Rahner's supernatural existential to integrate the sacred and the secular in 'one call to salvation.' He argues that this 'places more value on what is historical and concrete.' But the fear is that this is precisely what it does – it places more *value* on the historical, but does not result in an historical embodiment of the theological.[33] It merely 'evaluates' the facticity of the historical and the concrete; it finally does not integrate theology with the social, but merely grants the social its own space and relegates the theological to the evaluational. The Weberian strategy is not undone.

This reading of Gutiérrez is indebted to John Milbank's critique. Milbank describes Gutiérrez's position as 'naturalizing the supernatural' because of its reliance on Rahner's version of integralism rather than upon Blondel's, de Lubac's and Balthasar's notion of integralism that 'supernaturalizes the natural.' Rahner, Milbank suggests, loses the 'historical events, the human acts and images which can alone be the site of supernatural difference.'[34] In turn Rahner, and Gutiérrez, produce an 'asocial notion of salvation,' and this is why Gutiérrez in particular can so thoroughly draw on 'secular social science with enthusiasm.'

While I find this critique compelling, several caveats do arise. First, if, as Milbank suggests, 'there is no gratuity in addition to the gratuity of creation,' how would we know when someone has naturalized the supernatural rather than supernaturalized the natural? Doesn't the critique assume the distinctions it seeks to dismantle? Second, is it the case that liberation theologians have embraced 'secular social science with enthusiasm'? They have indeed suggested the need to do so, but they have been unable to pull it off. Their theology continues to get in the way of social science, such that the latter cannot be taken seriously in the work of the former.

Gutiérrez does suggest that his method begins with a socio-scientific analysis of oppression that is then presented to the theologian. He writes that 'recourse is had to social analysis in order to understand a situation – not in order to use this analysis in the study of matters more strictly theological.'[35] This implies that the social situation itself is not 'of matters more strictly theological.' This accepts a basic datum of capitalist economics: the fact–value distinction. Matters are not helped much by his explanation of his use of the particular social science of Marxism: 'since we are dealing with a social reality here, the situation and its causes must be analyzed by means of the social sciences.'[36] Why? Is theology incapable of analyzing a social situation? Is it an asocial science? In this use of his method Gutiérrez indeed does not concede too much of theology to the social sciences: he concedes too little. He makes little effort to theologize social science. He seems insufficiently suspicious of the social sciences, which are overwhelmingly committed to marginalist rationality.[37] In this respect, he is insufficiently Marxist. Theology and social science remain rather distinct realms of activity: each has its own autonomy and its own object of investigation. They interact in a confusing manner, given the whole of his theology.

This interpretation of his method conflicts with Gutiérrez's efforts to integrate theology with social analysis. His insistence that theology 'is an ecclesial function' that is not to be ruled by the social scientists, either in matter or in form, is laudable; but it does not explain how the ecclesial function of theology fits with the social analysis arising from sociology.[38] We still have two distinct realms not yet melded together: Milbank's critique is sound.

But there is a different interpretation of Gutiérrez's method, one that seems to fit quite well with his recovery of the witness of Bartolomé de las Casas, and which more thoroughly integrates theology with the social and the social with theology. His theology works out of an historical tradition, much neglected, that arose and continues to arise from situations of oppression. References to such an interpretation of Gutiérrez's method can be found at certain points in his work. He suggests that 'All through history there has been a repressed but resurgent theology, born of the struggles of the poor.'[39] Moreover, 'Liberation theology is an expression of a dialectical opposition to bourgeois ideology and the dominant culture that comes up out of the popular classes.'[40] This alternative tradition is not set over and against traditional Christian theology, but explicates what is implicit in that tradition against that tradition's neglect of the development of its own insights. It is essentially Christological because 'what makes a Christian a Christian is being caught up into the messianic sufferings of God in Jesus Christ.'[41] Because persons exist who are completing what was lacking in the sufferings of Christ, these persons and their locations provide the occasion for a 'repressed and resurgent theology.' This is not an *a*social notion of salvation but a rendering of the 'natural' inseparable from the 'supernatural.' Gutiérrez's theology is, then, essentially ecclesial and genuinely emergent. Yet perhaps the most troubling theological development in his work is precisely his revised ecclesiology.

## IV    Gutiérrez on ecclesiology

Milbank critiques Gutiérrez for failing to recognize the church as the site for 'a new social perspective.' The inability to properly theorize ecclesiology results in the abandoning of a social salvation: for the church is the only site where the political and social can be read salvifically. To fail to develop the social ecclesiologically is to lose the 'logic of the incarnation.'[42] Only a commitment to the orthodox assertion of the hypostatic union can integrate supernature and nature. It is this union that makes the church possible.

Gutiérrez has suggested that we need 'a new ecclesiological approach,' one which also begins with Christology. It sees

> Christ as the poor one.... In this approach one gradually comes to see that what is ultimately important is not that the church be poor, but that the poor of this world be the people of God – that disquieting witness of a God who liberates.[43]

This seems to suggest that the poor are the true church independent of their desires, commitments, beliefs, or actions – independent of their histories. Gutiérrez accepts a peculiar logic of the incarnation. Because God assumes flesh, flesh can be that which reveals the presence of God. Because God became poor humanity, poor humanity can become God. But this understanding of the incarnation renders the visible church as secondary to the historical reality of poverty. The poor appear to have been sacramentalized into the body of Christ over and against the visible church with its hierarchy and sacramental structure.

The role of the visible church with its hierarchy and sacramental structure in Gutiérrez's theology is ambiguous. On the one hand, his work cannot be understood without this church. He responds to the Magisterium's criticisms, quotes the encyclicals extensively, and seeks to present liberation theology as enriching rather than opposing orthodox Christianity.[44] On the other hand, he denounces 'ecclesiocentrism,' asserts that the memory of a faithful Christian like de las Casas 'lives on in resistance to ecclesiastical apparatus,' and he suggests that the church's structures 'are inadequate for the world in which it lives.'[45]

Gutiérrez rejects an 'ecclesiocentrism' as found in the 'Christendom mentality' that refused to concede autonomy to temporal realities. But he rejects also the 'New Christendom' model of Jacques Maritain and Catholic liberalism that allowed for the autonomy of the temporal realm, but which, for Gutiérrez, still maintained traces of an 'ecclesiocentrism' that insures the church's privileged position within its own distinct realm and prevents Christianity from being 'oriented towards radically new social forms.' Gutiérrez does find a theological advance in Maritain's 'New Christendom' model: it led to a 'distinction of planes,' which differentiated the roles of the church and the world, giving each its own autonomy.[46] This position was further developed by Yves Congar and French Catholicism, and became the basis for the teachings of Vatican II. But this 'distinction of planes' model has undergone a crisis, and it will no longer do. Where it once was used as a way for the 'vanguard' to limit the church's inappropriate exercise of power in the temporal realm, reactionary forces now use it to remove the church from all political interference. Thus the 'distinction of planes' model is no longer useful. A new model is needed which would avoid, on the one hand, a unitary model of church and world that makes the world merely a means to serve the church's ends, and, on the other hand, a bifurcated church–world division that will render Christianity politically inert. For a solution Gutiérrez turns to Karl Rahner.

The resolution is found in Rahner's 'supernatural existential,' which Gutiérrez recognizes was developed 'to avoid the difficulties encountered' by a theologian like Henri de Lubac. De Lubac was silenced by the Church for his challenge to the doctrine of pure nature. He thought this doctrine resulted in two distinct realms of human activity – grace and nature – that lost the unity between them. He was accused of immanentism. In making grace a feature of human nature, it was argued, he made redemption an obligation on the part of God to human creatures. Rahner's '*supernatural existential*' avoided the problems of abandoning altogether the concept of pure nature: it became a 'remainder concept.' At the same time he did not bifurcate grace and nature into two separate histories or two different and not easily integrated ontologies.[47]

Gutiérrez defines the 'supernatural existential' as the creation by 'the universal salvific will of God' of 'a gratuitous ontological–real determinant of human nature' in the human person.[48] He states that this is an advance because it means that we no longer need to speak of a 'supernatural end' or a 'supernatural vocation': we can speak of 'integral vocation.' Rahner's 'supernatural existential' functions in Gutiérrez's theology as a warrant for the following claim:

> This affirmation of the single vocation to salvation, beyond all distinc-
> tions, gives religious value in a completely new way to human action in

history, Christian and non-Christian alike. The building of a just society has worth in terms of the Kingdom, or in more current phraseology, to participate in the process of liberation is already, in a certain sense, a salvific work.[49]

Now we are prepared to sort out how Gutiérrez avoids the two extremes of, on the one hand, a bifurcation of the church from the world and, on the other, ecclesiocentrism. Rahner's supernatural existential allows Gutiérrez to find in non-Christian human activity an orientation toward the salvation Jesus reveals, a salvation described as 'God's reign.' Both church and world are caught up in a movement toward God's reign because of this 'gratuitous ontological–real determinant of human nature.' The church and the world are united under the single category of 'the Kingdom of God,' which insures unity to history, relativizing the role of the church while elevating that of the world.

Although this use of Rahner's supernatural existential moves us beyond two distinct ontologies called grace and nature, that it integrates church and economics is open to question. This is because the relationship between grace and nature may proceed in either of two directions. It could make the church more central to the economy of salvation: for what the world knows only vaguely – through a nature which is not grace but a determinant of grace – the church knows through *gift*. This would be the position of Henri de Lubac and Hans Urs von Balthasar. For von Balthasar, a metaphysics of nature can lead us to a realization of the ontological difference between Being and our being, but it cannot resolve that difference. When nature via a philosophical metaphysics (or one of its many offspring, such as the social sciences) seeks to resolve the difference it does so by collapsing the difference into an identity. The result will be the loss of theological substance and an embrace of nothingness as identical with God.[50] To counter this metaphysical incompletion, the historical practices of the church are necessary to an adequate understanding of our nature in all its facets. This interpretation could allow for the church's central role in the economy of salvation, and at the same time recognize that the church's knowledge of God's reign does not always insure that every aspect of the church's life is faithful to it. In a particular situation, the world can be present to the church as an implicit witness to God's reign against the church's faithlessness. But this nothingness would never be identified as faith itself. The positive role of the church is always also necessary to integrate grace and nature.

Such an interpretation would allow liberation theology to maintain a privileged position for the poor, believers and unbelievers, without sacralizing them into the body of Christ and relativizing the role of the visible church. It would also fit well with de Lubac's and von Balthasar's work. It would allow the centrality of the church, the language of a supernatural end and supernatural vocation integrated with human nature, and allow us also to explain why faithfulness sometimes appears outside the church rather than within it. It would have significant implications for the relationship between theology and economics because it would deny that economics is an autonomous discipline that could work without any theological analysis of social reality. Rather than the social sciences presenting 'facts' for incorporation into theology, those 'facts' would need to take into account a theological rendering of the social. However, this interpretation does not finally fit Gutiérrez's work. He distances himself from such a position: it still smacks of ecclesiocentrism. Despite the centrality to his theology of the church's teachings, he eschews making the church central to the economy of salvation.

For Gutiérrez, the movement has a different direction. The unity of history (as explained in his method) begins with an autonomous reading of the social, which is then given 'religious value.' The result is not just a relativization of the church and an elevation of the world, but a relativization of theology and an elevation of a non-theologized social science. Unlike Thomas Aquinas, in whose work extra-ecclesial and extra-theological sources of insight are genuinely integrated in a narrative whole that subordinates all to the vision of God, Gutiérrez's liberation theology remains dualistic, and thoroughly modern, failing to move beyond the 'factual' analysis of the social sciences with an added theological 'evaluation.' We have not yet emerged beyond Weber.

We have, however, moved beyond scarcity. A curious contradiction arises between Latin American liberation theology and some North American theology. A people who know scarcity and death will often construct theology from the perspective of an original plenitude that overcomes death to promote life, while theologians from more plentiful lands often construct theology assuming the threat of a scarcity that takes consolation in death. For Gutiérrez, the resurrection reminds us that God is the God of life who seeks to lift up the poor from their poverty and to extend to them life in its abundance. The resurrection 'signifies the death of death.'[51]

The redemption Jesus brings certainly contains positive political implications in Gutiérrez's theology, particularly in Jesus' victory over sin. Unlike its function in the dominant tradition, sin does not here become an anthropological given that renders any utopian quest for holiness not only useless but dangerous: instead, sin is political in that it falls under the category of idolatry. From a Christology that views Christ as Liberator, an understanding of sin develops that refuses to make it a comfortable doctrine which excuses our lack of holiness. In fact, Gutiérrez can go so far as to state unequivocally that 'for a Christian there is but one sadness: not to be a saint.'[52] Sin is not an anthropological given so much as it is a contingent social and political reality against which Christians must fight.

Although what Jesus is *against* is certainly political, what he is *for* remains somewhat formal. The two themes of universal love and preferentiality for the poor that characterize Gutiérrez's theology do not in themselves produce much of a political theology. This is perhaps due to the unproblematic definition of 'politics' he accepts – at least in *A Theology of Liberation*, where he used Weber's definition: the political as an orientation to power. Gutiérrez stated:

> For Max Weber this orientation constitutes the typical characteristics of political activity ... [which] are all based on the profound aspiration of a humankind that wants to take hold of the reins of its own life and be the artisan of its own destiny. Nothing lies outside the political sphere in this way.[53]

Weber's standard definition of politics remains intact in Gutiérrez's work, even though he argues that he has overcome the 'first Enlightenment.' But one cannot use Weber's definition of politics and claim, at the same time, to eschew Kantianism. Thus, I fear, the politics of Jesus that Gutiérrez discovers does not challenge the dominant tradition's view of 'politics,' but assumes it. And the dominant view of politics he assumes is defined not by Marx but by Weber. So when Gutiérrez writes that 'the political arena is necessarily conflictual,' he appeals not to Marx but to Weber's politics as orientation toward power. So, he suggests, 'the building of a just society means the confrontation – in which different kinds of violence are present – between groups with different interests and opinions.'[54] Charity cannot exist in Weber's political world as anything more than an irrational remainder.

How the 'political' is construed makes a difference, and there is a discrepancy between Gutiérrez's development of Christian charity and this Weberian account of politics as a formal power. All politics is viewed as an assertion of formal power. 'Nothing lies outside the political sphere understood in this way. Everything has a political color. It is always in the political fabric – and never outside of it – that a person emerges as a free and responsible being.'[55] Once this definition of politics is accepted, then Christianity is reduced to 'norms and criteria,' while the realist power analysis must effectuate these norms in the concrete situation.[56] Liberation theology, like the dominant tradition, has not been sufficiently skeptical of the social sciences, or of the 'political' as it is presented to us from that dominating tradition.

## V    Sobrino on ecclesiology

Like Gutiérrez, Sobrino appeals to the historical Jesus as the starting-point for Christology, but this is primarily an appeal to his practice, and this practice is not ecclesially determined but grounded in the Kingdom of God. The subordination of the church to the Kingdom of God provides access to a reality wherein the 'true Church' can be identified, sometimes in opposition to the visible church.

This emphasis on the kingdom of God is certainly not new in theological scholarship.[57] It was the central theme of German liberal Protestants such as Harnack and Troeltsch, who understood the Kingdom to be an inward and metaphysical reality associated with a spirit of liberty. This understanding of the Kingdom marked (and continues to mark) liberal Protestantism in much of North American theology. This tradition is hard to overcome. Even the nineteenth- and twentieth-century 'quests for the historical Jesus' continue to perpetuate this tradition. For instance Albert Schweitzer did argue that the 'Jesus of Nazareth who came forward publicly as the Messiah who preached the ethics of the Kingdom of God ... never had any existence. He is a figure designed by rationalism.' Nevertheless when he concludes his work and tells us of Jesus' contemporary significance, Schweitzer returns to this Kingdom ethic of a metaphysical spirit of liberty. He stated:

> It is not Jesus as historically known, but Jesus as spiritually arisen within men, who is significant for our time and can help it.... But in reality that which is eternal in the words of Jesus is due to the very fact that they are based on an eschatological worldview, and contain the expression of a mind for which the contemporary world with its historical and social circumstances no longer had any existence. They are appropriate, therefore, to any world, for in every world they raise the man who dares to meet their challenge, and does not turn and twist them into meaninglessness, above his world and his time, making him inwardly free, so that he is fitted to be, in his own world and in his own time, a simple channel of the power of Jesus.... They shall learn in their own experience Who He is.

It is the noumenal Jesus who secures freedom for us in our inward being that is relevant to the modern world. This certainly seems similar to the Kingdom promoted in German liberal Protestantism. Walter Rauschenbusch can put both the historical work of someone like Schweitzer and the liberal Protestant tradition together in his understanding of the role of the Kingdom for modern theological ethics. He replaced Jesus' eschatology with ethics in order to make the Kingdom relevant to the modern world; Rauschenbusch was one of the first demythologizers. He looked behind the church's traditional accretions to the real historical Jesus, and, like Schweitzer, he found Kant. That is to say, he found an idea of liberty that can be used to transform society. Rauschenbusch then used the idea of the Kingdom as a call to 'Christianize' American culture and make it more like the ethical ideal of the kingdom. In fact, once the heart of Jesus' teaching becomes the Kingdom as a noumenal freedom then the church becomes rendered more contextual and subordinate to the nation and its culture. Rauschenbusch argued that the

American churches are part of the American nation. They are not a foreign clerical organization grafted on our national life, but an essential part of it from the beginning, a great plastic force which has molded our public opinions and our institutions from the foundation up.[58]

Of course, the Kingdom understood as a metaphysics of liberty resulted in an anti-ecclesial theology. The mediator of the Kingdom idea becomes the state's search for justice, not the church's advocacy of charity.

The central role of the Kingdom of God within nineteenth-century liberal Protestant theology and within twentieth-century Catholic modernist controversies called into question the role of the church in salvation. Alfred Loisy perhaps put it most succinctly when he stated that Jesus announced the Kingdom but what we received was the church instead. Both liberal Protestant and Catholic modernist theologians who begin theology with the Kingdom of God often end by reading the creation of the church as a mistake. Sobrino's emphasis on the Kingdom of God as the place where we encounter the practice of the historical Jesus does not appear to differ substantially from this tradition of liberal Protestantism and Catholic modernism. However, when Sobrino argues that access to this historical practice is found through the martyrs and the deaths of the innocent, then his doctrine of the Kingdom radically differs. It does not suggest that we look behind the church's accretions of tradition to some reconstructed historical Jesus. We find Jesus precisely in those 'accretions.'

Yet a residual element of that German liberal theology remains in Sobrino's work. In fact, he acknowledges that this emphasis on the Kingdom of God stems from German liberal theology. He criticizes their interpretation of the Kingdom because it underwrote a 'bourgeois Jesus,' but he nevertheless suggests that the positive contribution of this theology was 'the de-absolutization of all historical institutions based on the discovery of the Kingdom of God.'[59] In making this move, Sobrino calls into question the extent to which his theology has sufficiently disengaged with the dominant ideology present in capitalist society. We have already noted how Schumpeter recognized that the ideological power of capitalist society was the 'critical frame of mind,' which it produced against all forms of traditional society, and which he thought would finally turn against and destroy capitalism. Weber accepted and developed capitalism's critical stance toward all traditional forms of rationality. Likewise Troeltsch read this back into the very essence of Jesus' proclamation of the Kingdom of God and this critical stance became a foreign import into the Protestant tradition, as Tillich and Reinhold Niebuhr baptized it 'the Protestant principle.' As we shall see, even Karl Barth's reading of Protestantism was not free of this innovative understanding. He likewise challenged all historical representations of the divine. What is lost in these theologies is the compelling doctrine of the church's ability to re-present in history a form of life that is good, true and beautiful. Rather than a debate about the manner in which the church's teachings can be grounded in truth, Protestant theology, influenced by capitalism's critical evaluation of all things historical and traditional, forsook altogether any doctrine of infallibility. The only remaining infallible teaching after neo-Protestantism is that the church cannot but err – this is what we now know with absolute confidence.

Sobrino's use of the Kingdom of God as a 'de-absolutization of all historical institutions' in no way calls into question this tradition. The Kingdom, he suggests, 'criticizes and makes relative any and every created reality.'[60] To argue that Jesus' practice of proclaiming the Kingdom of God produces a criticism of all historical institutions, including the church, does not show liberation theology to have emerged beyond and outside of the tradition of dominant theological scholarship. This is to be seen especially clearly in Sobrino's development of the relationship between *prophet* and *institution*.

Sobrino develops two dimensions to the church: one is prophetic, the other institutional. While this division bears some resemblance to the traditional ecclesiological distinction between the Petrine office and the Marian vocation to holiness, it actually reflects more Weber's analysis of social institutions where an original charism becomes routinized and then institutionalized. Sobrino states: 'The institutional church embodies for the long run what begins as pure prophecy.' The institution is the routinization of charisma. But, for Sobrino, the institution seeks constantly to stifle the prophetic charism.[61] The prophetic charism and the institution are pitted against one another. Archbishop Romero himself is a sign of this tension.

Sobrino acknowledges that Archbishop Romero 'prophesied from within the Church,' but then qualifies this claim with such arguments as that 'prophets speak directly in the name of God,' and 'the prophet has criteria of sinfulness unavailable to the Church.'[62] Does this distinction between *prophet* and *institution* – so prevalent in Weberian social analysis – adequately capture Romero's own sense of mission? In his first pastoral letter Romero stated that it is as church that the 'prophetic, priestly and social functions' are carried out. And it is as church that Romero denounced capitalism when he proclaimed that 'the church now lays down a condemnation of the capitalist system as well. It is denounced as one version of practical materialism.'[63] This is not to suggest that the prophetic word is found only within the confines of the church; certainly it is not. Thus the above comments are not intended to imply any opposition to Sobrino's intent when he states, for example:

> The prophetic word is one of the forms of God's own self-manifestation in history – one of the ways in which God overflows the limits in which historical institutions could wish to enclose the divine transcendence and thereby diminish it, 'cut it down to size.'[64]

But when Sobrino suggests that 'Jesus did not preach or establish (in the conventional sense of the term) any Church; he simply proclaimed a

Kingdom of God that was at hand. The ultimate definitive reality in the eyes of Jesus was the Kingdom not the Church,'[65] one is led to wonder if he has sufficiently distanced his work from 'European' scholarship.

The church plays a dual role in Sobrino's work: it is both a source of resistance and an accommodation to capitalist political economy. It represents the social institution capable of resisting capitalism; and it represents a social institution too often in collusion with the powerful against the poor. It is an infallible institution and one that demonically resists hearing, producing, and responding to God's word. On the one hand, it is the social institution that 'as depository of the tradition about Jesus, has been guaranteed indefectibility throughout history'[66] – a claim one would not likely find present in Protestant liberalism. On the other hand, Sobrino seems to accept the Protestant interpretation of 'early Catholicism' as an inevitable but necessary compromise of the original gospel ethic, centered on the Kingdom of God.

Sobrino finds an ecclesiological rupture within liberation theology. He suggests that the 'Church of the poor breaks away from traditional ways of being Church.' He defines the true church as the church of the poor and argues that this church cannot be construed as 'mystical body' or as 'hierarchical.' Instead it is the poor who are the primary site for the presence of Jesus in the world: 'The Spirit of Jesus is in the poor and with them as his point of departure, he re-creates the entire Church.' Do the poor function as a sacrament mediating Christ's presence to the world? Sobrino denies this interpretation, stating: 'There is no question here of idealizing, much less sacralizing the poor. The point is to recover an ancient idea that has been often repeated in Catholic theology.' But when he explains this ancient idea his defense is unconvincing. For the ancient idea that he repeats is that 'certain structures play a privileged role in the coming into existence of Christian reality,' such as the magisterium and the sacraments, and the presence of the Spirit in the poor *ex opere operato* is one such privileged structure.[67] How does this not sacralize the poor?

The poor function as church in two distinct, and not necessarily reconcilable, ways. First, 'the poor constitute the very basis of the Church.' Second, 'the poor within this church become the hermeneutical principle for a primary concrete expression of important Christian concepts and realities.'[68] That the poor 'constitute' the church irrespective of any criteria other than that they be poor would lead one to conclude that they do function sacramentally. But that they become a necessary 'hermeneutical principle' within the Christian faith does not imply the strong version of the *ex opere operato* principle Sobrino employs with respect to the poor.

Even if the poor are sacralized, we must still raise the question whether such a claim is theologically appropriate. Scripture provides warrant for such a claim, in Matthew 25, a passage to which Sobrino constantly appeals. Given what Sobrino has argued about the poor, why does he draw back from the obvious implications that he himself explicates – a life with the poor mediates God's presence *ex opere operato*? Of course, sacralizing the poor is first and foremost unfair to them. It would place too great a burden on them and prompt an inappropriate identification with the poor by which those of us who are not poor use them for our own salvation. This would raise several problems. The poor cannot save us; only Christ achieves this. Moreover, to sacralize the poor could too easily sanctify those same oppressive conditions from which liberation theology seeks liberation. Involuntary poverty becomes sanctified as a means for the rich's salvation. For these reasons Sobrino appears to draw back from the more extreme version of his own claim. Rather than sacralizing the poor, he views their sufferings Christologically. He then challenges the entire church to 'migrate to the periphery and share the powerlessness of the poor at the feet of a crucified God, so that it might there cultivate Christian hope and develop effective (and in this sense powerful) activity.'[69]

But there is yet another reason the poor cannot be sacralized, one that Sobrino does not emphasize. The poor are not the elect; the Jews are. To sacralize the poor is to de-scandalize the particularity of the biblical narrative. God does not call the poor; God calls the Jews. And this election can never be undone, only expanded to include the Gentiles. Christian theologians cannot replace the call of the Jews with the call of any group of people, including the poor. The Jews do not stand as a symbol for some other social group.

In this sense, liberation theology often reads Jesus in too decisive a break with Judaism. For instance, Sobrino asks whether the Father allows religious leaders to kill the Son 'so that he might overcome the old religious schema once and for all, so that he might show that he is a completely different sort of God who serves as the basis for a completely new kind of human existence.'[70] This borders on Marcionism, and it loses the sense of God's particular action in history, substituting for it something more vague such as that 'Jesus defends the law insofar as it is God's law acting in support of human beings.'[71] But how helpful is this? What does it mean to act in support of human beings? Isn't God's law to be the measure by which we recognize what it might mean to support human beings? How then can the latter be used to judge the former? Such an interpretation of Jesus' relationship to God's law is too amorphous. It does not help as an ethical principle because of its vagueness.

## VI   Theological and natural virtues displaced

The vagueness of Sobrino's interpretation of Jesus' politics is evident also in his elevation of the natural virtue of justice, and its transformation into a formal social process. The subordination of the theological virtues to the natural virtues is a common characteristic of the emergent tradition. Justice and courage become more decisive for the Christian life than charity or faith. The latter are treated with suspicion. To invoke them is to deny the dialectical and antagonistic nature of being itself.

For the tradition of the theological virtues stemming from St Thomas, justice was important but inferior to the theological virtues, the gifts and beatitudes, and the central role of phronêsis in politics. For Thomas justice was a straightforward virtue: it regulated the relationships of exchange between people. As a virtue, justice was concrete and material, embodied in principles such as the just wage and the prohibition against usury. But justice needed to be completed through the theological virtues. A right ordering of the virtues ultimately required the infusion of the theological virtues – faith, hope and charity – for the completion of the natural virtues. Thus the church was central for righteousness: it contained the means of the production and reproduction of the theological virtues that completed, made intelligible, and also corrected the natural virtues necessary for political and economic existence.[72]

Even though Sobrino finds a political theology present in biblical teachings such as the Sermon on the Mount,[73] he does not find 'faith' itself to be sufficiently political, and this is why 'justice' becomes more determinative than is faith. Thus Sobrino can speak of the 'promotion of justice as the essential requirement of the Gospel message' which assumes a sharp distinction between faith and justice.[74] Faith concerns the 'aspect of meaning' and justice concerns 'historical practice.' Faith becomes something subjective; justice is objective. In fact rather than a faith-infused justice being necessary for the human creature to achieve her spiritual vocation, Sobrino argues that 'in justice, faith is sustained.' This turns a faith-infused justice into a justice that sustains faith. Faith is a 'subjective act elicited by a subject,' but the subjective act is 'not enough': for a true ecumenism we need not so much a unity of faith as a 'call to a common practice of justice.'[75]

What is meant here by *justice*? Even though he emphasizes the 'objective' character of justice and the performance of justice as the essential element of the Gospel, Sobrino does not give us an extended description of justice. He argues against the ancient tradition that viewed justice as a 'virtue' and instead suggests that justice is 'the way in which the Kingdom is built and becomes a reality.' Justice appears to be a process of social construction, and faith is reduced to the 'meaning' given to that construction.[76] The way he develops the relationship between justice and faith de-politicizes the theological virtues.

This transvaluation of faith and justice results from Sobrino's attempt, similar to Gutiérrez's, to integrate faith and politics, theology and economics, through Rahner's 'supernatural existential.' A number of theologians have argued, both positively and negatively, that some of the impetus behind liberation theology stems from Rahner's theology. Stephen Duffy offered this argument in his *The Graced Horizon* and sees Rahner's influence as a positive shift in Catholic theology that makes possible a social ethic separate from overtly theological language.[77] But this is not radical

Catholicism. Rather it seems homologous to pre-Conciliar neo-scholasticism. A basis for a social ethics is found where people can participate in works of Catholic moral action without such actions having any explicitly thematic or categorical connection to theological language. Whereas the neo-scholastics did this through the doctrine of 'pure nature,' post-conciliar Catholic theologians seem to achieve the same end through the 'supernatural existential.' Where, before, 'pure nature' made possible a double finality that allowed the political to pursue its own ends on the basis of nature alone – conceding it a certain autonomy – now the 'graced horizon' of the supernatural existential allows the political to be a site for theological activity, but still with its own autonomy, or at least anonymity from specific theological language. Political economy becomes separate from the need for any specific supernatural end or vocation (and still free from the church's interference) precisely because of the transcendental revelation which is the basis for all human knowledge and action.

The relationship between transcendental and categorical revelation in Rahner is not easily deciphered. Rahner clearly argues that the transcendental is '*a posteriori*,' because it is 'mediated by a categorical encounter with concrete reality in our world, both the world of things and of persons.'[78] Rahner can be read as developing the transcendental as a necessary possibility because of the actuality of the incarnation. R. R. Reno provides such a reading when he states, 'Rahner reasons from God's designs for us (grace) to our capacities and purposes, not the other way around.'[79] Fergus Kerr, however, finds in Rahner's theology the culmination of Cartesian preoccupations with the cognitive subject. Theology becomes dependent upon some transcendent reality located in the human subject.[80] Likewise Hans Urs von Balthasar reads Rahner's work in the stream of German idealism's 'metaphysics of spirit' where an *identitas entis* replaces the Christian revelation with its *analogia entis*. This *identitas entis* denies the necessary distinction between Being and our being, and between God and creation, and in so doing, the transcendental subsumes the categorical.[81]

Whether or not Rahner himself is guilty of this subsumption is an open question, but that Rahnerians find in it a source with which to subsume categorical revelation under a transcendental philosophy is not. For instance, Stephen Duffy argues that 'categorical revelation makes transcendental revelation known for what it is and is the condition for its possibility, while transcendental revelation is hypothetically necessary for the reception of categorical revelation.' Nevertheless he can still speak of the transcendental as the *a priori*. And he suggests that 'Rahner will not reduce revelation to categorical revelation, embodied in the Jewish and Christian covenants,' because it must be linked to 'catholicity' rather than to these particular historical manifestations of faith. This catholicity is now freed from characterizing the church and becomes joined to the transcendental conditions of human knowledge and action; it functions in much the same way catholicity did when it was employed in the dominant tradition: Kant, not the church, defines what is catholic. Duffy suggests that revelation, as thoroughly normed by the Christian and Jewish covenants, is a 'reduction.' What then is the role for 'categorical revelation'? It 'brings awareness that the horizon encompassing all human life is the saving God.'[82] But this horizon has now relativized the ecclesiological role as the site where specific social practices can be expected to be produced as a social alternative in and of themselves.

Sobrino appeals to Rahner's theology as that which 'awakened' him 'from the dream' of his own dogmatic slumber. Rahner did this by revealing to him the significance of the 'mystery of God,' which 'helped us realize that the church is not itself the most important thing, not even for God.'[83] Rahner accomplished this through his transcendental philosophy, but Sobrino argues that this is not what wakened him from an earlier ecclesial triumphalism. Instead it was the recognition that 'the most pressing aspect of reality' is 'not in what happens to me, but in what is happening to the suffering people of the world.'[84]

Rahner's transcendental revelation provides the philosophical form by which Sobrino reinterprets the natural virtue of justice as a transcendental process through which persons participate in the gospel by participation in acts of liberation. Faith then gives some persons the explicit meaning behind their actions, but the language of faith itself is not constitutive of the action. Two things are, however, lost when Christian tradition is reversed so that justice sustains faith rather than faith completing justice. First, the concrete reality of faith is abandoned, and faith then must be made concrete through justice. Faith itself remains, as it was for the neo-scholastics, a-political. It is made political only through mediatory works of justice.[85] Second, the significant correction of ancient pagan virtue by the Christian tradition is undone. No longer is the moral life viewed as a gift mediated through the sacramental structures of the church, empowering persons to live the new law through the Holy Spirit. Instead, the essential reality of pagan virtue, where justice is an achievement accomplished through struggle, returns.

Justice loses its concrete specificity and instead becomes defined by Jesus' desire to seek change. Nowhere do we find traditional regulations of justice, such as the just wage, the prohibition of usury, the interesting interpretations of 'do not steal' that assume the universal destination of all created goods. Sobrino neglects these concrete manifestations of justice from the Catholic tradition. Not only are the natural virtues conceded an autonomous space, but they are transmuted into the formalized values that constitute modern ethics.

# 9 Scarcity, orthodoxy, and heresy

Tillich and Rahner are the two theologians who open a way for theology as liberation in the emergent tradition. This is not to deny that liberation theologies arise primarily from the protest of the household, the option for the poor, and the history of the black church. It is to suggest, however, that the formal identification of liberation as an ontological determinant of a graced human nature arises from those theologians who explicitly produced a theological apologia for modernity. Because God is now known through an identity with emancipatory negation and practice, specific Christian theology and practice are rendered secondary to this primary negation. This results in a diminished role for ecclesiology in favor of a theology grounded in a transcendental reality: a reality that becomes so certain that it can too easily dispense with the categorical, i.e. the historical language produced and embodied in the church's tradition, and ongoing historical existence. The result is the subordination of theological virtues to natural ones, but also theological language becomes viewed in terms of a scarcity that makes the distinction between orthodoxy and heresy difficult to maintain. All theological language becomes inadequate because it is grounded in a lack. This scarcity of theological language does not provide a form of theology that can emerge out of and against modernity. It can be only its ally.

## I    Theological, economic, and postmodern scarcity

Surprisingly, capitalist economic analysis, postmodern 'responsibility,' and theology in the emergent tradition all assume lack and scarcity, whether in economic practice, moral possibility, or theological language. Capitalist economics assumes scarcity. For instance, the economists Baumol and Blinder ask the question: 'What is the basic task that economists expect the market to carry out?' And they answer that 'the market resolves THE fundamental problem of the economy: the fact that all decisions are constrained by the scarcity of available resources.'[1] Notice the language these economists invoke: '*all* decisions are constrained by scarcity.' While this lack assumes a scarcity of resources, it assumes also a more fundamental scarcity – in *anthropology* itself. This anthropology is indebted to modernity's turn to the subject. After this turn, the human person becomes construed as grounded in a finite rationality but with an unlimited will. For instance, the critical idealism of Immanuel Kant posits our reason as bound by its ability to synthesize concepts based on sensible intuitions that are never adequate to things in themselves, but our will as grounded in a freedom that assumes the infinite. This modern anthropology fits well with capitalist economics' analysis of scarcity. An individual consumer confronts objects of desire that are limited by time and space, but the consumer confronts these finite commodities with an infinite desire grounded in an unencumbered freedom. Faced with myriad possible consumable choices that could satisfy me, once I choose one I have foregone all others. All exchanges assume a doctrine of human action where every transaction exchanges the infinite (freedom) for the finite (objects located in space and time.) Thus my choice at any historical moment is always already connected with lack. The moment I choose $x$ rather than $y$, I shall forever lack $y$ in that moment; my response to $x$ makes $y$ an 'opportunity cost' to me. I always live and act in a situation of scarcity where to decide for something at a particular moment is at the same time to decide against something else. The historical realization of my decisions can be only partial, determined beforehand by an inevitably scarcity. Curiously, a version of this account of human agency appears in Derrida's arguments for ethical responsibility and for Derrida (like Kant) it demands the superiority of heresy over orthodoxy.

Derrida's argument for ethical responsibility is found in his *The Gift of Death*, and is based on a poor interpretation of the *Akedah*. Derrida overlooks the interpretation of Abraham's 'sacrifice' as found in Hebrews (11:19): 'Abraham considered the fact that God is able even to raise someone from the dead – and, figuratively speaking, he did receive him back.' Thus for the Scriptures, unlike for Derrida, death is no gift. Yet, for Derrida, Abraham's sacrifice of Isaac must be beyond ethics because it is based on 'silence and secrecy,' which 'infinite responsibility' requires: it is the gift of death.[2] Thus Abraham's silence 'assumes the responsibility that consists in always being alone, entrenched in one's own singularity at the moment of decision.' The moment someone speaks, 'one loses that very singularity.' Now 'substitution' replaces the 'nonsubstitution, nonrepetition, silence, and secrecy' of 'absolute singularity.' Substitution is, of course, another key principle in capitalist economics. For instance, Paul Samuelson, in his classic textbook *Economics*, states that 'Substitution is the law of life in a full-employment economy.' This suggests that when all resources are employed, the only way to produce more butter is to substitute it for something, such as guns. Scarcity produces the need for substitution: I cannot have it all, so to act requires the substitution of one commodity for another.

Derrida appears to be rejecting this analysis. He recognizes that substitution allows for an account-ability, and this is the problem of ethics. It is a temptation that must 'sometimes be refused in the name of a responsibility that doesn't keep account or give an account.'[3] The other requires of me a complete sacrifice, including the gift of death, which gives with no expectation of a return. Ethical responsibility becomes incommensurable with any formal substitution. And this is also why, for Derrida, responsibility must be heretical:

> The absoluteness of duty and responsibility presume that one denounce, refute and transcend at the same time, all duty, all responsibility, and every human law. It calls for a betrayal of everything that manifests itself within the order of universal generality, and everything that manifests itself in general, the very order and essence of manifestation; namely the essence itself ...

This 'absolute duty' stands before the 'name of God as completely other, the nameless name of God.'[4] But rather than rejecting the key anthropological considerations behind capitalist substitution, Derrida repeats them. In an understanding of human action consistent with capitalist economics he asserts: 'What binds me to singularities, to this one or that one, male or female, rather than that one or this one, remains fully unjustifiable (this is Abraham's hyper-ethical sacrifice), as unjustifiable as the infinite sacrifice which I make at each moment.'[5] To choose to care for my spouse, my children, my cat or dog rather than all spouses, children, cats or dogs is always already grounded in an infinite sacrifice. Derrida may have challenged substitution, but his ethics remains just as much defined by lack as does capitalist economic analysis. Derrida's ethical responsibility is no radical account of the ethical life: it is nothing other than the capitalist's opportunity cost.[6]

Ruether's 'flight to critical freedom' also seems bound to the assumption of language and human action as always already grounded in scarcity. She assumes that the truth of God is always out in front of us in some transcendental realm, so that the moment I name God from within a particular historical tradition I foreclose on the possible transcendence not yet here: I dogmatize the historical. God then becomes negation. Her theology thus assumes that to name God, or to identify God with any particular historical work as orthodoxy does, is of necessity a lack of that fullness that is unnamable. The selection of eschatology as a central theological theme with which to critique capitalism fits well with this lack, because a specific use of theological language violates the future-oriented presence of God. God is always ahead of us yet never embodied in the fullness of any moment. But this understanding of theological language is not significantly different from capitalism's opportunity cost and Derridean responsibility. All three assume that to select this commodity, to care for this neighbor, to speak God's name in this way, must be bound to a lack. This lack is not simply the opportunity cost to an individual consumer: it is a metaphysics whereby every choice is mired in scarcity. Thus the answer to the problem of scarcity becomes either to recognize it and realize the world is fundamentally antagonistic (capitalism) or merely never to settle on a specific object, on a particular 'choice' or meaning (Derrida's *difference*, Ruether's eschatology).

The suggestion that these three philosophical positions share a common theme will certainly be a surprise to many readers. Even if this argument is accepted, what does it demonstrate? That such different voices all speak and act from an assumed scarcity could demonstrate merely that capitalist economics is philosophically sound. Can we deny the reality of this scarcity, this lack, at the heart of economics, morality, and theological language? Is it not the case that in choosing this commodity, I sacrifice an infinite number of other commodities? In caring for my wife, I sacrifice an infinite care for all other wives? Is it not the case that in calling God 'Father, Son and Holy Spirit,' I sacrifice an infinite number of other names for God? No, it is not. And to assume that it is shows how intrusive capitalism's critical culture is in both philosophy and theology.

Theologians must deny this narrative of scarcity for it forces our language and actions into the inevitable embrace of death. The moment my will and intellect are bound to some particular good entails a sacrifice of all other objects only if that good itself implies lack. But God is not defined by lack: God is an original plenitude never able to be exhausted. While we do not have an immediate access to God based on our being alone, we can recognize that our being participates in that fullness that makes our being possible, while at the same time that fullness is never exhausted nor diminished in our being. God's goodness in history cannot be exhausted by that history, but neither does the fact that it is in history mitigate against it being fully God's goodness. This makes possible my caring for my children, spouse, and neighbors, and my naming of God, without assuming that in so doing I shirk my duty toward all others. In fact, I do not know that by my living in a house I thereby make necessary homelessness for others. There may very well be no lack of shelter, food, clothing and above all charity and friendship. All these things may exist in plenitude. My love for my children, spouse, neighbors and even enemies is not borne out of an inevitable scarcity, but participates in a plenitude which discloses to me the possibility that all others can also enjoy these same goods and thus participate in God's inexhaustible goodness.

While some goods may indeed be scarce, this does not require that all goods – economic, ethical, and theological – must of necessity be scarce. That I argue for the specificity of Christian theological language as true does not imply a lack whereby I must deny any truthfulness to all other specific theological languages. In fact, the fullness of Christian theological language requires just the opposite. What I cannot do is expect to inhabit some neutral, olympian space whence I can view all religions as legitimate expressions of some unnamable *a priori* religious experience; for in claiming such a space I have always already named that experience. Only because I can speak a language that always contains more can I recognize truths in other religions. But such truths will of necessity be narrated within, and never from without, the truths of some specific theological language.

Ruether's eschatology functions as a critique of all historical and linguistic mediations of the Christian gospel.[7] But this seems to be because a more fundamental *a priori* religious experience is known without the mediation of this particular history. Once theological language is subordinated to some more metaphysical real, the result inevitably seems to be that theology becomes fundamentally about ethics and we lose the enchantment of ritual, the sacred, and the eternal:

> The mediation between God and man has been removed from all sacred settings, persons and sacraments and becomes the secular sacrament of the encounter with the neighbor that cuts across our self-enclosed egoism and opens us up to a new possibility of an open, loving relation with our fellow man. In this Christ event the alienation of man and man is overcome and the possibility of community is founded.[8]

This has dire consequences for Christian theology, particularly in ecclesiology and pneumatology. The concept of the church is flattened and de-particularized. And, as I argued with regard to McCann, the catholicity of the church becomes analogous to the Kantian universalization premiss.[9] Likewise the Spirit is no longer recognized by its particular role within the Trinity: the Spirit is not the Spirit of Christ poured out on the church at Pentecost, but has become a principle of liberty. It is not 'the captive of ecclesiastical ministries and channels, but is a free spirit abroad in the land ... whose presence is recognized wherever alienation is being overcome and human community built up.'[10]

Of course, the Spirit cannot be the captive of ecclesiastical institutions. An orthodox ecclesiology must always insist upon this as well. The role of the Spirit is not to maintain the ecclesiastical institution, but to produce in the world lives of holiness. As von Balthasar noted: 'The magisterium is a means; the life of the Church is an end.'[11] The Vatican II document *Lumen Gentium* illustrates this when it states that mere compliance with the church is inadequate; something more is still needed: 'He is not saved, however, who, though part of the body of the Church does not persevere in Charity' (paragraph 14). Thus, as von Balthasar also noted, the role of articulating doctrine entrusted to the Petrine office serves the purpose of producing the 'holiness of life within the (Marian) Church of the saints.'[12] It is always possible to have the second without a clear articulation of the first, but, when the second becomes set against the first, then grace inevitably loses its Christoform. The result is a secularizing of the sacred in that the sacred makes explicit merely what is already present in the world, yet what is already present in the world can be known without the sacred. In fact, the sacred becomes intrusive. The Spirit's free activity becomes not merely independent of the church, but in opposition to it. To adhere to the church's teachings becomes an act of infidelity against the Spirit. What role remains for the church and the particularities of Christian doctrine? They become subordinated to a putatively more universal reality marked primarily by the ethical. Christology itself can offer no real finality to human history: it is merely the way certain cultural groups point to that more universal reality.

Ruether's difficulty with particularity becomes most evident in her efforts to find a role for Christ within theology. This is for laudable reasons. The problem of Christ's role arises because of her commitment to feminism and her opposition to anti-Semitism. She argues that 'Christ as symbol is problematic for feminist theology.' Much of the church's traditional confessions about Jesus will not liberate women. Her argument is, in part, undeniable and based on Christianity's historical performance. She suggests that Christ becomes the 'founder and cosmic governor of the existing social hierarchy and as the disclosure of a male God whose narrative representation can only be male' because in Catholic tradition 'only the male represents the fullness of human nature.'[13] What is undeniable about her argument is the patriarchal assumption, found in Thomas Aquinas and others, that women cannot represent Christ because they lack the fullness of human nature. Although such an argument is not the basis for the present Catholic prohibition against the ordination of women, the suspicion that it is the suppressed premiss behind this prohibition lends credibility to Ruether's argument. Even if we argue that Christian tradition has never contended that God is male, the fact that only men are allowed to represent God does lend credence to the persuasive power of such protestations.

Any Christology that makes Jesus' *maleness* the soteriological center should be repudiated. But do such repudiations then entail the relativization of Christology, its reduction from necessary theological center to the role of theological support? After explaining that Christology is problematic for feminist theology, Ruether states:

> This does not mean that feminist theology may not be able to affirm the person of Jesus of Nazareth as a positive model of redeemed humanity. But this model must be seen as partial and fragmentary, disclosing from the perspective of one person circumscribed in time, culture and gender something of the fullness we seek.[14]

This suggests that Jesus is a 'partial and fragmentary' disclosure of that fullness because he is 'circumscribed in time, culture and gender.' If so, then it certainly assumes the metaphysics of scarcity that defines modernity.

Does feminist theology demand this Christological reductivism? Or is it Ruether's grounding of theological language in a classical metaphysical scarcity that inevitably leads to such claims? This metaphysics assumes that because we know Being, or the true and the good, outside of history, we know also that historical manifestations of that being lack its fullness. Her explanation of the incarnation resonates with this metaphysics:

> A religious culture may pick out a particular place where this appearing is seen 'normatively'; i.e. Jesus or the Torah or Buddha, but this doctrine of 'incarnation' is not just about this one place or person, but this one place or person operates as a norm for discerning the nature of this 'presence' wherever it happens.[15]

The incarnation becomes a metaphysical category within which particular historical manifestations are only partial and incomplete signs.

Ruether's Christological reductivism is also the result of her fear that high Christologies inevitably lead to anti-Semitism. She has combated Christian anti-Semitism since her earliest work. She warns against separating Jesus from Judaism; a warning many other theologians have made this century and one that too often goes unheeded. But her argument is much stronger than that of Karl Barth who admonished us to never forget that when God assumed human flesh that flesh was Jewish. Ruether suggests that any universal claims for Lordship based on Jesus' particularity have the inevitable consequences of anti-Semitism:

> The anti-Semitic heritage of Christian civilization is neither an accidental nor a peripheral element.... Anti-Semitism in Western civilization springs, at its root, from Christian theological anti-Judaism. It was Christian theology that developed the thesis of the reprobate status of the Jew in history and laid the foundations for the demonic view of the Jew that fanned the flame of popular hatred.... The understanding of Christology is, I believe, at the heart of the problem. Theologically, anti-Judaism developed as the left hand of Christology. Anti-Judaism was the negative side of the Christian affirmation that Jesus was the Christ. Christianity claimed that the Jewish tradition of messianic hope was fulfilled in Jesus. But since the Jewish religious teachers rejected this claim, the church developed a polemic against the Jews and Judaism to explain how the church could claim to be the fulfillment of a Jewish religious tradition when the Jewish religious teachers themselves denied it.[16]

If we concede this criticism, it strikes at the heart both of traditional Christology and of ecclesiology. To view Jesus as the restorer of Israel and the church as the social embodiment of that restoration is deemed anti-Semitic.[17] One possible response in rescuing Christianity from its own history is Ruether's – Jesus is 'the only name *for us.*'[18] This relativistic contextualization of Christology fits also with her understanding of liberation: 'Incarnation, Revelation and Resurrection cease to point backward to some once and for all event in the past, which has been reified as a mysterious salvific power in the institutional Church and becomes instead paradigms of the liberation which takes place in people here and now.'[19] But the difficulty with this strategy is that liberation becomes a category more fundamental to theology than is Christology, and not only Christology but Judaism itself becomes a historical manifestation of a more profound and readily available experience of the transcendental Spirit. The significant differences between Judaism and Christianity are sublimated into a putatively more certain transcendence that lets us know they are both partial manifestations of that transcendence. Rather than a necessary ongoing argument about the historical narratives Jews and Christians share and differ over, both the Christian and the Jewish tradition are re-read from the perspective of a more secure and certain liberation.[20] Both are relativized: conversion to either is less significant than is recognizing the transcendental reality of liberation to which they both point.

Re-reading tradition constitutes no theological problem. The incarnation must never be simply behind us; it is always *also* in front of us. In her serious engagement with questions of patriarchy and anti-Semitism, Ruether rightly suggests that tradition cannot merely be the repetition of earlier, putatively infallible, forms of theological production. That traditions are, and must be, re-read is, in fact, tautologous. If this does not occur, a tradition would die. When she states that 'an affirmation of the messianic even in Jesus in a contextual and open-ended, rather than a "once for all" and absolutistic way, is demanded by the exigencies of Christian theology itself,' there can be no serious objection. What it means for Jesus to be the Messiah has a surplus to it which can and must be re-presented daily: each representation both maintaining the 'original' event and through its historical performance making the 'original' event present itself anew.

Yet we seem to be caught on the horns of an unnecessary dilemma – either affirm the tradition and with it misogyny and anti-Semitism; or affirm liberation and break with tradition, selecting out of it what is useful for liberation. If these are our alternatives, any person concerned with living a good life will opt for the latter. But is this an adequate account of what tradition is? And does it neglect the fact that all knowledge will be situated within some historical tradition? To assume that we are outside of history is to lose the ability to recognize and work within the tradition(s) that shape us. That Ruether falls prey to the latter can be seen in her conclusion to the de-absolutizing of Christology: 'The Christian experience can parallel rather than negate the liberation experiences which are the community symbols of other faiths.'[21] Once again we find the loss of theological particularity in favor of something considered more universal – liberation experience. Ruether's criticism of Christianity's anti-Semitism does not lead her explicitly to adopt a different historical particularity – Judaism itself, for instance – a position that would be reasonable. Instead, we find something *outside* all of these traditions – liberation. But does such an outside exist? How would we be able to recognize it?

## II   Universality as ordering theological discourse: the embrace of death

Ruether re-situates Christian tradition by subordinating it to a more universal yet formal religiosity. This religiosity gives to human creatures a power to fashion new gods at will: 'With Jesus' death, God the heavenly Ruler has left the heavens and has been poured out upon the earth with his blood. A new God is being born in our hearts, to teach us to level the heavens and exalt the earth and create a new world without master and slaves, rulers and subjects.'[22] This free power to create new gods seeks to ameliorate differences through a more universal space than any one god could fill by incorporating the different gods into an overarching framework of a 'new humanity.' Women have a central role to play in the construction of this new humanity. Ruether suggests: 'Women must be the spokesmen for a new humanity arising out of the reconciliation of spirit and body.' Such a reconciliation will occur by 'combining the values of the world-transcending Yahweh with those of the world-renewing Baal.'[23] This ordering of theological discourses by combining the partial and particular gods into a 'universal' framework defined by liberation receives its fullest articulation in Ruether's 1992 *Gaia and God*. It is here that the implications of this strategy are seen to result in an embrace of death.

The combination of Yahweh and Baal in *Gaia and God* strikes a Malthusian chord. Ruether writes: 'Humanity has no real alternative to population control. The question is do we want population control to happen voluntarily, before conception, or violently, by war, famine and disease?'[24] Such statements approximate nineteenth-century Christian political economy. This should create a theological pause precisely because the appearance of this socio-scientific claim in the nineteenth century led to the giving over of Ireland to such 'natural' causes as famine and disease as a providential judgment against the Irish people's non-scientific attachment to Catholicism. Famine and disease were viewed as God's discipline against a superstitious people. Thus, in the midst of the famine Charles Treveleyan could state:

> I think I see a bright light shining in the distance through the dark cloud which at present hangs over Ireland…. The deep and inveterate root of Social evil remains, and I hope I am not guilty of irreverence in thinking that, this being altogether beyond the power of man, the cure has been applied by the direct stroke of an all wise providence in a manner as unexpected and unthought of as it is likely to be effectual.[25]

This classical account of capitalist economics embraces death as the great disciplinarian civilizing superstitious people into the universal providential order. Ruether's work is certainly not antagonistic toward the poor as had been these nineteenth-century Christian political economists, but the apocalyptic analysis and embrace of death resembles their natural theology of providence. The divine orders the world so that scarcity provokes human responsibility.[26] Death becomes our friend.

Ruether's reliance on eco-theology also seems to embrace death. She concludes her efforts to synthesize God with Gaia by stating:

> As we gaze into the void of our future extinguished self and dissolving substance, we encounter there the wellspring of life and creativity from which all things have sprung and into which they return, only to well up again in new forms. But we also know this as the great Thou.[27]

We are told that 'holy death' is 'the means by which all living things are returned to earth to be re-generated as new organisms,' and that 'in nature death is not an enemy but a friend of the life process.'[28] On the one hand, this embrace of death is a criticism of capitalism's necrophobia. The fear of death is another form of scarcity. To secure ourselves against death is a motivational force behind economic exchanges. On the other hand, the statement quoted above expresses precisely what capitalist economics demands – death and scarcity as the conditions for the possibility of an efficient life. It is through the gaze of my extinguished self that I realize the limitations that make scarcity necessary. Through this gaze into my own limitedness – a limit always established by the impending cessation of space and time for me – through this *gift* of death, I discover in nature the best way to be efficient. Thanks to death I must choose *x* rather than *y*. This has become a feature of 'nature' – a demystified 'nature' that bears no possibility of participation in the eternal. This is consistent with capitalism.

Capitalist economic analysis produces both necrophilia and necrophobia at the same time. Capitalist (micro)economic analysis begins with scarcity assuming death as a limit that necessitates choices, and (macro)economic analysis defends capitalism because of its efficiency. Through acknowledging the limitations death always imposes, the most efficient productivity can be established. On the one hand, death is the enemy, the limiting condition that means I must choose *x* rather than *y*, and I do not have the time or the ability to choose both *x* and *y*. The imminence of my death makes economics possible. On the other hand, this 'natural' condition makes efficiency possible: it discloses to us 'nature,' or the 'facts,' that make possible economic 'laws.' These laws tell us that, given the metaphysics of scarcity, capitalism provides the social formations within which human creatures can achieve the best possible economic outcomes.

Capitalism's necrophilia and necrophobia do not imply a contradiction. Fear is a form of worship and adoration: what we fear we implicitly worship. What we worship we love. What we worship and love we become. Death is embraced; the nihil, void or negation becomes our god. But this conflicts with a classical Christian understanding of creation that is secure neither in itself nor in its extinction, but only in its gratuitous generation from an eternal God.

Is Ruether's embrace of death analogous to the economists' basic principles? On the one hand, Ruether's analysis of nature is millenarian: in the year 2030 we will have no more fuel; war, scarcity, and famine await us. The cosmic matrix does not seem so gracious: she seems to impose scarcity upon us. On the other hand, we are suppose to trust her, to give ourselves over to her. Does gazing into the void of our future extinguished selves, and into the death of our loved ones, result in the possibility of life? Or is it a vision of putrefaction and worms, a return to the dust that is not another act of creation but a dissolution of body and therefore of memories as well?

Christian hope requires some understanding of the resurrection of the body. This theme is absent from Ruether's work even though she rightly critiques the church fathers for their non-corporeal eschatology. Without the orthodox understanding of the resurrection of the body some form of dualism is inevitable, a dualism too easily found in the fathers themselves. Ruether is suspicious of traditional eschatology because, she suggests, the 'operative Christian eschatology for the most part is one of an immortal soul that escapes from and is not limited by the mortal fate of earth's creatures.'[29] She challenges this doctrine of the immortal soul, but not by insisting upon the resurrection of the body – she fears that such an orthodox account of the body will lead to neglect of the earth. But if we are part of the dust of the earth, as the church teaches, then an appropriate theological understanding of the resurrection of the body cannot lead to a 'neglect of the earth.' That mortality is overcome in our participation in the life of God does not mean that mortality itself is eschewed. In fact, only through the mortality which God assumes in Jesus does Christianity extend the possibility that the mortal can put on the immortal. This is Christian hope.

Ruether's theology is suspicious of traditional orthodox Christianity. She sees it fundamentally as dogmatizing the historical. As an alternative she seeks a more inclusive and pluralistic theology which finds even in the heresies a partial and fragmentary glimpse of the transcendent Spirit that can never be captured in historical concretions. That the Spirit is more than its historical expressions is undeniable. But the assumption behind this understanding of the partial and fragmentary nature of historical theological language is that a metaphysics of Spirit is in fact present to us outside of any historical particularity. This metaphysics of Spirit is the basis for an understanding of scarcity. Because the infinite is assumed as present to us in contradiction to the historical, the historical is viewed as mired in lack.

## III  Critical reflection on praxis and on theological language

The theological content in Gutiérrez's work embodies a fullness that cannot afford scarcity. God is the God of an abundant life. The resurrection of Jesus challenges the reality of poverty and death among the poor, creating a new reality in history, a history that must be embodied in social and political life. While this content maintains the fullness of Christian orthodoxy, his theological *method* appears to present something quite similar to the metaphysics of lack that does not always capture the fullness his theological *content* presents. He defines this method as 'critical reflection on praxis.'[30]

The straightforwardness of this definition does not result in an easily deciphered methodology. It suggests that theology is a second-order discourse that utilizes critical modes of rationality to render praxis intelligible. Moreover, Gutiérrez appears to signify something unusually specific by his use of *praxis*: 'Theology is an attempt to do a reading of the faith from a point of departure in a determined situation,' and that determined situation is 'the exploited classes, despised ethnic groups, marginalized cultures.'[31] So it appears that theology begins with the praxis of the marginalized and then seeks to find a language appropriate to their social and historical conditions. Yet, because faith itself is not a political or social plan, theology must look also to contemporary socio-scientific thought to assist it in its social and political applications. It is here that the contingent character of that historical analysis slides into the social scientists' natural laws. The contemporary rationality to which Gutiérrez turns is that of Marxist social analysis, and the justification for this inclusion is that 'every theology' exists 'within a cultural time.' So just as St Thomas utilized Aristotelianism to express the truths of Christian faith, Gutiérrez employs Marxist social analysis.[32]

But St Thomas gave us a radically re-worked Aristotelianism that subordinated the latter to an overarching theological vision. Thus the cardinal virtues of justice, prudence, courage and temperance are fulfilled only with the infusion of the theological virtues, faith, hope and charity. Thomas never allowed Aristotle's work to stand as the historical vehicle that made an idealized Christianity relevant to thirteenth-century culture. Thomas had a more radically historical understanding of Christianity than that. Gutiérrez does not seem to have sufficiently historicized theology in allowing Marxist social analysis to be the vehicle for historicizing a Christian vision that still remains radically ahistorical. For Gutiérrez, the transcendent continuity within theology is the Word. But contingently new situations arise, and these need to be addressed theologically. The Word then becomes the constant, the transhistoric reality, such that the theological task is to 'search out new ways of reformulating the word.' Thus we have a 'theological reflection' that 'even as it breaks new ground ... retains all its validity and grows rich in its ongoing dialogue with the sciences.'[33]

Gutiérrez's method appears similar to the idealism found in the so-called 'Protestant principle.' I suggest this because of such claims of his as that 'the gospel message is a message that can never be identified with any concrete social formula, however just that formula may seem to us at the moment,' and that Christ is a 'challenge to every historical incarnation.'[34] While appearing to recognize the contingency of the social sciences, such claims rather demarcate the historical production of theology from the social sciences and insufficiently historicize theology. The Word becomes a transcendent reality that must be embodied in historical forms but can never adequately be contained in those forms, so that we must constantly criticize and reevaluate each historical form used to embody that which may not be historically embodied. A method which assumes that Christ challenges all 'historical incarnations' of the divine ultimately turns on Christ himself. The hypostatic union is challenged, and Christ is relegated to the metaphysical margins of history.

To see in Gutiérrez's work a reflection of the Protestant principle might be unjustified. However, the confusion over his method may not always be the reader's fault. For his method – theology is critical reflection on praxis – seems to function in at least three distinct ways. First, theology appears to be critical reflection on the *experience* of poverty and oppression. Second, theology is critical reflection on *socio-scientific analysis* of the conditions that produce poverty. Third, theology is an *historical tradition*, much neglected, that arose and arises still from situations of oppression.

If Gutiérrez's method is best described by the first option, then he assumes a pre-thematized experience expressed in theological language so that the adequacy of that language will be measured by its ability to explain this experience. If this is the method, then Gutiérrez's theology could be viewed as a variation on 'experiential expressivism.'[35] His theology certainly does not begin with a common-core human experience of transcendence or with anything that could be termed a religious *a priori*; but it does suggest that theology begins with a privileged core experience of oppression and exploitation, on which experience it then reflects and seeks to express it in language. The language is secondary to the experience.

This understanding of his method has the merit of theologically addressing concrete social reality but at the expense of a specifically theological language about that oppression. Yet Gutiérrez does not proceed on the basis of an unthematized observation of 'oppression.' Because he sees the world already theologically encoded, he sees 'oppression' and 'exploitation' where others see only a 'lack of development,' 'a residual mercantilism' or an 'inefficient allocation of scarce resources.' And central to the theological vision that already codes what he sees is *charity*.

At the heart of Gutiérrez's theological vision is the life of charity as participation in the life of God, a life to which we have access through the revelation of Jesus. In as early a work as *A Theology of Liberation* he wrote: 'To be saved is to reach the fullness of love; it is to enter into the circle of charity which unites the three persons of the Trinity; it is to love as God loves.'[36] This theme has been continuous throughout his work.[37] Related to it is the important role Christology plays as the 'center of all theology.'[38] These theological themes alone allow for the problem of oppression to occur in the way that it does for him. His method appears analogous to Barth's. As Gutiérrez himself put it: 'The one who starts with heaven is sensitive to those who live in the hell of this earth.' Participation in the life of charity is occluded by a social system that exploits the work of the many for the gain of a few. But before vision can be occluded, it must be clear.

Although his theological method sometimes suggests otherwise, Gutiérrez's theology does not begin with a neutral analysis of social conditions and *then* bring theology in as a transcendent reality that addresses those conditions. He begins, as St Thomas did, with the fullness of the vision of God. And he sees what he does because that vision conflicts with the social reality of Latin America. He does not begin with Marx to define a reality that then is presented to theology. He uses theology to reveal an absurd contradiction: in a world created and redeemed through the Blessed Trinity, Ayacucho exists.[39] Any deficiency in his use of theological language arises because his method has not sufficiently absorbed and integrated other cultural discourses, such as Marxism, within the content of his theology. Instead, such discourses are allowed too much autonomy.

Of course, Gutiérrez is not dependent on Marxism for social analysis. He finds it present in the Scriptural promise of Isaiah 65:21–2: 'They shall build houses and inhabit them; they shall plant vineyards and eat their fruit. They shall not build and another inhabit; they shall not plant and another eat.... My chosen shall enjoy the fruit of their labor.'[40] Anyone vaguely familiar with the use of migrant labor by which grocery stores in the United States of America are kept filled with agricultural produce could only be struck by the dissonance between this most basic economic reality and the economic vision of Isaiah.[41] The Isaiah passage is viewed as a defining characteristic of the Kingdom both the prophets and Jesus proclaim. This theological vision easily lends itself toward an absorption and a re-working of a Marxist social analysis. Charity could be construed as the virtue, emanating from the Trinity, that defines our lives by being embedded in material production.

Drawing on Paul VI, Gutiérrez defines charity as 'political charity,' because

> to offer food or drink in our day is a political action: it means the transformation of a society structured to benefit a few who appropriate to themselves the value of the work of others. This transformation ought to be directed towards a radical change in the foundation of society, that is, the private ownership of the means of production.[42]

It is *here* that Marxist analysis becomes essential to Gutiérrez's theology: Christian charity cannot be cultivated in a capitalist society, because it exploits the value of the worker's labor power for the benefit of the capitalist; workers do not eat from the fruit of their own labor. This constitutes the major difference between Gutiérrez and the dominant tradition: capitalism is incompatible with an emancipatory framework within which human beings will flourish. Scarcity does exist in Gutiérrez's theological world, but it exists primarily as an absurdity that can be eradicated because of the fullness of love present in the incarnation, death and resurrection of Jesus of Nazareth. Such an understanding qualifies his assumption that theological language remains always inadequate.

The inadequacy of theological language in Gutiérrez bears too much resemblance to Barthianism. Barth himself too closely approached the neo-Protestant principle of Tillich when he argued: 'By existing in the public sphere and therefore in time and in the world as such, the Church can never evade the possibility of a total or partial defection from Jesus Christ.'[43] Barth seems to suggest that because the church exists in history it must be subject to defectibility, to lack. Here is where Hans Urs von Balthasar found the decisive difference between Protestant and Catholic doctrines of grace. He challenged this very idea, noting that it was incapable of adequately expressing the incarnation, the sacraments, and Mary's 'yes' to God. He countered Barth, the Protestant principle, and the metaphysics of scarcity by asserting:

> But we reply: Does the Church – knowing as she does that she has been founded by Christ – not have the right to regard herself as true? Can she relativize herself without abrogating her obedience to her Lord? And where would such a self-relativization come to an end? The 'absoluteness' that the Catholic Church must claim for herself really represents her obedience, her refusal to countenance any detriment or constriction to the sovereignty of the freedom of God's grace. The Church has never equated the place of her visibility with that of the elect and the justified. And the certainty that she possesses depends entirely on her mission and charge. For every member of the Church, even for the infallible Pope, the essence of the Church is the *promise* of salvation and not its 'guarantee.'[44]

The self-relativization of the historical church in neo-Protestantism knows no end, and thus it turns itself, like capitalism, against all things historical that could be called beautiful, good, and true. The 'useful' subordinates all these 'transcendentals' to its own critical ends by producing a critical posture based on the assumption that interests alone, rather than the good, the true, and the beautiful, motivate human action. Creation becomes disenchanted, and its mystery is replaced by its consumability. Protest becomes an end in itself.

This is not to suggest that the protest is over: the reason for protest is not yet finished. We still need to protest against a counter-reformation Catholic church that has the potential to emphasize authoritarianism and the institution at the expense of holiness and mission. This potential comes to fruition in concerns such as women's ordination, a non-conciliar basis for authority and a moral theology that often finds the 'natural' alone as sufficient for its work.[45] But the protest should never be an end in itself. It should not be reduced to some principle that declares an unending war on any possibility that the authority of the church arises from truth rather than mere interests. The protest must have an end, or it is no longer a protest. If it has no end, it is but an ally of capitalist desire. The fullness of the theological content in the work of Gutiérrez needs something more than the all-too-modern (and Protestant) method of critique and protest.

## IV   Jon Sobrino's protest of the *polis*: Christology, ecclesiology, and holiness

 Like Gutiérrez's theology, Sobrino's arises not out of lack but out of a theological fullness that should be socially embodied. His implicit critique of a metaphysical scarcity can be seen in his understanding of sin. He does not make sin the foundation for political and economic existence. Sin is not, for Sobrino, an inevitable anthropological condition that must be appeased by counter-balancing diverse structures of interest that recognize and accommodate this sinfulness. This is not because he lacks 'Augustinian realism.' He recognizes that we are all sinful: even the poor, he argues, 'are sinners' who 'must have conversion preached to them.'[46] Sin can be finally remedied only when all things are subject to Christ. But sin is also 'a historical product of human wills, crystallized in structures that produce injustice,' which becomes a 'manifestation of anti-life,' produces social and ecclesial division, and must therefore be confronted and destroyed.[47] Scarcity is not an ontology for Sobrino. It is absurd, and is to be countered by a unified ecclesial body. For Sobrino, catholicity defines a goal for which the church's common life should strive. The soteriological necessity of the church's unity challenges capitalism's corrosive culture, which emphasizes pluralism, preference, and an insatiable proliferation of difference and desire.

Sin must be construed Christologically and 'taken on historically,' if it is to be eradicated. This is because 'the Servant can eradicate it. It becomes light and salvation and the scandalous paradox is resolved. Then the crucified people become the bearers of "historical soteriology".'[48] This correlation of Jesus with a 'crucified people' is the reason Sobrino can suggest that the 'oppressed are their own agents of liberation.' This point can too easily be misunderstood as a species of political liberalism, but for Sobrino this is not an anthropological claim where autonomy is the condition necessary to the expression of human dignity. It is instead a Christological affirmation indebted to Colossians 1:24, where St Paul proclaimed: 'in my flesh I complete what is lacking in Christ's afflictions for the sake of his body, that is the church.' The sufferings of the poor and the marginalized are viewed by Sobrino as also completing what is lacking in Christ's afflictions, and in this way the poor become 'their own agents of liberation.'[49]

For Sobrino, such afflictions are produced through capitalism's vicious effects. His estimation of a capitalist economy is clear: it is idolatrous because it sets itself up as a social structure that claims ultimacy and requires for its perpetuation that some people sacrifice their lives. 'The present prevailing structures – a capitalism of dependence and national security, whatever their forms – function as real deities with divine characteristics and their own cult.' They claim 'ultimacy, definitiveness and inviolability' and they 'demand daily and violent sacrifices.'[50] But these sacrifices are not redemptive; they are pagan sacrifices, mired in scarcity, and forced on others for the sake of a false god. To bear sin historically, then, is to suffer not because suffering is some noble end in itself, but rather because suffering characterizes the lot of those who protest against the forces of power, which demand sacrifices to secure their own power.

Knowledge of God is not easily attained in Sobrino's theology. Neither the 'starry heavens above' nor the 'moral law within' produces sufficient wonder to attain knowledge of God. We do not find some positive symbolism between God and humanity in nature, nor even in the cross itself. The vestiges of an *analogia libertatis*, which functions more as an identity between human liberty and God's liberty, are not present. In fact Sobrino insists on 'the element of discontinuity in our knowledge of God' because the cross reveals a discontinuity, a rupture between us and God that is only mediated through suffering.[51]

Knowledge of God arises from knowledge of crucifixion. However, this does not make knowledge of God scarce: there is 'nothing mysterious in Jesus' death, it is a frequent occurrence.'[52] Jesus' death gives us direct insight into the political oppression of the poor, and the political oppression of the poor gives us insight into the death of God on the cross. This dialectical structure drives Sobrino's work. It has the advantage of taking the scriptures seriously (Colossians 1:24, Matthew 25) and of inviting his readers to see how theology matters in the political context of El Salvador. It has the disadvantage of, perhaps, inscribing the death of Christ with an alien politics, of using Christ, perhaps, to inscribe the heart of Christian tradition with an historical dialectic between oppressor and oppressed. In so far as it suggests the latter, then the fullness of Christian theology is subordinated to a dialectic of struggle that will always reinscribe lack back into the theological narrative. In seeking to show the world the dialectical workings of capitalism, the dialectic also becomes the only way out. The moral life becomes reactive, and necessarily violent.

## V    James Cone: the courage to be and the protest of the black church

Cone finds theological speech grounded in lack because it must be historical. Drawing upon the work of H. Richard Niebuhr, he suggests that because Christian theology is human speech about God, it is also 'culturally limited.'[53] Following Niebuhr he distinguishes sharply the universality of divine revelation from the particularity of theological talk. This leads him naturally to a criticism of Thomas Aquinas whom he accuses of 'absolutizing what is relative' and of the 'materialization of the dynamic.'[54] The latter statement reveals Cone's indebtedness to the work of Tillich, who also found Catholicism suspect precisely because of doctrines such as transubstantiation. For Tillich this is a 'doctrinal distortion' because 'one can only speak of the ultimate in a language which at the same time denies the possibility of speaking about it.'[55] Cone adopts Tillich's understanding of theological language. Such an adoption reveals continuities between Cone and the dominant tradition and it places unnecessary limitations on his condemnation of white theology and white churches as heretical. Only when Cone asserts the fullness of orthodoxy, does his charge of heresy make sense.

On the one hand, Cone's theology is not intended for a white audience; at least not a white audience prepared to do anything other than listen.[56] On the other hand, Cone's work *demands* a white audience. He has done something revealing: he has broken the silence that exists between the black and white communities in the United States by saying in public what often is said, or assumed, in private. Like Malcolm X's prophetic utterance, 'I came to tell the white man the truth about himself, or die trying,' Cone has revealed, for public digestion, a black strategy for survival in white America.[57] That strategy includes the recognition that, given the gospel message, the white churches can be viewed only as heretical. Cone states: 'the question of heresy must be reopened in our time – for the sake of the Church's life.'[58]

To re-open the question of heresy assumes an 'orthodoxy' which has been violated, a proper theological speech that the church should embody. Cone both affirms and disavows such speech. For instance he notes: 'In our time the issue of racism is analogous to the Arian controversy of the fourth century. Athanasius perceived quite clearly that if Arius' view were tolerated, Christianity would be lost.'[59] This suggests an orthodoxy pertaining both to fourth-century Christological language and to twentieth-century ecclesiology.[60] It also implies that orthodoxy must be historically embodied. Nevertheless, Cone concurs with Ruether that the church of the third and fourth centuries betrayed the gospel through its accommodation to Roman power, and thus that the heretics' discourse is more compelling than that of the orthodox: 'Black theology believes that the spirit of the authentic gospel is often better expressed by "heretics" than by the "orthodox" tradition.'[61] And this implies that specifically *orthodox* theological language is dispensable to the true essence of the gospel. In fact, theological language itself is of secondary importance. 'It does not matter in the least whether the community of liberators designate their work as Christ's own work.'[62]

Once again we find evidence of an *analogia libertatis* read over and against specific theological language. The question is not whether Cone is right or wrong in asserting the dispensability of theological language for the liberation of people. Of course, liberation has occurred both outside the church and in opposition to it. That much is undeniable. The question is how can that work be described as the essence of the gospel despite the language used by 'the community of liberators'? The answer to that question is that Cone assumes a transcendental metaphysics of being that allows for the dispensability of specific Christian theological language. He identifies all works of liberation with 'being,' 'being' with 'Being,' and 'Being' with God. Thus we know that works of liberation are the works of God because of the *identitas entis*. The *analogia libertatis* discernible in the work of some theologians in both the dominant and the emergent tradition is problematic because it results in this *identitas entis*. This has the deleterious effect of providing an apology for the gospel without the need for it to be embodied in the church. The soteriological significance of the church's unity is sacrificed to an *a priori* metaphysics of being. That the church's historical performance has, again and again from the earliest days, sacrificed such a unity is undeniable. But for theology to dispense with the need and call for the historical embodiment of this unity is to sacrifice the gospel to metaphysics. A liberation that is more ontological than the language used to define it reduces the gospel to a metaphysical essence.

Delores Williams finds the rupture between Cone's work and the historical traditions of Christianity to be the strength of black theology. She states: 'Obviously Cones' theological project has been participating in and helping to bring about Western Christian theology's radical break with its past' and 'People are now beginning to consider seriously effective strategies consistent with the ethical theme of "liberation by whatever means necessary".'[63] But such an apparent 'radical break' can too easily be one more repetition of the modern impulse wherein we discover a tradition of protest requiring each generation to break with the past. The result is a people who no longer recognize the historical conditions of their own existence. Wouldn't this too easily liberate white people from their own history?

Alasdair MacIntye has noted how breaking with the past is precisely the normal mode of ethics within that individualism which constitutes the modern subject, is foundational for capitalism, and perpetuates racism. He writes that

> from the standpoint of individualism I am what I myself choose to be. I can always, if I wish to, put in question what are taken to be the merely contingent social features of my existence…. Such individualism is expressed by those modern Americans who deny any responsibility for the effects of slavery upon black Americans, saying 'I never owned any slaves'…. And of course there is nothing peculiar to modern Americans in this attitude: the Englishman who says, 'I never did any wrong to Ireland; why bring up that old history as though it had something to do with me?' or the young German who believes that being born after 1945

means that what the Nazis did to Jews has no moral relevance to his relationship to his Jewish contemporaries, exhibits the same attitude.[64]

To suggest either that we can or that we should decisively break with the past could contribute merely to furthering the myth of the modern subject whose all-determining will is capable of affirming self against all historical inheritances of both vice and virtue. Such an individualism is the result of a complex metaphysics where an ontology is asserted independent of the historical existents that participate in being. It is because the essence of the individual somehow transcends the contingent features of actual existence and participates in some mode of being separate from, even if related to, that actual existence that these contingent features can be dismissed or viewed as limitations. Tillich perpetuated this very metaphysics. Cone's work bears an irreconcilable tension between Tillich's metaphysics of being and actual historical existence mediated through the necessity of tradition.

Cone does recognize the significance of tradition: 'Theology cannot ignore the tradition. For only through the tradition are we given the freedom to move beyond it.'[65] And he is also suspicious of the use of tradition. After all, tradition is a passing on from one generation to the next, which is often accomplished through authorized powers serving their own interests. 'What is usually called "tradition" represents the Church's theological justification of its existence on the basis of its support of the state in the oppression of the poor.'[66] Cone seeks to find a more secure form of theological knowledge through historical appeals to Jesus.[67] But of course, some authority still legitimizes any historical appeals. Tradition is inescapable. The question is not whether one can break with tradition: the question is what authorizes any reading of history, which is always a participation in tradition. What makes tradition true, good, or beautiful?

Cone's work is itself a traditioning – a re-telling of the narrative so that it can withstand its critics. To accuse the white church of heresy is to expose its falsity, evil and ugliness, and preserve the tradition. It also risks disclosure: it risks a loss of power to the black community, for the unspoken can be a form of resistance. As Cone notes: 'The folklore of black people centers on the ability of the weak to survive through cunning, trickery and sheer deception, in an environment of the strong and powerful.'[68] If Cone's analysis is correct, no reason existed for stating publicly what the majority members of the black church already knew – white churches in America are heretical because race more than baptism is determinative of their identity. To state these things publicly is to speak primarily to a white audience. The fact that white Christians are unaware that they, of necessity, are heretics gives to black Christians a power of insight unavailable to a self-deceived white church. To break that silence is to invite white Christians to see what they could not see. It is, without a doubt, an extremely gracious act. (Of course, as Cone points out, this gracious act was not initiated by him, or even by Malcolm X: it is a message that has a long history, stemming back at least to 1906 with W. E. B. Dubois.) This was a risk precisely because it then meant that the silence could no longer function as an unspoken form of resistance making possible black survival within the dominant white culture. It makes possible a white response, an anti-heretical defense that diminishes the power of the message.

But Cone's indictment of the white church as heretical assumes also an orthodoxy, a correct way of living and telling the Christian message. He seems to have been less troubled by this in his early work, though even there an *analogia libertatis* is present that allowed him to break with the tradition wherever it did not appear to side with the liberation of the oppressed.[69] His later work seems more apt to break with the theological tradition. He denounces Christological exclusiveness as European and hegemonic: 'God's reality is not bound by one manifestation of the divine in Jesus but can be found wherever people are being empowered to fight for freedom.'[70] Cone still affirms Jesus as divine and human, but he subordinates the understanding of the divine in Jesus to an overarching architectonic – the fight for freedom. This becomes the real manifestation of the divine, and because this fight can be known with certainty Christology becomes relativized. So Cone tells us that he has undergone a 'radical development' in his theology. Jesus is, for him, now 'an important revelatory event among many.' This is not so much a critique of European thought as its predictable outcome.

## VI    Contingent truths of history and the philosopher's protest

Cone's theology arises out of his location in the black church, particularly Macedonia African Methodist Episcopal Church. This intimate connection between social location and theological production is a significant alternative to the dominant tradition and its formal universalism. In fact, Cone insists that this connection, symbolized by 'blackness,' must intrude into the putatively universal space of theological production.[71] Theology, which cannot address the history of blackness in America, cannot be genuine: for without encountering that particular history, theology cannot speak about what is undeniably true. But this unique aspect of Cone's work becomes a limitation when in order to critique the formal universal space of the dominant tradition he adopts a philosophy that is quite similar to Lessing's wide ditch in which 'contingent truths of history can never prove necessary truths of reason.'[72] Cone maintains that 'our finite existence cannot qualify us to postulate absolute value judgments.'[73] But is not that statement itself an absolute value judgment? For all of his efforts to think against 'European' reason, Cone has reproduced a central element of the western (Continental) philosophical tradition. Indeed he breaks with certain elements of Christian orthodoxy, but in doing so he also reproduces key themes of western (Continental) philosophy that privilege a metaphysics of being over any particular revelation.

Cone's work produces and reproduces these two claims – a particular social location is epistemologically privileged and theological judgments are finite and limited in scope because they arise from a particular social location. The latter claim seems to gain emphasis in his later work. Thus two decades after *A Black Theology of Liberation* Cone states: 'Since theology is human speech and not God speaking, I recognize today, as I did then, that all attempts to speak about ultimate reality are limited by the social history of the speaker.'[74] Consistent with the tradition of liberal Protestant theology, and its indebtedness to the Kantian tradition, Cone can assert only the 'limitation' of historical speech about God – finite reason is always limited, whereas the assertion of the will knows no bounds because it is grounded in freedom. But this limitation to theological reason is misleading. It must be based on a univocal access to the 'ultimate reality.' Otherwise his statement would not make sense. Cone can only construe theological speech as a 'limitation' because he implicitly claims recognition of some ultimacy. Such a position reveals his indebtedness to Paul Tillich's view of the symbolical nature and operation of language employed in theological discourse.

Cone regrets that his early theology was influenced by Karl Barth, but he does not confess an equal regret about Tillich's – deleterious – influence. Barth's influence led the early Cone to reject any natural theology or too close an identification between the gospel and culture. In rejecting these things Cone seemed to find in Barth a criticism of North American theology. He noted: 'Americans have generally agreed that Barth's rejection of natural theology was a mistake. Is that because American theologians still see a close relationship between the structures of this society and Christianity?'[75] Because North American theology assumed Christianity's compatibility with societal structures, Barth's theology never made serious inroads into North American theology. But Cone later rejected this Barthianism. In 1986 he stated the limitations to his early Barthian perspective stating that 'there is no abstract revelation,' and that 'although God is the intended subject of theology, God does not do theology. Human beings do theology.'[76] In 1989, he stated: 'I had been greatly miseducated in theology and it showed in the neo-orthodox Barthian perspective of *Black Theology and Black Power*.'[77] Cone does not seem to find as much social and political relevance in Barth's theology as does Gutiérrez. But in assuming that the historical and social contextualizing of theology is at the same time a limitation of theological truth-claims, Cone still embodies the neo-Protestant principle that Tillich developed and Barth never overcame. This principle does not provide sufficient resistance to the dominance of Kantian philosophical claims that truth cannot be predicated upon contingent historical locations, but must be found in some transcendental realm of being. In suggesting this, Cone's work becomes insufficiently radically historicist.

Cone criticizes Barth's theology for not taking into account the historical location of the speaker. Cone is not alone in his objection. In fact, this critique bears a resemblance to the Catholic theologian Hans Urs von Balthasar's criticism of Barth. Von Balthasar likewise objected that Barth's theology of actualization did not sufficiently take into account the human recipients of revelation. Barth certainly taught that any theological production, which insisted on the priority of the natural or socio-historical recipients of revelation, would have the adverse effect of legitimizing that historical structure over and against the Lordship of Christ. In fact, his concern seems to have been that Roman Catholic ecclesiology does precisely this. So he critiqued Catholicism, stating:

> Their presupposition is that the being of the Church, Jesus Christ, is no longer the free Lord of its existence, but that he is incorporated into the existence of the Church, and is thus ultimately restricted and conditioned by certain concrete forms of the human understanding of His revelation and of the faith which grasps it. Again there can be no mistaking the common Christian character of this faith to the extent that the concept of the acting God, of that which is radically beyond all human possibilities, is taken seriously as the source of dogmatic knowledge, at least in intention. But again our fellowship with this faith is broken by the way in which grace here becomes nature, the action of God immediately disappears and is taken up into the action of the recipient of grace, that which is beyond all human possibilities changes at once into that which is enclosed within the reality of the Church, and the personal act of divine address becomes a constantly available relationship between God and man in this revealedness. It affirms an *analogia entis*, the presence of a divine likeness of the creature even in the fallen world, and consequently the possibility of applying the secular 'There is' to God and the things of God as the presupposition, again ontological, of that change or transformation, of that depriving of revelation and faith of their character as decision by evasion and neutralization.
>
> (*Church Dogmatics*, I, 1, p. 41)

Given that this expresses Barth's concern, Cone's criticism seems both sound and unsound. It is unsound in that Barth here sides with Cone. Grace is 'beyond all human possibilities.' No language, particularly the language of Roman Catholic ecclesiology, is adequate to the revelation. But Cone's critique is sound in that Barth then has difficulty in narrating how this revelation becomes embodied in human agents. Barth's attempt to explain the embodiment of faith resulted in doublespeak about human agency. He stated:

> If it is true that man really believes (1) that the object of faith is present to him and (2) that he himself is assimilated to the object, then we are led in conclusion to the third point that man exists as a believer wholly

and utterly by this object. In believing he can think of himself as grounded, not in self, but only in this object, as existing indeed only by this object. He has not created his own faith; the Word has created it. He has not come to faith; faith has come to him through the Word. He has not adopted faith; faith has been granted to him through the Word. As a believer he cannot see himself as the acting subject of the work done here. It is his experience and act. He is not at all a block or stone in faith but self-determining man. He does not sink into passible, apathetic contemplation in faith, and even if he did he would still do so as self-determining man.... Nevertheless, the point is that in faith he must regard this in no sense diminished self-determination, himself in his own activity, in the living of his own life, as determined by the Word of God. In his freedom, in the full use of his freedom as a man, he must see himself as another man that he had no power to become, that he still has no power to become, that he is not free to become or to be (though he is free as he becomes and is), in short, that he can be only by being this man. Man acts as he believes, but the fact that he believes as he acts is God's act. Man is the subject of faith. Man believes, not God. But the fact that man is this subject in faith is bracketed as a predicate of the subject God, bracketed in the way that the Creator encloses the creature and the merciful God sinful man, i.e. in such a way that man remains subject, and yet man's I as such derives only from the Thou of the subject God.[78]

Although Barth seeks to develop a notion of a self-determining human agency already determined by the Word of God, he finds himself in the odd position of 'bracketing' human agency in the divine–human encounter.

Cone, like von Balthasar, finds this too limiting, but for different reasons. Von Balthasar critiques Barth for not affording sufficient room in theology for the historical role of the Catholic Church; Cone critiques Barth for not making sufficient room for the historical role of both the black church and of blackness as an ontological symbol for knowledge of God. Yet Balthasar has been sufficiently influenced by Barth to reject any return to a scholastic argument that would allow for a pure nature that gives us access to the world – including the world of economics and politics – separate from grace. Cone actually comes closer to this possibility than does the Catholic Balthasar. And this is because of the lingering influence of Paul Tillich on Cone's theology.

Tillich's work assisted Cone in synthesizing liberal Protestant theology with the challenges the Black Power Movement presented to Christian theology. In his very first work Cone stated:

A further clarification of the meaning of Black Power may be found in Paul Tillich's analysis of 'the courage to be,' which is 'the ethical act in which man affirms his being in spite of those elements of his existence which conflict with his essential self-affirmation.' Black Power, then, is a humanizing force because it is the black man's attempt to affirm his being, his attempt to be recognized as 'Thou,' in spite of the 'other,' the white power which dehumanizes him. The structure of white society attempts to make 'black being' into 'nonbeing' or 'nothingness.' In existential philosophy, nonbeing is usually identified as that which threatens being; it is that ever present possibility of the inability to affirm one's existence.[79]

Cone understands the 1968 rebellions as precisely such an act of self-affirmation against the powers of nonbeing and death. Although this has resonance with the work of W. E. B. Dubois, it also explicitly draws on Tillich and his affirmation of a nominalist theology that affirms the centrality of the will. Tillich's affirmation of the will to life was indebted to nominalism, Luther, and Nietzsche, whose work Tillich called 'the most impressive and effective representation of what could be called a "philosophy of life".'[80] With an extreme Lutheranism, Nietzsche recognized that a faith that says 'yes' to life must do so against all appearances: only a faith that lives within the unsettled world where God is dead can finally say 'yes' to life, *sola fide*. This 'yes' is to be said as an act of will, an act of power, against all appearances of truth.

Drawing on Tillich, influenced by this extreme Lutheranism, Cone developed black theology. The first step in this development is to recognize the 'symbolic nature of all theological speech.' Here Cone develops Tillich's 'analogical' method.[81] But Tillich's understanding of analogy is much more akin to that developed by Duns Scotus than by Thomas Aquinas. Tillich does state: 'We cannot describe God directly; we must use symbols that point to dimensions of reality that cannot be spoken of literally.' Yet Tillich seems to confuse analogical speech with symbolic speech. For his symbols possess a metaphysical reality that signs lack. The symbol 'participates in the reality' in a way that a sign doesn't. Because the symbol participates in the ultimate, it possesses a fundamental sameness across religious traditions at the same time that all historical linguistic expressions of the Ultimate are inadequate.[82] Thus theological speech requires symbols, embodied in myth, that speak of God's relationship to us such that this symbolic speech is both a participation in God and at the same time always marked by a lack – an attempt to express the inexpressible. Symbols, as Tillich explained it, 'point beyond themselves to something else' even though they participate in that which they signify.[83] The symbol has an univocal ontological reality; it expresses the nature of God's being even when the language used will itself always be marked by limitation.

Tillich's use of symbol makes both too much and too little of theological speech. It makes too much when it assumes the formal character of the symbol can participate unequivocally in the nature of God's being. This results in a univocal understanding of God across traditions, communities and languages that loses the capacity to discriminate among the languages used to name God. It makes too little when it can then confidently treat traditional theological language as important for its symbolic merit, but the actual language itself inadequate because it is historical.[84] This also led Tillich to contrast the 'ultimate concerns' of theology with the 'preliminary concerns' of politics, culture and economics. He only allows the latter to be the 'vehicle' which bears the former. To make them more than that is to be idolatrous and violate the first commandment. So Tillich asserts that although symbols are indispensable, a religion must nevertheless 'remain aware of the conditional and non-ultimate character of its own symbols.' For Tillich, Protestant theology does this best precisely because it takes as its theological center the cross. The cross functions here, however, not as a concrete historical reality of God's assumption of human nature and its profound expression of God's charity, but as a dialectical process between the divine and the human. The cross becomes a symbol of God's dynamic relationship with creation. Jesus and 'the Christ' are played against each other so that essence and existence become reconciled through an agonistic relationship. Only the death of historical existence overcomes the estrangement between essence and existence. The hypostatic union is altogether lost in Tillich's work. His theology is Nestorian, and that is why economics and culture are preliminary concerns only and not the domain of theology proper. The form of human embodiment and the divine form can never be brought together in his work. They always exist in a dialectical tension where the former must be sacrificed to the latter.

This is why Tillich makes unconditional and ultimate demands for Protestant theology based on its recognition of the conditional and limited nature of theological speech – 'the radical self-criticism of Christianity makes it most capable of universality.'[85] This is a brilliant theological strategy to impose faith upon the modern world. Tillich's ultimate criterion of negativity implies that the true believer will be the person who negates the 'symbols' of faith precisely because such a power of self-assertion, of being in the face of non-being, is itself the ultimate act of faith. So Tillich concludes *The Dynamics of Faith* with the statement: 'It is the triumph of the dynamics of faith that any denial of faith is itself an expression of faith, of an ultimate concern.' It is Tillich's commitment to a univocal ontology – the courage to be – that allows him to be so certain of faith that faithlessness finally becomes an impossibility, and explicit works and acts of faith become suspect.

Tillich remains, however, insufficiently agnostic. Like Duns Scotus, his theological predecessor, Tillich can assert that 'the primary object of the human understanding is being.'[86] Both share a univocity of being where the symbol used to speak of God shares in an unequivocal formal reality.[87] To this extent, Tillich's use of symbol is not analogical: it remains far from Thomas' understanding of theological language. In fact, it makes theological language secondary to a formal language about 'being.' For Tillich, to assert one's being, through the will to power, is the essence of faith. The natural virtue of courage subordinates to its power the supernatural virtue of faith.

Can Tillich's symbolic language of 'being' distance itself from the dominant sense of agency found in democratic capitalism? Tillich himself recognized the similarity between them. This equation is found in his defense of 'individualism.' Although he is critical of the 'modern individualism' that is found in economic liberalism, Tillich recognized it as a positive step toward a true 'existential' individualism, defined as the 'courage to be as one self' rather than the 'courage to be as a part.'[88] Tillich objected to Roman Catholicism for producing an insufficient courage, the 'courage to be as a part.' Likewise he rejected contemporary Marxism because it led not to 'liberation of everyone,' but instead to a 'system of enslavement' where a person is only valued for his or her communal role.

Tillich's influence is, without a doubt, given a new twist in Cone's 'existential absurdity' of the social positions of African Americans in the United States.[89] Tillich's formal ontology of being is enriched by Cone's integration of it with the content of the history of blackness in America. In so doing, Cone implicitly challenges Tillich's individualistic courage to be. Cone's work has a decided advantage over Tillich in that Cone seeks to incorporate the history of the black church and the Black Power Movement with Tillich's theology, but this does seem to be an unstable mix.

The mix is unstable because blackness begins to function more as an ontological symbol than as a tradition with specific practices embodied in a particular history. Thus, Cone states, 'to say God is creator means that my being finds its source in God. I am black because God is black! God as creator is the ground of my blackness (being), the point of reference for meaning and purpose in the universe.'[90] The equation of blackness with 'being' suggests the subsumption of history by ontology. The logic seems to work like this. The Creator and creature share in 'being.' We know this through ontology itself and must then express it in historical language, but the language will always be inadequate. The symbol 'blackness' is an historical vehicle to designate this ontological reality. As an ontological symbol it specifies this relationship between being and its ground. An obvious conclusion is that everything, insofar as it has being, can also be designated 'black.' But this is to elide the history of blackness into an *a priori* ontological assertion. A white person can now assert 'I am black because I too share in this formal being.' How does that capture the sense of history Cone himself has taught us?

To suggest that blackness still functions more as a symbol than a history in Cone's work is not to deny the importance for theology of his research and analysis of the history of the black church. It is to suggest merely that the latter, found in such works as *The Spiritual and the Blues*, seems to exist in tension with the lingering ontology of the 'courage to be.'

Tillich's 'courage to be' subordinates the supernatural virtues to the natural virtues. Faith becomes dependent upon the uncertainty that must reside in the 'limitations of any finite act.' For faith to exist, it must first accept this uncertainty, which is deemed 'courage.' Thus, Tillich suggested: 'Courage as an element of faith is the daring self-affirmation of one's own being in spite of the powers of "nonbeing" which are the heritage of everything finite.'[91] But courage functions here as much more than a mere element of faith: courage becomes the precondition for faith. A supernatural virtue becomes dependent upon the prior assertion of a natural virtue; and this makes faith fundamentally a product of the human will, despite Tillich's protestations to the contrary.[92] One can see this in Tillich's criticism of Aquinas for falsely correlating faith with theoretical knowledge. For Tillich, 'the term "faith" should not be used in connection with theoretical knowledge.' He then suggests that such a connection in Aquinas led to an 'intellectualistic distortion' of faith. And because all our knowledge is limited and uncertain, Aquinas' 'intellectualistic distortion' led also to a 'voluntaristic distortion' where 'the lack of evidence which faith has must be complemented by an act of will.' But as Herbert McCabe has pointed out, this is a poor reading of Thomas' account of obedience, for it is not fundamentally an act of will but of reason – of doing what one is *told* where the reasonableness of the *telling* is central for a proper obedience.[93] In fact, it is Tillich's emphasis on the 'courage to be' that finally leads to a voluntaristic distortion of the faith. And this voluntaristic distortion can easily be viewed as having its roots in nominalism, the Protestant Reformation and Martin Luther's theology where the reasonableness of the world is sacrificed to a voluntarism by which one does what 'love' demands 'by any means necessary.' Once this transformation occurs, the distinction between orthodoxy and heresy becomes impossible to maintain. Faith as a function of the will – separate from reason – need not be bound by the truth of any doctrine nor by the beauty of any pleasing narrative.

Luther's influence on Cone's political strategy can be found in his recognition that Tillich's courage to be is a development of Luther's alien work of charity. Cone writes: 'Taking his clue from Luther, Tillich speaks to the essence of Black Power and the uniqueness of Christianity when he says, "It is the strange work of love to destroy what is against love".'[94] James Cone follows both Luther and Malcolm X in arguing that Black Power is the 'complete emancipation of black people from white oppression by whatever means black people deem necessary.'[95] In assessing this claim, readers of Cone should exercise some caution. Such a claim has led some of his readers to accuse him of fascism. If no limitations on the possible means employed are present for this liberation, it could easily resemble fascism. But it is unclear that black theology advocates any possible employment of violence based purely on its effectiveness. Malcolm X was clear that violence was legitimate for blacks in America based upon the traditional teachings of the just war theory: 'with people who are nonviolent with us, we are nonviolent with them; with people who are not nonviolent with us, we are not nonviolent with them.' In fact, Cone's own defense of violence could be construed as consistent not with Luther's voluntaristic conception of warfare (which seems ineluctably to lead to Clausewitz) but with that of Thomas Aquinas, who argued for the legitimacy of tyrannicide if it furthered the common good. Cone also suggests that black theology 'came into being when the black clergy realized that killing slave masters was doing the work of God.' And the 'any means necessary' that Cone asserts has primarily to do with 'selective buying, boycotting, marching or even rebellion.'[96] He does suggest that 'all acts which participate in the destruction of white racism are Christian,' but he also maintains that it 'is not possible to speak meaningfully to the black community about liberation unless it is analyzed from a Christian perspective which centers on Jesus Christ.'[97]

Cone's liberation theology makes freedom central to the gospel message, but this freedom is a far cry from the freedom to make individual preferences extolled by Hayek. Cone's freedom requires a common *telos*. He states that freedom 'is not doing what I will but becoming what I should be,' and this freedom is inextricably connected with the crucifixion and resurrection.[98] He contrasts this freedom with that found in capitalism, which he finds related to either the 'profit motive' or the 'pleasure principle.' Instead this freedom is found whenever a people finds itself prepared to assert its own being against the forces that threaten it with non-existence. Therefore, he asserts: 'What we need is the destruction of whiteness, which is the source of human misery in the world.'[99] But Cone never suggests genocide. It is his use of Tillich's 'symbol' that allows him to use 'whiteness' and 'blackness' as he does. The difficulty with his analysis is not that it is fascist, but that 'whiteness' and 'blackness' become something other than their concrete, particular, historical manifestations. They become ontological symbols.

# 10 Conclusion to Part II

The emergent tradition seeks to incorporate an analysis of economic matters within a theological perspective. In so far as it offers a theological reading of particular historical events and institutions, such as the conquest, slavery, the rise and longevity of the black church, the protest of the household, and the alternative cooperative power of women, it succeeds in incorporating economics into theology. When, however, the formal opening for this incorporation becomes a metaphysics of being, drawing upon theologians such as Tillich and Rahner, then the theological rendering of the economic is unsuccessful. Instead, theological production is subordinated to metaphysics. The work of liberation and God's work are so identified that this analogy becomes the architectonic within which Christian doctrine must now proceed. Christology and ecclesiology become problems to be overcome. The result is a re-evaluation of any distinction between heresy and orthodoxy such that traditional orthodoxy is eschewed. Instead, ethics, particularly the ethics of liberation, becomes the decisive criterion for knowledge of God. This bears a resemblance to the dominant tradition's Weberian strategy. It remains within a modernist emancipatory framework that still renders the theological irrelevant or marginal. Theology gets only the role of adding 'value' or 'meaning,' but the 'facts' remain impervious to theological claims.

This is not to deny the substantive gains in theological production in the emergent tradition. Rosemary Radford Ruether's rebellion of the household and of women, Gutiérrez's theological descriptions of social realities, Jon Sobrino's compelling narratives of holiness and martyrdom, and James Cone's suspicion of sociology and unashamed privileging of the black church all represent significant theological advances over the dominant tradition. The role of holiness and historical recognition produces a less formal and less abstract theology; one more readily open to scripture and to historical arguments. In fact, despite the repeated calls for a socio-scientific analysis of economic realities, theologians in the emergent tradition maintain the primacy of theology over sociology more so than do the theologians in the dominant tradition whose reliance on Weber betrays theology into the hands of an autonomous sociology.

This is surprising, because liberation theologians seem united in calling for theologians to incorporate a social analysis of economic relations within theology. This call often assumes that such an analysis is out there, just waiting to be made evident, and will expose the injustices of the capitalist order. But within the emergent tradition such an analysis is either neglected, assumed or superficially presented. In as much as liberation theologians depend upon the reasonableness of this social analysis to expose the injustices of capitalism, they have failed. Yet whether liberation theology as such depends upon socio-scientific analysis remains an open question. As I have attempted to demonstrate, certain elements of Gutiérrez's and Sobrino's work do suggest such a dependency. Cone's earlier work was mistrustful of such an analysis; but as he becomes increasingly suspicious of Christological claims, his wariness of such a sociological analysis lessens.

But perhaps theology does not need the reasonableness of an independent social analysis of capitalism's injustices for its own critical power, and the fact that theologians in the emergent tradition have not delivered on these claims may in fact prove to be the strength of their work. Perhaps the difficulty capitalism poses to Christianity is its threat to not so much justice but to faith and charity. This difficulty cannot be assessed through any social analysis of the natural alone but requires a theological sociology, one that would be in direct contradiction of Hayek's sociology because such a theological sociology must assume a common *telos*. Even if capitalism could deliver on its promise to increase the real wages of most people through private property and social inequality, it is still the case that Christian theology must treat it with suspicion. For capitalism assumes the catholicity of a social institution – the *agora*, and this is a false catholicity that ineluctably leads to a mis-presentation of the divine–human drama discovered in Christ.

Catholicity cannot be based on the useful but only on the good, the true and the beautiful, and for Christian theology this is inextricably inter-related with Christ and with the strong ecclesiology that makes Christ present. But the two traditions noted here as dominant and emergent share a common theme in their formal understanding of the first mark of the church, *catholicity*. Both are able to abstract from the visible catholicity of the church to a catholicity either loosely related to the visible structures of the church or one that opposes those visible structures altogether. This is accomplished through the common theme of an *analogia libertatis* by which theologians give the *libertatis* content through competing narratives. For those in the dominant tradition, that narrative is provided by democratic capitalism. For the emergent tradition, liberty arises from socialism. But socialism, of course, is the stepchild of liberalism, and thus the tradition of liberation theology can be viewed at most as 'emergent' out of the dominant tradition: it is not decisively in opposition to it. Ruether alone, it seems, recognizes this – hence her efforts to include liberal, radical, and Marxist feminists within her liberation theology.

The dominance of the metanarrative of liberty seems to produce a subordination of the theological to the natural virtues. Once liberation becomes the essence of the gospel that liberation, in separation from explicit theological language, functions as the identification of God's work in the world. The result is a certain and foundational apprehension of God through either a metaphysics of being or through an assertion of the will. Once this takes place the theological virtues no longer have a central role in the divine–human drama. Justice or courage becomes the mediator of God's presence in the world. Charity, faith, and hope play secondary roles: they are reduced to giving 'meaning' to – in other words, an 'evaluation' of – the facts. Gutiérrez's appeal to the primacy of charity could be an exception to this claim, but the formal nature of this appeal and his Weberian understanding of politics prevent the appeal from being persuasive.

A common feature of both the dominant and emergent traditions is that 'liberation' is thwarted by an elitist conspiracy, whether those elites are constituted by Novak's intellectual classes, Ruether's 'male elites in power who deny their interdependency with women,' Cone's white powers, or Sobrino's European theologians. But this overlooks how power is diffused in capitalist society. No conspiracy of elites exists: hierarchies have been flattened for several centuries. Capitalism has long since destroyed the ancient regime. This makes resistance to its power even more difficult: there is no recognizable group or class the destruction of which thereby insures emancipation from capitalism's grip. The conditions of eighteenth-century France are not *our* conditions, and even in the eighteenth century lopping off royal heads did not result in the freedom anticipated.

Part III of this work contrasts a residual theological tradition with capitalism. It argues that this tradition should be viewed in opposition to capitalism – more so than the emergent tradition, because it opposes liberalism altogether. This is not to argue that Christian orthodoxy itself is sufficient for the Christian moral life. Scripture bears witness to this when it reminds us that belief alone is insufficient, for the demons also believe and tremble. In fact, the insufficiency of orthodoxy alone is itself an orthodox pronouncement: orthodoxy must be connected to the life of faith. The liberation theologians constantly remind us of this. Traditional Catholic ecclesiology also recognized the importance of this connection through the centrality to ecclesiology of both Peter and Mary. The Petrine office should be in service to the Marian vocation to holiness.[1] Holiness is possible without orthodoxy if some impediment exists to prevent a right understanding of the faith, but ordinarily holiness arises from right teaching. It is also possible to stop at orthodoxy and miss holiness altogether. Nevertheless, orthodoxy and orthopraxis should not be rent asunder. We cannot begin with some self-evident 'Christian practice' if we do not know what constitutes Christianity in the first place.

# III
# The residual tradition

Virtues and the true, the good,
and the beautiful

# 11 Introduction to Part III

If theology is not to concede the description of reality to Weber's fact–value distinction, then theology itself must be recognized as constitutive of the real. Creation is not adequately defined in terms of a brute mathematical facticity that can be interpreted only at a secondary level through the meaning or value given to those facts. Theological descriptions are as constitutive of the real as are economic ones. If this point is conceded, then it should lead to a theological suspicion of any economic analysis that assumes the fact–value distinction. But this distinction has become so determinative in contemporary intellectual discourse that alternatives to it are seldom countenanced. However, such an alternative can be found in a residual tradition that either ignores or refuses to take the modern era as the benchmark against which theology must be measured.

By 'residual' is meant something that 'has been effectively formed in the past, but it is still active in the cultural process, not only as an element of the past, but as an effective element of the present.'[1] Because the residual tradition is found outside of the familiar twentieth-century theological landscape, in order to recover it more is required than just theological works. Bernard Dempsey's theological economics and certain aspects of Roman Catholic social teachings put forth an economics grounded in the true rather than merely the useful. Although this account of the truth looks back to Thomas Aquinas for support, it also contains modernist assumptions that produce an ambivalent theological reading of the *natural*. Alasdair MacIntyre's recovery of virtue likewise looks back to Aristotle and Thomas to recover the ancient notion of a functional economy in service to humanity's true and good end. MacIntyre, the philosopher, identifies the potential for a more theological rendering of the natural than do theologians in either the dominant or the emergent tradition. But John Milbank's poetic Christology 'supernaturalizes the natural' to such an extent that any distinction between the natural and the Christological collapses. Dempsey and Catholic social teaching grounded in truth, MacIntyre's good and Milbank's appeal to beauty all represent elements formed in the past, yet which are still effective in the present. These elements make possible another option with which to counter the dominant tradition, and while bearing some similarities to the emergent tradition is ultimately an alternative to that as well.

This residual tradition bears traces of a time prior to that in which the useful has been predominant. It does not seek to be relevant to the modern world through Kant, or Weber, or Marx, but seeks instead to present a rationality rooted in the thirteenth-century work of Thomas Aquinas. It assumes, unlike the two traditions already discussed, that modernity and secularity are mistakes that must be undone – or, as in MacIntyre's case, that will undo themselves. A capitalist political economy is the 'fruit' (or the 'weed,' according to one's viewpoint) of the modern era. What binds together Dempsey, MacIntyre, and Milbank is a critique of the basic assumption that makes possible the fact–value distinction. They all deny that a human assertion of will gives *value* to objects in the world. Instead, they draw upon the residual notion of the transcendental predicates of being to show us a world that already bears goodness, truth, and beauty prior to the emergence of individual choice. Dempsey reads modern economics theologically by setting it against the benchmark of a truthful social life capable of producing virtue. MacIntyre's quest for a substantive goodness reveals how such a quest will, of necessity, put us at odds with the modern world. Milbank presents a beautiful creation where creatures participate in the poetic act that makes the creation possible by re-presenting the contingent historical reality of God made flesh. All of creation, including the necessity of exchanges, is to be read through this particular form that shapes the beautiful. MacIntyre and Milbank, unlike Dempsey, do not present the good and the beautiful in terms of a foundational epistemology through which our knowledge of the good and the beautiful becomes more certain than the good and beautiful themselves.[2] Although they draw upon a residual tradition, their work cannot be relegated to some archaic premodern realm. If, as they both suggest, the modern ends in nihilism, this residual tradition bears resources with which to resist the dominance of the useful. Precisely because it is *residual* this tradition contains hope against the inevitable breakdown and dissolution of the modern. The modern is *not* our *only* possibility.

Part III begins with a discussion of Roman Catholic efforts to create an alternative economics that is grounded in a theological vision. To understand the significance of these Roman Catholic efforts, the natural theology that formed the basis for nineteenth-century Anglican political economy will first be presented. Roman Catholic social teaching represents an alternative to that Anglican natural theology, even though the Catholic effort itself failed. Leo XIII's *Rerum Novarum* first attempted to express the Catholic alternative. *Rerum Novarum* gave rise to a tradition of Catholic social teaching that held forth promise for a reconstruction of the social order. Forty years later Pius XI, in his *Quadragesimo Anno*, invited Roman Catholic intellectuals to begin work on that social reconstruction. One person who answered that call was the twentieth-century Jesuit economist

Bernard Dempsey. He developed one strand of Catholic social teaching that finds in Thomas' account of the natural law a basis for a rapprochement between economics and theology. Dempsey thought modern economics had arisen in opposition to the church and had been corrupted by its break with medieval economics. He sought to integrate the study of economics with theology, or more precisely with Christian philosophy. Dempsey's strategy closely resembles that of the dominant tradition, except for the important difference that he denies the reasonableness of the fact–value distinction and the presumed irrationality of a premodern economics. He develops the scholastics' economics in conversation with its modern study and finds the latter in need of the former's insights.

Dempsey's work, along with that of others, gave rise to the Catholic Economic Association. It originally worked within the auspices of the American Economic Association, but was soon transformed into the Association for Social Economics. This group of interesting, predominantly Catholic, intellectuals works on the margins of the discipline of economics. They no longer seek to reconstruct the social order, but merely to find a space for a Catholic social economy. They preserve the notion of a 'functional economy.'

Having traced the Catholic effort to develop an alternative economics, Alasdair MacIntyre's work is examined. MacIntyre is a philosopher who does no theology, but his work makes room for a recovery of St Thomas' *theology* of the virtues. MacIntyre looks to Thomas for a reasonable argument, based on tradition, virtue, and a common *telos*, concerning the resolution of moral differences, a resolution that can not be tolerated within liberalism, as we witnessed in the work of Hayek. Thomas can help move us beyond the soft nihilism that pervades modern moral discourse and practice. MacIntyre first recovered this tradition in his *After Virtue*, where he displayed the profound problems with the dominance of modern values in moral philosophy. The importance of that work for our thinking about economics has not always been adequately recognized. For MacIntyre the recovery of virtue requires a critique of capitalism due to capitalism's inability to integrate the cultivation and reception of virtues with necessary daily exchanges. His philosophy also needs theology for its fulfillment: MacIntyre not only recognizes this, he seems to welcome it. But MacIntyre welcomes a *particular* theological tradition. He finds in Roman Catholicism the form of life capable of sustaining the good in a world where the dominance of the will's power has left us with such thin characters as bureaucratic managers, psychotherapists, and romantic aesthetes. Because Roman Catholicism bears a truth and a goodness that all reasonable persons should embody, it makes possible the fulfillment of our otherwise frustrated natures. Such natures know desire but that desire contains no intrinsically good end. St Thomas proposes friendship with God as our true end, and that calls for a radical re-formation of our desires.

John Milbank's 'radical orthodoxy' has developed the significance of a revised Thomistic socio-political theology for contemporary market considerations. His work fits within neither the emergent nor the dominant tradition, but represents both a premodern and a postmodern theology through a 'poetic Christology' and the primacy of ecclesiology. He is, however, at odds both with MacIntyre and with Roman Catholic social teaching. He does not think MacIntyre has yet freed virtue from its ancient origins in conflict. Nor does he find Roman Catholic social teaching sufficiently anti-modern. In fact, he finds the present configuration of the magisterium to be utterly modern. It is a species of 'ideal modernist absolutism.'[3] He finds both positions inadequate in rendering economics theological.

Milbank's revised Thomism develops more thoroughly the theological dimensions of Thomas' work. Because MacIntyre does not sufficiently distance his account of the virtues from antique virtue, with its dependence on heroism and victory in conflict, Milbank finds it, too, wedded to a non-Christian understanding of 'self-possession.' The Roman Catholic tradition of social teachings also loses the infused character of Christian virtue and associates the cultivation of virtue with the self-possession assumed in individual property rights. Thus it does not sufficiently recognize that capitalism, with its advocacy of individual property rights, is as much of a threat to the Christian life as is socialism. The result, argues Milbank, is a crypto-fascism – a charge that he levels also against contemporary eco-theology.

What binds together these disparate voices is the assumption that the theology of Thomas Aquinas provides a useful critique of modern political economy and tools for the reconstruction of economic relations. Each of the three residual movements seeks to maintain a distinct transcendental predicate of being against modernity's loss of all such transcendence in its reduction of human exchanges to the useful.[4] Dempsey's work relies upon a *true natural order* potentially accessible to all people outside of a particular tradition, but this true nature is fundamentally present in Catholic social teaching. Although he argues for a nature that potentially can be read by anyone, church councils, papal encyclicals, Christian tradition, and scripture are primarily the vehicles that present the true to us. All persons of good will should find no conflict between natural reason and divine teaching. Dempsey's work embodies the interesting contradiction that Christian tradition and scripture make possible access to the truth without Christian tradition and scripture.

MacIntyre holds to *the good*. He has stated that 'the good life for man is the life spent in seeking the good life for man, and the virtues necessary for the seeking are those which will enable us to understand what more and what else the good life for man is.'[5] This quest for the good conflicts with the two dominant efforts to secure morality in modernity – Mill's utilitarianism and Kant's practical reason. Both, suggests MacIntyre, require the development of fictive notions of utility or rights as that which can adjudicate moral disagreements; but as fictions these notions lack any substance that can do more than conceal the will to power behind them.[6] MacIntyre's turn toward the virtues entails a turn toward narrative and historical tradition that eschews a foundationalist epistemology based on the individual as *res cogitans*.

Milbank draws upon Hans Urs von Balthasar's theological aesthetics to argue for the primacy of the beautiful as that which incorporates the true and the good. The beautiful here is the form of revelation itself that maintains continuity with worldly beauty even as it expresses it more fully. This beauty is a contingent historical event, which must then be transmitted through human making. The result is not just the priority of Christology to any rendering of the natural, but the primacy of ecclesiology to Christology itself. The primacy of ecclesiology also entails the central importance of *poesis*, a human making which participates in the divine simultaneity of act and power. All three movements within the residual tradition find themselves at odds with contemporary economic arrangements. All three call for a reconstruction of the social order.

# 12   A true economic order

## I   Catholic and Anglican social teaching and its failure: the non-necessity of theology for reading the natural

In its zeal to bear witness to the congruity obtaining between grace and nature Catholic social teaching often neglects the role that the revelation of God through Moses, the prophets, and the New law of Jesus play in constituting the natural. Although the congruity of grace and nature must be maintained if Christianity is to be credible, so must the possibility remain that we are frustrated in both our assent to, and our understanding of, the natural. The meaning present in the natural order is not self-evident, and cannot become so by objective human reasoning because such investigation itself participates in the natural. In fact, that the natural will always in part be open to revision is neither a modern nor a postmodern insight. St Thomas himself argued that because our recognition and assent to the natural is also always dependent on social and political promulgations, it can be revised at the level of secondary prescriptions; those that affect us most directly.[1] Although they do not constitute the natural, human speech and action participate in its possibility. Thus the natural cannot be appealed to without there being at the same time a recognition of those social and historical contexts that make such appeals possible.

John Milbank argues that Roman Catholic social teaching has failed in part because of its understanding of *nature*. It has created a monstrous hybrid between liberalism and patriarchal corporatism, which he accuses of fascism. But A. M. C. Waterman argues that Catholic social teaching failed because Leo XIII 'destroyed the intellectual foundation of economic liberalism,' and the result has been 'an insulation of official doctrine from economic science that persists to this day in the public utterances of the hierarchy.'[2] Milbank finds Catholic social teaching insufficiently theological and overly reliant on a modern conception of nature. Waterman finds Catholic teaching too theological and insufficiently reliant on the modern conception of nature. Both imply that an adequate understanding of Roman Catholic social teaching requires that it be situated in terms of the natural theology characteristic of the nineteenth century. This natural theology was the means by which theology and economics were related.

Waterman finds nineteenth-century Anglican theologians such as Malthus, Paley, Sumner, Coplestone and Whatley preferable to Catholic theologians because they represented a middle way between the systems of Calvinism and Catholicism. Their middle way allowed for an accommodation of Christian orthodoxy to economic science. But they accomplished this not by relying on orthodoxy, but through their evaluation of what natural reason could accomplish separately from faith. Waterman recognizes that Malthus was anything but orthodox, denying the resurrection of the body, the incarnation, the possibility of revealed knowledge, God's omnipotence and the necessity of Christ's sacrifice to redemption.[3] But he finds Sumner capable of salvaging the natural law of Malthus' population principle within a more orthodox Christian framework. Sumner appears more orthodox for Waterman simply because Sumner allows Malthus' population principle to cohere with God's benevolence:

> For whereas Malthus himself and virtually all of his readers had looked on the principle of population as producing an uncommonly nasty case of the problem of evil to be reconciled as well as might be with the divine *goodness*, Sumner lifted it out of the icy realm of theodicy altogether, transplanting it to the genial soil of Paley's teleology, there to flourish as an example of divine *wisdom*.[4]

Anglican theologians incorporated Malthus' principle of population, grounded in natural reason alone, with an orthodoxy that refused to deny God's benevolent ordering of creation. This was accomplished through Paley's teleology.

Paley denied that scarcity adequately explained human action. If human action were capable of description solely in terms of the problem posed by scarcity, then the consequences for theology would be dire. He recognized that such an explanation too easily rendered God evil. In a much more Thomistic fashion he argued that creation was ordered to a particular end and that pressures of scarcity, where they existed, were to serve that end, an end constituted by fullness. Any pressure of scarcity was not an end in itself but an occasion for sharing possessions. For this reason, Paley, unlike both Bentham and Mill *et al.*'s philosophical radicalism and the 'liberal conservatism' of Malthus and nineteenth-century Christian political economy, did not argue that charity and the Poor Laws were the cause of poverty. Instead, he noted, 'the poor have a claim founded in the law of nature upon the resources of the rich.'[5] But this was a possibility that Malthus' economic science could not bear, for it argued that on the basis of utility alone cash transfers do not resolve the problem of population; they provide only the occasion for increased propagation, and thus they exacerbate the problem of poverty.

Although Paley should be credited with resisting the dominance of the law of scarcity in describing human action, he did not then provide us with a theological description of human action. He remained convinced by religion's critics that revelation was solely based on authority and thus needed to be both defended and supplemented through a natural reason universally accessible. He feared that the enthusiasm of the Methodists, in particular, threatened the reasonableness of faith. But the result of his 'natural theology' was a bifurcated world where grace and nature function in their own autonomous domains.[6] Such a de-socialized space for theology could easily maintain an orthodoxy that never impinged on the newly discovered laws of political economy. Moreover, no space remained for the infusion of theological virtues. Instead, for Paley, the 'foundation of everything which is religious' becomes human striving, through 'continued meditation upon a subject, placing a subject in different points of view, induction of particulars, variety of examples, applying principles to the solution of phenomena, dwelling upon proofs and conclusion.'[7] Here we have one more version of the two-tiered structure of scholasticism. Paley's natural theology does not represent any decisive alternative to scholasticism.

Roman Catholic social teaching was not as enamored of economic science as were the nineteenth-century Anglicans. Perhaps this was because the test case for English Christian political economy was Ireland. The response put forward by the Christian political economists failed miserably – a failure that should make us suspicious of all attempts to implement it as a policy. Catholic theologians did not develop an overtly Catholic alternative in response to the failed Irish policy, but Villeneuve 'reasserted the ancient sovereignty of theology over all other inquiry' against Anglican parsons like Malthus. Thus Villeneuve refused to make the distinction between a value-neutral economics and questions of virtue and wealth.[8] Villeneuve suggested that 'What one should strive for is a synthesis of English efficiency and a Christian sense of mutual responsibility. Otherwise violence and class warfare would erupt.'[9] Catholic social teaching then gave rise to what became known as the 'charitable economy' which searched for a third way between economic liberalism and socialism.[10] It was this search that gave rise to Leo XIII's 1891 encyclical *Rerum Novarum* in which Catholic social teaching made an official response to the dominance of capitalism and the threat of socialism. This initiated a tradition of papal teaching on the relationship between theology and economics. Encyclicals such as *Quadragesimo Anno* (Pius XI, 1931), *Mater et Magistra* (John XXIII, 1961), *Populorum Progressio* (Paul VI, 1967), *Laborem Exercens* and *Centesimus Annus* (John Paul II, 1981 and 1991) developed themes present in *Rerum Novarum* in an effort, as John XXIII noted, to correlate economics with morality.

How successful have these efforts been? They have failed for a number of reasons. One reason is that in the waning years of the twentieth century the bishops' authority in economic matters is simply not conceded by the laity.

Those teachings are not judged on the basis of the theological and moral traditions the bishops preserve and produce, but by the economic science embodied in the laity and, increasingly, among the clergy themselves. A second reason is that these teachings were intended for all persons of good will and thus they did not develop out of specifically theological language capable of forming people within the church. The teachings became ensconced in the language acceptable to modernity, the language of *rights* and technological *calculations*. In this way, the teachings became so formal and general that they became utterly ambiguous. All sides to the debate could claim their applicability.

## II   Leo XIII, the holy family, and economics

Catholic social teaching sought to present its conclusions in terms that would be universally accessible. It did not often assume the necessity of theology to illumine economic matters. In fact, it tended to reproduce the scholastic theology of a double finality to human existence such that economics can be viewed within the natural alone. Catholic social teaching did not substantially move us beyond the natural theology of the Anglican parsons – Malthus, Paley, Sumner and Whately.[11] An analysis of *Rerum Novarum*, however, shows that the beginnings of Catholic social teaching had the potential to connect theology and economics in a substantive way, particularly through Leo's analysis of the holy family as making the incarnation possible. The logic of the incarnation generated Catholic social teaching on the economy, although that logic does not always sustain it. Once these encyclicals became 'social teachings' they were used to extract principles such as 'human dignity' for a reconstruction of the social order beyond the confines of the church. The result was a loss of an economics embodied within a theological narrative, an adaptation of Catholic social teaching to economic science, and the search for an economic system that will have catholic applicability without Catholic theological presuppositions.

In *Rerum Novarum* Leo XIII established a close connection between the life of Christ and our understanding of labor. Leo proclaimed that contemplation of Christ's work as a carpenter led to the conclusion that a person's worth and nobility is found in his or her work. He stated:

> As for the poor, the Church teaches insistently that God sees no disgrace in poverty, nor cause for shame in having to work for a living. Christ our Lord confirmed this by his way of life, when for our salvation he who 'was rich became poor for our sake.' He chose to be seen and thought of as the son of a carpenter, despite his being the Son of God and very God himself; and having done so, made no objection to spending a large part of his life at the carpenter's trade. Contemplation of this divine example makes it easier to understand that a man's worth and nobility are found in his way of life, that is to say, his virtue; that

virtue is the common inheritance of mankind, within easy reach of high and low, rich and unpropertied alike; and that the reward of eternal happiness is earned only by acts of virtue and service, by whomsoever they are performed. Indeed, the will of God himself seems to give preference to people who are particularly unfortunate.[12]

Here we see the priority of internal goods of virtue over external goods, and at the same time a recognition of the importance of external goods for the cultivation of virtue.[13] This theological pronouncement reveals a Catholic understanding of labor as intimately associated with the cultivation of virtue and as a re-presentation of the life of Christ. Labor cannot be interpreted as a commodity capable of explanation through supply and demand alone because the incarnation, and the mission of Jesus, sanctifies labor as a central component of the divine economy. God assumes the form of flesh. Such a form is inextricably connected to the daily exchanges such flesh requires. The labor of Joseph and Mary provided the conditions for them to receive Jesus as a gift to be nurtured.[14] The example of Jesus shows that his own virtue was associated with his work, and the task of his followers is to repeat his pattern. Labor is necessary for virtue.

Leo XIII was not pleased with the industrial capitalist order at the end of the nineteenth century. He found it marked by the 'inhumanity of employers, the unbridled greed of competitors,' and a 'voracious usury.'[15] Its culminating error was its abandonment of workers. This resulted from the wage contract, which reduced laborers to mere commodities. Labor lost its dignity, and therefore the possibility of cultivating virtue. Although Karl Marx made a similar point,[16] Leo does not look to socialism for the answer to the workers' dilemma. Instead, he draws upon the Holy Family as an example of an alternative social practice.

Through reflection on the Holy Family, Leo XIII viewed labor not as a mere commodity subject to free competition, but as a dignified vocation. Labor provided the necessary condition both for Mary to give birth to the Messiah, and for Jesus to grow, develop and mature. Thus in *Quamquam Pluries* Leo wrote that 'Joseph devoted his life to labor and by his hands and skill produced whatever was necessary for those dependent upon him.' The word 'necessary' in that sentence is no accident. When Leo reiterated the church's traditional teaching on the just wage, he claimed that 'human work has stamped upon labor by nature two marks peculiar to it.' First, it is 'personal'; second, it is 'necessary.'

Labor is personal because it is a function of the person acting. Thus a singular person should have the power of disposal over his or her acts. The personal aspect of labor requires some measure of freedom for people to obtain property and enter into contracts. This obviously resonates with the teaching of John Locke, but for Leo this freedom is not absolute: for labor is not only personal, it is also necessary. The necessary aspect of labor prompts Leo to have serious reservations about the free-market system.

In the free-market system, workers must be 'free' to enter into any contract they choose without either political or church interference. This system was first articulated by Adam Smith 100 years prior to *Rerum Novarum*. Jeremy Bentham developed it more thoroughly when he wrote that 'no man of ripe years, and of sound mind, ought, out of lovingkindness to him, to be hindered from making such bargain, in the way of obtaining money, as, acting with his eyes open, he deems conducive to his interest.'[17] For Leo XIII, however, such so-called freely entered contracts between workers and employers are unacceptable. Each person has a duty to stay alive, and labor is the precondition *necessary* to fulfill that duty. No one, then, has a right to enter into any contract that conflicts with this duty. But that is exactly what the wage-contract, with its so-called 'freedom,' does: it refuses to take account of the duty both employers and employed have to 'produce whatever is necessary for those who are dependent on us.'

Even the incarnation depended upon the necessary duty of labor, a duty fulfilled by St Joseph and Mary. When God assumed human flesh, it was flesh like ours that was assumed. Therefore, it was a life bound by the conditions of family and labor, a life subject to all the vicissitudes our fleshly existence bears. Had Joseph worked for an employer who denied him a just wage, it would have been a threat equivalent to that of Herod's slaughter of the innocents. Yet Joseph could, through his own labor, provide 'whatever was necessary for those dependent upon him.' Had Joseph worked for a mining company, for the railroads or in textiles at the latter part of the nineteenth century, had he worked for a fast-food restaurant in the twentieth century, his labor could not have provided for his family. The incarnation itself would have been threatened. The Holy Family then provides evidence for the dignity of labor and of the duty of employers to provide a wage which can sustain life. No one has the right to establish a wage-contract for anything less than this. Such an act would be intrinsically evil.[18]

Because of labor's necessity, Leo argued also against the socialization of private property. Rather than common ownership, justice demands workers are given more 'power of disposal over ownership.' Here we find the beginnings of a Catholic accommodation to modernity through Locke's insistence on the will as the basis for property rights. Although in *Rerum Novarum* this argument serves the purpose of conceding more property rights to the poor, it also paves the way for later arguments about 'individual dignity.' Individual dignity is located in freedom, and this becomes associated with individual property rights and the need to 'extend dominion over nature' for the sake of development, as is particularly found in the encyclicals of John XXIII.[19] But Leo was not Locke. The similarity between them should not be overstated.[20] For Leo, labor's necessity requires that a worker has disposal over certain types of property, which forms the precondition for a way of life older than the state itself, familial life. Thus, his appeals to the Holy Family resist both capitalism's wage-contract infringements on the family and socialism's call for common ownership.[21]

One argument against Leo XIII's analysis of work is that, wittingly or unwittingly, it serves merely to keep the poor in their place and then designates those forced circumstances as 'virtue.' In other words, it is symptomatic of a traditional, paternalistic, hierarchical ordering of economic relations. If in 1891 such an ordering of economic relations was preeminent, then perhaps this charge would have been sound. However, by the end of the nineteenth century economic relations were far from based on a hierarchical traditionalism. Instead, economic liberalism, with its opposition to all things traditional, was firmly entrenched. In fact, a transformation had occurred that based economic relationships solely upon the *free*-market system. Thus, if the argument against the papal teaching is that it serves the interests of a patriarchal ruling ideology, then the teachings are, at most, potentially harmless, a residual form of hierarchical relations which buttress the power of few who actually wielded it, particularly in the United States or England in the 1890s.[22]

## III   Modernity, the tradition of economic liberalism, and the role of church and family

When compared to the dominant understanding of economic relations of the time, Leo XIII's insistence on the Holy Family as the exemplar of economic virtue is more than a mere residue of some long-since discredited hierarchy. It is, in fact, a stinging critique of the most powerful economic philosophy of the day, the liberalism that was the foundational discourse, or perhaps the consequential discourse, of capitalism.

This discourse is marked by the loss of authority based in traditional social roles. People's moral actions are no longer intelligible because of their role within a community, but people are reconstituted as *individuals* who through their autonomous activities give value to the things in the world. This understanding of human action shapes moral significance. No longer is moral significance found outside the individual subject *per se*, but it must be imposed on the world through our volitional activities. Thus morality, like the price of commodities in general, becomes viewed as a matter of *value*, determined through subjective preference. This transformation is 'modernity.' Modernity is characterized by an emphasis on freedom, particularly a freedom from all constraints. Such traditional constraints were the church and the family. And among the economic philosophers who scripted our baptism into modernity, both the church and the family, especially the poor family, were recognized to be fundamental threats to the so called 'perfect liberty' of the economic system.

Adam Smith set the questions that formed the tradition of economic liberalism. A sign of the transformation that occurred is that whereas St Thomas Aquinas discussed economic relations under the virtue of justice (which could be completed only with the infused virtue of charity), Smith, a moral philosopher, taught them under the virtue of prudence, now understood in terms of expediency. His famous book, published in 1776, *The Wealth of Nations* developed out of his lectures on moral philosophy, forming the fourth part of those lectures that came under the category of expediency. For Aquinas, justice was the moral virtue that regulated relationships between persons and between persons and things. For Smith, justice was a derivative of 'perfect liberty'; and perfect liberty was the precondition necessary for the market system to work out its logic and thus create plenty for all. Smith was specific in arguing that perfect liberty required a curtailment of interference in the market: whether that interference be political, based on justice, or ecclesial, based on charity. The central virtue necessary for the logic of Smith's system was the prudence to seek one's own advantage. When this was done without undue interference by either the church or the state then justice would result. Therefore, conflictual means would lead to a harmonious end.[23]

The conflict Smith envisioned was between two groups of people, laborers and owners:

> What are the common wages of labor depends every where upon the contract usually made between those two parties, whose interests are by no means the same. The workmen desire to get as much, the masters to give as little as possible. The former are disposed to combine in order to raise, the latter in order to lower the wages of labor.[24]

The masters pay the laborers' wages based on the 'natural price' of labor, now viewed as a commodity. The natural price is that price which will sustain the laborer so that he or she can work. It includes the cost incurred for the basic necessities of life, such as food, clothing and shelter. But the value of the commodity produced depends on the market price. If the natural price is lower than the market price, then profit results. If not, the laborers must be forced to live on a less than subsistence wage.

Economic liberalism narrates the relationship between owners and workers as conflictual and even violent.[25] Karl Marx often gets blamed for viewing economic relations as rooted in conflict, but in truth he is merely the inheritor of the liberal tradition that already assumed such conflict. When this economic analysis becomes received wisdom, then family and children become a threat to a stable economic order. Adam Smith repeats a common expression of his time: 'The rich get richer and the poor get children.' Children increase the natural price of a worker's labor and thus decrease profits for owners and threaten the possibility of a subsistence wage for laborers. The lowest natural price was from those commodities produced by slavery. Smith calculates that four children can be maintained for the cost of one slave. Thus, the marginal efficiency of a family with four children would have to be equal to that of one slave for their work to be profitable. The only exception to this is where land is abundant, as in the New World. There, labor is needed and thus children do not pose as much of a threat to the system.[26] A greater return can be had from more laborers, and until the land is no longer plentiful large families will be economically profitable. In such places, Smith stated, 'the value of children is the greatest of all encouragements to marriage.'[27]

For large families to survive they must be mobile. They must be able to move, much like commodities, to those places where there is need; otherwise the labor market becomes saturated and those families cannot be sustained. Because of this need for families to be mobile, Smith attacks the Poor Laws in England. The Poor Laws were the result of the English usurpation of the Catholic Church's property. The parish system provided poor relief through charity in each parish location. Smith argued that one of the important first steps toward perfect liberty was the dismantling of that system. It was a sign of churchly interference in the free workings of the market. So, he wrote, the

> constitution of the church of Rome may be considered as the most formidable combination that ever was formed against the authority and security of civil government, as well as against the liberty, reason and happiness of mankind, which can flourish only where civil government is able to protect them.... The gradual improvements of arts, manufactures and commerce, the same causes which destroyed the power of the great barons, destroyed in the same manner, through the greater part of Europe, the whole temporal power of the clergy.... Their charity became gradually less extensive, their hospitality less liberal or less profuse. The ties of interest, which bound the inferior ranks of people to the clergy, were in this manner gradually broken and dissolved.... As the clergy had now less influence over the people, so the state had more influence over the clergy. The clergy therefore had both less power and less inclination to disturb the state.[28]

For Smith's perfect liberty to become a social reality, the power of the state had to increase and the temporal power of the church had to be defeated. The latter occurred in two ways. First, the poor were released from this 'oppressive' charity doled out by the church. Second, the power of the church over the educational system was broken. Smith derided the European educational system because it was 'meant for the education of ecclesiastics,' and was geared toward 'a proper introduction to the study of theology.' But, he argues, 'the greater part of what is taught in schools and universities does not seem to be the most proper preparation for the real business of the world.'[29]

For Smith, the advance of freedom required the loss of the church's influence over the educational system and over the poor. The state accomplished this by confiscating church properties, thereby rendering the church's hospitality less profuse. But then the state erred by maintaining the church's work of charity through the introduction of what were know as the Poor Laws.

When by the destruction of monasteries the poor had been deprived of the charity of those religious houses, after some other ineffectual attempts, for their relief, it was enacted by the 43rd of Elizabeth that every parish should be bound to provide for its own poor and that overseers of the poor should be annually appointed, who, with the churchwardens, should raise by a parish rate, competent sums for this purpose.[30]

Smith was not as vicious as had been James Stewart, an earlier economist who 'scorned all public charity' and argued that wage-labor alone should discipline the needs of the poor.[31] Smith does not deny the legitimacy of relief. However, the relief of the poor still maintained vestiges of the parish system, and thus an unwarranted ecclesial interference now mediated through state intervention. To be eligible for poor relief one had to secure a settlement, that would demonstrate one actually resided in a particular geographical location and others there could testify to one's poverty: 'the poor' were not to be strangers, but people who were known by their neighbors. But because such settlements were difficult to come by outside one's parish of origin, the mobility of the labor pool was severely restricted. Therefore Smith argued for the eradication of the laws of settlement upon which the Poor Laws depended.[32] For Smith, the Poor Laws were the residue of the ancient practice of regulating wages by laws or justices. He wanted the labor pool deregulated so that the poor would be able to move on from their geographical place of origin to places where labor was in demand.

Although Smith did not himself argue against the need for poor relief, the logic of his 'perfectly free' market system led the next generation of economic philosophers to so argue. Malthus, in his 1798 'Essay on the Principle of Population as It Affects the Future Improvement of Society,' developed the population principle, which stated that population was increasing exponentially while food could only increase arithmetically. Unless the 'preventive check' of 'moral restraint' slowed human reproduction then, by inevitable natural laws, the preventive checks of vice and misery would do so. A cataclysmic famine was inevitable in which 'epidemics, pestilence and plague advance in terrific array and sweep off their thousands and ten thousands.'[33] Large families posed an economic threat.

Malthus' principle of population had a profound impact not only on the Christian political economy of Senior, Sumner and Paley but on the philosophical radicalism of David Ricardo and John Stuart Mill. The latter used it to argue for human perfectibility through voluntary birth control, while the former used it to suggest that such schemes were impossible. Human perfectibility was 'utopian.'

For Ricardo, who published his *Principles of Political Economy* in 1817, the Poor Laws 'formed the habits of the poor' and caused them to act irrationally by bearing too many children. These laws needed to be abolished.

The clear and direct tendency of the poor laws, is in direct opposition to obvious [economic] principles: it is not, as the legislature benevolently intended, to amend the condition of the poor, but to deteriorate the condition of both poor and rich; instead of making the poor rich, they are calculated to make the rich poor; and whilst the present laws are in force, it is quite in the natural order of things that the fund for the maintenance of the poor should progressively increase, till it has absorbed all the net revenue of the country, or at least so much of it as the state shall leave to us, after satisfying its own never failing demands for the public expenditure. This pernicious tendency of these laws is no longer a mystery since it has been fully developed by the able hand of Mr Malthus and every friend to the poor must ardently wish for their abolition.

Natural and obvious economic laws revealed that economic transfers from the wealthy to the poor do not help the poor. They only allow the poor to have too many children. For the sake of the 'prudence' necessary for the market system, the government has an obligation to regulate their numbers by refusing to support them.

It is a truth which admits not a doubt, that the comforts and well-being of the poor cannot be permanently secured without some regard on their part, or some effort on the part of the legislatures to regulate the increase of their number and to render less frequent among them early and improvident marriages. The operation of the system of poor laws has been directly contrary to this. They have rendered restraint superfluous, and have invited imprudence by offering it a portion of the wages of prudence and industry.

Notice that not only the economy but marriage and family are now defined under the virtue of prudence. And prudence now means sexual restraint. Ricardo concludes:

By gradually contracting the sphere of the poor laws; by impressing on the poor the value of independence, by teaching them that they must look not to systematic or casual charity, but to their own exertions for support, that prudence and forethought are neither unnecessary nor unprofitable virtues, we shall by degrees approach a sounder and more healthful state.

For the 'perfect liberty of the market,' the Poor Laws must be rescinded, and the poor taught to accept this and live accordingly 'with as little violence as possible.'[34]

John Stuart Mill and the Benthamite radicals perpetuated the idea that a large family is a threat to the free working of the economy. Mill concretizes the intellectual underpinnings for this way of life with his development of that moral philosophy known as *utilitarianism*. He also made note in his autobiography, posthumously published in 1873, of his embarrassment that he himself came from a large family. Commenting on his father's life, he wrote:

> In this period of my father's life there are two things which it is impossible not to be struck with: one of them unfortunately a very common circumstance ... that in his position, with no resource but the precarious one of writing in periodicals, he married and had a large family; conduct than which nothing could be more opposed, both as a matter of good sense and of duty, to the opinions which, at least at a later period of life, he strenuously upheld.[35]

Such an objective criticism of his father for siring so many offspring makes one wonder which of his siblings Mill thought it would have been more prudent that his father had not brought into the world? The necessity of economics is set against the contingency of family life .

Notice how Mill and Leo XIII conflict in their understanding of *duty*. For Leo, life is a good to be received. Families should have children and even practice social reproduction so that they are open to life, perhaps lots of it. The economy should then serve the interests of those families by providing a just wage that will sustain them in their entirety. For Mill this is reversed. The economy comes prior to the family. The role of the economy is not a function of the family, but the family is a function of the economy. Now we have a duty not to have children until we can be assured that individual family units can provide for them.[36] The church's teachings on the family must be challenged, because the family is now to be disciplined by the market rather than the church.

The classical liberal economic philosophers envisioned a world where the social institution of the market would be freed from all interference, whether it be political, moral, theological, or familial. The fact that Leo XIII recognized the threat this world posed both to the church and to the family makes his work much more than a longing for a defunct hierarchical and paternalistic world. Instead, we are reminded of three things. First, economic relations should not be based on prudence alone, but on the virtues of charity and justice. Second, labor is not a commodity, but is prerequisite for the cultivation of virtue. Virtue serves the interest neither of the state nor of the market, but of the family. But this understanding of the family takes its meaning from its role within the church. The Holy Family itself provides the example for a proper understanding of labor. Any wage preventing a family from fulfilling the necessity of subsistence is intrinsically evil. No amount of future possibilities can justify such exploitative means. Third, the family is one social community that should be freed from infringements by free-market logic. The family holds forth the possibility of an internal good. It is a social community (like the church) that should not be justified in terms of its usefulness for external ends. The family is good because it is a family.[37] This is not to suggest that the family can be self-interpreting. For Christian theology, the family's goodness is also related to that goodness which is God alone. Such goodness is attested to primarily in the social community called the church. It is where social reproduction into the life of God occurs. The reproduction within the family should be in service to that (super)natural reproduction.

Does this understanding of economics merely neglect Malthusian mathematics and thus, as Waterman noted, deserve its irrelevance? Can the claim that the market should serve the family, and not vice versa, be more than a pious platitude? The tragic world of Malthus stated that the family's reproduction needs the market for its possibility, but its reproduction also threatened the market's capacity to provide that possibility. He saw no way out. The philosophical radicals thought that subordinating the family's reproduction to the disciplinary mechanism of the market through the value of *prudence* would provide a way out of this tragic world, and result in progress and the possibility of human perfectibility. But this simultaneously tragic and progressive perspective judged economic exchanges based upon their 'utility.' They assumed that the purpose in such exchanges was solely to support life in its longevity and pleasures. Only a sadist would deny some such role for the economy, but can this be its sole purpose, its true end?

In Roman Catholic moral theology the purpose of economic exchange is considered to be broader than that which was assumed in either nineteenth-century Christian political economy or philosophical radicalism. This is the direct result of the centrality of Thomas' theology and the assumption that the vision of God rather than the survival of life itself is our true end. Such an end is open to the newborn (even the unborn) as much as it is to those who live long and rich lives. This different end results in a different context within which economic exchanges are judged. But the Catholic effort to integrate Catholicism and political economy did not always maintain the distinctiveness of this *super*natural end.

Many Catholic efforts to reconstruct the social order perpetuated scholastic theology's teaching of a double finality by its rigid distinction of natural reason from divine teaching. This was the dominant strategy of the Catholic Economic Association (CEA). It originated during a meeting of the American Economic Association, in 1941, and was initiated by such Catholic notables as the Right Reverend John A. Ryan, Thomas F. Divine SJ, and Bernard Dempsey SJ. Its task was to discuss 'scientifically problems of economic policy the solution of which requires a knowledge both of economic science and of Christian social principles.'[38]

How these Christian social principles were, and were not, integrated with their economic science is the issue to which attention now turns. In examining the work of the economist Bernard Dempsey, I argue that this strategy to reconstruct the social order has been unsuccessful partly because it was incapable of maintaining the priority of the theological virtues; thus it assumed, but did not give due emphasis to, the role of the church within political economy.

## IV  Bernard Dempsey and a theological economics

Bernard Dempsey SJ (1903–60) developed an economic theory called 'the functional economy.' It assumed that the economy, like the human person, should orient a person toward her or his true end. For Dempsey this true end was primarily the common good defined in terms of justice. But Dempsey, like Father Ryan before him, did not seem to integrate the natural virtue of justice with the supernatural virtue of charity. Nevertheless, his functional economy set forth an understanding of exchanges that was based on something other than the will's power alone.

Dempsey was an economist who taught at St Louis University, Nirmala College in India, and Marquette University. He was also a Jesuit well versed in scholastic moral theology. He was a trained economist, receiving his PhD in economics from Harvard University in 1940, having studied under Joseph Schumpeter.[39] Schumpeter wrote the introduction to Dempsey's book *Interest and Usury*. He stated that Dempsey's training as a theologian 'made it easy for him to read the scholastic thought on interest and usury without any danger of misunderstanding.' 'Moreover,' said Schumpeter, 'his professional training as an economist put the methods and results of modern professional analysis at his command.'[40] Schumpeter thought Dempsey's 1943 work worthy of the attention of both economists and theologians.

Dempsey's theological economic analysis fits within a conversation on church teaching initiated not by the theologians but by the economists. No less significant an economist than John Maynard Keynes had reassessed the scholastics' theological economics and, for a brief moment in the latter part of the 1930s, the scholastics were recognized as valuable contributors to economics. This is surprising, because most economists had long since dismissed them as irrationally committed to an authoritarian tradition-dependent morality that failed to analyze economics on its own terms. Thus a pre-condition for the rise of the rational or modern study of economics was the death of the scholastic theological economics.

Economists often explain the history of their discipline as the victory of modern rational economic thought over the authoritarianism of the irrational Middle Ages. A recurring theme of that story is that the mark of the medieval church's irrationality was its prohibition of usury. A version of this story is found in the work of Adam Smith. He did not set his work specifically against the usury prohibition. In many ways, his arguments for interest were quite consistent with those of the scholastics of the seventeenth century. He found interest legitimate because the borrower risks the lender's profit by employing it on potentially productive enterprises.[41] The scholastics agreed that this was an acceptable reason for a non-usurious profit. Still Smith thought that those European countries that enforced usury laws were only furthering the 'evil of usury.'

> In some countries the interest of money has been prohibited by law. But as something can everywhere be made by the use of money, something ought everywhere to be paid for the use of it. This regulation, instead of preventing, has been found from experience to increase the evil of usury; the debtor being obliged to pay, not only for the use of money, but for the risk which his creditor runs by accepting a compensation for that use. He is obliged, if one may say so, to insure his creditor from the penalties of usury.[42]

Smith's language is not as careful as that of the scholastics: he did not distinguish between charging solely for the use of money (which *would* be usury) and any profit received for the employment of one's legitimate savings in a productive enterprise at communally agreed upon levels of profit (which *would not* be usury). Nevertheless, Smith's argument was less a refutation than a restatement of the usury principle; he still called usury 'evil.'

Jeremy Bentham took issue with Adam Smith for not going far enough toward 'perfect liberty,' because Smith still allowed the civil magistrate to fix the interest rate. This allowance, he suggested, 'is inconsistent with some fundamental ideas of Dr Smith.'[43] The central issue for Bentham remained what he had learned from Smith: the need for 'perfect liberty' when it came to market matters. But Bentham wanted Smith to be more consistent and to refuse all restrictions on interest rates.

The narrative that a rational economy arises against the church's resistance is also present in the Austrian school.[44] Böhm-Bawerk's monumental 1884 publication *History and Critique of Interest Theories* contained chapter titles such as 'Resistance of Economic Practice to the Canonistic Prohibition of Interest,' 'Victory in the Netherlands of School of Economists Who Approved of Interest,' and 'Backwardness of the Romance Countries: French Legislators and Writers Cling Tenaciously to the Canonistic Doctrine.'[45] He obviously did not find the scholastics to be reasonable. He began his historical assessment of the period with the claim: 'Since [the interest] controversy was at its height during the heyday of scholasticism, it can well be imagined that the growth in number of arguments and counter-arguments was by no means a measure of the growth in knowledge of the subject itself.' Much like Adam Smith before him, Böhm-Bawerk sets Roman society against medieval society and found the former more economically rational than the latter because the Romans were tolerant of interest. Medieval society saw 'a relapse in industry to the circumstances of primitive times.' The triumph of interest was the triumph of practical businessmen over abstract and theoretically minded ecclesiastics.[46] Such a triumph was the first victory necessary for a rational free market.

Böhm-Bawerk was not alone in his assessment within the Austrian school. Ludwig von Mises discussed the canonist influence as a 'well known example of the failure of authoritative interference with the markets.'[47] Even the otherwise rebellious Schumpeter originally told a similar story. In his early work *The Theory of Economic Development*, he found the medieval theologians woefully inadequate. They 'only observed economic things fleetingly and only paid attention to the interest which was observed in their sphere.'[48] They mistakenly viewed all loans as consumptive and therefore prohibited usury. However, by the time he wrote his *History of Economic Analysis*, he gave a more sympathetic portrayal of the scholastics.

Schumpeter's careful analysis of the scholastics earned him Dempsey's admiration. In his 1958 publication *The Functional Economy*, Dempsey wrote: 'Probably for the first time in the English language the period of the scholastics is treated by a competent economist who is able and willing to read them.'[49] That 'for the first time' is telling. Keynes, before Schumpeter, had treated the schoolmen sympathetically, but according to Dempsey, incompetently.

As a trained theologian, Dempsey recognized that many economists spoke about the Middle Ages with a complete lack of theological resources. As a trained economist, he also recognized that many theologians *applied* theology to economics without seriously undertaking a study of the subject matter. He sought to avoid both errors. However, the greater error was to be found among the economists. Their contempt for the medieval theologians was symptomatic of an Enlightenment arrogance that refused to read or take seriously predecessors' work. These economists therefore deceived themselves as to the uniqueness of their teachings by caricaturing the thought of earlier generations. Dempsey drew upon seventeenth-century scholastics to show their relevance to modern economics, while at the same time maintaining their moral and theological teachings. What the Enlightenment had rent asunder – economics, theology, morality – he attempted to join back together.

Dempsey did not explicitly state what precipitated his work on usury. One factor must have been the tradition of papal encyclicals, particularly *Rerum Novarum* (1891) that claimed 'voracious usury' was rampant in industrial society. Likewise *Quadragesimo Anno* (1931) elaborated and applied the principles set forth in *Rerum Novarum*. Certainly these encyclicals prompted theologians like Dempsey to turn toward economic matters. But another important factor was John Maynard Keynes' reappropriation of the scholastic tradition to support his attack upon classical liberal economics. Dempsey dedicated the final chapter of *Interest and Usury* to a refutation of Keynes' solicitation of the schoolmen for support.

In 1931 a debate began in the *British Economic Journal* with a brief essay by H. Somerville entitled 'Interest and Usury in a New Light.' In this essay, Somerville stated that Keynes' *Treatise on Money* raised a number of questions and 'unexpected consequences,' one of the most startling of which was his 'vindication of the Canonist attitude to interest and usury.'[50] Keynes vindicates the canonists, or perhaps the canonists vindicate Keynes because of his distinction between savings and investment. For Keynesian economics, savings alone do not provide the capital necessary for economic growth. If savings are not immediately transformed into purchasing power, effective demand is diminished and therefore supply as well. The result is unemployment and economic stagnation. As Somerville stated it, 'the worst thing is the sterile saving of money.' Sterile money results from interest on accumulated savings without employing it in productive enterprises. But when the interest rate is held low, this practice is discouraged and sterile savings can be transformed into productive investment. Therefore, as Somerville suggests, in the 'Keynesian analysis, interest is the villain of the economic piece.'

This analysis opposed liberal orthodox economics where interest and profits were correlated, and high interest rates would entice savings, which would then provide a pool of capital out of which profits could be earned. Savings equals investment. But Keynes set interest and profits in opposition. Interest on money saved did not necessarily equal profits from capital usefully employed. He then distinguished capital (investment) from money (sterile savings). And this, stated Somerville, placed him in the camp of the canonists who 'never quarreled with payments for the use of capital, but they disputed the identification of the lending of money with the investment of capital and denied the justice of interest as a reward for saving without investment.'[51]

Somerville's understanding of usury was based on Ashley's *Economic History*. Ashley drew upon the distinction made by the medieval church between a legitimate *societas* – a partnership where capital was pooled for the purposes of profit and the lender was a partner who undertook risk – and usury where the lender was only a creditor, lending money without risk. This early usury proscription was undone in the sixteenth century when canonists such as Johann Eck (1486–1543) began to defend the triple contract which allowed investors to enter into a 'partnership' without risk because they entered a second contract where they were guaranteed a return. But, given the Keynesian revolution, Somerville prophesied: 'There may be reasons for thinking that the world will go back to the early Canonist doctrine.'[52]

Somerville's essay led to a symposium on savings and usury in the March, 1932 edition of the *Economic Journal*, with contributions from Edwin Canaan, B. P. Adarkar, B. K. Sandwell and Mr Keynes himself. The symposium focused on 'Mr Keynes' conversion to the doctrine of the Medieval Church.' And this raised the question whether interest should be approved or condemned. Is it the case, as Somerville suggested, that interest is the villain? If so, then the early canonists were on to something.

All the respondents, except Keynes, found Somerville's suggestion ridiculous. Canaan, although finding Somerville's argument unpersuasive, used it to attack Keynes. The problem, however, was not the adequacy of Somerville's analysis but Keynes' economics. Somerville had rightly interpreted Keynes and thus had unwittingly demonstrated Keynes' central error: he misunderstood savings. The canonists were not vindicated. Canaan distinguished savings as accumulation of 'the excess of income over consumption' from savings as 'mere refraining from expenditure.' If we understood savings as the former, then interest was 'both natural and useful.' Interest is what people pay for access to this surplus for further profitable enterprise. It is useful because interest encourages the surplus savings. If however, savings were mere abstinence, then interest would be 'mysterious and indefensible,' for no one should make money just by not spending their money.[53] But, for Canaan, savings are not mere abstinence. Savings are a form of investment, and the two cannot be separated, as Keynes had attempted to do. Orthodoxy still held: 'The old orthodox view is right – that banks, far from paying interest on idle money and delaying its investment, facilitate and quicken the necessary transactions between passive savers and active producers.'[54]

B. P. Adarkar defended Keynes against Somerville's discovery. He found Somerville's correlation of Keynes and the early canonists a misreading of Keynes which, he wrongly assumed, Keynes would surely repudiate. The canonists' doctrine, he wrote, 'has been buried long ago by both classical and modern economists.' And Keynes cannot be placed in the canonist camp. Yet Adarkar was proven wrong by Keynes' response to Somerville's essay, as well as by Keynes' 1936 publication *The General Theory of Employment, Interest and Money*. Keynes did not leave the canonists buried: he tried to dig them up.

B. K. Sandwell did not dismiss Somerville's essay as thoroughly as had Canaan and Adarkar; but, he argued, the similarities between Keynes and the canonists were less than profound:

> The Canonists held that there is a form of investment which involves no risk, and that because it involves no risk it should not be allowed to receive remuneration. Mr Keynes holds that there is a form of holding of savings which involves no investment, and that at times when the amount of such holding becomes excessive it might well be discouraged by reducing the rate of its remuneration, if necessary to zero. If the proposition that savings' deposits might in certain circumstances advantageously be deprived of interest is a 'vindication' of the proposition that no interest should ever be allowed on safe investments of any kind, all I can say is that the Canonist doctrine must be very hard up for vindication. Which, of course, at the present time it is.[55]

Sandwell found no value in considering the relationship between the canonists and Keynes. The usury prohibition, he argued, is merely an effort to 'impose upon mankind the ethics of the early Hebrews,' and it was there that those ethics 'first and foremost' broke down. The usury prohibition reflected only an irrational theological ethic, and Somerville's essay was a disguised attempt to challenge 'personal ownership and the exchangeability of capital goods.' The canonist doctrine, Sandwell concluded, 'affords a splendid springboard for the transition to a full Soviet economy.'

These criticisms of Somerville's essay underestimated Keynes. His response came 'to the support of Mr Somerville' on 'one main issue.' Keynes took exception to Cannan's interpretation of savings. He reiterated that there is no necessary connection between savings and an 'increment of capital wealth.' And, he stated:

> If an increment of saving by an individual is not accompanied by an increment of new investment – and in the absence of deliberate management by the Central Bank or the Government, it will be nothing but a lucky accident if it is – then it necessarily causes diminished receipts, disappointment and losses to some other party, and the outlet for the savings of A will be found in financing the losses of B.

How did this, then, relate to the teaching of the scholastics? Keynes agreed with Adarkar that the canonists did not fully understand the difference between interest on savings by debts and savings by assets. Nonetheless, he raised the question: 'May not Mr Somerville be right that the social evil of usury, as conceived by the Canonists, was essentially due to the fact that in the circumstances of their time savings generally went with the creation not of assets but of debts?' Somerville's essay certainly prompted Keynes to rethink the scholastics' position – although not from any theological perspective. The scholastics were defended as implicitly recognizing what Keynes himself would later make explicit. By the time he wrote *The General Theory*, he had emphasized the similarities between himself and them.

In 1936 Keynes published his *General Theory*. The scholastics were now called upon as allies. He wrote:

> I was brought up to believe that the attitude of the Medieval Church to the rate of interest was inherently absurd, and that the subtle discussions aimed at distinguishing the return on money-loans from the return to active investment were merely Jesuitical attempts to find a practical escape from a foolish theory. But I now read these discussions as an honest intellectual effort to keep separate what the classical theory has inextricably confused together, namely, the rate of interest and the marginal efficiency of capital. For it now seems clear that the disquisitions of the schoolmen were directed towards the elucidation of a formula which should allow the schedule of marginal efficiency of capital to be high, whilst using rule and custom and the moral law to keep down the rate of interest.[56]

Keynes argued that the soundness of the usury proscription resided in the scholastics' effort to reward investment by keeping 'the marginal efficiency of capital high,' and not to reward mere savings by keeping the rate of interest low. Thus, for Keynes, the beauty of the scholastic teaching resided in the just reward for investment risk and the denial of a reward merely for the lending out of one's savings. This fit well with the Keynesian revolution, for it emphasized investment and deemphasized savings.

Keynes revivified the scholastics to support his attack on the classical economists. Of course, he never analyzed the scholastics' work with any depth.[57] His arguments are haphazard and were employed merely for the sake of supporting his own position. They occurred in that portion of *The General Theory* (Chapter 22) which Keynes called 'his way of honoring cranks who have preferred to see the truth obscurely and imperfectly rather than to maintain error reached by easy logic on hypotheses inappropriate to the facts.'[58]

As an economist and a Jesuit, Bernard Dempsey had a stake in this debate. As indebted to Schumpeter's economic thinking as he was, he obviously could not find palatable Keynes' appropriation of the Jesuitical theological tradition for the Keynesian revolution.[59] Dempsey did not defend the liberal orthodox theory, but he found Keynes' re-appropriation of the scholastics backward. He recognized, with Keynes, the legitimacy of profit for investment risk, which is 'a special case of emergent loss.' He agreed that this was an important aspect of the scholastic teaching, but considered it the only aspect of the teaching that Keynes had understood. Concerning Keynes' famous passage in *The General Theory*, Dempsey wrote:

> This statement contains a truth, but one very poorly presented. To a Schoolman, the marginal efficiency of capital would be another name for the loss emergent or gain cessant upon the relinquishing of money, the true cost of the alternative opportunities. In communities where these alternatives were numerous and would be competed for, there would arise a common price based on the community appraisal of an average profit opportunity, an average rate of marginal profit from investment.[60]

The modern economic assumption of the marginal efficiency of capital, that rate of return which can be expected from the employment of a particular amount of capital, was correlated with the scholastic assumption of *lucrum cessans*, or cessant gain. This was the principle that allowed one to receive a return for a loan. This return was not viewed as interest on a loan but as the fair profit one would have received had that money been employed in some other venture. The loan becomes a good deed whereby a lender employs his savings and accepts the risk of the borrower's venture.

Usury did not imply that one could not make a profit on one's investment. Usury implied that one could not make a profit merely by loaning money. For although money itself does not fructify, money employed in useful ventures can, through those ventures, fructify. For instance, if I purchase a pear orchard for a certain amount of money, I hope that those pear trees will fructify and bring me a return for my investment, a profit. If, however, I loaned that same amount of money to another when I could have used it to purchase the pear orchard, I can receive as a fair return the same amount of money that I would have received on the investment but which I have now foregone so that I could make the loan. That fair return depends on 'the community appraisal of an average profit opportunity.' Such appraisals arise from the real possibilities of profit given the intrinsic value in the created world: they were not the result merely of the will's power to give the world its value. Risking that 'average profit opportunity' for the sake of offering a loan, was known, among scholastic theologians, as *lucrum cessans*: I was not obligated to make the loan; I could have invested the money myself and kept the profit. Because I loaned the money, I am entitled to the profit I would have received based on the community appraisal had I invested it.

Thus, as Dempsey pointed out, the scholastics taught that, if a sin against commutative justice was to be avoided, marginal profit should equal the rate of interest. And Keynes was consistent with the scholastics, against the classical theorists, in distinguishing marginal profit from the rate of interest. Yet Keynes was incorrect in his conclusion. Dempsey wrote:

> But though this possibility of de facto divergence meant that the concepts are distinct, it may be very misleading to say that the Scholastics labored to keep them separate when concretely their whole purpose was to keep them together. A high marginal efficiency of capital meant a true emergent loss to him who relinquished capital goods or the money means to them. The just price of present money, the rate of interest, was therefore high and a consistent Scholastic would work to keep it up, and to allocate the benefit to him to whom in commutative justice it was due, namely, to the one who incurred the emergent loss. Keynes is right in the distinction which he draws; but the use he makes of it is so different from the Scholastic application that it might readily be the source not only of confusion of ideas but also of imputation to the Schoolmen of ideas directly contrary to what they held.[61]

Although Keynes wrongly applied the scholastic teaching on usury, Dempsey agreed that the scholastic teaching was relevant to the modern economy. In fact, he found the modern acceptance of usury one of the central reasons for violations of distributive justice. We live in a maldistributed economic system because that system institutes usury.

## V   Institutional usury

At mid-century, in his landmark book *The Scholastic Analysis of Usury*, John T. Noonan found no direct application of the usury proscription to our credit economy. He wrote: 'Usury today is a dead issue, and except by a plainly equivocal use of the term, or save in the mouths of a few inveterate haters of the present order, it is not likely to stir to life.'[62] The usury proscription can be applicable only to loan sharks and pawnbrokers. It cannot be used as an indictment of our current economy. Those persons who seek to invoke it do so only as a foil for their hatred of the present economic system. They are not in any way committed to scholastic principles.

Although Noonan began his historical analysis with this moral judgment, he found Dempsey's work to be an exception: 'Far more scientific and subtle than the rhetoric of the Viennese circle and the indignation of Beloc and Benveinisti is the criticism launched against the present order under the banner of the usury theory by Bernard Dempsey.'[63] Dempsey was no 'inveterate hater of this world.' He did not rush to judgment on the question of the viability of usury to the modern economy. Only after a careful analysis both of the scholastic position and of profit and interest in the modern economy did he reach his conclusion – modern economics is founded on 'institutional usury.'

Dempsey's *Interest and Usury* divides into two sections. First, he analyzed modern interest theory. He did this through an examination of the theory of interest as found in Knut Wicksell, Ludwig von Mises, Friedrich von Hayek, Irving Fisher, Joseph Schumpeter, Gunnar Myrdal and John Maynard Keynes. Second, he explained the scholastic prohibition of usury in the seventeenth century through the work of de Lugo, Molina and Lessius. Then he compared the two economic theories.[64] He concluded his comparison with the following assessment:

> The modern situation to which theorists have applied the concepts of divergence of natural and money interest, divergences of saving and investment, divergences of income disposition from tenable patterns by involuntary displacements – all these have a sufficient common ground with late medieval analysis to warrant the expression 'institutional usury.'[65]

Why this conclusion?

To understand Dempsey's judgment, we must first observe the three divergences he examined. The three divergences – 'natural and money interest,' 'savings and investment,' and the divergences of 'income disposition from tenable patterns by involuntary displacements' – referred, respectively, to the work of Knut Wicksell, John Maynard Keynes, and Ludwig von Mises. Having examined the second divergence already, I turn now to the first and the third.

### Wicksell and the divergence of natural and money interest

'Institutional usury' suggests that our modern economic system has the effect of usury without personal culpability.[66] How does this happen? Wicksell's analysis of the divergence of natural and money interest helps explain this. In *Interest and Prices*, Wicksell hypothesized a 'pedagogical economy' in which goods were lent *in natura* without a monetary medium. Dempsey found this compelling in part, because it fitted with the traditional scholastic possibilities of exchange: 'If goods did not have the characteristic of producing a greater volume of goods in time, interest as a production factor would not exist.'[67] Using one's goods to increase one's goods is not usury. Thus Wicksell's natural rate of interest fits with scholastic possibilities for legitimate profit.

Wicksell stated that the natural rate is 'the rate which would be determined by supply and demand if real capital were lent in kind without the intervention of money.'[68] Yet while this understanding of interest falls within the limits of the usury prohibition, Wicksell did not advocate the natural rate of interest as something beneficial or desirable. For in this natural economy prices would fluctuate at the discretion of nature, dependent more or less on the 'beneficent influences of nature.'[69] This prevents the achievement of Wicksell's ideal future state, in which prices will have a certain invariable stability not subject to natural contingency. As we rely more on 'our own strength and foresight' and less on nature we will become 'masters' rather than 'slaves' of nature. Monetary theory and practice had not yet improved to this point, but Wicksell's work was an effort to determine the factors that influence interest and prices in an effort to rationalize them against natural contingencies.

At this point in his argument, Wicksell rehearsed the modern theory of value where supply and demand are conditioned by marginal utility. Each person continues the process of exchange as long as 'he continues to acquire commodities which represent more than the equivalent of the commodities that he gives in exchange.'[70] In so far as these exchanges will be indirect, which is inevitable, money will be required. But here the purpose of money is merely to effect the exchange or to serve as a store of value over time until the exchange is transacted. However, money becomes something other than this once it 'derives a marginal utility and an exchange value against other commodities.' To the extent that money serves either to facilitate exchange or as a store of value for future exchange, then the usury proscription would not be violated. However, when money does not express the *value relationships* between the commodities exchanged, then it clearly does violate the usury proscription. The exchange of money alone now provides the possibility of an income that was never earned and yet can be used for future gain, whether that gain goes to the individual employing it or to someone else.

By showing how the money rate of interest diverges from the natural rate of interest and does not need to come into equilibrium with it, Wicksell demonstrated no necessary connection between money and commodity exchange.[71] As long as commodities are lent in kind, the physical commodities themselves establish the objective limits of their relationship. Once, however, commodities are bought and sold, and money lent for that purpose, then such limitations are no longer extant. And money does not possess the same limits as do commodities. The market rate of interest is determined by the credit institutions separately from any necessary connection with the natural rate of interest

At this point, Dempsey found the usury teaching applicable. If Wicksell has explained adequately the modern economic situation, then no emergent loss is possible, and money violates the purposes it should serve:

> If money does not so change hands as to express accurately these value relationships [of physical objects], then the relations themselves are altered rather than expressed by the money sums paid for them. When investment is made with funds that have never been income, and before being income have never been cost, such a derangement is theoretically inevitable.[72]

The problem with this 'derangement' is that it distorted just distribution.

### Von Mises and divergences of income disposition from tenable patterns by involuntary displacements

How 'institutional usury' occurred can be seen also in the work of Ludwig von Mises and his discussion of the nature of fiduciary media. Von Mises argued that 'it is a complete mistake to assert that the nature of an act of exchange is altered by the employment of fiduciary media.' Dempsey disagreed.[73] Fiduciary media are employed in credit transactions. Von Mises divided credit transactions into two types. The first comprises those which 'impose a sacrifice on that party who performed his part of the bargain before the other does' through the 'foregoing of immediate power of disposal over the exchanged good.' This first type of credit transaction is called commodity credit. In this sense, credit transactions would not be usurious because *lucrum cessans* could be demonstrated. The second class of credit transaction comprises those which are 'characterized by the fact that in them the gain of the party who receives before he pays is balanced by no sacrifice on the part of the other party.'[74] In this second class of credit transaction, referred to as circulation credit, no sacrifice is made by the issuers of fiduciary media. They could never incur a loss, for they have not given up the power of disposal over any commodity. The issuance of fiduciary media for the second class of transaction would not be usurious if it were kept within certain natural limits – that is to say, if it were contained by the natural rate of interest, as Wicksell described it, in terms of commodities lent *in natura*. Economists such as Tooke had argued that the elasticity of fiduciary media was the effect and never the cause of 'fluctuations in business life.'[75] Therefore, the banking industry, which issued fiduciary media, was merely 'passive.' But von Mises showed the error in this way of thinking, an error that resides in a misunderstanding of the 'fundamental nature of fiduciary media.'

His argument had four steps. *First*, fiduciary media is issued, i.e. a bank discounts a bill or grants a loan, as an 'exchange of a present good for a future good.' This is why fiduciary media are employed. A bank provides a loan (the present good) in exchange for future goods that the borrower will receive through employing the present good. But what makes possible the present good? This question gave rise to the *second* step in von Mises' argument: 'the issuer creates the present good that it exchanges, the fiduciary media, practically out of nothing.' This leads to the *third* step in his argument – because fiduciary media are issued practically out of nothing, no 'natural limitations' exist for the quantity of fiduciary media. In truth, the future goods that will be produced are limited, but no limitations are present in their possibilities for exchange in terms of present goods, as circulation credit, in the market. And the *fourth* step is that the issuers of fiduciary media can

> induce an extension of the demand for future goods by reducing the interest demanded to a rate below the natural rate of interest, that is below that rate of interest that would be established by supply and demand if the real capital were lent *in natura* without the mediation of money, whereas on the other hand the demand for fiduciary media would be bound to cease entirely as soon as the rate asked by the bank was raised above the natural rate.[76]

The conclusion is that 'the quantity of fiduciary media in circulation has no natural limits.' For von Mises, this was just how the market worked. For Dempsey, this was institutional usury.

Dempsey did not argue that these theorists advocated usury, but rather that their analysis show us the usurious and negative effects of the modern economy. He stated:

> Apart from enrichment of politicians by confiscations, and exploitation of natives in imperial areas, whence do the modern aggregates of free capital funds arise if not from profits of credit-financed innovations, including the periodic innovation of military enterprise requiring the complete re-direction of the economy, with credit-financed windfalls to those holding assets with special wartime values? ... If innovation had always paid a full just price for the saved resources employed to the persons whose income-curtailment furnished the savings and upon whom the consequent emergent loss descended, how different would distribution of income be from what it is? What its shape would be we

may not say, but we can safely hold that it would be very definitely less askew than it is.[77]

The capital which financed the modern economy violated the usury proscription because it was based either on confiscation, conquest and exploitation, or credit that had little connection with savings from legitimate earnings. All of these acts of accumulation were usurious because no *lucrum cessans* could be named when capital was formed in this way. This is obvious in the case of confiscation and exploitation, but the use of credit is the heart of the matter. Following von Mises, Dempsey found credit to be created without foundation in any present income or savings. Therefore, access to credit provided a gain for which no corresponding risk or loss could possibly be found. Profit was made solely on one's access to this credit separately from any corresponding debt or obligation to another.

What does it matter that profit can arise separately from one's earned savings and investment? Usury still mattered for Dempsey because of his Thomistic account of economic life. The fullest articulation of this is found in his 1958 publication *The Functional Economy: The Bases of Economic Organization*. Dempsey argued that the 'goal of the economic process' is 'the development and perfection of human personality.' Notice how this goal conflicts with McCann and Stackhouse's argument that the central purpose of economic exchanges is to produce wealth. Dempsey was as favorably disposed to the free market as are the members of the dominant tradition, and he does not seem to have had socialist leanings. Still he critiqued twentieth-century capitalism for theological reasons. Because he inherited this *telos* of the perfection of human personality, capitalism as it existed had to be reconstructed. Economics must recognize something more than a bare exchange of commodities: human personality contained an (Aristotelian) *ergon*, a proper work or function that each person has through which one is to become what one ought to be. Each person has a proper work, and this Dempsey viewed theologically as a mission to be performed. The *is* of the human person cannot be adequately defined without this *ought*, and exchanges in the market are central for both.

Because of this residual element of an Aristotelian–Thomistic understanding of the human person and economy, Dempsey could not accept the fact–value distinction. Economic exchanges could not be based solely on the abstract value of fiduciary media because each such exchange also embodies a relationship between human persons, between persons and creation, and therefore also between the person and God. But without some understanding of what our true end is, we will not be able to measure these exchanges by anything other than the sincerity of the will itself. This was the only criterion left with which to regulate exchanges after Bentham's defense of usury. But, for Dempsey, the task of each agent is to perfect his or her personality. This is accomplished by the identification of one's actions with the objects for which one aims. And this occurs only within a social community.[78]

Within a social community a person is called upon to do a certain work, and that person should be adequately compensated to be able to perform that task. This compensation can then be employed for the good of the community through 'contributive justice.' By this a worker perfects both his work and the community's good. The 'work' a person perfects is not simply her labor, but also her self. These exchanges are integral to the mission to which God calls each person. But once profit on investment is separated from savings, it is separated also from one's work. Perfection of personality cannot occur, and the economic life is reduced to a large lottery system wherein profit can be made, but this profit will have no connection to a person's *ergon*.

A restored social order is required if economic life is to achieve its appropriate *telos*. For Dempsey, neither liberalism nor Marxism allowed for the form of social activity that could perfect human personality, because each assumes conflict and antagonistic social relations. Dempsey sees too much commonalty between Adam Smith and Karl Marx for either of them to be used to create a society that can fulfill the appropriate theological function of economic life. Therefore, the moral demands of a Thomistic theology require the 'restoration of the social order.' He invited theologians and others to create those forms of economic life that can be oriented toward theological ends.

The state cannot function as the social community which will allow for human perfectibility to proceed as it should, but neither can 'privatization,' for that is merely the securing of the power of the individual (the corporation) by the state.[79] Instead, something like the medieval guild economy needs to be in place. Dempsey's work was a call for local communities to have some control over their economic life; it was a call for 'intermediary associations' based on the Catholic principle of subsidiarity. Local social institutions are necessary for people to fulfill the tasks of responsibility, loyalty and liberty that allow for the perfection of one's end. This cannot occur within modern economic arrangements because the class conflict written into liberalism reduces workers' labor to a mere commodity. Here Dempsey's work finds resonance in the work of John Milbank, who also argues that a 'complex space' is necessary to mediate between individuals and the state. The problem with modernity, suggests Milbank, is that it produces a 'simple space' where all that is left is the state and the individual. The result is that workers have no forms of resistance against the state's encroachment in all aspects of their lives. Members of the dominant tradition also often point in the direction of the importance of intermediary associations as well; but, by finding the 'corporation' as the intermediary association, they fail to recognize something that both Dempsey and Milbank point out. This is that corporations are not based on any substantive goods that would provide persons with refuge, resistance, or an alternative to the purely formal assertion of power (negative right) that defines the state in the modern era.

For Dempsey, the institutionalization of usury means that workers are not adequately compensated for their contributions. Thus, they themselves cannot cultivate the virtue of justice by contributing to a common good. The savings that provide a pool of capital are separated from human activity. It appears as though money fructifies, even though we all know that it cannot.

The fact that Dempsey could position economics as a tradition and then interrogate it with the scholastic tradition of moral theology is itself a great achievement. Dempsey took economists seriously, not as mere accountants but as philosophers of human action. This meant that their work had theological relevance. Although for Dempsey economics has a relative independence, upon which the theologian should not tread, economics and theology can never be thoroughly separated just as no human action can be seen as theologically irrelevant.

## VI   The natural and the theological

Dempsey assessed human action by a normative ethics grounded in the Thomistic tradition. Although this meant that he took seriously the usury proscription, his work was more than an ethics of obligation that posited laws which are to be obeyed. He situated the usury proscription in the social context of a functional economy. Participation in economic life was a theological task. While increased productivity, efficiency, and the production of wealth are important elements of a functional economy, so too is the life of virtue. If the economy, while managing to increase productivity, is incapable of contributing to the life of virtue, then it is a social organization failing to achieve its true and proper end.

Nevertheless, the nature of that true theological end is not adequately set forth in Dempsey's work. As the above analysis of his work reveals, Dempsey assumed that economics can be discussed within the categories of the 'natural,' separate from the theological. His analysis remained within the medieval doctrine of 'pure nature.' In fact, his method for relating theology and economics appeals to the natural law as an impersonal, universal, and objective form of morality.[80] While Dempsey's work maintains residual elements of the Thomistic world, particularly in its functional understanding of the human person, it also sets the stage for the emergence of a *natural* that can be determined by the social sciences *per se*.

An assumption commonly encountered in the work of Catholic moral theologians is that the moral life may be grounded in the natural law alone and thus Catholic moral theology can be divorced from the theological particularities of Catholic theology. Although it was John Courtney Murray's 1962 publication *We Hold These Truths* that popularized this strategy, Dempsey had advocated a similar position decades before him.

Dempsey sought to bring theology and economics into conversation while maintaining the semi-autonomous identity of each discipline.[81] He developed an economic theory from a theological perspective but without his economics assuming his theological convictions.

Like Dempsey, Murray argued that Catholicism's unique contribution to modern life was the natural law. 'Only the theory of natural law,' claimed Murray, 'is able to give an account of the public moral experience that is the public consensus' which he thought America needed: Catholicism has a unique contribution to make to American politics because its ethics are grounded in the natural law. However, 'the doctrine of natural law has no Roman Catholic presuppositions.'[82] This creates the odd situation that the contribution Catholicism makes to the political and civil realm is something separate from and independent of Catholicism itself.

This strategy has become a commonplace among Catholic moral theologians. In fact, it forms a basic method that begins with nature and a philosophy of action, and then moves to supernature and the particularities of theology, Christology, the sacraments, and the theological virtues.[83] It has also resulted in a truncated Thomism because it severs Thomas' moral theory from his theology. It makes the natural law that which integrates morality with Catholic theology when in fact Thomas works in the *opposite* direction. The *lex nova* alone rightly orders morality into theology.

Dempsey, like most Catholic moral theologians, applies Thomism to economics based solely on the natural law. However, unlike Murray and Novak, Dempsey does not argue that modernity was based on the principles of Thomistic natural law rather than on British liberalism. Dempsey traced the rise of the philosophical basis for capitalism to the rise of secular revolutionary movements and the suppression of the Jesuits in 1774, which 'terminated what had been a flourishing system of colleges and universities.' At the precise moment when the industrial revolution required a cultural discourse, one which would keep economics humane, the voice of the church was 'systematically stripped of the cultural resources that would have enabled her to influence the spread of industrialization.'[84] Therefore, the only cultural discourse to guide the industrial revolution was that of liberalism. By liberalism, Dempsey meant the British tradition of classical economics – Adam Smith, Malthus, Ricardo, J. S. Mill, and Karl Marx. Dempsey viewed Marxism not as outside of the tradition of British liberalism but as a variation within it.

Dempsey objected to modern economics for three main reasons. First, it is based on conflict. It assumes that only two classes of people exist – owners and workers. These two classes are viewed as incompatible and in constant conflict. A choice must be made whether we side with the owners against the workers, as most of the classical liberal tradition suggests, or with the workers against the owners, as the Marxist trajectory suggests. Dempsey, following Joseph Schumpeter, suggested that this conflict is an illusory social construct.[85] It does not adequately describe economic reality. In fact, like Schumpeter, Dempsey stated: 'There is no such thing as capitalism.'[86] The concept of 'capital' eludes precise definition. Both its defenders and its critics employ it for ends extrinsic to the actual ways in which property and production work. Dempsey argued that the term itself originated within Marxist analysis, which had the unfortunate consequence of then creating a group of theorists antagonistic to Marxism who set out to defend 'capitalism.' This led to a defense of capitalism that lacked substance. Rather than a defense of private property within the guidelines of medieval theology, this defense secured the practices of an abstract concept which then prevented Catholics from an analysis 'of institutions as they are,' particularly as they need to be governed by 'social justice.' In fact, this defense of capitalism resulted in a defense of 'banking, monetary and fiscal institutions which facilitate the institutional usury by which the benefits of saving are swept to those who have not saved.'[87] If the British liberals' economics of conflict is not to become our only reality, then a different cultural discourse is needed. 'Conflict as a fact and as an immutable principle are quite a different thing,' Dempsey observed.[88]

The second reason Dempsey objected to modern economics is that it is irrational. It is based on a fiction, a false theology of providence. This theology is false because it is a providence by which vices can be miraculously transubstantiated into virtues. This results in a 'piecemeal' economics that works from some sort of divine predestination where possessions are distributed by some inscrutable invisible hand in separation from people's actual labor. Thus, modern economics is much more irrational than was medieval theological economics. 'Not before the Enlightenment could men place their faith in an "invisible guiding hand" that required no human cooperation.... Ends [however] are attained through order not through chaos or competition.'[89] The not-so-divine providence behind modern economics delegates economic matters to a private realm. Medieval society, in contrast to modern society, was 'public and unblushing.'

The third reason Dempsey opposed modern economics is that the cultural discourse on which it depends gives no common consensus to allow for the cultivation of natural virtues that might provide the basis for economic associations.[90] The only social institution on which modernity can depend is the state. In this sense, Dempsey traced the decline of the theological economics of the Middle Ages to the nationalism let loose with the emergence of Protestantism.[91]

Dempsey set up conflicting economies – the economics of modernity against the economics of the medieval world. Unlike Novak, he recognized that modernity involves a decisive rejection of the Thomistic world. Dempsey found that world far superior to the modern one. Yet, despite the conflict between these two economies, they could be brought into conversation because both had their basis in the 'natural law.'

In *Interest and Usury*, Dempsey argued that his comparison of modern with scholastic economic theory was warranted because of the natural law.

Both modern and scholastic economic theory assume the employment of reason alone:

> As far as the radical problem was concerned – is usury wrong, and if so why? and under what conditions is a loan otherwise usurious legitimate? – the answer given was no different than if the canon and civil law and the councils were silent. Not that the medieval writer would not have listened to them respectfully had these sources said something new on this basic subject; but they had not. On a specific contract Lugo chides Scotus for giving as a reason for its unlawfulness that it is forbidden by divine law – 'which is not to the point since the whole wickedness of usury proceeds from the natural law.' By this limitation our unwieldy material can be trimmed to tractable dimensions and, though certain interesting points will thus be lost, we shall be enabled to gain in clarity and precision…. In this way, moreover, our comparison with contemporary writers is facilitated in that there is no irreconcilable conflict of basic principle: both parties proceed from truths known from natural reason alone.[92]

Although Dempsey recognized the conflict between these two economies, the conflict was not incommensurable because both assume 'reason' alone as their basis. This allows Catholic theologians to address economic issues without the loss of any 'basic principle.' The divine law, embodied in canon law and church councils, need not be appealed to in the case of usury because reason alone allows for rational persons to recognize that usury is always wrong. Nature discloses the truth independently of the contingencies of traditional teachings. Dempsey shows that the seeds of the fact–value distinction on the basis of which economics operates antedate Weber; they are found in seventeenth-century scholastic thought where a pure nature is posited and used as the basis for economic teaching.

Dempsey reads a rigid distinction between the natural and divine laws back into Thomas himself. He speaks of access to the natural law via 'natural reason alone.' Because economics depends upon natural reason alone, he can develop an economics that does not depend upon church teaching even when he takes church teaching as the norm. The semi-autonomous nature of economics frees it from any explicit connection to divine law. Thus the relationship between church teaching and economics is the same for Dempsey as his understanding of the relationship between faith and reason. Faith adds nothing to the reasonableness of the proscription against usury.

This is not to suggest that Dempsey was unwilling to abide by the church's teachings without reserve. He was even willing to consider Jesus as the economist par excellence. He wrote: 'We may usefully recall here that Jesus Christ, being God as well as man, was and is a better economist than Adam Smith or John Stuart Mill. Had He chosen to do so He could have taught us all the economics we would ever need to know ...'. But such pious sentiments do little theological work for Dempsey. They only point out that Jesus did not teach us economics and therefore we are free to do so ourselves, but within the general truths Christ did teach which are the 'basic truths about the nature of man and his ultimate destiny.'[93]

Just as Jesus did not give us an economics, nor did St Thomas. Dempsey readily admits that Thomas was no economist. Thomas' development of 'fundamental economic ideas' always occurred as a 'byproduct of some other activity,' particularly his explication of the virtue of justice.[94] But Dempsey left this intriguing insight undeveloped. Instead of recognizing the significance of the need in Thomas' work for a narrative wholeness between theology and economics, Dempsey went about separating out these two areas of discourse and then 'easily and logically' extending Thomas' basic principles to 'this new economic order.'[95] This extension was based upon the premiss that Thomas' fundamental economic ideas are generally accessible synchronically and diachronically because they are based solely in the 'natural law.'

Thomas' economic principles are generally accessible because they depend mainly on 'social justice.'[96] According to Dempsey, social justice is not something new and unique. It is a form of legal justice that goes under the title of 'contributive justice.' Like all the various forms of justice, social justice is a virtue: 'Social justice is the virtue which prompts a man to those acts which contribute to the common good even though they may not be required by positive enactments.' Dempsey finds this virtue of 'social justice' in Thomas' *Summa Theologia* (Ia IIae Q 94), and it arises from basic natural inclinations – self-preservation, sexual procreation, the need to live in community and to provide for one's own needs and the needs of others.[97] It does not require any specific connection to the life of faith.

This article in the *Summa Theologia* (Ia IIae Q 94, art. 2) is the central text used, not only by Dempsey but by other Catholic moral theologians, to find in Aquinas warrant to proceed with certain modes of reasoning independently of specific theological considerations. Here Thomas explicates the 'first precept of the natural law' in response to the question: 'Whether the natural law contains several precepts or one only?' He argues for a *first precept* from which the others are derived. The first precept is that 'good is to be done and pursued and evil is to be avoided.' *Good*, here, has for Thomas the 'nature of an end,' and *evil* the 'nature of a contrary.' Thomas suggests that 'all those things to which man has a natural inclination, are naturally apprehended by reason as being good and consequently as objects of pursuit, and their contraries as evil, and objects of avoidance.' Thomas then suggests an 'order of inclinations' correlative to the 'precepts of the natural law.'

> First of all, an inclination to good in accordance with the
> nature which humanity has in common with all substances:

inasmuch as every substance seeks the preservation of its own being, according to its nature: and by reason of this inclination, whatever is a means of preserving life, and of warding off its obstacles, belongs to the natural law.

Secondly, there is in humanity an inclination to things that pertain to him more specifically according to that nature which he has in common with other animals: and in virtue of this inclination, those things are said to belong to the natural law, which nature has taught to all animals, such as sexual intercourse, education of offspring and so forth.

Thirdly, there is in man an inclination to good, according to the nature of his reason, which nature is proper to him: thus man has a natural inclination to know the truth about God, and to live in society: and in this respect, whatever pertains to this inclination belongs to the natural law; for instance, to shun ignorance, to avoid offending among whom one has to live, and other such things regarding the above inclination.

Dempsey works in the direction of these 'natural inclinations.' His economic theory begins with basic 'elementary drives' all people have in common and proceeds to develop economic theory from these 'natural inclinations.' The first precept of the natural law begins with basic inclinations like self-preservation. To fulfill the precept, God gives human beings 'reason and hands.' Self-preservation forces people to be industrious to provide for themselves. The second natural inclination prompts people to procreate. This necessitates that we live in families. We find ourselves dependent upon others. That dependence broadens by way of our third inclination. To be human is to live in community. These three inclinations are all that Dempsey needs to develop economics. He does not even discuss the natural inclination for truth about God, Thomas' third inclination, for all he needs to do his economic work is the basic 'natural' inclinations to self-preservation, procreation and communal life.

The direction within which Dempsey developed a Thomistic economics has actually reversed Thomas' order and omitted to discuss what is most central to Thomas, the relationship between the New law of the gospel and the old law. What is central and foundational for Thomas is not 'basic elementary drives,' but conformity to God. Question 94 of the *prima secundae* cannot stand alone as a basis for moral action. It fits within a broader discussion of the relation between the New law of the Gospel and the old law, primarily found in the decalogue. To begin moral theology at question 94 in the *prima secundae* disrupts the thematic coherence of the narrative Thomas has been developing. The result is a sundering of nature from the necessity of grace for nature's intelligibility.

## VII  The old and New law

For Thomas, the relationship between the New law and the old is the same as the relationship between grace and the natural law. He maintains throughout the *prima secundae* that the New law is necessary for the natural to be understood *as* natural. A sign of this is found in the very order of the decalogue. The decalogue is the manifestation of the precepts of the natural law.[98] The first command is also first in the order of nature. Thomas stated that

> since the order of reason starts with the end envisaged, what is most contrary to reason is for man to be wrongly oriented to his end. But the end of human life and society is God. Consequently, the precepts of the decalogue had first to direct man to God, since the reversal of this direction would be the worst of disorders.[99]

To be turned toward God in worship and adoration is that which makes us most consonant with nature. Neither self-preservation, sexual procreation, education of the species, nor life in community is naturally prior to worship of God. But herein lies the problem. Although the decalogue (and therefore the natural law) contains all that is sufficient for people to be oriented toward their own end, the end has not adequately elicited our will. In fact, the decalogue itself was given because 'the natural law began to be obscured by reason of the proliferation of sin.' Thus Thomas calls the decalogue an 'intermediary' between the law of nature and the law of grace.[100] This could be confusing if we think of the law of nature as something separate from the law of grace, because Thomas also identifies the decalogue as the law of nature. How can it be both the law of nature and an intermediary between grace and nature? Because the law of nature is obscured and what the New law of the gospel accomplishes is to clarify for us the law of nature.

Thomas takes up the question of whether the divine law works only where human reason fails; in other words, he takes up the question of a two-tiered nature–grace distinction where grace works only when natural reason reaches a dead-end. He asks whether 'the divine law had to come to man's assistance where his human reason failed,' only to reject this understanding of the divine law. Here we have the actual method used by Dempsey, as well as by the scholastics and nearly all exponents of natural theology. We begin with human reason and use it to develop our ethics. When human reason fails, divine law is invoked. But this is not the position of Thomas. He stated: 'It was consistent with the divine law that it should provide for man's needs not only in matters unattainable by reason but in matters in which man's reason may be prevented from its proper function as well.'[101] The authority of the divine law lessens the confusion concerning the natural law.[102] Sacred doctrine helps us understand the natural *as* natural. No two-tiered rationality exists.

The question of the old law, like the question of the natural and the New law, is first and foremost a question about the appropriate ordering of human action to the good.[103] The decalogue is good precisely because it turns people toward their appropriate end – God revealed in Christ: 'For the old law turned men towards Christ in two ways. The first is by bearing witness to Christ.... The second way in which the old law turned men towards Christ was by predisposing them for him in a certain way.' It is this sense of predisposition that helps make most sense of the relationship between the New law and both the natural and the old law. Nature, rightly understood, predisposes one for the truth of God, which is Christ.

To fulfill what is natural, the *lex nova* must elicit our desire so that this order can be maintained, not only in external action but in internal action. Therefore, Thomas could not have meant his three inclinations to be an order which people follow for their perfection. Such an order reverses the order of nature. It would be a state of disorder.

The *lex nova* sets in order a person's actions so that a person is directed toward his or her proper, and ultimate end – the state of blessedness. Thomas makes explicit that the end toward which the New law orders action, and the means by which that end can be achieved, is the vision of blessedness Jesus pronounces in the Sermon on the Mount, entrusted and passed on through the Apostles.[104] This compelling vision orders nature properly, and then requires ongoing human promulgation.[105] This ordering is not merely added to nature in some mysterious sense: it re-directs it by instituting in human history the language and vision of blessedness and by requiring its ongoing institution through human language and act.[106] God takes form in the flesh and that form makes possible God's in-forming all our being and action. The term *lex nova* describes this form. It is not confined to some *super*natural realm: it is that which is added to nature to make it truly *natural* in view of the consequences of sin.

Thomas insists that the reason for the New law was that the old law, i.e. the natural law and the decalogue, contained the appropriate precepts, but not an adequate power to orient our actions toward their true end. Thomas does not argue that the ten precepts are deficient; for his argument has to do with two forms of *actus*, one interior, the other exterior. This is important to bear in mind so that the New law will not be relegated to an inner realm of the person, separate from external action. The *lex nova* needs and builds on the ten precepts. It cannot do without them. It does not separate a person from them. Law and grace are not opposed, or even dialectically related. The New law draws the person more fully into the ten precepts by ordering his or her actions not only externally (which is an unquestionable good) but internally.[107] This internal ordering occurs because the New law produces the desire for the Lord's blessedness, and desire is the first necessary impulse for action. So what we find is not a method that moves from basic, common, human inclinations (nature) to more particular theological considerations (grace), but rather a fuller specification of that which is natural found in the appearance of our true end, the Lord of the Sermon on the Mount pronouncing blessedness.

The New law as the grace that orders nature is not some otherworldly and anti-natural event working through an ineffable theophanous mystery. It is a form that can elicit our vision, and is found in the teaching and the pronouncements entrusted to the apostles. This constitutes a tradition of thought, language, and vision capable of eliciting our will and our reason toward our final end – the God who as Trinity is charity. This vision must necessarily be repeated, and in so doing the natural is graced. The natural alone cannot be the basis for Christian teaching on morality precisely because the natural alone no longer exists (if it ever did) because God has assumed human flesh. In so far as Catholic social teaching recognizes that what is found in *nature* will be the same as that which the New law discloses, it offers to theological reflection on economics the service of overcoming the fiction of a 'natural theology' that falsely assumes a rigid division between nature and *super*nature and provides autonomous space for economic analysis. Such a division, in whatever form it appears – in Scholasticism's two-tiered grace and nature, or in Weber's fact–value distinction – always reduces theology to the non-historical irrational remainder: it becomes that to which appeal can be made when reason fails. In so far as Catholic social teaching assumes that what is found in the 'natural laws' to which economists appeal are reasons sufficient in and of themselves, then the bifurcation between theology and economics remains. Theology will be relegated to the ascribing of 'values' or to fundamental orientation. Little recourse will be had to the end of human life as *super*natural, and thus the theological virtues become irrelevant. Economics can be discussed under the virtue of justice alone. Once the theological virtues are rendered irrelevant, the rules prescribing and proscribing certain actions will lose their signifi- cance and so will appear arbitrary – or, worse yet, they can *be* only arbitrary – insisted upon solely for the sake of the power of some authority.

# 13  Theology and the good

The central place of the New law for the relationship between supernature and nature has been preserved in the present age not so much by theologians as by the philosopher Alasdair MacIntyre. He revealed the formative social assumptions behind the is–ought distinction, which gave rise to the separation between fact and value. A connection exists between MacIntyre's preservation of the New law and his criticism of the is–ought distinction. The New law of the Gospel is an *ought*, or *telos*, that determines and constitutes the *is* of creaturely being. To maintain the logic of the New law, the is–ought distinction must be understood as contingent upon a prior social formation. That an *is* occurs prior to, or separately from, an *ought* is not a necessary feature of human action. If this distinction is not challenged, then the *is* of modern social formations will define the real such that a moral or theological *telos* never disturbs nature-as-it-*is*. But if the is–ought distinction is shown to be something other than a necessary feature of human action, then new possibilities for understanding the sociality of human existence are opened. These new possibilities will be in conflict with modernity and capitalism. They will also allow a greater role for theology and moral philosophy in defining the *is*-ness of human action. Like Dempsey, MacIntyre calls upon the ancient notion of a 'functional economy' as an alternative to modern economics. Unlike Dempsey, MacIntyre recognizes that the *is* of modern economics can be finally challenged only when the *ought* of a theological *telos* re-orders that *is*.

Alasdair MacIntyre is not a theologian: he has produced no theological treatises, and he remains a moral philosopher. We cannot look to his work for an analysis of specific theological themes and their relationship to economics. However, his work is significant for any discussion of the relationship between theology and economics because it makes room for the primacy of the theological virtues over the a-rational attachment of modernity to *values*. MacIntyre's work shows why the dominant and emergent traditions fail as reasonable attempts to relate theology to economics. They are insufficiently opposed to modern values. The formal nature of those values results in formal and bureaucratic efforts to effect change but such changes inevitably arise solely through an assertion of power. Not the reasonableness of a good, true or beautiful life assists us in negotiating economic exchanges, but only the assertion of one will against the other is the basis for such negotiations.[1]

MacIntyre suggests that a 'contemporary vision' based on a Weberian formal rationality sustains the appearance of morality in modernity without its substance. This contemporary vision gives morality a certain coherence, but this coherence is a-rational because it is a formal *rationality* that functions by refusing to order desire to anything other than what the individual wants. We can still use moral language intelligibly, but not substantively, because all morality is now reduced to *values*. This reduction of morality is a result of the ever-encroaching power of the capitalist global economy in every facet of our lives.

MacIntyre may have left his Marxism behind in his turn to Aristotle, St Thomas, and Rome, but not so his trenchant criticisms of capitalism. He does not critique capitalism based on a socio-scientific analysis of its inevitable failures; his critique is a moral one. Capitalism destroys the possibility of a virtuous life because it separates our labor from any meaningful contribution it can make to a common good. Christian theologians can take heart from MacIntyre's analysis because he has led a foray into hitherto sacred territory. He has torn down the walls that rigidly separated academic disciplines from one another and has revealed that, especially when it comes to economics and theology, we are discussing not two different realms but the same realm of human action differently. Both descriptions cannot be correct. MacIntyre finds the theological description of our human action more reasonable than its reduction to value-preferences by the economists. Thus he finds traditional Catholic moral theology's 'functional economy' a compelling alternative to both capitalism and Marxism.

## I  The contemporary vision of an a-rational inheritance

MacIntyre begins his *After Virtue* with a 'disquieting suggestion': after a nuclear devastation a know-nothing movement blames the scientists for the destruction and revolts by burning all books in an effort to destroy the knowledge that has ruined their lives. Later efforts are made to recover this knowledge but the narrative context that would render it intelligible has been lost, perhaps irretrievably. This disquieting suggestion bears a striking resemblance to Walter M. Miller's novel *A Canticle for Leibowitz*. Reading MacIntyre's 'suggestion' in light of that novel illuminates why it is so 'disquieting.'

Miller's novel contrasts conflicting moral traditions that arise after a nuclear holocaust: the 'simpletons' who survive revolt against all knowledge in a frenzied book-burning, and a monastic order that preserves books in the hope that one day the context that rendered those texts intelligible will once again appear. However, they soon discover an unexpected problem. Cultural inheritances are difficult to do without because our lives cannot exist at a level that is fragmented and unintelligible. When one cultural context has been destroyed another soon arises to narrate those fragments into a coherent whole:

> The monks of the earliest days had not counted on the human ability to generate a new cultural inheritance in a couple of generations if an old one is utterly destroyed, to generate it by virtue of lawgivers and prophets, geniuses or maniacs; through a Moses, or through a Hitler, or an ignorant but tyrannical grandfather, a cultural inheritance may be acquired between dusk and dawn, and many have been so acquired. But the new 'culture' was an inheritance of darkness, wherein 'simpleton' meant the same thing as 'citizen' meant the same thing as 'slave.'[2]

In light of Miller's novel, MacIntyre's disquieting suggestion is not simply that our moral language is fragmented. Rather, it is the less obvious and more disquieting idea that we lack the tools with which to recognize our morality's fragmentation because of a new dominant cultural inheritance that bandages up that brokenness, concealing its wounds. MacIntyre alludes to this in the concluding sentences of his disquieting account when he says that

> the language and appearance of morality persist even though the integral substance of morality has to a large degree been fragmented and then in part destroyed. Because of this there is no inconsistency in my speaking ... of contemporary moral attitudes and arguments.[3]

In other words, MacIntyre does not deny that a contemporary agreement on morality exists: modernity is not so fragmented as to be obviously disjointed. Modern morality exists within a contemporary vision, but MacIntyre, like Miller, finds it to be a cultural inheritance of darkness.

MacIntyre does not argue that we live in a wasteland of incommensurability, unable to speak with each other because we lack the contexts that make our moral languages intelligible. His argument is more profound and subtle. Thus the numerous people who have criticized him for exaggerating our fragmentation have missed his point. For instance, Ronald Thiemann appears partially sympathetic to MacIntyre's thesis when he writes:

> It is now clear that America's historic civic piety has disintegrated and that no new public philosophy has arisen to take its place. Consequently we live among fragments of shattered moral and religious traditions, no one of which has yet shown its ability to provide a basis for our common public life. Some commentators – most notably Alasdair Mac-Intyre – have suggested that our moral disagreements are so profound that we will never reach consensus on the most basic policy issues.[4]

But this misses MacIntyre's point, and can too easily lead to the fascist conclusion that the only remedy we have is for one tradition to impose its dominance over the others. Because no reasonable person wants that alternative, liberalism is viewed as the lesser of two evils. We remain trapped in a false dualism: either liberalism or fascism. But when we recognize the subtlety of MacIntyre's disquieting suggestion, then the either–or of fascism or liberalism loses its persuasive power. MacIntyre does not argue that we cannot reach consensus on public policy issues and therefore that we must reassert by power one dominant tradition over all others; rather he argues that we have no '*rational* way of securing moral agreement in our culture.'[5] We have no *rational* way to do so because of an overarching consensus in our culture about basic policy issues that 'obliterates any genuine distinction between manipulative and non-manipulative social relations.'[6] A dominating tradition is already present.

The threat to moral reasoning is not, as Thiemann suggests, 'that America's historic civic piety has disintegrated and that no new public philosophy has arisen to take its place.' The threat to moral reasoning is that America's public consensus has not disintegrated enough and thus the narrative rendering intelligible our moral language conceals its manipulative character. We have a public consensus, and it is embodied in dominant social characters, particularly the bureaucrat–manager. But this consensus and its social embodiment is a-rational – a form of will to power concealed behind a formalized Weberian rationality.

The greater part of MacIntyre's *After Virtue* does not focus on moral fragmentation so much as on the homogenizing effect of our 'contemporary vision.' He returns to this 'contemporary vision' in the key chapter 'Nietzsche or Aristotle?' which he begins by stating: 'The contemporary vision of the world is predominantly, although not perhaps always in detail, Weberian.' This is because 'we know of no organized movement towards power which is not bureaucratic and managerial in mode and we know of no justifications for authority which are not Weberian in form.' To anyone who objects that MacIntyre has erred by finding in our putatively multi-differentiated and pluralistic society a single, all-embracing, contemporary vision, he states: 'belief in an irreducible plurality of values is itself an insistent and central Weberian theme.'[7] MacIntyre reveals how modern morality and theology conceal our moral fragmentation behind the apparent reasonableness of value-free facts mediated to us by socio-scientific experts. Those experts are the economists whose 'logic' is taken for granted by those in key posts in the government, in educational institutions, and right through the public arena to the leadership of the church. These managers are neither liberal nor conservative, neither radical nor traditionalist; they are the product of a new cultural inheritance wherein all of life, including moral and theological life, is reduced to 'value' and we all become consumers.

Perhaps the best image for this new cultural inheritance is the food court at the mall, where difference is affirmed: as many 'cultures' are represented as is possible. Food is available from places all over the world and is even served by persons from those ethnic backgrounds in traditional dress. From the inside, it appears as though no single culture has gained dominance. Everyone is welcome; all are included. But such 'difference' is utterly illusory. The presentation of a pluralistic society is necessary to conceal the reality that all this difference is contained by a formal edifice that can be entered only if one has assumed the role of consumer. Consumers move about the food court sampling different cultural products only because all these products now have the status of a formal (and therefore a form*less* ) value potential of being exchanged. Behind the apparent multi-cultural difference in the food court lies the singular power of the owners of the formal edifice. Their power is now dispersed through the various cultures, but it is still *their* power and interests that this multi-cultural formation serves. For MacIntyre, Weber's formal rationality supports this social formation.

Chapter 9 of MacIntyre's *After Virtue*, 'Either Nietzsche or Aristotle,' would perhaps have been better titled 'Either Weber or Nietzsche or Aristotle.' For the latter two options are necessary only because the first describes contemporary reality. Why is Weber to blame for our cultural inheritance of darkness? Because Weberian rationality 'disguises and conceals rather than illuminates and it depends for its power on its success at disguise and concealment.'[8] Once this passes for reasonableness, then the social embodiment that bears this rationality will be found in technicians, i.e. the sociologists, psycho-therapists and bureaucrat–managers who take the value-free facts and use them to produce human action in predictable ways. Weber creates law-like generalizations that supposedly govern human action and generate predictive power. The assumption behind this worldview is that things are constantly changing and the only way to negotiate the future is to develop the skills to predict it and then manage change accordingly through the formal and natural laws that the social scientist discovers, laws that are independent of any commitments, beliefs, or traditional practices. The social scientists provide the occasion to manage objectively and impersonally such that the person implementing the policy is merely doing what the *facts* require. To what end does one manage? What good, true, or beautiful form of life is possible in this world? This question becomes not only unanswerable but no longer possible. Management takes place solely for what is useful, i.e. for the congruence between a person's actions and interests. But which person? Whose interest finally predominates? Because the rational has become associated with the useful and someone's interest, the rational loses all connection to any teleological understanding of human life. The result is a formal power in service to someone's utility calculations for reasons that are difficult to establish.[9]

The new cultural inheritance of darkness that renders intelligible our broken moral language and conceals its fundamentally a-rational nature is the language of economics. It is the market's values that relegate morality to a private space of value preference. It advocates the universality of its own formal rationality, and it constantly encroaches on new territories, defining and delimiting their possibilities.

## II   Morality and theology as private value preference

A brief look at any introductory economics textbook will reveal the congruence that obtains between a marginalized morality and the economistic advocacy of a rigid fact–value distinction. Mansfield's popular *Principles of Macroeconomics* begins, as nearly all such textbooks do, with a distinction between 'positive economics' and 'normative economics.' Positive economics appeals to 'facts.' Normative economics appeals to 'values or preferences'; terms which, for Mansfield, function interchangeably to describe any concern for 'what *ought* to be.' Morality is based on individual value preference. Positive economics describes what *is*. Normative economics describes what we would wish life to be. The latter has its place, suggests Mansfield, but the economists' task is to describe, first and foremost, what is, not what ought to be.

But Mansfield's text has erroneously bifurcated the moral and the economic life, concealing this error behind the fact–value distinction. This bifurcation arises because no substantive knowledge of either moral philosophy or theology has been incorporated into his analysis. Moral philosophy and theology are relegated to evaluation: they are concerned with what *ought* to be. But in this analysis 'what ought to be' is not an intrinsic feature of creation, but rather a function of individual preference. Thus morality and theology are reduced to value consumption. The result is that economics positions the logic of theology within its own fact–value logic. This overlooks the similarities obtaining between economics, morality, and theology. Moral theology traditionally has been defined as the 'science of human action.' Likewise, economics is nothing but a science of human action. Thus, moral theology and economics are not two distinct disciplines each with its own autonomous realm. Both function as descriptions of human action.

Perhaps only John Maynard Keynes among the economists has glimpsed the reality of this point. He recognized that economics was primarily a moral science.[10] It gives a vision of how humans do and should act in the world and then seeks to transform those actions into a global 'economic' vision. Keynes' moral science had little to do with the 'economic' vision of traditional Christian theology. In fact, the rise of economics and the dominance of socio-scientific models celebrated the 'death of God.'[11] But Keynes recognized at least that economists and moral theologians were discussing the same thing – human action. As we have seen, Keynes sought even to coopt the Christian tradition for his own modest economic 'revolution.'

Many, if not most, economists, however, have not advanced to Keynes' basic insight. Mansfield, for example, settles the debate between economists and moral theologians by retreating to Weber's value-free world of formal rationality. He suggests an account of human economic action that can describe the *facts* independently of historical, moral, political, or theological considerations. But the account of human action that drives his positive economics is identical to the account of human action that he asserts to be the basis for normative economics. Positive (fact-oriented) economics works on the assumption that individuals make choices based on their preferences. As we saw with the marginalist revolution, this insight provides economics with its 'scientific' basis. Normative (value-oriented) economics works on the assumption that morality is concerned with individuals making choices based on their preferences. Both positive and normative economics assume the moral agency of an individual who 'legislates for himself in matters of value.' In both cases, the economist frees himself from judgments on the content of those choices. An economic analysis requires no underlying 'value' commitments. But this is obviously wrong.

Mansfield has misled us in telling us that his portrayal of positive economics does not seek to 'convert us to a particular set of values.' Instead, he suggests that positive economics teaches us 'how to obtain better solutions to economic problems, whatever set of values you may have.'[12] Here the damage is done. Generations of unsuspecting students are introduced into a specific form of the moral life under the pretense that it is value-free and neutral. We should not be surprised that in a capitalist society this account of human agency encroaches on the moral–theological realm and defines all moral agency in terms of value preference. For anyone with a minimal training in moral philosophy can recognize the error in Mansfield's argument. His account of human agency is far from morally neutral. It advocates a particular tradition of moral agency wherein the moral life is a matter of choices, which are then indexed to reveal what is good in terms of the pleasures we seek or the pains we avoid. John Stuart Mill, like Adam Smith a *moral philosopher*, writes the script for Mansfield's science of human action. His economics makes sense only within that particular moral tradition. But Mansfield seems incapable of recognizing that he, too, is a moral philosopher working out of a contingent and historical tradition. We do not have a distinction between facts and values, but conflicting traditions about the questions that should be asked when describing human actions: what narrative should render those actions intelligible, and which social institutions (i.e. the market and corporation or the church) should we serve? For human action never merely arises as an isolated event; it is always already bound by interpretive conditions – which in turn are bound by social institutions historically embedded – such that *facts* are intelligible only on the basis of those interpretative conditions.

MacIntyre's work re-situates the economic question. He challenges the distinction between the *is*-ness of the world (its facticity) and its *oughtness* (its evaluation). He does so by recovering the notion of a 'functional concept' in Aristotle. That is to say, if we recognize the *is*-ness of things as already embodying a particular goodness, then *is*-ness is a function of a thing's *ought*-ness. For instance, a maple seed is what it is not simply because it has being *qua* being, but because it has present within it the potential for a perfection – it ought to become a maple tree. Likewise, a human person is what she is based upon what a good person ought to be. We cannot describe something's *is*-ness without reference to its function within its movement toward its goodness. As MacIntyre puts it: 'To call something good therefore is also to make a factual statement.'[13] Likewise, economics cannot be understood merely as a neutral socio-scientific discipline that gives us the facts no matter what our values might be. Factual statements already assume a particular evaluation of the ends our necessary daily exchanges should embody. The *is* arises from its participation in the possibility of perfection. This is inescapable even though factual descriptions can be hidden behind fictive *teloi*, such as utility. Such a fictive end always speaks in formal terms such as 'economic growth,' or 'opportunity cost.' MacIntyre's turn to Catholicism and a functional account of human nature seeks to recover a different end grounded in a 'functional economy.'

## III   The functional economy

In the 1995 'Introduction' to his 1953 publication *Christianity and Marxism*, MacIntyre draws upon Catholic moral theology's 'functional economy,' although he does not use that term. First, he honors those Christian laity and clergy 'who recognized relatively early the systematic injustices generated by nascent and developed commercial and industrial capitalism.'[14] Then he explains that systematic injustice:

> The relationship of capital to labour is such that it inescapably involves an entirely one-sided dependence, except insofar as labour rebels against its conditions of work. The more effective the employment of capital, the more labour becomes no more than an instrument of capital's purposes and an instrument whose treatment is a function of the needs of long-term profit maximization and capital formation. The relationships which result are the impersonal relationships imposed by capitalist markets upon all those who participate in them. What is necessarily absent in such markets is any justice of desert. Concepts of a just wage and a just price necessarily have no application to transactions within those markets.... It becomes impossible for workers to understand their work as a contribution to the common good of a society which at the economic level no longer has a common good, because of the different and conflicting interests of different classes.[15]

The impersonal relationships of the capitalist market constitute the cultural inheritance that we should resist for the sake of a good life. MacIntyre's own philosophical development from Marxism to Catholicism does not leave behind his 1953 work. In fact, the later work is a reasonable development of those earlier critiques.

As early as 1953 MacIntyre argued that Marxism required some foundation other than the supposedly socio-scientific one that Marx and Engels had provided it with: Marxism was 'unintelligible' without a 'secularized version of Christian virtue.' Likewise, it needed a teleological understanding of human nature that functioned as a critique of the contemporary accepted vision of what it is to be human, assuming as that vision does an individual who 'legislates for himself in matters of value.'[16] This alternative teleological Marxist understanding was to be mediated through a social understanding of human action.[17] However, suggested MacIntyre, these insights of Marxism have been left undeveloped and, in turn, like capitalism Marxism became concerned merely with future consequences of action rather than with intelligible action based on a functional concept of human nature. Thus, it failed to provide a serious alternative to liberalism's utilitarianism, which absorbed the Marxist analysis time and time again. This occurred despite the fact that Marxism rejected liberalism's sense of moral agency.

Marxism fails to provide an adequate alternative to the contemporary vision. It poses an ineffectual challenge to the dominance of the social sciences and the reduction of the moral life to a formalized value preference. MacIntyre's analysis helps us recognize why a soft nihilism pervades our lives. Morality has become a private choice, and thus one person should not judge the morality of another person. MacIntyre, however, does much more than merely lament these deplorable circumstances: he explains why they are so entrenched in the modern world. Modern rationality works at crossed purposes: it produces and thrives on managerial modes of 'rationality' and then appears surprised that the moral life has become reduced to those same forces. Only when we can recognize the conflictual natures and the incommensurability of the economic and moral descriptions of human action will we make any dent in the soft nihilism that protects against a cultivation of a virtuous life. Such a recognition is difficult to achieve because it requires acknowledging the need to reconstruct the social order based on substantive notions of the good.

Catholics once spoke of the 'reconstruction of the social order.'[18] Such language suggested that the economy should be a function of the working person and not the working person a function of the economy. Thus an inevitable tension existed between capitalism, with its wage-contract (and its contemporary manifestation known as 'downsizing'), and what Catholics called 'the functional economy.' This tension seems to have been relaxed in recent years, as Catholics have become consumed by modernity's central economic question – *either* capitalism *or* socialism – in an attempt to produce a universal economic vision. Now that the former has won, many

Catholic theologians operate as if no tension existed between capitalism and Catholicism's functional economy. We seldom hear of the need for a reconstruction of the social order among Catholics these days. Instead, we find essays in the *Wall Street Journal* applauding Catholic teaching for its pluralistic accommodation of capitalism. Robert A. Sirico writes of 'The Bishop's Big Economic Tent' and states: 'To the joy of Catholics who support capitalist institutions, the US bishops have at long last applied the principle of ecumenism to economic issues.' He explains why they have done this by quoting from their ten-point 'Catholic Framework for Economic Life,' published ten years after their letter 'Economic Justice for All.' Sirico suggests that the first principle – 'The economy exists for the person, not the person for the economy' – is somehow an endorsement of capitalism because it recognizes that 'the economy is, in the first instance, made up of individuals who act, choose, and plan for the future.'[19] Marginalism becomes consistent with Catholic social teaching. But this is a profound distortion of the ancient Catholic notion of the functional economy. This first principle is not, as Sirico suggests, an endorsement of the economists' marginalist rationality. It is the traditional way of expressing both Aristotle's and Thomas Aquinas' point that the economy should be in service to human beings who are moral, political, and theological actors, not merely consumers of values.

Sirico's essay does not understand the idea of the functional economy in Catholic teaching. The functional economy is not consistent with marginalism. It is quite different. The 1995 'Introduction' to *Christianity and Marxism* illustrates this difference in the way MacIntyre writes against capitalism on the basis that 'concepts of a just wage and a just price necessarily have no application to transactions within those markets.... It becomes impossible for workers to understand their work as a contribution to the common good of a society which at the economic level no longer has a common good.'[20] This – work understood by those who do it as a contribution to the common good of society – is a description of the functional economy. MacIntyre's turn to Rome is not incidental to his critique of capitalism.

Perhaps MacIntyre best describes the need for Roman Catholicism's narrative framework in his 'How Can We Learn what *Veritatis Splendor* Has to Teach Us?'[21] There he notes that what philosophy 'is and what it can legitimately hope to achieve has to be understood in the light afforded by the Christian Gospel.'[22] Needless to say, this is an unusual admission for a twentieth-century philosopher to make. This does not mean that philosophy must be absorbed by theology, only that it must recognize that the natural is not self-interpreting outside of a theological narrative. MacIntyre states:

> Part of what we have to learn, or rather to relearn, from *Veritatis Splendor* is that, at least so far as the fundamental and central precepts of the moral law are concerned, the truths about those precepts declared

to us by God through Moses and the prophets, in the revelation by Jesus Christ of the New law and in the teaching of the Catholic Church, culminating in this very encyclical, are no other than the truths to which we have already assented as rational persons, or rather to which we would have assented, if we had not been frustrated in so doing by our own cultural, intellectual and moral errors and deformations.[23]

Grace then perfects, completes, and 'corrects' nature. To explain human nature, descriptions of human action must be open to the teaching of Moses and Jesus' New law. And this means that they must be open to the fact that certain actions are never to be performed based on their presumed usefulness alone because the useful cannot be prior to the true, the good, and the beautiful. But this is precisely what the marginalist rationality of the economists cannot tolerate. For that rationality assumes that we do, and we should, act on the basis of weighing perceived foreseeable benefits against perceived foreseeable harms – without explicit knowledge of what a true, a good, and a beautiful life is. Such an account of human action can only conflict with the theological tradition that sees in the teaching of Moses and the New law of Jesus the appropriate ordering of our desires for the sake of charity, justice, and the common good.

The functional economy is intelligible only on the assumption that the church's teaching of a just wage and its endorsement of labor as both a personal and necessary vocation are not value suggestions to be consumed by individuals who *might* prefer them.[24] These teachings describe the good order of justice and charity for which creation exists. A just wage is what employers owe employees. According to Leo XIII's encyclical, *Rerum Novarum*, a just wage is one that 'ought not to be in any way insufficient for the bodily needs of a temperate and well-behaved worker.'[25] Leo XIII's advocacy of the just wage preserved a tradition that arose from Thomas Aquinas.

Thomas takes the example of wages for services rendered to explain the importance of *ius* as the object that determines the virtue of justice.[26] Thomas takes up the question of whether the human will alone can make something *ius*. He argues that through 'common agreement' the will can make something 'just' provided that it does not conflict with natural *ius*. Natural *ius* provides the created form within which exchanges can be ruled as justly proportionate to one another. In fact, Thomas follows Aristotle in arguing that 'justice is first of all and more commonly exercised in voluntary exchanges of things, such as buying and selling, wherein those expressions are properly employed; and yet they are transferred to all other matters of justice.'[27] Justice arises from the necessary practice of exchanges: it is preeminently known in these practices. It should be based on natural *ius*, but we do not know what that is without these practices and the prudence to determine how such practices embody *ius*. Unlike Aristotle, Thomas then relates all of these practices to charity. Any injustice, such as denying a just wage, is unjust precisely because it does not allow our will its proper movement, which is to be turned *toward* a neighbor. Thus all injustice is contrary to charity: charity makes justice intelligible.[28] A just wage is necessary because of this functional understanding of human exchanges.

While Thomas recognizes an important place for the will in exchanges, he does not argue that the will alone provides the basis for ownership, as is the case for liberalism. As the just wage was developed in Catholic social teaching, it did merge with this liberal understanding of property rights. For instance, John Ryan argued that the just wage was based on three principles:

> The first is that God created the earth for the sustenance of all His children; therefore, that all persons are equal in their inherent claims upon the bounty of nature.... The second is that the inherent right of access to the earth is conditioned upon, and becomes actually valid through, the expenditure of useful labour.... The two foregoing principles involve as a corollary a third principle: the men who are in present control of the opportunities of the earth are obliged to permit reasonable access to these opportunities by persons who are willing to work.[29]

Here the just wage teaching and liberalism begin to merge. Although the first principle provides a functional account of exchange within which they must occur, the latter two assume the priority of the will as determining ownership. Ryan's second principle qualifies the first. Now creation is shared only through the individual laborer's will. Locke triumphs over Thomas and what is lost is the virtue of charity to which the laws of justice regulating these exchanges should direct our actions.

The principle of the just wage assumes that to hire someone to work as a laborer for a wage that is less than sufficient for the worker's daily sustenance and that of her or his family plus enough to then contribute to the common good is intrinsically evil. The necessity of daily labor would not be ordered to a charitable life. To deny a just wage would be to violate the seventh commandment, 'You shall not steal.' It is 'unjustly taking or keeping the goods of one's neighbor and wronging him with respect to his goods.'[30] Thus wage contract negotiations alone cannot determine a just remuneration. The moral life is not based on value judgments that people make based on individual preferences. The moral life has an objective reality over and against us to which we must conform, and not vice versa. This reality is best known through the teachings of the church, but it is also reasonable. Because God has so construed the world, any achievement of a common good can occur only when this teaching is honored.

For MacIntyre there is no neutral realm to appeal to in order to adjudicate the differences between descriptions of human action within the market, on the one hand, and the church, on the other. No 'public' space can objectively mediate the conflict – no secure realm of 'facts,' independent of the narratives and social institutions that render those facts intelligible, exists. Thus *either* the church and its spokespersons *or* the contemporary market and its spokespersons must finally persuade us. To begin to acknowledge that they describe our actions in incommensurable ways is itself to begin to challenge the cultural inheritance of darkness. The 'unity' of the contemporary vision is called into question. To appeal to virtue is to challenge 'value.'

Because workers' labor is unintelligible in capitalist societies in terms of a 'contribution to the common good,' the prospect of labor's exercise being viewed as a training in virtue is rendered limited if not out of the question. Capitalist modes of production separate a person's labor from her just rewards and from her contribution to a community's good. A worker who is a faithful and conscientious employee of a company for the majority of her life is not viewed as contributing to that company such that she has produced its good with her labor and her labor marks that corporation with her identity. Instead, the goods of that company are owned by owners and consumers (that is, those consumers whose holdings of stock in a company constitute part-ownership). No intrinsic connection exists between a laborer's identity, even over a complete lifetime, and the good of the corporation. In fact, the goods of the owners and owner consumers actually conflict with the goods of the laborers. Thus, the relationship between a person and what is proper to him or her (including both virtue and property) excludes a proper exercise of both virtue and property.[31] One's property is not a function of one's work, but of one's consumption. What someone *does* is not rewarded, but what someone buys or sells is. The rewards to consumers for buying and selling are based neither on any goodness intrinsic to the products bought and sold nor on the relationship of those products to the goodness of the human labour required in their production. Consumers are rewarded solely for understanding (guessing correctly?) the formal mechanics of the marketplace. Proper exercise of one's property would assume some intrinsic connection between one's character and one's labor. Without this connection, virtue is seldom possible.[32]

Virtue assumes 'goods internal' to certain 'forms of activity' which can be 'realized' through one's participation in those forms of activity.[33] Internal goods cannot be scarce. Any person's possession of such goods contributes to the good of all the participants in a particular community.[34] These internal goods differ from external goods because the latter do not achieve the good of the whole community, but are achieved at the expense of others. They are antagonistic. Yet for internal goods to flourish some connection must exist between them and external goods. This is where capitalist societies create problems for the cultivation of virtue. Because the success and advancement of capitalist societies have little if any bearing on the relation of the internal goods of participants in those societies to their achievement of external goods, such societies make the exercise of virtue difficult. External goods are widely available, but the efficient production of these external goods lacks connection with internal goods. Without some connection between internal and external goods virtue is difficult to cultivate.

But how would we know what relationship should exist between internal and external goods? Why shouldn't a CEO be disproportionately reimbursed in comparison to the person who cleans his toilet? Here is where historical tradition becomes important. Internal goods depend on an acknowledgment that our lives are embedded in histories and traditions that give us the resources to be moral agents. Without historical traditions, there are no internal goods. Without acknowledging that my life comes as a gift already embedded in a narrative, I cannot be an adequate moral agent. I lose the practices that make possible a virtuous life. But capitalism denies this sense of embeddedness. Neither the pursuit nor the production of goods is 'intelligible in terms of the larger and longer history of the tradition through which the practice in its present form was conveyed to us.'[35] Instead, the production of goods is viewed as a unique process that subverts and destroys the old by introducing to the process of production an element new and hitherto unknown.[36] Capitalist societies deny that laborers' identities are embedded in the histories of their own corporations. The practice of work lacks tradition.

By recovering the 'narrative phenomenon of embedding,' MacIntyre calls us to account for those inheritances that contribute to the narrative unity of our lives, in their potential for both vice and virtue. This recovery of the narrative unity of life should include an acknowledgment of the embeddedness of a laborer's work in the common good of a corporate community. But this is precisely what is not recognized when wealth is supposedly produced either by the introduction of completely new ideas (new growth theory) or by managing class antagonisms to favor the employment of capital (classical liberalism).

Once the narrative phenomenon of embedding is lost, traditional moral rules about economics either become unintelligible or are transmuted to serve new interests. This is precisely what has occurred within the Christian tradition: rules such as the just wage, the prohibition of usury, and specific forms of the admonition not to steal are no longer viable for us. All we have are the fragments of these rules, but we lack the narrative context within which they could be intelligible. For these rules to make sense, we must recover the theological narrative out of which they arise.

MacIntyre's virtue ethic sets him at odds with capitalism because capitalism is a form of traditioning that refuses to acknowledge its history. For a similar reason his virtue ethic sets him at odds with the poststructuralists. Their efforts to subvert, disrupt, expose and interrupt the inherited totalities do not fundamentally challenge modern economic configurations. The denial of any continuity to personal identity lodges no objection to the disacknowledgment of the narrative phenomenon of embedding.[37] Creative destruction poses no threat to a capitalist economy.

## IV   The church's virtues

An alternative to capitalism's inability to produce virtue could be embodied in a community capable of recognizing its inheritances, both virtuous and vicious. Such an alternative can be found in 'the rationality of traditions.' A tradition is by definition an acknowledgment of an inheritance. The logic of a tradition eschews both the illusion of modernist self-made individuals (especially the entrepreneur) and postmodernist linguistic revolutionaries exploiting fissures in the totalities. As a participant in a tradition I need not destroy to create; I can instead discover, confess, repent, and constantly seek the unity of reconciliation that might give my life integrity. Although MacIntyre has not himself developed a theological economics, he points us in a direction where traditional rules can be made intelligible through their relationship to a virtuous life.

The sources for a Christian economy are the virtues of charity and justice, the practices of baptism, repentance, and reconciliation, the narrative of God's self-revelation in Jesus, and his continual presence in the life of the church. These three sources are not fundamentally different, for they all assume the centrality of Jesus and of the theological virtues.

### The centrality of Jesus

For Christians, a good human life is discovered in the blessedness pro-nounced by Jesus in the Sermon on the Mount. All of our actions are to be directed toward such beatitude. For only a blessed life can be an ultimately happy and useful life – useful within the context of the divine economy. Jesus' blessings are eschatological verifications of forms of life pleasing to God. One of the best articulations of this vision is that of Thomas Aquinas who takes these blessings as the heart of a Christian social ethic:

> [The] discourse given by the Lord on the Mount contains all that a Christian needs to conduct his life. In it man's interior motions are perfectly regulated. For after announcing blessedness as the end, and recommending the dignity of the Apostles by whom the Gospel teaching was to be promulgated, he regulated man's interior motions, firstly in regard to himself and secondly in regard to his neighbor.[38]

The Lord of the Sermon on the Mount pronouncing blessedness is the central image of the moral life. This vision properly orders nature, but it is a nature that is embedded in a contingent historical tradition, beginning with the Apostles' promulgation.

For Thomas, we cannot fully embody perfect moral virtue without the gift of grace, which is the New law of the Gospel. This New law is the life of Jesus present to the community of faith through his ongoing presence mediated by the Holy Spirit. The significance of Jesus for economics is not merely that he gives rules, but that he himself rules. He orders a person's actions so that she is directed toward her proper and ultimate end – the love of God – through her participation in his life. Contained within this proper end is an order of one's life to one's neighbor. Thus a properly oriented moral action will be congruent with the order of charity.

### The virtues of charity and justice

Charity is not a formal principle; it names the relationship between the Father and the Son through the Holy Spirit, in which by grace we can participate. Charity is the life of God and it is the structure on which creation rests. Because of this we should not be surprised that Thomas explains the order of charity before he discusses the natural virtue of justice. This is significant, because under the virtue of justice Thomas develops rules for ordering economic relations. However, these rules cannot be explained by the natural virtue of justice alone: they also require the supernatural virtue of charity. This fundamentally qualifies the ancients' political economy.[39]

Thomas' discussion of justice begins with the traditional Roman definition, as articulated by the jurist Ulpian, in which justice is the rendering to each person his or her due. Consistently with this classical definition, Thomas defines justice as 'some work adequate to another according to some mode of equality.'[40] Justice, then, is a right ordering based on some rule for recognizing the equality obtaining between people and things. However, Thomas drastically alters this order by finding the ultimate good to which all things are to be ordered to exist outside of human nature, in God. This poses a serious problem to the traditional rendering of justice. As MacIntyre notes, Aquinas does not find our ultimate good related to any 'state available in this created world.' Instead, Thomas draws upon scripture to argue that the *summum bonum* is God. This could leave the soul finding itself 'directed beyond all finite goods, unsatisfiable by those goods, and yet able to find nothing beyond them to satisfy it,' and thus in a state of 'permanent dissatisfaction.'[41] This permanent dissatisfaction was exacerbated in Thomas' understanding of the moral life because of 'a rooted tendency to disobedience in the will and distraction by passion which causes obscuring of the reason and on occasion systematic cultural deformation.' However, suggests MacIntyre, rather than leading to despair or the loss of any intelligible conception of human nature,

> it is in fact this discovery of willful evil which makes the achievement of the human end possible. How so? The acknowledgment by oneself of radical defect is a necessary condition for one's reception of the virtues of faith, hope and charity. It is only the kind of knowledge which faith provides, the kind of expectation which hope provides, and the capacity for friendship with other human beings and with God which is the outcome of charity which can provide the other virtues with what they

need to become genuine excellences, informing a way of life in and through which the good and the best can be achieved. The self-revelation of God in the events of the scriptural history and the gratuitous grace through which that revelation is appropriated, so that an individual can come to recognize his or her place within that same history, enable such individuals to recognize also that prudence, justice, temperateness and courage are genuine virtues, that the apprehension of the natural law was not illusory, and that the moral life up to this point requires to be corrected in order to be completed but not displaced.[42]

Repentance gives our lives integrity by preparing us to receive the virtues of faith, hope, and charity. These virtues come to us as a gift and not as an achievement. They do not arise from our own integrity, but through confession of our lives' lack of continuity. This point in MacIntyre challenges Milbank's argument that MacIntyre remains too indebted to antique virtue and its understanding of virtue as a self-possession. Rather than self-possession, the moral life comes as gift based upon an acknowledgment that we can never securely possess our own integrity. But this does not imply that we have only a forensic righteousness. These infused virtues must be our own if they are to be truly infused; otherwise *super*nature and nature remain bifurcated. While they are our own, they are so only as more than our own. They are a participation in the life of God, an inexhaustible source of goodness.

Faith gives the knowledge that our lives can be recognized within God's life. Hope expects continuity, constancy, and permanence. Charity establishes friendship with God and our neighbor. Once our lives are founded on these grace-infused virtues, then we can properly order the natural virtues. Natural virtues alone, such as justice, courage or prudence, cannot establish a Christian economic ethic. The rules that justice advocates assume the narrative of God's self-revelation, our full knowledge of which requires the infusion of faith, hope, and charity. This is God's economy: it comes as gift, and it is present in the material practices of the sacraments.

### Baptism, repentance, and communion–reconciliation

In baptism we receive faith, through which we recognize our place in God's economy. This recognition is sealed, strengthened, and renewed in the celebration of the Eucharist. The blessed meal is our participation in the life of God, and all of our life is to have its intelligibility from the centrality of that meal. Such a meal makes us holy and cultivates in us the practice of *koinonia*, which is both our communion around the table and our communion with God.

*Koinonia* can be translated as participation, fellowship or communion. The narrative contexts for this virtue are found in the Acts of the Apostles (2:43–7 and 4:32–7) and in the Second Letter of Peter (1:4). These passages convey the double movement of a Christian economy wherein our communal life with our neighbors is a participation in the life of God and our life with God is a participation in the communal life of our neighbors. In the Acts' passages, as a response to Peter's preaching of the Gospel, people are converted and the result of the life of faith is 'they held all things *koinâ*' (2:44). This is not surprising, because we have already been told that these new believers devoted themselves to the apostles' *koinonia*. Precisely what this devotion to *koinonia* is, we do not know. However, a description of it is found in Acts 4:32, where it is related to a believer's relationship with her or his property:

> Now the whole group of those who believed were of one heart and soul, and no one claimed private ownership of any possessions, but every-thing they owned was held in common.

The contrast here is between holding our property *idion* – as our own – and holding all things *koinâ* – in common. The former speaks of one's property as one's own, and implies the antique virtue of self-possession. The latter is to hold one's property as a participation within the community of faith, as a gift and not a self-possession. It is a life of *koinonia*, of participation in a community mediated by the way one uses one's property.

The term *koinonia* refers to one's participation in the community of faith, but it is at the same time a participation in the life of God. For when Second Peter informs us that all things have been given to us which we need for life and godliness, he reminds us that all of what is given us is so that we might be *koinonia* of the divine nature. But this participation in the life of God includes not only what is needed for a pious and spiritual life but what is needed for life itself – *zoên* – as well as *eusebias* (piety). The things necessary here are not only spiritual or there would be no need to include the *zoên* with the *eusebias*. Participation in the life of God is at the same moment a concrete, material participation in the life of one's neighbor. This double movement of the life of charity finds its ultimate expression in the sacrament of the Eucharist.

The virtue of a charitable justice should find its measure of equality in the communion practiced at the Eucharist. The Eucharist is a meta-practice that renders intelligible a Christian's daily activities of producing and consuming. What we discover embedded in the Eucharist is a glimpse and foretaste of the ultimate good for God's creation, which is God himself. Such resources are neither scarce nor subject to competition, but everyone can be satisfied and each person's satisfaction only increases that of her neighbor. Christ is inexhaustible. Distribution is made subject only to the condition of one's baptism and one's willingness to repent and seek reconciliation. There need be no poor among us.

A Christian economy assumes a life of charity ordered toward God and one's neighbor. Such a discovery will entail also a broader conception of the moral life; we then recognize that the natural law is not illusory. But this broader conception of the moral life is not separate from its theological particularities. The second table of the decalogue cannot be rendered intelligible separately from the first table. In fact, the negative commands of the second table assume the virtues implicit in the first table, otherwise the negative commands become 'arbitrary prohibitions.'[43] This means that commands such as 'do not steal' and 'do not covet your neighbor's possessions' cannot in and of themselves be the condition for an economic ethic. Instead, they require the virtues of faith, hope, and especially charity for their intelligibility.[44] And these virtues assume a particular narrative, the narrative of God's revelation in Jesus. The gifts of the theological virtues are necessary for moral virtue. And since justice assumes the significant practice of economic exchange, faith, charity, and hope as *theological* virtues become central for a right ordering of the economy.

A just ordering of economic life assumes the order of charity. This assumption entails the specifics of Christian theology, for charity is not natural to us. As Thomas put it, 'charity, since it greatly exceeds proportion to human nature, does not depend on any natural virtues, but only on the grace of the Holy Spirit infusing it.'[45] A problem is here posed for moral agency, because this could be misconstrued to suggest that the human will is either forced to be charitable or else reduced to the status of a mere instrument for the Spirit's activity. Thomas rejects both such options, and suggests instead: 'It is chiefly necessary for charitable action to exist in us that some habitual form be superadded to potential nature inclining itself to charitable action and to do it with ease and pleasure.'[46] This requires charity to be a virtue, and a virtue that is both outside of us – we cannot achieve it through our natural powers – and within us, forming our interior action.

The virtue of charity is both *extra nos* and *intra nos*. Thus it has a motion similar to that of the biblical practice of *koinonia*. In fact, Thomas defines charity as the divine essence, and gives it a Trinitarian determination: 'Charity can be in us neither naturally, nor through acquisition by the natural powers, but by the infusion of the Holy Spirit who is the love of the Father and the Son and the participation of whom in us is created charity.'[47] As the natural law is our participation in the divine reasons for creation, the life of charity is our participation in the divine life itself. Perfect justice cannot be had without the life of charity.

Thomas does not state explicitly that justice requires charity for its completion when he develops the natural virtue of justice in the *secunda secundae*. This could mislead one to think that Thomas argues for a justice that is separate from charity; in which case, we could develop an economic ethic based on the natural moral virtues alone, such that justice orders relations within political and economic society and charity orders relations among Christians within the church, or provides motivation for, or meaning to, the practice of justice. But this two-tiered interpretation of Thomas cannot make sense of his discussion of either charity or of injustice.

Thomas has already explicitly stated in the *Summa Theologia* that charity is necessary for all the moral virtues.[48] And we see specifically how charity is necessary for justice in his discussion on injustice. He defines injustice in terms of a person wanting to have 'more of goods, namely wealth and honor, and less of evils, namely labor and toil.'[49] This particular vice requires restitution for the good not only of the political or economic order but for salvation itself.[50] Political, economic, and theological matters coincide. To seek to accumulate external goods without labor jeopardizes one's salvation.

## V    The just ordering of commands

Having established the narrative context within which the virtues of charity and justice reside, we can now better understand some of Christianity's traditional rules about economics.

### Do not steal or covet your neighbor's property

The decalogue occupies a significant place in any Christian economy. The meaning of the commandments is not, however, self-evident. They are unique in that they are both *revealed* and *natural*. The sequence of the ten reveals the order of charity, which should be natural to us, even though it often seems otherwise. Our first motion should be toward God. Once our lives are directed toward God and established in faith and hope, then we can be turned toward our neighbors in charity.[51] Because of this order of charity, Christian tradition gave a startling interpretation to the command not to steal. St Thomas argued that 'by natural law whatever people have in abundance should sustain the poor.' Therefore if a clearly urgent need arises, someone can take the property of another, even secretly, and such taking does not have the nature of theft.[52] The basis for such an understanding of 'do not steal' resides in the order of charity.

Our property, like our virtue, finds its purpose in the life of charity. Thus, any right to our property has a direction that makes such a right intelligible. We are to use our property in service to ourselves, our family and our immediate neighbors. If we have a neighbor in need and we do not share our goods with such a neighbor, our neighbor does not steal by taking our surplus property to meet her basic needs. No violation of the seventh commandment occurs. However, any neighbor who is unwilling to share from his surplus with his neighbor has violated the tenth commandment. God has given him his property, not as an inalienable right but as a means for him to participate in a life of charity. By refusing to share his goods with others in need, he covets what actually belongs to them.

For a similar reason, Christian tradition forged rules about a just wage. A just wage was what an employer *owed* an employee. Since the just wage regulated exchanges between people, it obviously fell under the virtue of justice. But the mode of equality by which such exchanges were regulated was also normed by the demands of charity. A worker's labor contributes to the common good. Thus he should be rewarded for his labor with a wage sufficient for the basic necessities of life. Without paying such a wage, an employer commits an intrinsically evil act.[53] Such acts are intrinsically evil because they are deprived of any possibility of being ordered toward the life of charity. Even though the laborer's skills might command a lesser wage based on market analysis, this alone cannot determine just reimbursement. A wage that does not allow a laborer's work to be directed toward the good of her family or neighbors does not allow her to participate in the life of charity. It would be better for her not to work, and to live from the gratuity of others, than it would be to work under such circumstances where her actions are made intelligible from another's intrinsically evil actions. Her refusal to work under these conditions would increase the possibility of the internal good of charity, whereas her working in an unjust environment would lose all connection with the possibility of any internal goods.

### Lend expecting nothing in return (Luke 6:35)

Central to the life of charity for premodern theologians was the ancient philosophic and biblical admonition to lend without expectation of gain. The usury prohibition was, until the emergence of the modern economists, the dominant economic regulation put forth by the church. In fact, modern economists freed the market from the theological and political interference that the usury prohibition represented. Adam Smith objected to the usury prohibition, arguing that a fee should be paid for the use of money since gain could be made from it. The resounding judgment of the economists on the church's traditional teaching was that it was irrational, based on a false notion of economics which was assumed to be a zero sum game wherein all loans were by their nature exploitative of the debtor. Thus, the economists suggest, the theologians were incapable of recognizing how loans may be productive.

This, however, is a false reading of the theologians' efforts to integrate the ancient philosophic prohibition of usury with Luke 6:35, where Jesus says 'Lend expecting nothing in return.' Thomas Aquinas clearly recognized that both the loaner and the debtor could benefit from a loan. Thus he wrote:

> He that entrusts his money to a merchant or craftsman so as to form a kind of society does not transfer the ownership of his money to them, for it remains his so that at his risk the merchant speculates with it, or the craftsman uses it for his craft and consequently he may lawfully demand as something belonging to him part of the profits derived from his money.[54]

Thomas did not argue that employing one's money in enterprising activities could not make a profit: he was not so foolish as to argue against the need for and the fruitfulness of exchanges. What the ancient prohibition sought to insure was a connection between one's labor and one's compensation. As St Albert the Great, Thomas' teacher, stated it: 'Usury is a sin of avarice; it is against charity because the usurer without labor, suffering or fear gathers riches from the labor, suffering and vicissitudes of his neighbor.'[55] And Thomas notes that usury is intrinsically evil because 'we ought to treat every man as our neighbor and brother, especially in the State of the Gospel whereunto we are called.'[56] The principle behind the ancient prohibition is not as absurd as the modern economists tell us it is. The principle is quite simple: money does no work; people do. So when we assume our money to be working for us to make more money, we have not accurately described God's economy. We lose the ability to describe how our lives are embedded in the narratives of others. The food that we eat, the clothes we wear, the transportation available to us, clean restrooms, floors, etc. – all these things are provided for us without any awareness on our part of the practices that make such external goods possible. We cannot name our debts; thus we cannot pray well. And we are incapable of receiving the virtue of charity that directs our lives toward our neighbors adequate to our redemption in Christ.

The usury prohibition did not deny the legitimacy of profit. To use one's money to assist another in a joint-adventure could be an act of charity. But to use one's money only to make money, especially when it is made through layoffs, exploitation, and the production of unjust things, is intrinsically evil because it cannot be ordered to that which should become natural to us – a life of charity.

### Buying and selling

The same narrative that prompted the usury prohibition and the Christian tradition's odd notion of stealing also seeks to order our buying and selling. According to an early church father like Tertullian, how a person earned his or her living was a matter that required examination prior to baptism. Christians were to refrain not only from the production of idolatrous commodities but from trades that would require mendacity or covetousness.[57] This concern for one's occupation remained a consistent Christian theme at least up to and through the Protestant Reformation. St Thomas sought to regulate buying and selling through the virtue of justice by emphasizing the importance of truth-telling in exchanges. He also guarded against greed by prohibiting trading merely for the sake of gain:

> Trading, considered in itself, has a certain debasement attaching thereto, in so far as, by its very nature, it does not imply a virtuous or necessary end. Nevertheless gain which is the end of trading, though not

implying, by its nature, anything virtuous or necessary, does not, in itself, connote anything sinful or contrary to virtue: wherefore nothing prevents gain from being directed to some necessary or even virtuous end and thus trading becomes lawful.[58]

The stipulation here seems to be that trade is 'payment for labor' and that it serves the common good.

Because law directs human acts to virtuous ends, laws without virtues can be only a source of disguised tyranny. This includes both the laws of the state and the laws of the market. Whenever they take precedence over the virtues that direct us to our final end – life with God – our lives will be distorted, particularly in our request for our daily bread through our labor.

Human labor is not a commodity to be bought and sold. It is a vocation God gives us by which we preserve our families, participate in the common good, and produce sufficient resources so that we can act charitably toward our neighbors. It is a theological reality. Our labor should be intelligible only within the context of God's economy of salvation. If our labor does not allow us to fulfill this vocation, then it is disordered. But this economy of salvation functions differently from the global economy, where labor is a means only for increased productivity. Labor can be rewarded not because of the work done, the 'justice of desert,' but because of its relationship to 'long-term profit maximization and capital formation.' If labor serves these ends, it is useful. If it does not, then corporate rulers feel a moral obligation to shareholders to remove laborers from their work. If they experience a sense of moral compunction about their actions, some social scientist will be present to grant them absolution on the premiss that this is the only route toward economic growth. The future benefits will outweigh the present harms done.

How will we ever know if the economists have adequately defined human action? How can we critique a system that tells us the present utilitarian rationality will best serve the future? Is this a more sure form of knowledge than moral and theological knowledge? MacIntyre reveals deep problems confronting this contemporary vision. It gives us *values*, but it lacks virtue. In lacking virtue, it cannot help us to see God. It dissolves all goodness and beauty into interest.

# 14  The beauty of theology

## Uniting the true and the good, and subordinating the useful

Neither the true nor the good can stand on brute facticity alone. Truth is something more (even though it is not less) than an adequate representation of an object by a corresponding description. Thomas Aquinas recognized that because creatures participate in being, they cannot step outside being to evaluate it. However, this participation does not result in a subjectivistic epistemology that denies or relativizes human knowledge of creation and its Creator. We know what is because we also know what it can and ought to be. Our participation in being is a gift because being itself makes possible our participation in the perfections of being. The true, the good, and the beautiful are such perfections. They are also predicates of being. Truth, then, is not merely a correct description of reality: it is a compelling vision grounded in the beautiful that conforms our intellect and will to itself.

Hans Urs von Balthasar recognized that the modern era had lost the beautiful and with it a significant understanding of the truth. Von Balthasar noted that beauty had been destroyed by 'interests.' His theological trilogy reversed the order of Kant's three critiques by beginning with beauty, proceeding to the good and ending with the true.[1] In his *Theological Aesthetics* he stated:

> Beauty is the word that shall be our first. Beauty is the last thing which the thinking intellect dares to approach, since only it dances as an un-contained splendour around the double constellation of the true and the good and their inseparable relation to one another. Beauty is the disinterested one, without which the ancient world refused to understand itself, a word which both imperceptibly and yet unmistakably has bid farewell to our new world, a world of interests, leaving it to its own avarice and sadness.[2]

Without beauty, truth too easily loses its relationship to vision and story. The result is that truth can be conceived only as brute facticity. Interests then predominate, because those facts stand alone and do not exist within a rich world of beauty that gives them their intelligibility. *Meaning* becomes a volitional activity of human *techne*: something that is accomplished after the facts have been presented. This should never be satisfying for Christian theology. It proceeds from the gift of the incarnation, crucifixion, and resurrection. Christ is the form of beauty and all human exchanges are called to participate in that form.

## I    John Milbank's particular narration of dialectic

Novak found capitalism to be identical with Catholic social teaching; Stackhouse found it grounded in Protestant covenant theology, while Ruether, Sobrino, and Gutiérrez condemned it as idolatrous. MacIntyre found it to render virtue nearly impossible and Dempsey argued that although capitalism technically doesn't exist, modern economics institutionalizes usury. John Milbank, like James Cone, regards capitalism as a Christian heresy.[3] But, unlike Cone, Milbank is willing to insist on a normative Christian orthodoxy against which capitalism fails. He traces the intellectual background to capitalism's rise to an heretical deformation within Christianity by which God becomes defined solely in terms of absolute power. Whereas the dominant tradition remains indebted to Mill or Kant (primarily through Weber) and much of the emergent tradition draws upon Marx, insisting that the latter is for contemporary theology what Aristotle was for Thomas' theology, Milbank, like MacIntyre and Dempsey, draws upon the work of Aquinas. But it is a revised Thomism, one that eschews the account of the *natural* found in Dempsey and Catholic social teaching – for the easy compatibility it allows between the social sciences (particularly economics) and theology – through an autonomous, or even semi-autonomous, acknowledgment of two spheres: nature and grace. (In fact, one wonders if Milbank does not finally collapse nature into grace altogether.) The advantage to Milbank's theology is that no social science can exist on its own: the particular form of the Christian narrative functions as a 'metanarrative' that positions all other discourses within its own *logos*, rather than being itself positioned by those other *logoi*.

Milbank invokes the particularity of the Christian narrative as a way to avoid the dialectical retrieval of virtue that makes violence and victory necessary for virtue. This 'pagan' conception of virtue is found to be always embedded in striving and overcoming something; thus it was 'reactive.'[4] Postmodern philosophers, such as Derrida, trace all morality via this reactivity back to an original act of violence. Milbank's invocation of the particularity of Christianity functions as an apology for Christianity against postmodern efforts to trace it, along with all morality, to this original violence. This has the advantage of drawing moral theology into the beauty of its particular form. God's inexhaustible self-giving becomes the basis that generates not only the production of theology but theology's narration of creation, including the necessity of daily exchanges. Death and scarcity become disordered signs of that inexhaustibility rather than sources of hope or the basis for political economy. As Milbank puts it:

It is, of course, quite simply impossible to be a Christian and to suppose that death and suffering belong to God's original plan, or that the struggle of natural selection (which one doubts is even proven as a full account of evolution) is how creation *as creation* rather than thwarted creation genuinely comes about. To do so is to embrace a sickly masochistic faith against the explicit words of scripture (and one notes here the co-belonging of 'kenotic' and evolutionary Christologies). To believe in plenitude is to believe in the already commenced and yet-to-come restoration of Creation as Creation.[5]

Milbank contrasts a plenitude based on the particular form of Christianity with a pagan virtue, reproduced in much of classical western metaphysics, grounded in lack and ending in nihilism.[6] At times, however, all possibilities for virtue appear to arise more from that scarcity than from fullness, and Milbank becomes suspicious of all accounts of virtue. One result is Milbank's suspiciousness of MacIntyre.

Like MacIntyre, Milbank recognizes that the value of modern social theory rests on its compatibility with the political and economic practices it assumes. It does not present to us pure nature, but *a* natural made possible through a capitalist political economy. That economy is based on a formal power of the will, which ineluctably leads to nihilism. Milbank agrees with, and builds upon, MacIntyre's critique of modernity as nihilism concealed behind social science. Yet Milbank finds MacIntyre's general appeals to tradition and virtue insufficient. He is less convinced that a rational *argument* exists capable of refuting the liberalism–nihilism both he and MacIntyre oppose. Thus Milbank states that

> MacIntyre wants to *argue* against this stoic–liberal–nihilist tendency, which is 'secular reason'. But my case is rather that it is only a *mythos* and therefore cannot be refuted, but only out-narrated, if we can persuade people – for reasons of 'literary taste' – that Christianity offers a much better story.[7]

Whereas MacIntyre remains wedded to the power of the good as that which can stand over and against the liberal reduction of the moral life to *rights* alone, Milbank, drawing upon the theological method of Hans Urs von Balthasar, appeals to *beauty*. Milbank's theological aesthetic does not eschew reason, but he is suspicious that the antique virtue to which MacIntyre appeals remains wedded to arguments grounded in conflict, scarcity, and self-possession in such a way that the contents of particular narratives are subordinated to an overarching antagonistic dialectic.

Whether this is a sound criticism of MacIntyre remains an open, yet important, question. It certainly applies more to the MacIntyre of *After Virtue* and *Whose Justice? Which Rationality?* than to the MacIntyre of *Three Rival Versions*. MacIntyre has more fully incorporated the work of

Thomas and the theological virtues within this latter publication, as my description in the previous chapter sought to show. But even in *After Virtue* MacIntyre's conception of a practice suggests limits to Milbank's criticism; limits that imply something other than an antagonistic economic structure. In his definition of a practice MacIntyre states that the excellences involved are cooperative and cannot be scarce. This already moves MacIntyre's account of virtue away from Aristotle's self-possessed, great-souled, man and toward Thomas's disciple, who receives virtues not as a self-possession but as a gift from God's charitable plenitude mediated through the church's sacraments. MacIntyre's notion of excellence is based on a distinction between internal and external goods, which suggests that the latter remain scarce and antagonistic. A suspicion remains about whether he himself has overcome a scholastic distinction between two realms: one (external goods) ruled by nature and subject to scarcity and competition, the other less subject to scarcity and competition and ruled by supernature (internal goods).

Although his work is not possible without MacIntyre's critique of modernity, Milbank still seeks a more theological rendering of the virtues. So he challenges the relationship between virtue and 'victory in conflict.' He seeks a peaceable theological reconciliation of virtue and difference. Christianity's 'fuller invention of virtue' makes possible a conception and practice of virtue based on charity, forgiveness, and peace which is not 'dominated by warfare, heroism,' and the overcoming of difference.[8] This makes Christian virtue less subject to postmodern deconstruction, in that it cannot be traced back finally to an original act of violence, scarcity, and will-to-power. This is because God, as conceived in Christian theology over and against antique philosophy, is 'no longer finite.' God is not understood in terms of a univocity between our being and God's Being, though this is not to suggest that God is without being.

Milbank characterizes God as 'superabundant being, and not a Plotinian unity beyond being and difference, [but] he is also nevertheless, as Dionysius also saw, a power within Being which is more than Being, an internally creative power.'[9] To suggest that God is a 'power within Being' could be construed as subordinating God to a metaphysical ontology (and thus it is imperative to couple this claim with the one that follows: God 'is more than Being'). But this is a position that the entirety of Milbank's work eschews. God is not subordinated to being: God is conceived neither as pure power nor as pure act, but as both at the same time, as a 'power–act' that is not '*stasis*,' but is dynamic and moving, always flowing beyond unity, being or any self-contained act. The Trinity itself is this movement because the 'first difference,' which is the Son, also gives rise to the 'second difference,' the Holy Spirit:

> Therefore difference, after first constituting unity (the Son causing 'backwards' the Father), becomes a response to unity that is more than

unity, which unity itself cannot predict. The harmony of the Trinity is therefore not the harmony of a finished totality but a 'musical' harmony of infinity. Just as an infinite God must be power–act, so the doctrine of the Trinity discovers the infinite God to include a radically 'external' relationality. Thus God can only speak to us simultaneously as the Word incarnate, and as the indefinite spiritual response, in time, which is the Church.[10]

That God is the creative power within being does not lose the ontic difference between God and creation which theologians such as Karl Barth and Jean Luc Marion have taught us to uphold. This creative power does not posit a univocity of being that subsumes beneath it both God and creatures. But neither does it lose the ability to narrate all being theologically, and thereby it refuses to concede a *natural* space that can lead to troubling distinctions such as nature–supernature or fact–value.[11] This makes possible a discussion of 'human co-creation' so that the ontological distinction is not jeopardized as it is in the dominant tradition's *analogia libertatis*.

Milbank, like Novak, can speak of 'human co-creation,' but in a much more profoundly *theo*logical sense. The foundation upon which Novak relates faith to the economy is an anthropology in which God has created us and a world such that we are at liberty to fashion it and ourselves into something better. We know God because we know this freedom we possess. For Milbank, our 'co-creation' is based not on an anthropology of liberty but in this Trinitarian surplus. The key themes he draws upon are Trinity, Christology, and the primacy of the church. God's 'radical external relationality' makes possible a human participation in God's creative power that can be designated as co-creation, or *poesis*. This is not Aristotle's 'modification of existing forms,' nor is it assisting God in bettering creation (as Novak seems to imply with his anthropologically founded *poesis*). Instead it is a participation in God's 'continuously generated ex nihilo' creative power–act. Such human making is a 'participation in divine understanding.' However, the priority of theology over anthropology must be maintained if this account of *poesis* is not to degenerate into an anthropological claim that will finally ground human making in an *analogia libertatis* that frees us from God and generates a 'secular' space with its reduction of all exchanges to a formal power alone. The result will be all the theological problems posed by secular reason and its anti-theological account of nature.

## II    Milbank, Kant, Marx, and liberation theology

Milbank finds MacIntyre indebted still to antique virtue and thus subordinating the specific content of a narrative tradition to an overarching dialectical adjudication. He also faults liberation theologians for reproducing a two-tiered world wherein theology becomes subordinate to a sociology based on the false assumption that Marxism can present a non-theological, or an anonymously theological, account of the natural that will expose the contradictions of capitalism. The result is that in liberation theology the social

> is an autonomous sphere which does not need to turn to theology for its self-understanding, and yet it is already a grace-imbued sphere and therefore it is upon pre-theological sociology, or Marxist social theory, that theology must be founded. In consequence, a theological critique of society becomes impossible.[12]

The central problem Milbank finds with the liberation theologians is their insistence on the autonomy of the social sciences. The theological justification for this autonomy becomes, as was noted in the earlier discussion on Gutiérrez, Karl Rahner's transcendental theology, in which every human thought and act becomes a pre-thematized form of grace. The result is one more 'theology of providence' where God is working behind the scenes in nature to bring about liberation, now equated with salvation. Milbank does not deny the usefulness of Marxism for theology, but he identifies that usefulness in a manner contrary to how Marx is employed by Gutiérrez and Sobrino.

Milbank is *for* Marx in that Marx deconstructs the secular 'by denying that civil society is a permanent natural aspect of human community.' Milbank argues that Marx's historicization of the putatively natural exchanges in capitalist society is commensurable with a theological rendering of such exchanges: it begins to recognize the historical and contingent character of exchanges. Milbank is, however, *against* Marx precisely because Marx himself remained too much a sociologist of the natural. Through his assumption of necessary phases of development on the way to socialism he failed 'to realize the sheer contingency of the capitalist system as a whole and to see [that] it can only be morally criticized and opposed in the name of another, equally contingent vision and practice.'[13] By arguing for the autonomy of the social sciences as offering us insight to the natural, liberation theologians also fail to realize this 'sheer contingency,' and they ignore the one profound source that offers a critique of capitalism – the church's virtues.[14] Rather than merely using Thomas as warrant for incorporating Marxism into theology, as Thomas did Aristotle, Milbank reminds us that for Thomas no science was autonomous in respect of theology. To concede such an autonomy to the social sciences is, at the practical level, to maintain Kant's ethics of freedom. Liberation becomes equated with salvation, and theology serves merely as the 'regulative apparatus to secure this content.'[15] The supernatural becomes naturalized with a dogmatic account of human freedom as the symbolic site for knowledge of God. Milbank, in contrast, appeals to a revised Thomism that (following de Lubac) seeks to *supernaturalize* the natural.

Milbank gives us a careful and profound critique of Kant, contrasting his metaphysical dogmatism with the more open and charitable metaphysics of Aquinas. He shows how the dominance of *right* over *good* in contemporary ethical thought and practice arises from Kant's apparent agnosticism concerning 'things-in-themselves.' Kant's boundary demarcation between the phenomenal and noumenal appears to be a form of agnosticism, but it is in fact a metaphysical dogmatism upon which abstract *right* becomes 'the very mode of being of our practical and political existence.'[16] All persons stand equally before the unknown; no one has the *right* to transgress this boundary demarcation and proclaim that he or she knows the good, the true, and the beautiful in-themselves. Rather than a political and moral existence based on the good, the true, and the beautiful it becomes based on the formal character of *right*. This formalism is also quite consistent with the contractual mode of exchange in capitalist economics. As I will show, Milbank finds this abstract right a Christian heresy because it represents a deformation of power relationships between God and creatures and among creatures themselves. But this right-based politics assumes Kant's boundary demarcation. In other words, it posits dogmatic statements about what can be known about the true, the good, and the beautiful, which then become impossible to transgress.

Milbank's critique of Kant is quite consistent with Karl Barth's earlier critique, although the latter was taken in a different direction. Barth argued that Kant's critique of the 'ontological proof' for God served theology well in that it made possible an acknowledgment of the 'limitations' of natural or speculative reason, so that God's self-disclosure can become the basis for theology (a rational basis always related to practical reason). Nevertheless, Barth suggested, Kant had not gone far enough. By stating specifically what we cannot know about the relationship between God and the world, Kant was also stating what could be known. Barth, like Milbank, found Kant too dogmatic in asserting what can be known about God. But the theological implications Milbank and Barth draw from this criticism differ markedly. For Barth this meant that theology should eschew analogical language about God and the world altogether. But Milbank suggests that 'theology must always speak "also" about the creation, and therefore always "also" in the tones of human discourse about being, nature, society, language and so forth.'[17] It is this *also* that Barth would find objectionable. But it is this *also* that requires Milbank to read economics theologically. Theology has no 'proper subject matter' of its own, so it must use analogical speech drawing upon other discourses and fitting them into its own logic. This distances Milbank from Barth.

Kant had stated that 'if God really spoke to man, he would never be able to know that it was in fact God who was speaking to him.' Barth found this statement partially acceptable because it safeguards theology against any *a priori* 'criterion in the sphere of our experience' for analogizing our conception of God. Yet Barth suggested that even this statement assumes too much *a priori* knowledge of God's relationship to us. In acknowledging that he knew the empirical limits to God's act of communication, Kant still had a metaphysical preconception of who God is. Barth argued that it was impermissible

> to exalt [such knowledge] to the level of empirical knowledge on account of its incomprehensibility ... since in order to do this we should already have to have some prior knowledge of what revelation is, and of what God is.[18]

Such knowledge leaves open the possibility for the very kind of analogical thought about creation, being, nature, language, and society that Milbank finds to be *also* necessary for theology. This latter tendency in Kant – which Milbank develops into an analogy of attribution in a direction opposite to Barth's – is what Barth finds objectionable. There is no analogy other than Christ himself. He alone is the object of theology for he is the 'Word which conditions all things without being conditioned.'

Milbank fears that Barth has turned Jesus into a 'proper object' for theology rather than viewing 'Christ himself as theologic.' This latter perspective recognizes that Christ is not the object upon which theology works, but the *way through which* it must work. Milbank fears that once Barth makes Christ the object rather than the (theo)logic 'theology will be distinguished only by the specificity of its empirical object, and the question of whether this object can call into question the methods and supposed "objects" of other sciences cannot really arise.'[19] Although Barth suggested the possibility of developing a Christian philosophy, he was not finally capable of producing one. Barth, however, assumed that any residual element of some knowledge of God grounded in an *analogia entis*, such as one finds in Milbank, inevitably 'leads to Rome.'[20] Were Barth alive he would certainly find Milbank treading far down that road, if not having already arrived and passed beyond. Not only does Milbank deny that theology has any proper object: he denies altogether the need to distinguish creation from grace. Milbank asserts, drawing on and extending the work of Henri de Lubac, that 'there is no gratuity in addition to the gratuity of creation.'[21]

This does not imply that Milbank denies the gratuity of Christ's life, or of Christian tradition. He denies an account of grace that de-naturalizes it and so thoroughly separates it from human history that it remains extrinsic, ineffably mysterious, and secure from critique in some noumenal realm. He denies Weber's relegation of theology to the irrational remainder. Grace and nature may not be convertible but, for Milbank, 'as the historical, the supernaturally given becomes also our nature, *all* of our nature.'[22] To understand this account of grace in Milbank, we must understand the centrality of *poesis* in his work. And it is from his revised Thomism that he develops this *poesis*.

'*Poesis*,' states Milbank, 'is an integral aspect of Christian practice and redemption. Its work is the ceaseless re-narrating and "explaining" of human history under the sign of the cross.'[23] Re-narration is how we act. And the supremacy of act over form in Thomas leads to this account of *poesis*. For the 'superadditions' of grace that Thomas insists upon are 'nothing mysterious':

> They involve, simply, further acts of intellectual synthesis, further strengthening in virtue, further insight into the truth that virtue, as, especially, charity, is not merely perfection in us but a constant spilling over into the strengthening of others after the pattern of the divine creative perfection itself.[24]

The superadditions God gives us through grace are not unnamable deposits, but concrete acts that are participations in, and repetitions of, God's original plenitude.

This theological understanding of God's plenitude is decisive for Milbank's narration of the relationship between theology and economics. As with Novak, it calls him to speak of 'co-creation,' but never with such an autonomous will-to-power as Novak, when he states: 'Now that the secrets of sustained material progress have been decoded, the responsibility for reducing misery and hunger is no longer God's but ours.' For Milbank, there is no underlying reality to be 'decoded.' God has not hidden the truth in some deep abyss where human creativity must strive to decode it. There is behind reality no secret waiting to be activated by human will. Instead, God is the overwhelming splendor of luminosity that continues to create *ex nihilo*, generating the codes through which human creatures then participate in God's creativity by way of participating in the Word God speaks. So Milbank can argue that we 'do not "assist" God, who supplies all power and all being, but rather participate in God.'[25] Nor does this suggest a realism such as Dempsey's where the just order simply exists and human making seeks to copy it. For Milbank, the Word God speaks is re-presented such that human making participates in God's making which as power–act is an infinite plenitude never unrealized and never exhausted.

Does this poetic theology give us insight into the relationship between theology and economics? We have already seen how Ludwig von Mises also drew upon a doctrine of *creatio ex nihilo* to argue for the legitimacy of interest. For von Mises, human making creates fiduciary media out of nothing: money does fructify. Can *poesis* function as a critique of the world capitalism makes? Why is that world not generated from God's power–act producing the possibility of the wealth of nations? *Poesis* alone obviously cannot sustain Milbank's critique of capitalist political economy, but he does not argue for *poesis* alone. He argues for a poetic Christology by which a specific, contingent, historical event is then promulgated in history through a non-identical repetition. The result is a privileging of the church as the historical site where this making occurs. As Leo XIII had claimed, the church is privileged because it made Jesus possible. Mary plays a central role in their shared theology. Of course, this human making will take place outside of the church as well, but the priority of the church establishes the central plot line. All other human makings refer to it as the site where the divine–human drama unfolded and unfolds: it is the pattern of true human making, for it is where the overwhelming splendor of luminosity takes form. This primacy of the church becomes the pattern for economic life and leads Milbank to condemn capitalism as a heresy that celebrates a formal power established in opposition to the divine–human drama. It leads him also to call for the recovery of a pre-1848 Christian socialism.

## III   Christological poetics and the primacy of ecclesiology

John Milbank's theology develops Hans Urs von Balthasar's theological aesthetics. Balthasar found aesthetics to be the only definitive inroad to the center of theology.[26] For him, the *formosus*, the beautiful, originates from *forma*, shape, and *speciosus*, the comely.[27] The shape of theology contains an intrinsic beauty that commands attention, and this shape, although the basis for and thus prior to, is also consonant with worldly beauty. Form is central to our being: its 'indissolubility' and 'determination by antecedent conditions' constitutes our humanity and our Christianity. But this does not imply that we can first develop an account of the beautiful and then fit theology to it. That would constitute an 'aesthetical theology,' which Balthasar distinguishes from his own 'theological aesthetics.' The former isolates some object called 'beauty' from the totality of its form and seeks to use it as an *a priori* criterion. Here Christianity is valued, but its value becomes subordinate to the more encompassing category of the aesthetic. Balthasar rejects this strategy in favor of one which assumes that theology and revelation have their own beauty, although this is a beauty that maintains a 'genuine relationship' with the 'beauty of the world.'[28] This makes possible analogical language about God. Such a recognition of the relationship between theological and worldly beauty also makes possible the appreciation of a *habitus*, a 'perduring, inherent *qualitas*' in the world. Balthasar recognized that some Protestant theologians viewed this *habitus* with suspicion. They thought it was 'something that can be manipulated,' and so it became associated with a 'demonic corruption.' Balthasar himself sought to avoid this interpretation without denying the possibility of such a *habitus*.[29] He maintained the possibility of a *habitus* without manipulation, that is to say, without the assumption that worldly beauty becomes the basis for theology, without the assumption that this *habitus* was solely a self-possession. Thus we cannot have the form of the beautiful without its specific content.[30]

'Christ's atoning life, death and resurrection' is the objective content of the beautiful, whereas subjective faith can never be separated from that content. A transcendental horizon of faith may be distinguished from its categorical object, but a theological aesthetics never allows this distinction to be a separation.[31] The reason for this should be clear. The beautiful never exists in the general alone: the beautiful is not merely the Kantian sublime – to think the infinite without contradiction – which becomes a subjective assertion about humanity's own powers and still assumes two separate spheres between the finite and the infinite. The beautiful exists as the universal in the particular; it is to think the infinite in and through the finite; it may be in the eyes of the beholder but it is *what* those eyes behold that matters. It must have an objective content, compelling and eliciting our desire. It is to gaze upon Jesus, and all those saints whose lives embody the beauty of Christ.

The influence of Balthasar's theology on Milbank can be seen in Milbank's statement that 'revelation needs to be understood in its aesthetic as well as its logical and ethical dimensions if it is to be adequately grasped at all.'[32] Neither the true nor the good alone can adequately convey the Christian revelation: for that, the beautiful also is required. For Milbank the beautiful arises in our 'poetic encounter with God,' because what we make and have is always more than what we make and have:

> Because our cultural products confront us and are not truly 'in our control' or even 'our gift', this allows that somewhere among them God of his own free will finds the space to confront us also. The transcendental possibility of revelation is the decision of God to create the poetic being humankind, and with this realization one can, at once, overcome a liberal, merely 'ethical,' reading of religion, and also an (equally modern and deviant) positivistic notion of revelation as something in history 'other' to the normal processes of historicity. The event of revelation itself may be defined as the intersection of the divine and human creations.[33]

Does this poetic encounter with God lead to an aesthetic theology rather than a theological aesthetics? For von Balthasar the latter can be maintained only when the objective content of Christian revelation provides the form of the beautiful, while at the same time this form will also always already be related to 'worldly' beauty. The objective content is not an ineffable positivist revelation that contradicts the creation in which it becomes incarnate.

Although he has been influenced by von Balthasar's theological aesthetics, Milbank does appear to eviscerate Jesus of any *substantial* content. The key to Christology is not the *substance* of Jesus in his two natures but the practice he initiates, which then becomes repeated as church. This is not to deny that Jesus is true God and true human, but it resituates Chalcedonian orthodoxy from a discussion of substantial notions of being to the assumption of historical being into the Divine Being.[34] In orthodox fashion, Milbank suggests, 'it is indeed true that incarnation cannot be by the absorbing of divinity into humanity, but only by the assumption of humanity into divinity.' In Jesus, God assumes human nature. However, Milbank then goes on to suggest: 'All that survives that is particular in this assumption is the proper name "Jesus".'[35] Here the question must be raised whether in Milbank's theology God has assumed humanity or consumed it? Is there a crypto-Appolinarianism in such an assertion? An answer depends on what Milbank means by 'the proper name' that remains. Because he denies all ontology of substance where language functions as nominaliza-tion, Milbank's claim does not dissolve the reality or being of humanity into the divine. Only if we think of humanity in terms of *substance* would that be the result. But language is not nominalization where scarce objects are determined by likewise limited signs. Instead, language is power–act, a participation in God's plenitude that is inexhaustible. The proper name of Jesus gives an enduring form to human speech that now makes possible a true and beautiful repetition of God's taking form in flesh. Because this is as real as our own being itself, humanity is not consumed by God: it is assumed.[36]

Milbank's reading of the Gospel of Luke speaks of two stories: the first is a 'straightforward, "apparently" historical tale' of Jesus and the announce-ment of God's reign. The second is a more mysterious meta-narrative that reveals to us 'the secret significance of what Jesus says and does.'[37] This meta-narrative or 'recoding' of the apparently historical tale of Jesus is Christianity. No one can go behind or beneath it to discover the real Jesus, the historical Jesus, because, as Milbank argues, the meta-narrative is itself warranted by the Gospel narratives' portrayal of Christ's life and work. And these, he asserts, disclose that 'Jesus cannot be given any particular content: for the founder of a new practice cannot be described in terms of that practice, unless that practice is already in existence, which is contradictory.'

For Milbank, the heart of the Gospel is not 'the story of Jesus and how he wrought human salvation': it is 'the (re)foundation of a new commu-nity.'[38] It is the establishment of an ongoing practice of non-identically repeating the gift of Jesus through the church. Otherwise the incarnation and death of Jesus become isolatable data to be believed separately from the meta-narrative that makes them significant. Once they become isolatable data then salvation is made necessary through a mysterious and ineffable violence. If the primacy of ecclesiology (the re-foundation of a new community) is maintained, then the incarnation and atonement can maintain their rich significance through the repetition of the historical creation of this new community.[39] Once the primacy of ecclesiology to incarnation and atonement is upheld, then the only remaining particular content to Jesus is his name. This implies that, there is nothing that Jesus does that he will not enable the disciples to do: they will be able to cast out demons, heal the sick, raise the dead, forgive sins. And just as Jesus's proper source and place is not contained within this world, so also his followers are to be 'born again', and so somehow exceed their temporal origins.[40]

Thus the evisceration of Christological content is rendered necessary by the incarnation whereby humanity is assumed into divinity rather than divinity into humanity. Jesus' words and works – as God made human – produce a 'plenitude of significance' which makes necessary their eternal poetic repetition.[41]

The contentless character of the real Jesus in Milbank's work reflects the theological reality that God has assumed into his own infinite plenitude the historical reality that we name 'Jesus.' Thus, says Milbank,

> the historical concreteness of Jesus is forever buried beneath – although at the same time preserved within – an avalanche of metaphors and typological stories which themselves tend in the direction of spelling out the mere formal grammar of the 'fact' of incarnation.... [The] 'textual' Christ, who has always been the Christ who saves us, is the real histori- cal 'person' Jesus, for 'real' human identity resides in its 'force' or the effect upon others made by an individual.[42]

Such claims may conjure up images of Bultmann, and the differences between those images and what Milbank is saying appear to be but a hair's breadth. Nevertheless the difference is decisive. Milbank does not demyth- ologize God language: he re-mythologizes human language. Human language becomes a participation in God's infinite plenitude.

The incarnation plays a central role in Milbank's Christology. His view of redemption seems most fitting with that of the early church fathers who recognized that salvation occurs through the assumption of human nature, though for Milbank this nature is viewed not in terms of substance, but of history, language, and culture. To *have* a human identity is to have a form that effects and affects others. When God assumes this humanity, God assumes its contingent nature. As death is part of that contingent nature, it also is assumed. But such an assumption is not because violence effects some change in God. This is not to deny but to resituate the significance of the crucifixion. It cannot be presented merely as an extrinsic event, which redeems in some mysterious way that we must believe through an act of will. This would be to make Judas the hero of the divine–human drama. Had he not betrayed Jesus, we would not then have Jesus' blood to save us. The cross becomes less something that exists in, or for, God, and more something that exposes the falsity of human politics. Here Milbank's and Sobrino's thoughts are actually similar: as Sobrino puts it, the cross is 'the immense power of the anti-kingdom triumphing over the kingdom' (although he should add that the triumph is apparent and not real, in that it lacks the goodness of being that can endure). But insofar as Sobrino follows Moltmann in seeing the cross as a site for divine passibility, he makes violence intrinsic to God's being, something which the orthodox tradition rightly avoided.

Milbank's emphasis on the incarnation does tend to diminish the importance of Jesus' teachings. The Sermon on the Mount does not seem to contribute significantly to Milbank's 'charismatic ethics.' But in this he follows Thomas, who argued that what Jesus instituted was not a new teaching *per se*, for what he taught was already present in the ten commandments. What Jesus institutes is a new community to promulgate this teaching, and his own vision and presence, to sustain it. We then participate in it through our own poetic activity.

For Milbank, Jesus does not represent an identifiable *telos* toward which we are moving in such a way that the present (and the past) are rendered merely transitory phases of becoming. Instead Christianity embodies a 'telos which subverts teleology' because 'no aspect of life is merely a stage on the way to a final outcome.' And this means that the church has less definite ideas about the roles and characters it seeks to produce than does the *polis*. As Milbank puts it, 'what must be done again is nothing specific and definable ... but ... a work of continuous judgment.'[43] At this point one wonders whether Milbank has blinked in his unrelenting criticism of modernity. Is this another version of the Protestant principle? Does not Jesus and the church also lose all objective content for the sake of avoiding Derrida's erasure?[44] Does Milbank point in the direction of Tillich, Ruether, and Cone where the fallibility of the church becomes its basis? Milbank's reversion to a form of liberalism appears evident in the lack of any doctrine of the church's ability to represent an unquestionably true form of life in his theology, as well as the lack of a strong doctrine of the saints. His argument against the contemporary Roman Catholic church is similar to the critiques of both Barth and Tillich: it needs to become a community capable of self-critique.[45] But the reason he argues against the current configuration of infallibility within Roman Catholicism is an important qualification to any ecclesiology understood in terms of the Protestant principle. Before examining Milbank's critique of ecclesiology, his fascination with Nietzsche's dismissal of virtue as necessarily reactive must first be presented. Milbank's reaction to Nietzsche prevents an adequate development of the role of the saints and of holiness in theology.

Although he recognizes that Christian virtue cannot be reactive, Milbank seems to concede too much to Nietzsche. He writes:

> Mother Theresa needs Calcutta: it is not just her literal burden, but also her burden of ambiguity.... Hence virtue is always reactive: it always secretly celebrates as its occasion a *prior* evil, lives out of what it opposes.[46]

This is a description of the position Milbank rejects, but the question remains of whether he does not himself concede too much to it in his *reaction* against it. At this point it is no longer necessary to out-narrate Nietzsche: one may simply laugh at his misunderstanding of the notion of holy mission. God first spoke to Mother Theresa and gave her a mission; *then* she found Calcutta.

Milbank does contrast reactive virtue with *gift*: 'In the beginning there was only gift: no demon of chaos to be defeated, but a divine creative act; this virtue of giving was not required, was not necessary, and so was a more absolute good, complicit with no threat ...'.[47] But then he concedes too much when he suggests that Christian virtue must be something other than virtue: it must be a 'charismatic ethics' of 'anarchic virtue.' He suggests even that the resurrection 'ruins the possibility of any moral order.' But the language of morality needs to be forsaken only if Nietzsche has adequately described virtue; and, as Milbank also shows us, he has not.

Forsaking the language of morality and virtue concedes too much to Nietzsche, whom Milbank recognizes is a 'remote and bastard descendant of Luther.' Nietzsche's reactive notion of virtue resembles the Lutheran doctrine of *simul justus et peccator* taken to an extreme. If taken seriously, holiness will no longer be present. Instead delight will be taken in the fact that no infallible performance of goodness is possible. Does the suspicion remain for Milbank that every good work is ambiguous because it also assumes the necessity of the evil against which it reacts, and that for this reason Christianity is beyond morality?

If no infallible performance of the good and the beautiful is possible, then Milbank points in the direction of Tillich and Cone, where the fallibility of the church becomes its basis. If the church is formed in infallibility then, as Tillich noted, protest is not an intermediary strategy but the basis for ecclesiology. Protestantism becomes wedded to a dogmatic ecclesiology that must err. It is in the church's fallibility that we discover its infallibility. Such a position does indeed become self-defeating. God's absence becomes more determinative than God's presence. Beauty takes a permanent holiday.

Milbank appears to concede this position when he critiques modern Roman Catholicism for reducing its premodern 'complex space' to the simple space of 'ideal modern absolutism' by the contemporary configuration of the papacy. This is not an unusual criticism for an Anglican theologian to urge against Roman Catholicism. Yet Milbank does not finally seem to argue against a 'genuinely desirable human life' set forth in truth, goodness, and beauty by the church. Milbank opposes modern Roman Catholicism for its inability to give a rich and complex theological rendering of the natural. *Poesis* is so central to Milbank's work that a refusal to recognize that any reading of the natural is at the same time a function of human making leads him to charge such theological approaches with crypto-fascism. He finds two forms of modern theology tending in this direction – Catholic social teaching and eco-theology.

His criticism of the work of Sallie McFague makes clear his concerns about eco-theology. It leads to an embrace of death wherein the

> only remaining imperative would be that of ecological sacrifice. The law of fatality would invite us, as the strong, to gloriously submit ourselves to the yet stronger, the planet as such, the self-maintaining totality. While we should, of course, respect ecological mechanisms, to expect from these mechanisms the key to all modes of evaluation is to acquiesce in the notion that there is such a 'readable' fatality, such a manifest possibility of knowing what 'the whole' requires. The danger is that claims to have identified 'optimum' environments, the most 'natural' and 'sustainable' balances, will often mask the ruses of human power and ambition. Eco-theology may not entirely escape the danger of under-girding this crypto-fascism, because, instead of finding in Biblical tradition ample support for recognition of animal subjectivity, the careful tending of nature, and divine glory and sublimity as disclosed therein, it insists (after little historical reflection) on jettisoning orthodoxy, and constructing a more purely immanent, embodied, developing, limited Godhead.[48]

Eco-theology claims to know what the whole requires from the mechanisms of nature itself. Although it does not make the state the bearer of this totalizing vision, as fascism assumed, it posits the planet in the role of the state and thus embodies a 'crypto-fascism.' For the sake of the natural, individuals must give themselves over to the planet, to the earth, and accept their fate – even their death – as contributing to its comprehensive totality. Because the natural appears to assert its power over us, independently of us or of any political and social mechanism with which we participate, this power takes on an unaccountable role. It produces a 'simple space' where all that remains is the over-powering planet and the resigned individual. Eco-theology is 'modern natural theology,' suggests Milbank. In truth, one could trace its parentage back to Malthus.

Milbank finds an odd similarity between eco-theology and Catholic social teaching, particularly on economic matters. Even though he recognizes that John Paul II defines 'unrestrained capitalism' (as does 'all papal teaching') as the 'surrender of justice to power and truth to opinion,' nevertheless Milbank charges the encyclicals of John Paul II, and the rest of Catholic social teaching, with another form of crypto-fascism because of its refusal to consider pre-1848 socialist thought.[49] He does not suspect Catholic social teaching of fascism because it promulgates 'prescriptive' statements on economic matters. He does not challenge the Catholic notion of 'intrinsic evils,' such as the refusal of employers to pay a just wage. His criticism of Catholic social teaching does not seem to arise from a liberal conception of freedom where the will's power becomes more basic than the true, the good and the beautiful. He suspects Catholic social teaching of a form of fascism because it takes its traditional 'advocacy of complex space' and fits it into a simple hierarchical space that subordinates the parts of this complex space to the greater whole. This is done primarily through the modern construct of the papacy.

The modern papacy propounded the doctrine of infallibility in response to the conquest of the modern (particularly capitalism) in the nineteenth century. The doctrine of infallibility was a direct counter to democratic and capitalist assumptions that the true and the good are found primarily in the power of the will to effect exchanges. In contrast to this, the doctrine of infallibility asserted that the magisterium of the Roman Catholic church had been granted the power to set forth teachings without error despite any combination of human wills affirming or denying that truth. Such a statement conflicts with Tillich's neo-Protestantism because it denies the possibility that truth or goodness may be articulated without any lack in history. Every historical expression of truth or goodness participates in finitude, and therefore is inadequate to what it expresses. It lacks the truth or goodness it seeks to express, simply by expressing it. Milbank, however, challenges the modern magisterium for a different reason. He does not appear to deny the possibility of truth and goodness in history; infallibility *per se* is not the problem. The problem is that in Catholicism such truth and goodness are predicated upon the *power* of the papacy to present the truth. Although John Paul II has well expressed the problem with modernity – freedom loses any relationship to truth – the form of the modern papacy merely repeats this problem. Infallible statements are not presented because they are true. Therefore their conclusions are not subject to conciliar discussion. These statements are rendered true because the power of the papacy presents them as such. Milbank seeks an alternative:

A truly Catholic critique of modernity, if it is not to be perverted, must include an element of self-critique, especially of the character of current ecclesial (and not just Roman Catholic) institutions. One can agree with Pope John Paul II: democracy risks surrender to propaganda, and the forgetting of the primacy of truth, yet the antidote to this cannot be merely entrusting of truth to a sovereign power or clerical/clericist caste (although the need for 'hierarchy in time' in the educative dimension of society, for an elite which nevertheless seeks to 'cancel itself' by passing on wisdom, does need to be reaffirmed, just as democracy must be complemented by a concern with objective truth and justice). In the end the only security for excellence resides in a republican but complex dispersal of guardianship and trusteeship.[50]

Milbank is trying to avoid both liberalism and papal absolutism. He does not deny the importance of the church's claim to teach truth. He denies that this truth will arise from a 'clericist caste' even though he allows a 'hierarchy in time.' But the final sentence of the quoted passage is something of a surprise.

Why is a republican dispersal of power the best way to preserve truth? Such a claim makes sense only in terms of Milbank's advocacy not finally of liberalism but of a 'complex space' patterned after the church itself.[51]

'Complex space' is Catholicism's traditional advocation of 'intermediate associations.' Here Milbank finds congruence between early Christian socialists and papal social teaching. Both recognized the need for a diversity of associations – such as the household, free associations, guilds, and even the university – that exist independently of the state and do not simply mediate state power to the individual. Here Milbank would find important allies in Ruether, Dempsey, and MacIntyre.

Milbank draws on the Gothic cathedral as an example of complex space wherein 'the whole exceeds the sum of its parts and the parts escape the totalizing grasp of the whole.'[52] But in Catholic social teaching the various parts of the modern economic system are subordinated to a patriarchal whole which is a curious hybrid between the ideas of Locke and Smith, and 'an organicist, patriarchal vision of society.' The result is 'kitsch,' albeit a dangerous kitsch.[53]

The natural organic whole of traditional Catholic teaching incorporates liberal understandings of self-preservation, individual dignity, the 'contribution' of capital to production, and an advocacy of property rights. Thus the conflict inherent within capitalism is not sufficiently challenged as a part of the system, and the harmony that should characterize the totality of the natural order is forced upon the conflictual parts. The result is the loss of 'a more "openly" liberal system to workers' generation of their own autonomous counter-authorities and wrestling certain rights and benefits that are guaranteed by political powers.'[54] Liberalism's formal recognition of blatant self-interest and power is preferable.

Milbank's criticism of Catholic social teaching does not lead to an endorsement of liberalism over and against the church. Instead it makes way for the emergence of the church as the pattern for a political economy: 'The Church as a whole was not an enclosed, defensible terrain like the antique polis, but in its unity with the heavenly city and Christ its head, infinitely surpassed the scope of the state and the grasp of human reason.'[55] The church provides the basis for a non-totalizing and non-fascistic socialism because the various parts exceed the whole while nevertheless freely participating in that whole.[56] The church as the pattern for political economy over and against the state leads Milbank to view capitalism as a Christian heresy and to advocate a Christian socialism that returns to pre-1848 socialism.

## IV   Capitalism as heresy

For Milbank, capitalism is a heresy because it celebrates and extends a formal, and manipulative, power of the will separately from any account of what is true, good or beautiful. It is a *Christian* heresy because it occupies that secular space produced within Christianity which gives our lives over to a nihilistic power:

> Dominium, as power, could only become the human essence because it was seen as reflecting the divine essence, a radical divine simplicity without real or formal differentiation, in which, most commonly, a proposing 'will' is taken to stand for the substantial identity of will, essence and understanding. [57]

Capitalism is a Christian heresy because of the loss of the orthodox doctrine of the Trinity according to which the world is created through, in, and for participation with God, who is not some bare divine unity defined in terms primarily of will, but who is a gift who can be given and yet never alienated in his givenness. Once the doctrine of the Trinity is reduced to bare divine simplicity, a new 'secular' politics emerges from within Christianity that makes capitalism possible. This new politics

> first of all ensured that men, when enjoying unrestricted, unimpeded property rights and even more when exercising the rights of a sovereignty that 'cannot bind itself', come closest to the imago dei. Secondly, by abandoning participation in Being and Unity for a 'covenantal bond' between God and men, it provided a model for human interrelationships as 'contractual' ones. [58]

Milbank finds a contractual economy problematic because it assumes a process of exchange which is not based on gift but merely on will. In modern contractual economies, my labor is an investment that goes out from me and is then alienated: it represents a sacrifice made by my will. It becomes a commodity that receives a return only in the form of abstract equivalence such as wages. Yet labor within Christian theology must be understood primarily as an 'aesthetic and liturgical work offered to God.'[59] It assumes the role not of contract but of gift, and gift is marked by a social reciprocity that eschews sacrifice. There is no place for a sacrificial economy within Christian theology: 'a self-sacrificial view of morality is first immoral, second, impossible and third, a deformation, not the fulfillment of the Christian gospel.'[60] The very idea that Christian love requires disinterested concern for the other, as Reinhold Niebuhr and Max Stackhouse have taught us, is for Milbank a Christian deformation, a misunderstanding of the necessary relationship between *agape* and *eros*. And it is the basis for a contractual understanding of exchange based on alienation and substitution. In contrast, the Christian notion of gift gives expecting a return, not in the sense of a formal equivalence but as a gift that cannot be alienated from us and thus whose givenness always returns. This is how the divine economy itself works – as 'inexorable gift and infinite return.' God on the cross receives our refusal of being, so manifesting the refusal as, after all, the reception of a gift. Here, however, infinite return is realized as perfect return, God's return of himself to himself, and it is disclosed to us that the divine created gift, which realizes an inexorable return, is itself grounded in an intra-divine love which is relation and exchange as much as it is gift.[61]

For Milbank, the divine economy, with its basis in gift, must be re-presented in our lives because our lives are also fundamentally based on exchange. We have no alternative to exchange: there is no self-sacrificial morality that gives without expecting a return; no heroic sacrifice that is redemptive in itself. Such an understanding of morality would be inhuman, not even fit for God.

The result is an insistence that Christian orthodoxy demands the abolition of capitalism and the production of a socialist market:

> [We] must insist that if community resides only in exchange, we must have a socialist market. We must strive still to abolish capitalism, albeit this must now be undertaken on a global scale and must often work within businesses, seeking to turn them into primarily socially responsible and not profit-making organizations. In every exchange, something other than the calculation of profit and loss must enter; we must at every turn, at every specific point (not of course from the centre), negotiate concerning what here, in this place, might be justice, what here might be a space of shared benefit.[62]

But how is this to be accomplished? What does it mean to socialize corporations from within? Clearly it implies that socialism is not to be produced through some central bureaucratic mechanism that merely perpetuates the *polis*. It is clear that this is what Milbank opposes; but what is the alternative? What is finally meant by a 'socialism of the gift and of grace?' Does this assume one more theology of providence? Will this socialism inevitably erupt in history through human poetic participation in God's creative power–act?

Milbank has pointed us in a fruitful direction. The church is the basis for a political economy that will flow out of God's original plenitude and not be grounded in an inevitable scarcity. Even though we see this political economy only through a glass darkly, we must in faith live it and participate in its presence. Natural laws alone will not provide its basis. Instead a theological poetics must seek to make possible a participation in daily labor and necessary exchanges as an aesthetic and liturgical offering, as an encounter with God. This 'supernatural pragmatics' demands that Christians work for the abolition of capitalism and the recovery of a Christian socialism destroyed by Marx and Engels' scientific socialism. The question remains of how is this to be accomplished by the *ecclesia* through the corporation without the state? Here indeed, a poetic encounter remains necessary.

# 15 Conclusion

Our cultural products, including theological ones, always exceed our reach. Because of this, an author should never be granted ownership of the definitive interpretation of his or her work. Our cultural products are too interconnected in necessary exchanges for them to be conceded such univocal meaning. Of course, neither does that imply that an author be conceded no say in the interpretation of her or his work. That would imply a nihilistic reading of texts that constantly seeks to destroy the past, the present, and the author for some unknown future. I have tried to be a faithful reader of the theologians cited here from the particular perspective of a theologian endeavoring to place their work within the question: what has theology to do with the economy? Which theological themes are selected to relate to the economy, and which neglected – wittingly and unwittingly?

The preceding chapters offer a critical analysis of various representatives of differing traditions and of schools within traditions. I have traced, developed, and critiqued the works of some representative theologians to see how they respond to this question. I have little doubt that not all those represented here will be pleased with my particular reading of their work or my placement of them within a given tradition. Even though their proffered economic prescriptions vary, I found sufficient commonalty within these various traditions, based on the three main strategies of values, protest, and virtues. What unites all three traditions is their concern to make theology credible and the recognition that to accomplish this theology must have something to say about economic exchanges.

Any theology that suggests our lives can be autarchic and free from exchanges can only be falsely utopian. Any theology that denies it exists within a structure of economic exchange simply has no awareness of the conditions for its own possibility. The question is not *whether* theology is related to economics, but what constitutes a credible articulation of this relationship? Should theology be judged by the legitimacy of its socio-scientific predictions? Should theology be judged by its practical effects? Should it be judged by its fidelity to tradition and the original vision of Jesus?

A credible judgment between these various traditions cannot be determined by a single criterion any more than one analyzes a play or football match based on the costumes or the colours worn. A sense of the entirety of the performance should be taken into account, which addresses questions such as: What is given the central role? How are the various themes ordered? What are the consequences for such an ordering? In addressing the relationship between theology and economics, the dominant tradition gave anthropology the central role. Other theological themes were subordinated to their understanding of the human person as fundamentally free to create, and in this freedom to identify God's activity. The result was that any more specific Christological and ecclesiological themes became problematic. Theology was given the place primarily of an evaluative discourse on facts. Those facts were seldom contested or influenced by particularistic theological themes. The emergent tradition drew on eschatology and emancipatory praxis. Although Christology received a central role in the work of Gutiérrez and Sobrino, it became problematic for Cone and Ruether. Like theologians in the dominant tradition, they sought a more cosmopolitan ethic. For all the theologians in the emergent tradition ecclesiology remained something that could be incorporated only with radical revisions of the tradition. Theological language is primarily protest – against the market and the church, often in the name of social facts that do not seem to have been given a theological reading. The residual tradition remains indebted to virtue and the primacy of ecclesiology. Christology, the Trinity and ecclesiology play the central roles. The church is viewed as the social formation that renders intelligible all other formations. The fact–value distinction is viewed as irrational and subject to critical revision from a theological standpoint.

I have argued that the market tempts us to view the world in terms of *values*. It produces a 'critical frame of mind' that reduces everything which is good, true and beautiful to a formal value based on usefulness and substitutability, flattening all hierarchies to formal equivalences. In contrast to this the church holds forth the possibility of an infallibly true, good and beautiful presentation of human action, incapable of reduction to the usefulness of its formal value.[1] A good theological performance of the relationship between theology and economy will give the church and the market their appropriate roles.

# I    Speaking of God

The theological performance of the three traditions indicates both similarities and differences. The first two traditions are more wedded to the liberative dimensions of modernity than is the latter, which views it as inevitably leading to nihilism and an embrace of death. I have argued that both the dominant and the emergent tradition integrate theology and economics in a way that does not fundamentally call modernity into question. They do this through an *analogia libertatis* characterized by four features. First, this shared understanding of liberty assumes a univocal account of human freedom and God's freedom. Second, this freedom becomes the identifying characteristic of God considered separately from contingent historical practice. Once God is identified based on this univocal freedom, theology becomes too easily subordinated to a more certain metaphysics. Third, Christology and ecclesiology become problems to be overcome because of their historical contingency. To locate them in history is to disclose their limitations rather than their fullness. Fourth, the result is a loss of traditional Christian orthodoxy. The respective members of the dominant and emergent traditions do not necessarily embody all four points, but both traditions provide too much space for this classical western metaphysics. This has social consequences.

Despite the similarities in their use of *analogia libertatis*, the members of the dominant and emergent traditions do not present a uniform emphasis on the role played in the divine–human drama by various social formations. Novak, Stackhouse, and McCann give a more prominent role to the market within the divine–human drama than do the liberation theologians. Wogaman and Preston have an important role for the market but maintain the state as the central character. Gutiérrez and Sobrino diminish the role of the market and elevate the role of some institution wedded to justice, such as the state. Ruether demotes both the state and the market to the background and brings out the household and women's labor as central for a proper theological performance. Cone does the same with the black church and the Black Power Movement. A different performance is found, however, in the residual tradition. Milbank decisively casts the visible church in the leading role.

None of these 'players' can be left out of the divine–human drama. In fact, different alliances and convergences take place across these three traditions. The latter two traditions still hold forth hope for some version of socialism while the first dismisses such hope as utopian and dangerous. Certain members within each of the traditions desire to be orthodox in their theology, while others find orthodoxy oppressive and seek to re-evaluate it. But even those who advocate orthodoxy do not use it in the same way. The first two traditions, along with certain elements of Catholic social teaching, present the possibility of a non-theological, or anonymously theological, nature in which political economy can be presented with theological language fashioning the natural either indirectly or not at all. But this, as I have argued, is consistent with a sharp nature–supernature distinction that antedates, and yet gives rise to, modernity itself. It offers no critique of the autonomy of the social sciences and their fact–value distinction.

The problem with the autonomy of the social sciences is not merely that modernity sets itself against Christian theology through some secular and atheistic conspiracy to subvert the Christian basis of society. Modernity obviously has continuities with certain aspects of premodern Christianity. The inability to integrate nature with theology and thus produce a secular space free from theological interference precedes modernity and establishes the conditions for its possibility. It was an internal Christian transformation that led to the independent, and then autonomous, explication of the *natural* over and against theology. To speak a theological word on the economy requires that this split is overcome, a requirement emphasized in modernity, but stemming from medieval theology itself.

The first theological task in overcoming this split is to confront the assumption of the scarcity of theological language with its plenitude. The so-called Protestant principle, which denies that human language and action can be anything more than a preliminary vehicle for some ultimate concern that always remains ineffable and unnamable, has had dire consequences for the necessarily human presentation of theological descriptions of economics. The Protestant principle assumes that once a theological description is located in history, it is rendered fallible. Because it is human, it errs. Likewise the juxtaposition of a transcendental with a categorical revelation produces a similar problem in Roman Catholic theology. This modern strategy to preserve the transcendent dimensions of the divine merely intensifies the nature–supernature distinction. The logic of the incarnation is split into a dialectic where the human and the divine can never be unified. The church is rendered of necessity fallible in all respects because it is a human, and therefore an historical, institution. The result is that interests and values replace truth, goodness and beauty. Too much space is conceded to an autonomous economics, and the critiques of ecclesiology issue in the unintended consequence that they become an ally in the missionization of the catholic market. Theological language is taken too lightly, and thus is easily dismissed without recognizing that the secular language embraced is not merely a negative theology, but it is already a positive natural theology.

When all theological formulations are viewed *a priori* as limited, as incapable of adequately expressing the divine, then to speak theologically will assume an 'opportunity cost.' To speak of God is to speak against God. Theology is reduced to silence and proclamation itself is rendered heretical. But of course this presumed scarcity in theological language can be present only because theologians implicitly claim to know the *more* that cannot be named, a *more* that is known outside of theology's historical promulgation. This assumed *more* is almost always some version of natural theology. The scarcity attributed to theological language arises not because theologians claim too little knowledge of God but because they claim too much for it outside a particular historical tradition and its linguistic performance. Thus they suggest that the language used in theology is an historical 'vehicle' (sometimes including the incarnation itself) that can be substituted with others without a loss of theological identity.

Once theology assumes a univocal understanding of God based on being or theophanous experience or liberty, then the logic of the incarnation will be lost. We no longer need to see the Word made flesh to find in finitude God who cannot be contained in finitude. Rather than the humanity of

Jesus being the way toward God, it becomes an obstacle we must look beyond to see the ineffable. A more analogical understanding of God language does not have to advocate a privileged positive revelation for an untouchable proper object that only theology knows. Instead such an understanding will depend more thoroughly on the social and historical presentation of human language about God as containing a fullness in which God is *made* known for us. The feminist liberation theologian Maria Clara Bingemer has captured this sense of the fullness of theology when she expressed 'the need to become conscious that a time for silence and discretion about one's conviction and adhesion to the Christian faith, characterized by modernity and secularization, has passed and is over.'[2] The final word about God is not silence in the presence of the ineffable, but the plenitude of language God gives us to speak God's name.

To argue that God gives God's self to us in an inexhaustible plenitude does not imply that we must therefore deny the limits of all resources. This plenitude should not lead to the false assumption that we can consume the creation with a titanic will to power that knows no limits. That surely cannot be the point John Milbank is trying to make through his Christological poetics. Such a titanic will to consume would really be only a demonic *techne*. Instead of this *techne* of strife, God's inexhaustible plenitude suggests that we need not try to consume creation as our own. We need not cling to creaturely life, nor seek to flee from it. Instead, its desires can be properly ordered. This plenitude invites us to learn to participate in God's own perfections, in a simplicity of life that rejoices in cooperation and gift rather than in conquest, competition, and acquisition. These latter arise precisely because of the fear of scarcity. Participation in simplicity is an alternative to the consumptive patterns capitalism lets loose. It teaches us that desire for its own sake is not the end of human exchanges; instead desire has an end. Friendship with God cannot be reduced to some formal equivalence with any other thing. In this sense, the residual tradition makes possible an ecological concern that does not need to accept the limitations of death imposed by a 'natural' life cycle. Such an eco-theology need not arise from a reaction against the fear of scarcity and nature's limits. It can proceed from a different basis, from the fullness of God's gift of creation that knows no limits and invites us to eternal life.

## II   Speaking of the church

A proper theological performance will not seek to control and regulate exchanges through the self-possession that constituted antique virtue. It will neither accept the antagonism intrinsic to the market nor turn from the market to the state for a forceful resolution of such antagonisms. Instead it will give free reign to the exuberance and boundless theological virtues that cannot be possessed, but come as dis-possessions drawing us into the life of God. Whether this is accomplished well cannot be recognized apart from an analysis of the roles given by theologians to social institutions such as the household, the market, the state and, particularly, the church.

For Novak, participation within corporations in a capitalist system of exchange is a participation in God's grace because it is a participation in creativity and liberty. But Novak's theology seems to embody precisely what Milbank deemed heresy – that secular space formed within Christianity of a free creative power that lacks the specific content of the Christian narrative. Novak's theology is a poor performance not because he misunderstands Marxism or capitalism, but because his theology too easily leads to heresy, to the substitution of the corporation for the *ecclesia*. This is readily disclosed when he equates the multinational corporation with the Suffering Servant. It should be obvious to all people of good taste that singing 'He was despised and rejected' during Advent as we meditate on the cross contains a sublimity that is rendered crass were it to be done by the shareholders of Microsoft as they contemplate the year's profits.[3] Novak's ability to find 'analogies' to Christ based solely on the formal principles of liberty and creativity threatens the heart of theology. The identification of human liberty and God's liberty actually breaks from analogy altogether and becomes an identity by which God's actions are now appended to a formal human freedom. What is certain is human freedom, and that certainty makes God credible. Novak's theological strategy is thoroughly modern. But this is not to say that his exaltation of human making has no place in theology. It just cannot take the place of Jesus and the role of the church. Although Novak's theology contains insights into the doctrine of creation, other themes such as Christology, ecclesiology, and the doctrine of the Trinity become subordinate to human creativity and freedom.

Stackhouse and McCann also suggest that participation in economic exchanges is a participation in God's redemptive activity. Again this claim should not be denied; the question is, however, whether the proper tempo and space are maintained for these exchanges. Like Novak, McCann and Stackhouse find themselves arguing for a plurality of visions and practices that cannot finally make sense of the church's unity or catholicity; indeed the corporation becomes a 'worldly church.' But the church does not seem to provide the pattern for the corporation; rather it is the corporation that provides the pattern for the church. This is because of the formal nature of their *realism*, which views the covenanting power of the will in service to the common good as that which rightly constitutes ecclesiology. The notion of *mission* in Christian theology loses its Christological form, and confessional particularity is rendered obsolete through a missional strategy that serves this unity and catholicity through 'capitalization.' Hymns, prayers, sermons, saints, and sinners cannot be formed through such a mission.

We must listen with care to Sobrino, for his work contains the beauty of holiness, and all people of faith should be able to recognize that this is the most profound form of theological argument. He identifies the sin intrinsic to the historical performance of corporations within a capitalist structure, a sin found present in Adam Smith's revolution at its inception. The 'freedom' of the market may free it from governmental intrusion, but a strong national defense goes hand in hand with this 'free' market. The role of government may be to leave the market alone, but it is also called upon to kill, maim, and destroy all who would question the market's unrivaled sovereignty. Romero's death and the death of countless others are undeniable signs of this truth. Even the innocent can be slowly starved through years of blockade, but the starving themselves must not depend upon aid that will upset the market's workings. From Smith to Ricardo to Mill to Marshall to our contemporary neo-liberals, who call themselves 'conservatives,' the 'poor laws' are the problem. Sobrino shows us from the margins the results of such an ideology.

But has he helped us recognize that 'our social nature is exchangist'? Does he give us a role for economic exchanges situated within the context of the *ecclesia* rather than merely against it? Has he demonstrated the inevitability of violence for the corporation's operation? Is there a necessary interdependence between the corporation's profits and the sacrifices and deaths of the poor and the marginalized? Sobrino's analysis suggests this is so, and his narration of the corporation's historical role in El Salvador is haunting, but he has not yet made the case that such interdependence is a *natural* and necessary feature of a global capitalist market. He makes the wickedness of capitalism too stark, too obvious, and thus he counters it with a reactive power, the power of a different kind of *polis*, one which is not yet here but will inevitably come into being. The theological strategy used to legitimize capitalism becomes the same strategy now sought to displace it – a natural theology of providence.

Cone and Ruether each contribute a crucial voice to the development of a complex ecclesiology. Any ecclesiology that refuses to take into account the marginalization of persons because of particular historical circumstances cannot finally be adequate as a 'complex space.' When the church is defined by a patriarchal *potestas*, then its own marginalization of persons makes them create alternative spaces to live faithful lives. Such spaces must constantly be welcomed within the church as belonging to an ongoing reform and as a corrective of its own historical performance. This need not, however, lead to a complete rejection of the church's historical tradition. If that tradition is based on nothing but a will to power, then Christianity is incapable of reform. The logic of the incarnation suggests that, despite the church's poor performance, God refuses to be absent. God becomes flesh and in doing so releases a power that makes the church possible as the site where we discover those practices which give us a glimpse of true exchange.

Milbank's work holds promise for a theological answer to the question posed by this book, because he maintains the primacy of the church in the divine–human drama and at the same time recognizes a place for the necessity of economic exchange. These exchanges are to be narrated as liturgical performances within the church rather than commodity transactions solely relegated to the market. He reminds us that the question of economics depends on the theological end our exchanges serve. If economic exchange requires abstract duty based on sacrifice and alienation, then it is inconsistent with Christian virtue. If it assumes reciprocating relations between and among persons whereby their lives could be based not only on contract but on gift, then it has a place within the divine drama. Contracts assume disinterested exchanges based on two individuals' sacrifice and alienation of their commodities. Gifts, on the other hand, assume that what we give – our daily labor, our professional activities, our time and energy – cannot be thoroughly sacrificed and alienated from us, but in fact extend our being as participants in the lives of those who receive them.

But Milbank's 'socialism by grace' seems to suggest that we reform capitalism from within the corporation by insuring that all transactions bear witness to justice. How this occurs and how it is to be related to the church are as yet not clearly presented. 'Socialism by grace' does, however, point us in a fruitful direction. It reminds us that we first think of economic exchanges in terms of the definitive social practice wherein the divine–human drama occurs – the Eucharist. This social practice provides the script within which all exchanges should take place. The *is* of necessary daily exchange finds its nature in the *ought* of God's self-gift in Jesus, mediated to us in the church through its repetition in the Eucharist. For our natures to be what they are called to be, this supernatural repetition must become our natures. We have no substance that exists separate and secure from the plenitude of this inexhaustible gift. Our 'substance' is secure only in the expressive repetition of this event. The question as to the relationship between theology and economics is not how do we make this theology relevant to current economic formations, but how do we make current economic formations consistent with this theology?

We do not do so by first going outside the church and seeking some neutral public space in which to create a policy based on something, such as liberty, universally accessible in the human person. Instead, we begin with the church. As Stanley Hauerwas has consistently advocated, the church does not have a social ethic: it *is* a social ethic. The repetition–reproduction of this form of life in the Eucharist is itself significant as a way to bear witness that not all our life is determined by marginalist exchanges. As the Roman Catholic Catechism notes, honoring the Sabbath is a protest against the servitude of work. It marks out some space and time where neither the enticement of marginalist exchanges nor their necessity rule us. Instead we discover the beauty of gift and charity. Together we present our gifts to God, and in so doing are not alienated from them, but we and they are taken up into God's own life. This is Christian theological economics.

Of course, such a theological economics cannot assume that its task is to rule the world. A single, univocal, catholic economy, whether it be capitalism or socialism, is not the economic vision Christian theologians should advocate. Such a vision cannot be put forward without subordinating truth, goodness, and beauty to power. It cannot avoid Weberian rationality because it assumes that exchanges can be made based on formal equivalences and thus that nothing is incommensurable. Rather than constructing an economic vision for a global empire, the task of the church is to produce countless alternatives to the marginalist domination of rationality by interests. The theological task is the proliferation of a complex space. Such a space will resist the questions posed by the search for a univocal catholic economy: How does this particular action fit into the whole? How does it fit with the maximization of profit? Does it fit with economic growth? Instead, it will seek to be inscribed into the Catholic vision of the church. Different questions and rules arise. Is charity furthered? Do our exchanges point us toward our true source? Does this fit the mission Christ has entrusted to us? Does it allow us to participate in holiness and in God's perfections? All Christian churches, orders, and vocations cannot be faithful if they fail to ask and answer this question: How do our daily exchanges promote that charity which is a participation in the life of God?

If our lives are to be understood in terms primarily of a mission that takes its form from the beauty of Christ's mission, then theological economics begins with the church; but it also must give itself for the world. The mission of the church always overflows its boundaries. Constant alliances must be made to produce alternative economic formations that bear witness to the expressive character of God's exchanges with us. Let me give an example. With the loss of small family farms in North Carolina a group of persons created the 'Seeds of Hope' ministry where small farmers could be assured of markets for their produce by members of the church. Church parking lots became filled with agricultural produce. The anonymous and impersonal exchanges that usually characterize the supermarket, where producers, consumers, and workers are alienated from one another, were replaced by friendship and personal relations. Such a ministry may not be able to withstand the encroachment of multinational corporate farming. But it bears witness to a different understanding of labor: one where human production is not about efficiency only, but is also about mission and vocation. If we lose such a witness, we lose the ability to recognize true exchanges.

The Seeds of Hope ministry is only one such ministry performed by church persons and others bearing witness to the truth, the goodness, and the beauty of a theological economics. All such ministries are signs of the hope and patience that remind us to be creative in the daily exchanges constituting our lives while we wait on God's complete and perfect rule. They remind us to raise such questions as how do we commute to and forth to work? What do such practices bear witness to? Do we treat creation merely as something to be consumed by our will, or can we find in it God's beauty? How do we eat? How are we clothed? What relationship exists between our eating, being clothed, and other people's lives? Can we avoid desire for its own sake, even if such avoidance is not necessarily good for economic growth? The questions that might be raised are inexhaustible. But they move us beyond the single question that predominates in marginalist rationality – at what point do our exchanges no longer serve our formalized interest.

What theology has to do with economics cannot be given a single answer sufficient for all time. Nevertheless, every answer to this question is not necessarily correct. How do we determine a correct or orthodox answer? From an orthodox theological perspective, the central question must be: How does any particular presentation position human creatures to receive from God those theological virtues which allow them to serve well within God's economy? This question seems at present to lead inevitably to conflict between Christian theology and capitalist political economy, but it does not require an inevitable or natural conflict between theology and economy. Such conflict should be remedied, but it will not be so by theology abdicating its role as the 'queen of the sciences.' Both theology and economics describe human actions. Economics seeks to do so from a purely formal account of rationality; theology does so from the concrete character of its contingent history. As absurd as it sounds, theologians must maintain the priority of their language over that of the economists; just as the church must maintain its priority over the market. Otherwise the true significance of *catholic* will continue to be eclipsed by the all-consuming formality of an insatiable desire. To teach us to desire the infinite with an infinite desire and the finite with a finite desire – that is the mission of the theologian and the role of the church. To teach us to desire ... *that* is the role of the contemporary market. Yet, if economics is to be reasonable, this cannot be the *vocation* of the economist.

# Notes

## Introduction

1 See Karl Barth, *Church Dogmatics*, vol. I, Book 1: *The Doctrine of the Word of God* (Edinburgh, T. & T. Clark, 1975), pp. 200–1.

## 1 Introduction to Part I

1 Raymond Williams, *Keywords: A Vocabulary of Culture and Society* (New York, Oxford University Press, 1983), p. 318.

2 In his *Keywords*, Williams seems to set these two in opposition. This is a result of his concern to critique the idea of tradition as a passive receiving of immutable knowledge. Yet his discussion of tradition in *Marxism and Literature* (New York, Oxford University Press, 1988, p. 115) emphasizes tradition as 'an intentionally selective version of a shaping past and pre-shaped present which is then powerfully operative in the process of social and cultural definition and identification.' Karl Barth gave a better interpretation of this account of traditioning through his analysis of hearing. Hearing, he suggested, is not passive: 'hearing is self-determination, act, decision.' To hear the Word of God in and through the tradition is like listening to music and tapping one's foot. The beauty of the music compels one to tap one's foot, but it is, nevertheless, the agent whose response to the music is at the same time a 'self-determination.' See Barth's *Church Dogmatics*, I, Book 1: *The Doctrine of the Word of God* (Edinburgh, T. & T. Clark, 1975), pp. 198–203.

3 Williams, *Marxism and Literature*, pp. 115–20.

4 Ibid., p. 125.

5 H. H. Gerth and C. Wright Mills (eds), *From Max Weber: Essays in Sociology* (New York, Oxford University Press, 1964), p. 281.

6 Max Stackhouse, Peter Berger, Dennis McCann, and M. Douglas Meeks, *Christian Social Ethics in a Global Era* (Nashville, Abingdon Press, 1995), p. 7.

7 Quoted in Gary Dorrien, *Soul in Society* (Minneapolis, MN, Fortress Press, 1995), p. 193.

## 2 The Weberian strategy

1 For his appropriation of Weber, see Michael Novak, *The Spirit of Democratic Capitalism* (New York, American Enterprise Institute/Simon & Schuster, 1982), pp. 36–48 and *The Catholic Ethic and the Spirit of Capitalism* (New York, Free Press, 1993), pp. 2–11. In his *Will It Liberate?* (New York, Paulist Press, 1986, p. 124), Novak writes: 'What is original about capitalism, as Max

Weber saw, is its spirit, although even Max Weber misidentified that spirit.' He misidentified it because he associated it with Protestantism rather than Catholicism.

2  Novak, *The Catholic Ethic and the Spirit of Capitalism*, p. 11.

3  How theology provides the basis for these necessary values is discussed below. Suffice it to say for now that for Novak a Judaeo-Christian anthropology provides the basis for this *geist*. This anthropology appears quite similar to the formal rationality of human economic action that Weber identified. It assumes that persons are to be understood primarily in terms of their capacity to choose, in their freedom, certain activities over others. The result is a co-creative process whereby a new spirit, not intended by the individual's actions alone, is let loose in the world.

4  Novak, *Spirit of Democratic Capitalism*, p. 14.

5  Ibid., p. 360. Notice Novak's unwillingness to argue for vocations to which people should be called. Instead he emphasizes the vocations to which they 'believe' they are called. This has led him, much like it led Hayek, to argue for an 'emptiness' at the heart of the public realm. Such an emptiness has been challenged by other neo-conservatives such as Richard Neuhaus. For an excellent discussion of this see Gary Dorrien's *Soul in Society*, pp. 214–15.

6  Smith wrote:

> By preferring the support of domestic to that of foreign industry, every individual intends only his own security; and by directing that industry in such a manner as its produce may be of the greatest value, he intends only his own gain, and he is in this, as in many other cases, led by an invisible hand to promote an end which was no part of his intention. Nor is it always the worse for the society that it was no part of it. By pursuing his own interest he frequently promotes that of the society more effectually than when he really intends to promote it.
>
> (*Wealth of Nations*, New York, Modern Library, 1965, p. 423)

This is also Niebuhrian realism, and is a central reason the dominant tradition finds it easy to apply Niebuhr's Stoical doctrine of sin to capitalism.

7  Novak, *Spirit of Democratic Capitalism*, pp. 88–9.

8  Weber, *The Protestant Ethic and the Spirit of Capitalism* (New York, Charles Scribner's Son, 1958), p. 181.

9  Gerth and Mills, *From Max Weber: Essays in Sociology*, pp. 240 and 229.

10  Novak, *The Catholic Ethic and the Spirit of Capitalism*, p. 101.

11  In his 1982 publication, Novak explicitly repudiated Weber's 'iron-cage' thesis. He denies that a bureaucratic rationality identifies the spirit of capitalism. Instead, he views it as 'the role of insight and practical wisdom in entrepreneurship and skillful management' (*Spirit of Democratic Capitalism*, p. 47).

12  Novak, *The Catholic Ethic and the Spirit of Capitalism*, p. 109.

13  Novak, *Spirit of Democratic Capitalism,* pp. 45–6.

14  Joseph Schumpeter (1883–1950) taught economics at Czernowitz, was minister of finance in Austria, then held the chair of public finance at the University of Bonn. From 1932–59 he taught economics at Harvard University. He is perhaps best known for his theory of 'creative-destruction.' Based upon the ideal state of a freely working market, Schumpeter asked how profit arose. A truly free market would result in equilibrium. Profit arose, Schumpeter suggested, when that equilibrium was disrupted by the destruction of old patterns and the creation of new ones. The key actor in the process of creative-destruction was the entrepreneur. Schumpeter also suggested in his 1942 publication *Capitalism, Socialism and Democracy* that capitalism would eventually collapse, not for economic reasons but because the cultural contradictions it created would destroy it.

15  Novak, *Spirit of Democratic Capitalism*, p. 32.
16  Ibid., p. 34. This is one of the reasons Novak can make his scandalous assertion that the top 300 multinational corporations should be understood in terms of the suffering servant passage in Isaiah 52. We will return to this argument in the conclusion as a sign of an improper theological performance of the relationship between the church and the market. See Novak, 'Toward a Theology of the Corporation,' in Stackhouse, McCann, Roels, and Williams (eds), *On Moral Business: Classical and Contemporary Resources for Ethics in Economic Life* (Grand Rapids, MI, Eerdmans, 1995), p. 775.
17  Novak, *Spirit of Democratic Capitalism*, p. 41.
18  For an excellent discussion of the relationship between global cultural industries, capitalist economics, and the church's accommodation to these industries, see Michael Budde, *The (Magic) Kingdom of God: Christianity and Global Culture Industries* (Boulder, CO, Westview Press, 1977). In *Soul in Society*, Gary Dorrien also notes this inconsistency in most neo-conservative analyses of the relationship between economics and culture. He states:

> While they inveigh against the spiral of divorce, drug addiction, hopelessness and social decay in American society, however, neoconservatives give a free ride to commercial interests that relentlessly manipulate baser human instincts. They carefully ignore the social and cultural effects of corporate elites that assiduously promote self-absorption, materialism, immediate gratification, and preoccupation with sex.
>
> (pp. 205–6)

19  Novak, *The American Vision: An Essay on the Future of Democratic Capitalism* (Washington, DC, American Enterprise Institute for Public Policy Research, 1978), p. 1.
20  Ibid., p. 10.
21  Ibid., p. 11.
22  Ibid. pp. 43–4.
23  Weber describes *ressentiment* as the teaching that 'the unequal distribution of mundane goods is caused by the sinfulness and the illegality of the privileged and that sooner or later God's wrath will overtake them' (*Economy and Society*, Berkeley, University of California Press, 1978, p. 493). The result is a moralism that compensates for deprivation through vengeance. This describes quite well Novak's argument against those who are critical of capitalism's production of wealth (see *The American Vision*, pp. 41–5 and *The Spirit of Democratic Capitalism*, p. 34). Novak argues in *The American Vision* that the adversarial culture employs moralism against corporate executives who are not up to the war of ideas. The cultural Left controls the media and uses it to press its moral concerns about such things as 'cigarette smoking, corvairs, auto emissions, and auto safety.' The corporate executives need to become more sophisticated in countering this adversarial culture (pp. 48–52).
24  Novak, *Spirit of Democratic Capitalism*, p. 186.
25  Joseph A. Schumpeter, *Capitalism, Socialism and Democracy* (New York, Harper Torchbooks, 1975), p. 143.
26  Novak, *Spirit of Democratic Capitalism*, p. 157.
27  Ibid., p. 214.
28  Schumpeter, *Capitalism, Socialism and Democracy*, pp. 123–4.
29  Curiously, despite his own creative use of Weber, the father of social sciences, Novak criticizes liberation theologians for 'an old fashioned faith in social science rather than in theology' (*Will It Liberate?*), p. 127.
30  Novak, *Freedom With Justice: Catholic Social Thought and Liberal Institutions*, San Francisco, Harper & Row, 1984, p. xiv.
31  Novak, *Freedom With Justice*, p. 107.

32 See Gertrude Himmelfarb, *On Liberty and Liberalism: The Case of John Stuart Mill* (San Francisco, CA, Institute for Contemporary Studies, 1990), p. 121.

33 J.S. Mill, *Autobiography* (London, Penguin Books, 1989), p. 94.

34 Novak, *Freedom With Justice*, p. 96.

35 Mill, *Principles of Political Economy* (Oxford, Oxford University Press, 1994), p. 127.

36 Ibid., p. 126.

37 Philip Wogaman, *Economics and Ethics* (Philadelphia, PA, Fortress Press, 1986), p. 16

38 Ronald Preston, *Church and Society in the Late Twentieth Century: The Economic and Political Task* (London, SCM, 1983), p. 167.

39 Robert Paul Wolff, *The Poverty of Liberalism* (Boston, MA, Beacon Press, 1968), p. 3.

40 In *Freedom With Justice*, Novak comments that 'many call an approach such as mine "neo-conservative". The proper designation for it, I believe, is "neo-liberal" or "realist." I prefer to call the approach as a whole "biblical realism" ' (p. xiv).

41 See *Freedom With Justice*, Chapter 5: 'A Quintessential Liberal: John Stuart Mill' (pp. 61–108).

42 Max L. Stackhouse, *Public Theology and Political Economy: Christian Stewardship in Modern Society* (New York, University Press of America, 1991), pp. 83–92.

43 Ernst Troeltsch, 'What Does "Essence" of Christianity Mean?' in Robert Morgan and Michael Pye (eds) *Ernst Troeltsch: Writings on Theology and Religion* (Atlanta, GA, John Knox Press, 1977), p. 129.

44 Ibid., p. 130.

45 Troeltsch wrote:

> Only the courage of an act combines the past and the future by so emphasizing the historically grasped essence of a cultural complex for the present that the future arises out of the essence in a manner demanded by the present and yet at the same time exhausting the depth of the historical impulse.
>
> (Ibid., p. 161)

46 Stackhouse is consistent methodologically, applying the same underlying method developed in his *Creeds, Society, and Human Rights: A Study in Three Cultures* (Grand Rapids, MI, Eerdmans, 1984) to his work on political economy, and to his more recent work on the family (see his *Covenant and Communities: Faith, Family and Economic Life*, Westminster/John Knox Press, 1997).

47 Max Stackhouse, *Creeds, Society, and Human Rights*, p. 4.

48 That the content of the creed is not that important seems warranted by the fact that a book entitled *Creeds, Society, and Human Rights* never addresses any particular creeds. In fact, what is affirmed in that book is the 'broadening' of this social space from the church to include 'a wider range of voluntary associations, interest groups, dissent committees, experimental associations, opposition parties, and "private assemblies" '(p. 4.).

49 Surprisingly, Stackhouse writes that the doctrine of universal human rights he is upholding 'represents a modest revolution against much of the treasured wisdom of modernity.' Since the doctrine he puts forward seems identical to Kant's explication of a similar theme in his 'Idea for a Universal History with a Cosmopolitan Intent,' published in 1784, I don't see how a doctrine of universal human rights can be construed as a revolution, modest or immodest, against anything modern.

50 Stackhouse, *Public Theology and Political Economy* (Lanham, University Press of America, 1991), p. 88.

51 Stackhouse, *Covenant and Communities,* p. 54. Stackhouse suggests that this is why great civilizations, such as pre-Columban Latin America, have been destroyed. Stackhouse earlier suggested ('Public Theology and Ethical Judgment,' *Theology Today* vol. 54, no. 2, 1997) that ancient civilizations disappeared because they were 'beset by a metaphysical–moral disease' (p. 167).

52 Stackhouse, *Public Theology and Political Economy*, p. 152.

53 *Covenant and Communities*, p. 4.

54 Ibid., p. 164.

55 Ibid., p. 25.

56 Ibid.

57 *Public Theology and Political Economy*, pp. 75 and 85.

58 Ibid., p. 115.

59 Ibid., p. 91.

60 Ibid., p. 92.

61 Ibid., p. 94.

62 Ibid., p. 84.

63 Weber, *Economy and Society*, p. 587.

64 Ibid., p. 567.

65 Adam Smith, *The Theory of Moral Sentiments* (Indianapolis, IN, Liberty Fund, 1976), pp. 165–6

66 This is not to deny that Smith also had a moral doctrine of disinterestedness. He did, but it was a disinterestedness that refused to be unnecessarily moved by another's sorrows, not by his joys. His doctrine of sympathy allowed for an interest in another's joys.

67 Stackhouse and McCann, 'Introduction', in Max L. Stackhouse, Dennis P. McCann, and Shirley J. Roels with Preston N. Williams (eds) *On Moral Business*, p. 19.

68 In *Creeds, Society, and Human Rights*, Stackhouse draws on Weber's *Economy and Society* to explain how the rise of the corporation makes possible this move toward a 'cosmopolitan future' (p. 43).

69 The full text of his statement is: 'Perhaps we have no choice but to be purely "confessional." If we believed this to be the case, however, we would undercut all truth claims about human rights' (ibid., p. 270).

70 Ibid., pp. 120–1.

71 Alasdair MacIntyre, *After Virtue* (Notre Dame, IN, University of Notre Dame Press, 1984), p. 71.

72 John Milbank, 'A Critique of the Theology of Right,' in *The Word Made Strange* (Oxford, Blackwell Publishers, 1997), p. 11.

73 Thomas Aquinas, *Summa Theologia*, Ia IIae Q 93, art. 6. Throughout this work all English references to the *Summa Theologia* come from the Benzinger brothers' edition: Westminster, MD, Christian Classics. All Latin references come from the Blackfriars' edition: Cambridge, McGraw-Hill. Reference to the *Summa Theologia* will appear as ST.

74 I recognize that Ricardo and Malthus first introduced scarcity into Smith's harmonious vision. Although Smith did not establish scarcity as a fundamental principle, he recognized that each exchange was fundamentally antagonistic. Thus scarcity for each transaction was assumed even if the end result of such transactions would be, unlike for Ricardo and Malthus, the 'wealth of nations.'

75 Smith, *Theory of Moral Sentiments* (Indianapolis, IN, Liberty Fund, 1982), p. 47.

76 It comes as no surprise that this aesthetic contempt for poverty finds a place in the tradition Smith founded. We shall see how it works its way through Malthus, Ricardo, and John Stuart Mill in Part III. This is not to suggest that these people personally disdained the poor. In fact, many of them did remarkable work for the poor. Yet they could find no virtue in poverty itself and thus

their desire to eliminate poverty is consistent with the Stoical contempt toward the poor and suffering one finds in Smith.

77  John Milbank, *Theology and Social Theory* (Oxford, Blackwell, 1990), p. 85.
78  Stackhouse, *Covenant and Communities*, p. 64.
79  A version of this appears in most of Preston's major works. In his *Religion and the Persistence of Capitalism* (London, SCM Press, 1979, p. 6), he discusses the contribution of Tawney and states:

> the church's traditional social doctrines had nothing specific to offer in terms of the growth of a capitalist economy, but were merely repeated when they ought to have been thought out again from the beginning.

Thus, the medieval church's teachings on the economy, 'deserved to be abandoned.' See also his *Church and Society in the Late Twentieth Century: The Economic and Political Task*, p. 136.

80  Preston, *Religion and the Persistence of Capitalism*, pp. 90–1.
81  The keyword in that sentence is 'traditional.' Preston's argument is against a pre-Vatican II Roman Catholicism. My statement should not be construed in such a way that it denies Preston's contributions in ecumenical conversations. Nevertheless, it would be less than honest to suggest that Preston does not remain quite critical of the notion that moral theology should be done under the guidance of the magisterium, a guidance that still seems significant for Roman Catholic moral theology.
82  Ronald Preston, *Religion and the Ambiguities of Capitalism* (Cleveland, Ohio, Pilgrim Press, 1991), p. 33. For a brief discussion of his views on usury, see Preston's Appendix 1 in that book (pp. 135–52).
83  Preston, *Religion and the Persistence of Capitalism*, pp. 140–4. Preston notes that 'the authority attached to the magisterium in the Roman Catholic Church has made the task of moral theology particularly difficult,' and that 'any tendency among Catholics to denigrate the Enlightenment is to be deplored until we are sure that we have learned from it all that we need to.' See also his *Religion and the Ambiguities of Capitalism* where it is argued that *Rerum novarum* is 'a largely unreconstructed medieval defence of private property'. The Middle Ages were 'repressive and protective' and the appeal to usury was a 'rearguard action.' He claims that 'Calvin made a better attempt to come to terms with the realities of economic life' (pp. 5–6).
84  Ronald Preston, *Religion and the Persistence of Capitalism*, p. 91. See also *Religion and the Ambiguities of Capitalism* where he argues that with Calvin we are 'in a different world' because of his critique of Aristotle and because he handled the biblical texts about finances 'flexibly' (p. 143). See also *Church and Society in the Late Twentieth Century*, p. 42, for a discussion of Calvin's superiority in economic matters.
85  Preston, *Church and Society*, p. 22.
86  Preston, *Religion and the Ambiguities of Capitalism*, p. 89.
87  Preston, *Religion and the Persistence of Capitalism*, p. 22; *Religion and the Ambiguities of Capitalism*, p. 95.
88  Preston, *Religion and the Persistence of Capitalism*, p. 48.
89  Wogaman, *Christians and the Great Economic Debate* (London, SCM Press, 1977), pp. 15 and 73.
90  See Wogaman's *A Christian Method of Moral Judgment* (Philadelphia, PA, Westminster Press, 1976), p. 241, n. 1. This self-designation as heir to the Kantian tradition is maintained in the 1989 revised edition of the same book (p. 174).
91  Wogaman, *Economics and Ethics: A Christian Inquiry* (Philadelphia, PA, Fortress Press, 1986), p. 34. Wogaman argued something quite similar in his 1968

publication *Guaranteed Annual Income* (Nashville, TN, Abingdon Press, 1968, p. 107):

> Christian ethics, as such, cannot supply answers to the technical problems involved in these areas. But it contributes a basic moral perspective in which we see problems in terms of their effect upon physical health, personal integrity and man's life with fellowman in community.

92 Wogaman, *Christian Moral Judgment*, pp. 73–97.
93 Wogaman, *Economics and Ethics*, p. vii.
94 Wogaman, *Christians and the Great Economic Debate*, p. 31.
95 Ibid., p. 32.
96 Wogaman, *Economics and Ethics*, p. vii.
97 Wogaman, *Great Economic Debate*, pp. 51–5.
98 Wogaman, *Economics and Ethics*, pp. 34–40.
99 Novak, *Freedom With Justice*, p. 218.

## 3  An anthropology of liberty constrained by original sin

1 Novak, *The American Vision: An Essay on the Future of Democratic Capitalism*, p. 58.
2 Michael Novak, *A Theology for Radical Politics* (New York, Herder & Herder, 1969), p. 29.
3 Ibid., pp. 11 and 69.
4 Ibid., p. 74.
5 Ibid., p. 92.
6 Novak's reliance upon human creativity does fit with Thomas' argument – to an extent. Thomas argued that what makes rational creatures more excellent than other creatures is that they can participate in divine providence by providing for themselves and others. ST Q 91 Ia IIae, art. 2, resp.: *Inter caetera autem rationalis creatura excellentiroit quodem modo divinae providentiae subjacet, inquantum et ipsa fit providentiae particeps, sibi ipsi et aliis providens.* In Chapter 3 I examine a proper role for *poesis* in relating theology and economics.
7 Novak, *Freedom With Justice*, p. 28. To say that God did not make the world perfect could be simply the result of carelessness except that Novak reiterates this theme. Later he states that the meaning behind Jesus' statement, 'Be ye perfect as God is Perfect' is that we must imitate God and, 'The Lord God could have created a perfect world, but did not. He allowed for the disobedience of Adam and Eve and all the rest of us. It is our vocation to bring the good things of creation which are never perfect to fruition' (p. 32). Capitalism becomes the means by which we bring to fruition God's imperfect creation.
8 See for instance *Catechism of the Catholic Church* (New York, Paulist Press, 1994), paragraphs 295–301.
9 In *The Spirit of Democratic Capitalism* Novak explicitly traces this view of the world to Adam Smith when he argues for a correspondence between Reinhold Niebuhr's realism and Adam Smith's 'insistence upon attention to unintended consequences rather than to virtuous motivations' (p. 326). Both are put forward as valuable contributions to a Christian worldview.
10 Whether this is consistent with Niebuhrian realism is much contested. Certainly Niebuhrians such as John Bennett, Robin Lovin and Ronald Stone would contest Novak's appropriation of Niebuhr's work.
11 Stackhouse, *Public Theology and Political Economy*, p. x.
12 McCann, *Christian Realism and Liberation Theology: Practical Theologies in Creative Conflict* (Maryknoll, New York, Orbis Books, 1981), pp. 4–5.

13 Tillich stated, 'Protestant theology protests in the name of the Protestant principle against the identification of our ultimate concern with any creation of the church' (*Systematic Theology*, Chicago, University of Chicago Press, vol. I, 1951, p. 37). I will subject this so-called Protestant principle to a critique in Part II. See Richard Fox, *Reinhold Niebuhr: A Biography* (New York, Pantheon Books, 1985), pp. 158–66 for a discussion of Tillich's influence on Niebuhr.

14 Dorrien, *Soul in Society*, pp. 143–4. For an account of Niebuhr's indebtedness to liberal Protestantism and his inability to make substantive use of Christian doctrine, see Cornel West, *The American Evasion of Philosophy: A Genealogy of Pragmatism* (University of Wisconsin Press, 1989), pp. 150–64. Inheritors of the Niebuhrian mantle take his lack of engagement with Christian doctrine as a sign of his realism. Henry Clark notes that 'Niebuhr was sufficiently honest to know that orthodox ecclesiastical dogma was not intellectually acceptable' (*Serenity, Courage and Wisdom: The Enduring Legacy of Reinhold Niebuhr*, Cleveland, OH, Pilgrim Press, 1994, p. 75). John Milbank, on the other hand, finds this Niebuhrian mantle to be the 'poverty of Niebuhrianism.' In opposition to Niebuhr, Milbank suggests that

> the Christian grasp of reality right from the start is utterly at variance with anything the world supposes to be 'realistic'. This is why it is so absurd deliberately to import the world's realism into the sphere of Christian ethics as if, when it came to the practical crunch, we could set our entire religious vision to one side. In Christian terms, it is the world that will never understand the world aright.
>
> ('The Poverty of Niebuhrianism,' in *The Word Made Strange*, pp. 233ff.)

15 Dennis McCann, *Christian Realism and Liberation Theology: Practical Theologies in Creative Conflict*, p. 200.

16 Ibid., p. 18.

17 Ibid., p. 205. Gutiérrez's usage of scripture is problematic for McCann because 'his use of biblical narratives is not disciplined by the usual canons of historical scholarship.'

18 Ibid., p. 194.

19 Ibid., p. 236.

20 See Frederick Jameson's 'Culture,' in *Postmodernism Or The Logic of Late Capitalism* (Durham, NC, Duke University Press, 1992), pp. 1–54.

21 Reinhold Niebuhr, *An Interpretation of Christian Ethics* (San Francisco, Harper & Row, 1963), p. 143. McCann does state:

> Since this book was written on the assumption that the conflict of practical theologies is not reducible to the confessional differences between Roman Catholics and Protestants, I have not found it necessary to outline a distinctively Catholic alternative to the Catholic liberation theology. There may be some readers, however, who find Christian realism too 'Protestant' to be of much use to Catholic theologians and social activists. My advice in that case is to consider Niebuhr's work as a model for creating a Catholic agenda in practical theology.
>
> (*Christian Realism and Liberation Theology*, p. 240)

22 Stackhouse and McCann, 'A Postcommunist Manifesto,' in *On Moral Business*, p. 950.

23 Ibid., p. 951.

**4 The subordination of christology and ecclesiology to the doctrine of creation**

1 Novak, *A Theology for Radical Politics*, p. 116.
2 In 'A New Vision of Man: How Christianity Has Changed Political Economy' (*Imprimis*, vol. 24. no. 5 (1995), p. 3), Novak writes:

> It is difficult to draw out, in brief compass, all the implications for political economy of the fact that history begins in the free act of the Creator who made humans in His image and who gave them both existence and an impulse toward communion with their first breath. In this act of creation, in any case, Jefferson properly located (and it was the sense of the American people) not only the origin of the inner core of human rights '... and endowed by their Creator with certain inalienable rights, including ...' but also the perspective of providential history: 'When in the course of human events ...' The Americans were aware of creating something 'new': a new world, a new order, a new science of politics. As children of the Creator, they felt no taboo against originality; on the contrary, they thought it their vocation.

3 Ibid., p. 7.
4 Novak, *Freedom With Justice*, p. 174.
5 Ibid.
6 Ibid., p. 175.
7 Ibid.
8 Novak, *Spirit of Democratic Capitalism*, p. 224. This theme is revisited in Parts II and III in discussing the work of James Cone and of Alasdair MacIntyre.
9 See John C. Cort's *Christian Socialism* (Maryknoll, New York, Orbis Press, 1988), pp. 12–15 and Alasdair MacIntyre's *After Virtue*, pp. 181–8.
10 Quoted in Cort, *Christian Socialism*, p. 13.
11 MacIntyre, *After Virtue*, p. 185.
12 Novak, *Freedom With Justice*, p. 194.
13 Novak, 'A New Vision of Man,' p. 7.
14 'The prognosis for Catholic countries of the Third World is far less good than that for countries shaped by Confucius. It makes me sad to say this, since nothing in Catholicism makes such outcomes inevitable, except current unnecessary weaknesses in theological reflection' (*Freedom With Justice*, p. 194).
15 Novak, *Confessions of a Catholic* (San Francisco, Harper & Row, 1983), p. 43. It is open to question whether this can be reconciled with John Paul II's claim: 'It is in the saving cross of Jesus in the gift of the Holy Spirit in the sacraments which flow forth from the pierced side of the Redeemer that believers find the grace and the strength always to keep God's holy law, even amid the gravest of hardships ...' ('*Veritatis Splendor*,' in John Wilkins (ed.) *Considering* Veritatis Splendor, Cleveland, OH, Pilgrim Press, 1994), p. 168.
16 'Liberalism arose as a defense of individuals against church and state' (*Spirit of Democratic Capitalism*, p. 209).
17 *Freedom With Justice*, pp. 55–6.
18 Novak, *The Catholic Ethic and the Spirit of Capitalism*, p. 248.
19 'There are no existing examples of the Catholic middle way. Catholic social teaching has, therefore, occupied a sort of utopian ground – literally no place. It came to seem uncharacteristically abstract, otherworldly, deracinated' (ibid., p. 246).
20 Ibid., p. 249.
21 Ibid.
22 Michael Novak, *The Open Church, Vatican II, Act II* (New York, MacMillan Co., 1962), pp. xi and 56.

23 *Confessions of a Catholic*, p. 45.
24 Ibid., p. 47.
25 *Gaudium et Spes*, in Michael Walsh and Brian Davies (eds) *Proclaiming Justice and Peace* (Mystic, CT, Twenty Third Publications, 1994, paras 78.2–3), pp. 210–11.
26 *Confessions of a Catholic*, p. 55.
27 Novak, *Will It Liberate?*, p. 37.
28 Novak, 'A New Vision of Man,' p. 3.
29 See for instance Gerhard Lohfink's *Jesus and Community* (Philadelphia, Fortress Press, 1982); Richard Hays, 'New Creation: Eschatology and Ethics,' in *The Moral Vision of the New Testament* (New York, HarperCollins, 1996), pp. 20–7; N. T. Wright, *The New Testament and the People of God* (Minneapolis, Fortress Press, 1992).
30 Stackhouse, 'Public Theology and Ethical Judgment,' p. 168.
31 In a 'personal note,' Stackhouse mentions that he once thought corporations were driven by greed and were caught up in 'demonic consumerism' (*Public Theology and Political Freedom*, pp. 120–3).
32 Stackhouse, *Public Theology and Political Freedom*, p. 126.
33 Stackhouse and McCann, 'A Postcommunist Manifesto,' p. 953.
34 Ibid., p. 951.
35 Ibid., p. 941.
36 Johnson stated: 'I consider it past time to renounce our long romantic attachment to the community of possessions and to look more deeply into the part of our tradition which has flourished in Judaism to our own day but which is equally part of our own Christian heritage' – i.e. almsgiving (Luke Timothy Johnson, *Sharing Possessions*, Philadelphia, Fortress Press, 1981, p. 132).
37 *The Didache*, in *The Early Christian Fathers*, ed. Cyril C. Richardson (New York, MacMillan, 1970), p. 171.
38 Tertullian, 'On Idolatry,' p. 67.
39 Justo Gonzalez, *Faith and Wealth* (San Francisco, Harper & Row, 1990), pp. 153–4. Hugo Rahner narrates this shift in his *Church and State in Early Christianity* (San Francisco, Ignatius Press, 1992), p. 46. He recounts Eusebius' tale of the great banquet prepared by Constantine for the bishops of the church during the Council of Nicaea. Eusebius explained how thoroughly the bishops enjoyed the goods set before them. However, Rahner noted: 'The kingdom of God has never been established by bishops reclining in imperial dining rooms.'
40 ST IIa IIae Q 77, art. 4.
41 See Plato's *Republic*, 541a.
42 Stackhouse and McCann, 'A Postcommunist Manifesto,' p. 952.
43 Ibid.
44 Ibid., p. 953.
45 That modern economists position the rise of their own discipline against the 'superstitious,' 'authoritarian,' and 'irrational' world of the theologians will be traced in more detail in Part III.
46 *Wall Street Journal*, Thursday, August 1, 1996.
47 Preston, *Religion and the Ambiguities of Capitalism*, p. 108.
48 R. H. Tawney, *Religion and the Rise of Capitalism* (New York, Mentor Books, 1954), p. 280.
49 Preston, *Church and Society*, p. 19.
50 Preston makes a similar claim in *Church and Society*, when he asks: given the demise of Christianity and the rise of 'moral pluralism,' 'where today is the source of disinterested good will to be found?' (p. 45).
51 Preston, *Religion and the Persistence of Capitalism*, pp. 132–3.
52 Preston (*Church and Society*, p. 19) defines this anthropology this way: 'In the Christian view men and women are meant to live in communities of mutual

giving and receiving and not to try to be as independent of everyone else as possible.' While this anthropology is identical to that of Novak, Wogaman, McCann and Stackhouse, its implications for economics practice differ slightly. Preston insists that this anthropology is different from the individualism undergirding classical liberal capitalism. Christian anthropology requires more socialization. This is only slightly different from the view of other theologians, however, because none of them accepts the argument that capitalism is based on possessive individualism. They all agree that a Christian anthropology requires life in community. They disagree only about whether capitalism as it is allows for that possibility. Novak, Stackhouse and McCann find this communal life more readily available in a free-market economy, whereas Preston argues that it necessitates a powerful state.

53 Although Roman Catholics use natural law to describe this, Calvinists, following in the tradition of Abraham Kuyper, often use the language of 'spheres of sovereignty.' Preston finds some agreement between his own theological understanding of the economy and the Kuyperian–Calvinist 'spheres of sovereignty.' He does make some qualifications to the latter since it tends to put together two contradictory elements: respect for the separate spheres; and the state's right to intervene if those spheres usurp the role of other spheres. This, argues Preston, violates participatory democracy (*Church and Society*, pp. 78–80). Despite all Protestant protestations to the contrary, that understanding also fits well with the neo-scholastic doctrine of the natural law. In his earlier work (*Religion and the Persistence of Capitalism*, p. 92), Preston argued that Catholic thinking has not been as flexible in relating to modern economic trends, because 'its understanding of natural law prevented it from arriving at a proper understanding of the autonomy of the secular law.' Yet he later critiques the US Catholic bishops for abandoning 'a natural law basis for a biblical one' (*Religion and the Ambiguities of Capitalism*, p. 144). Of course, this critique fits well with his view of the *distinctiveness* of the bearing of Christian ethics on the economy. Interestingly, Novak makes the same critique of the US bishops' pastoral. Scripture is too distinctly Christian to help us create a common morality. Both natural law and the spheres of sovereignty offer an ethic that is and, at the same time, is not grounded in the Christian life.

54 Preston, *Religion and the Ambiguities of Capitalism*, pp. 146–8.

55 Ibid., p. 74.

56 Ibid., p. 148. Preston argues also that 'the root problem of the modern Western democratic state is not that it has too much power but that electorates give it too little.' We need a strong state to counteract trades unions and other interest groups that form. Thus the state needs 'the back-up of churches,' although Preston does caution that 'we must not idealize the state' (*Church and Society*, pp. 116–18).

57 Preston, *Religion and the Ambiguities of Capitalism*, p. 107.

58 See Preston, *Church and Society*, pp. 102–4, for a discussion of love as the essence of Jesus' teaching on the Kingdom. Preston also states: 'The Kingdom of God relativized the institutions of the kingdom of the world' (ibid., p. 104).

59 Preston, *Religion and the Ambiguities of Capitalism*, p. 97.

60 Ibid., p. 71.

61 Ibid., p. 81.

62 Preston writes in opposition to Tawney: 'The idea that there is a new social order and some Christian law or principle which can be simply realized in it through the influence of the Church is quite alien to the teaching of Jesus' (ibid., p. 93). In fact, Tawney's teaching that such an order was present in Jesus' teaching is problematic: 'There is indeed a problem in elaborating a distinctively Christian way of life in the mixed societies in which Christians live' (ibid., p. 96). Preston finds all such talk of a new order as the sign of an

inappropriate 'apocalypticism,' to which the early church was prone, particularly as indicated by Acts 2 and 4 (see ibid., p. 137 and *Church and Society*, p. 97).

63  Preston, *Religion and the Persistence of Capitalism*, p. 147.
64  Ibid., p. 151.
65  Preston, *Church and Society,* p. 69.
66  Ibid., p. 72.
67  Pius XII, *Humani generis*, para. 2.8.
68  Henri de Lubac, *Mystery of the Supernatural* (New York, Herder & Herder, 1967), p. 61.
69  Heilbronner, *Crisis of Vision* (Cambridge, Cambridge University Press, 1995), p. 127. That this is true can be seen from economists' analysis of price rents. Invariably such analyses suggest that ceilings placed on rental property through political power will be ineffective because the end result is that landlords will invest their capital elsewhere if their returns are limited by political fiat. As long as the conditions of capitalist society are assumed, the mathematics will work. But it works only if those conditions are assumed. This particular issue will be addressed more fully in Part II.
70  Preston, *Religion and the Ambiguities of Capitalism*, p. 124.
71  See Novak, *Will It Liberate?*, p. 42 and Wogaman, *Christian Moral Judgment*, pp. 52–4.
72  Wogaman, *Guaranteed Annual Income*, p. 54. This notion of grace as free from the law seems to be indebted to Paul Tillich's understanding of grace as unconditional acceptance. This is the singular theological theme Wogaman develops. Wogaman's position borders on antinomianism.
73  Wogaman, ibid., pp. 70–1.
74  Wogaman, ibid., p. 48; *Great Economic Debate*, pp. 49–50; *Economics and Ethics*, p. 74.
75  Wogaman, *Great Economic Debate*, pp. 80–1.
76  Ibid.
77  Wogaman, *Economics and Ethics*, p. 30.
78  Ibid.

## 5  Conclusion to Part I

1  My own sense of this matter is that modernity is to postmodernity what the Pony Express is to the Internet.
2  Weber, *The Protestant Ethic and the Spirit of Capitalism*, p. 47.
3  Weber, *Economy and Society*, p. 18.
4  See Gerth and Mills, 'Introduction,' in *From Max Weber*, p. 55.
5  He suggests that 'strictly rational economic activity' would be 'unaffected by errors or emotional factors and if, furthermore, it were completely and unequivocally directed to a single end, the maximization of economic advantage' (Weber, *Economy and Society*, p. 9).
6  Ibid., pp. 24–6. The definition of marginal utility comes from Brannock, Baxter and Evans (eds) *The Penguin Dictionary of Economics* (London, Penguin Books, 1992), p. 272.
7  Weber, *Economy and Society*, p. 25.
8  Ibid., p. 85.
9  Ibid., p. 561.
10  Ibid.
11  Ibid., p. 226.
12  In his *Marx, Marginalism and Modern Sociology: From Adam Smith to Max Weber* (London, Macmillan, 1982) Simon Clarke has demonstrated the decisive connection between Weberian sociology, with its typology of human action,

and the marginalist revolution of the 1870s that established the 'rational' foundation for modern economics.

13 Alasdair MacIntyre, *After Virtue*, pp. 23–120.

14 For an excellent presentation of Nietzsche's prescience, and for a theology that does not simply ignore his profound criticism, see David Toole, *Waiting for Godot in Sarajevo: Theological Reflections on Nihilism, Tragedy, and Apocalypticism* (Boulder, CO, Westview Press, 1998). An account of Nietzsche's prescience can be found on p. 3.

15 To be fair, Novak argues both sides on this point. He argues that socialism cannot work because it asks the impossible of humanity on account of sin (see *Spirit of Democratic Capitalism*, p. 198); and he argues also that socialism should not be allowed to work because it requires a spirit of jealousy. He writes: 'Perhaps one reason I cannot be a democratic socialist is that I find it difficult to be envious' (*Spirit of Democratic Capitalism*, p. 213).

16 See Alasdair MacIntyre, *Whose Justice? Which Rationality?* (Notre Dame, IN, University of Notre Dame Press, 1988), p. 162.

17 Adam Smith, *The Wealth of Nations*, pp. 755–7.

18 See Novak, *The American Vision*, p. 24.

19 ST I II Q 78, art. 1.

20 I do assume that all the theologians in the dominant tradition would agree that this is the ultimate end of creation. One could hardly claim the role of Christian theologian and eschew this end. My question is whether their theological economics does justice to this end.

21 Stackhouse, Berger, McCann and Meeks (eds) *Christian Social Ethics in a Global Era* (Nashville, TN, Abingdon Press, 1995), p. 7.

22 'Few theologians have attempted to reflect systematically upon economic activities and economic systems' (Michael Novak, 'God and Man in the Corporation,' in Donald G. Jones (ed.) *Business, Religion, and Ethics: Inquiry and Encounter*, Cambridge, MA, Oelgeschlager, Gunn & Hain Publishers, Inc., 1982, p. 69). 'One has to be sure that one understands the market and the economic trends of one's own times if the precise role of the market and the framework needed around it are to be thought out' (Ronald Preston, *Religion and the Ambiguities of Capitalism*, p. 89).

23 For the accommodation of Roman Catholicism to the capitalist market, see William McGurn's essay, 'A Market in the Image of the Creator' (*Wall Street Journal*, March 20, 1996). He argues for 'a contemporary convergence between Catholic social doctrine and modern economics' based on the work of Cardinal Alfonso Lopez Trujillo. McGurn argues that this represents 'a growing sophistication within the church about the virtues of a market economy.' And, he says, it shows that capitalist economists are beginning to embrace traditional 'intangible virtues.' But what McGurn should say is 'values' rather than virtues. He has confused the two traditions. Values are intangible. Virtues are as tangible as is one's neighbor.

24 Quoted in Robert Skidelsky, *John Maynard Keynes: The Economist as Savior 1920–1937* (London, Penguin Books, 1992), p. 170.

25 Quoted in David Toole, *Waiting for Godot in Sarajevo: Theological Reflections on Nihilism, Tragedy and Apocalypticism*, p. 36.

26 Gertrude Himmelfarb (*On Liberty and Liberalism: The Case of John Stuart Mill*, San Francisco, CA, Institute for Contemporary Studies, 1990), often quoted by Novak, is much more forthcoming in explaining Mill's account of liberty, which forms the backbone of Novak's work. She states:

> In what is called the 'free world' today, Mill's doctrine of liberty is preeminent. It has usurped the place once occupied by the ideas of God, nature, reason and justice. In an age which prides itself on liberation from

all absolutes, which has succeeded in making the very word 'absolute' sound archaic, the one idea that has very nearly the status of an absolute is liberty.

(p. xx)

27 In this sense, I should say something about my theological use of Raymond Williams. After all, in *Politics and Letters: Interviews with the New Left Review* (London, Verso, 1981), Williams mentions that in 1935, at the age of 14, he declined confirmation in the Church of Wales. Can his work be used with integrity to discuss theological matters? Because I have no interest in writing from a Marxist viewpoint, I am basically indifferent to this question. Still, what is interesting in Williams is that he does not confine culture, tradition, and religion solely to superstructual phenomena. In fact, Williams was asked in one interview with the *New Left Review*, about his *Culture and Society*:

> There is one other interesting silence in *Culture and Society*. That is the relative absence of any attention to religion. For if one looks through the figures in the book, one notices immediately how central religion was to the development of the tradition. This was not just an adventitious or extrinsic phenomenon. Christian themes, whether in Anglican, dissenting, evangelical, Catholic forms – the whole gamut of possibilities of Protestant and non-Protestant variance – furnished one of the main ideological repertories from which an industrial capitalism could be and indeed was criticized…. Did you think it would clutter the book too much to refer to religion?

Williams responded:

> I think that it was much more a case of tone-deafness. Your criticism is utterly just, for of course religion was a very key issue. I think I was unconsciously making the assumption, characteristic of a Marxist tradition … that if religious terms occurred in a discourse they were a transposition of social terms. I didn't look at them in their own right.

(*Politics and Letters*, pp. 129–30)

## 6  Introduction to Part II

1 For a fuller discussion of this notion of *emergent* see Raymond Williams, *Marxism and Literature* (Oxford, Oxford University Press, 1977), p. 125.
2 This is something Williams does not seem to countenance and thus it has placed limitations on the theological usefulness of his categories.
3 As I show when examining Gutiérrez, this way of putting it does pose some problems. It assumes that the 'theological tradition' is something other than a 'historical social location' itself and thus implicitly maintains an idealist account of tradition.
4 Troeltsch, *The Social Teaching of the Christian Churches* (Chicago, University of Chicago Press, vol. 1, 1981), p. 44. It is not surprising that Troeltsch quotes Rousseau as confirmation of this sentimentalized view of the poor. Troeltsch stated: 'Poverty and simplicity are the foundation of truth; but an artificial and polished age neither sees nor believes this fact; Rousseau brought this out very clearly with reference to "natural truth" ' (ibid., p. 46).
5 Ibid., p. 58.
6 See Cone's *The God of the Oppressed* (Maryknoll, NY, Orbis, 1997), p. 249, n. 30.
7 Ruether does consistently argue against an 'other-worldly eschatology,' which she rightly finds to lose the historical and bodily aspect of Christianity. See Ruether's essay, 'Eschatology and Feminism,' in Susan Brooks Thislethwaite

and Mary Potter Engel (eds) *Lift Every Voice* (San Francisco, Harper & Rowe, 1990), and her discussion in *Women and Redemption* (Minneapolis, MN, Fortress Press, 1998), p. 8.

8 Yoder, *The Original Revolution* (Scottsdale, PA, Herald Press, 1971), p. 53.

9 Seyla Benhabib suggests that the role of utopia 'distinguishes critical social theory from positivistic sociology' because utopia gives critical social theory an 'emphatic *normative* dimension' (*Critique, Norm and Utopia: A Study of the Foundations of Critical Theory*, New York, Columbia University Press, 1986).

> For critical theory, consciousness is both immanent and transcendent: as an aspect of human material existence, consciousness is immanent and dependent upon the present stage of society. Since it possesses a utopian truth content which projects beyond the limits of the present, consciousness is transcendent.
>
> (ibid., pp. 4–5)

10 See for instance Karl Löwith's *Meaning in History* (Chicago, University of Chicago Press, 1970).

## 7 Marxism as a theological strategy to relate theology to economics

1 See Althusser, *Lenin and Philosophy* (London, New Left Books, 1971), pp. 177–83.

2 Ibid., p. 151.

3 Ibid., p. 181.

4 Ibid., p. 170: 'there is no practice except by and in an ideology.'

5 As Alastair Kee has noted, liberation theologians have not actually taken up this Marxian criticism of religion. Kee sees this as a failing in liberation theology, but his argument seems rather confused at this point. He states: 'Religion has thus inverted reality and created an ideology which has been all-pervasive. And this is Marx's second, ontological, criticism of religion. It does not apply only to bad religion, but to religion as such' (Alastair Kee, *Marx and the Failure of Liberation Theology*, London, SCM Press, 1990, p. 280). Kee wants liberation theologians to recognize and accept this Marxian criticism of religion and then do theology. But this seems impossible. If Marx is correct on this point, theology can have only the place granted it in the modern world – an intellectual discourse grounded in the irrational or ideological. The contradiction in Kee's argument can be found in his concluding paragraph, where he states (ibid., p. 283): 'Religion in its traditional form is inherently an inversion of reality. In this form it was appropriate and important in earlier epochs, but it is becoming obsolete in the modern world, and in this form deserves to be so. The future of religion, in the next epoch, depends on accepting Marx's ontological critique' – a bleak future indeed.

6 Louis Dupré, *Passage to Modernity* (New Haven, CT, Yale University Press, 1993), p. 4.

7 This influence can be seen in the phrase 'black theology' itself. As Cone states: 'The term "black" in the phrase refers to Malcolm's influence on my thinking and the word "theology" points to my solidarity with Martin' (*A Black Theology of Liberation*, Maryknoll, NY, Orbis, 1990 [1970], p. 199). For Cone's careful discussion and evaluation of the importance of King and X for theology, see his *Martin and Malcolm and America: A Dream or a Nightmare* (Maryknoll, NY, Orbis, 1991).

8 *Black Theology and Black Power* (Maryknoll, NY, Orbis, 1969), p. viii.

9 Cone argues that even Malcolm X's black nationalism had to draw upon themes from the Bible rather than the Quran:

Locating the origin of the Nation of Islam in the African-American experience is supported by Muhammed's and Malcolm's frequent quotations from the Bible. The Bible, not the Quran, is the central document in the black religious experience in America. Malcolm would never have gained wide acceptance in the African-American community without his profound knowledge and creative use of the Bible, the sacred book for black Christians.

(*Martin and Malcolm and America*, p. 161)

10  Cone, *A Black Theology of Liberation* (1970), pp. 123 and 134.
11  Cone, *The Spirituals and the Blues* (Maryknoll, NY, Orbis, 1972), p. 19.
12  Jon Sobrino, *Jesus the Liberator: Historical–Theological Reading of Jesus of Nazareth* (Maryknoll, New York, Orbis, 1993), p. 235.
13  Jon Sobrino, *Archbishop Oscar Romero: Memories and Reflections* (Maryknoll, NY, Orbis, 1990), p.10.
14  'In the midst of economic and political disenfranchisement, black slaves held themselves together and did not lose their spiritual composure, because they believed that their worth transcended governmental decisions' (Cone, *The Spirituals and the Blues*, p. 83).
15  Gutiérrez, *A Theology of Liberation: History, Politics, and Salvation* (Maryknoll, NY, Orbis, 1988), p.xxxviii.
16  'It is not in its spirituality that one has difficulties with liberation theology; it is, rather, in its interpretations of economics and social realities' (Novak, *Will It Liberate? Questions about Liberation Theology*, New York, Paulist Press, 1986, p. 10).
17  Gutiérrez, *A Theology of Liberation*, p. 24.
18  Novak, *The Catholic Ethic and the Spirit of Capitalism* (Toronto, Maxwell MacMillan Canada, and New York, Maxwell MacMillan International, 1993), p. 26.
19  From Jevons, *The Theory of Political Economy* (London, MacMillan, 1871), pp. 1–2, quoted in Stanley L. Brue, *The Evolution of Economic Thought* (5th edn, Dryden Press, 1994), p. 250.
20  Jevons in ibid., p. 251.
21  This will be examined more fully in Part III when I discuss Bernard Dempsey's work.
22  See Brue, *The Evolution of Economic Thought*, pp. 230–1.
23  The introduction of the supply curve obviously gives the 'factors of production,' including labor, some role in the determination of value. Alfred Marshall is usually credited with combining the marginalist revolution with classical economics to produce the supply and demand curves – the Marshallian scissors.
24  As Simon Clarke noted (*Marx, Marginalism and Modern Sociology: From Adam Smith to Max Weber*, London, MacMillan, 1982, p. 23), Smith's view of wealth production is ambivalent. Profit and rent sometimes represent 'deductions from the produce of labor' and sometimes 'correspond in some way to the original contributions made to the product of capital and labor.'
25  Ibid., pp. 30 and 37.
26  Smith, *The Wealth of Nations* (New York, Modern Library, 1965), pp. 30–1.
27  In *On the Principles of Political Economy and Taxation* (Cambridge, Cambridge University Press, 1990, p. 4) Ricardo stated:

Adam Smith, who so accurately defined the original source of exchangeable value, and who was bound in consistency to maintain that all things became more or less valuable in proportion as more or less labour was bestowed on their production, has himself erected another standard measure of value, and speaks of things being more or less valuable in proportion as they will exchange for hire or less of this standard measure.

28  Ibid., p. 11.
29  Clarke, op. cit., p. 36; Ricardo, *Principles*, pp. 69–72 (extract which follows is ibid., p. 73).
30  Marx, *Capital* (New York, International Press, vol. I, 1973), p. 55.
31  Ibid., p. 35.
32  Ibid., p. 36.
33  Ibid.
34  Ibid., p. 38.
35  Brue, *The Evolution of Economic Thought*, p. 232.
36  Böhm-Bawerk, *Capital and Interest* (South Holland, IL, Libertarian Press, 1959), p. 296.
37  Ibid., p. 262.
38  Ibid., p. 264.
39  Ibid., p. 265.
40  Ibid., p. 266.
41  Ibid., p. 270.
42  Ibid., p. 271.
43  Marx, *Capital*, vol. I, p. 168 (emphasis added).
44  Böhm-Bawerk, *Capital and Interest*, pp. 287, 297, and 302.
45  The labor theory of value, according to Böhm-Bawerk, has an ancient lineage. He finds it to be embodied in a tradition put forward only by the force of authority from Aristotle through the theologians to Locke, Smith and Ricardo and into the pages of Marx. The labor theory of value suggests that profit or interest arises from the exploitation of workers' labor value by the owners of the means of production. It is associated with the Scholastics' prohibition of usury.
46  As Simon Clarke has argued, 'political economy inverted the relationship between economics and political theory' (*Marx, Marginalism and Modern Sociology*, p. 10). In Adam Smith and classical political economy harmony was assumed to arise out of the natural liberty within which the market worked. Thus political order derived from a free and autonomous economy. This was further entrenched in the marginalist revolution of the 1870s when 'marginalists claimed to offer not a social theory but a pure theory of rational choice.' It was then buttressed by the dominance in social science of Weber's typology of action (Clarke, ibid., pp. 15ff.).
47  Of course, Marxists have brought their marginalization upon themselves once they accept the premiss behind Engels' 'Socialism: Scientific or Utopian.'
48  I recognize that this is a contested account of theology. For instance, see Max Stackhouse's contrast between 'theological ethics,' which provides 'ultimate warrants,' and 'historical social analysis' in his *Covenant and Commitments: Faith, Family, and Economic Life* (Philadelphia, Westminster/John Knox Press, 1997), p. 5. All theology that rests comfortably with the fact–value distinction will contest this understanding of theology.
49  William J. Baumol and Alan S. Blinder, *Economics, Principles, and Policy* (5th edn, San Diego, CA, Harcourt Brace Jovanovich, 1991), pp. 83–5. The scientific nature of their claims is then supported by showing how this is the inevitable result based on a supply–demand diagram for rental housing in NY City. The mathematics is uncontestable. That this math rests on a scientific natural fact was already questionable once these economists invoked a theology of providence – the invisible hand – to support their argument.
50  Cone, *The Spirituals and the Blues* (Maryknoll, NY, Orbis, 1995), p. 14.
51  Marx, *Capital*, vol. I, p. 168.

52 Eugene D. Genovese, *The World the Slaveholders Made* (New York, Vintage Books, 1969), p. 242.
53 Ibid., p. 177.
54 Ibid., p. 234.
55 James Oakes, *The Ruling Race: A History of American Slaveholders* (London, W.W. Norton & Co., 1982), p. 30.
56 This is not to suggest that Smith was pro-slavery. It suggests only that his economic analysis alone, based as it was on the principle of liberty, did not bring him to challenge slavery in his analysis in *The Wealth of Nations*.
57 Smith, *The Wealth of Nations*, p. 68. This is not to suggest that Smith favored slavery. It suggests only that nothing intrinsic to early capitalist economic analysis argued against slavery.
58 I do not put this forward as an uncontested claim, but only as Adam Smith's observation. Slavery did require housing and some form of care that would allow the slave to work. The difference between a slave and a Guatemalan migrant worker may in fact be such that the costs in producing fruits and vegetables are less with migrant workers than they were with slavery.
59 See Hayek, *The Road to Serfdom* (Chicago, University of Chicago Press, 50th Anniversary Edition, 1994), pp. 40–1.
60 Ibid., pp. 64–5.
61 Ibid., pp. 17–19. Christianity seems to begin for Hayek with Erasmus.
62 Ibid., p. xv.
63 One inevitable result of such an understanding of the relationship between economics and politics is something like Pinochet's Chile. For a good discussion of this, see William Cavanaugh, *Torture and Eucharist* (Oxford, Basil Blackwell, 1998), pp. 34–48.
64 Quoted in Genovese, *Roll, Jordan, Roll: The World the Slaves Made* (New York, Vintage Books, 1976), p. 143. Who knows what Ezra Adams would have stated in the privacy of 'the quarters'?
65 Ibid.
66 Peter J. Parish, *Slavery: History, and Historians* (New York, Harper & Rowe, 1989), p. 3.
67 Parish does, however, recognize the contradiction in slavery when he states: 'One of the most glaring paradoxes of the white South lay in its combination of fierce devotion to the idea of liberty, with a profound commitment to the institution of slavery' (ibid., p. 132). But while he recognizes this, Parish does not offer a critical interpretation of this liberty or expose the roots of this paradox. Genovese does offer such a critical, and persuasive, interpretation. One of the key difficulties in Parish's otherwise excellent historical review of slavery and its historians is that he seeks an analysis free of 'ideological distortion' and thus assume the problematic concept of the fact–value distinction (see ibid., p. 37). This makes him suspicious of Genovese's work, despite his praise for it.
68 Genovese, *Roll Jordan Roll*, p. 44.
69 Ibid., p. 53.
70 Ibid., pp. 48–9.
71 Ruether, *The Radical Kingdom: The Western Experience of Messianic Hope* (New York, Paulist Press, 1972), p. 191.
72 'This vast process of stripping the Americas of their gold and silver together with the slave and agro-export trades, laid the foundations for western European capitalism' (Ruether, *Gaia and God: An Ecofeminist Theology of Earth Healing*, San Francisco, Harper, 1992, p. 198).
73 R. R. Reno has characterized feminist theology in general as arising out of, and therefore still within, the project of modern theology. He identifies the commonalities between these two projects as 'the triumph of ethical criteria over the dogmatic, a distrust of tradition combined with a confidence in the perspi-

cuity of contemporary experience, and a vision of theology as saving the tradition from both error and irrelevance' ('Feminist Theology as Modern Project,' *Pro Ecclesia*, vol. V (fall 1996), p. 406). As a description of Ruether's theology Reno's identifying characteristics seem undeniable, with the one caveat that she does seem to recognize the problematic nature of the will in modern society. These characteristics place feminist theology within an inheritance that proceeds from a theologian such as Paul Tillich, who did not recognize the problematic nature of the will when he described faith as the courage to be against all 'intellectual distortions' of faith. Reno's descriptions characterize a type of feminist theology that still seeks to be *in* but not *of* traditional Christian theology, as opposed to those theologies that have left Christianity altogether. A different kind of feminist theology, however, is emerging that does not share these characteristics and would not fit within his overall categorization of 'feminist theology as modern project.' See for instance Sara Maitland's *A Big Enough God: A Feminist's Search for a Joyful Theology* (New York, Riverhead Books, 1995) p. 74, where she argues for the compatibility of feminism and a 'radical orthodoxy.' She also challenges the role of 'experience' within feminist and modern theology, recognizing it as one more form of modern dualism that seeks to ground theology in something certain, such as the modern subject (ibid., pp. 13–15).

74 Ruether, *Radical Kingdom: The Western Experience of Messianic Hope* (New York, Harper & Row, 1970), p. 99.

75 Ruether, *Liberation Theology*, p. 191, emphasis mine.

76 Ruether, *Gaia and God*, p. 200.

77 Ruether, *Sexism and God-Talk: Toward a Feminist Theology* (Boston, MA, Beacon Press, 1983), pp. 219–21.

78 Ibid., pp. 224–6.

79 Ibid., p. 227.

80 Ibid., p. 74.

81 See *Women and Redemption* (Minneapolis, MN, Fortress Press, 1998), pp. 62–97.

82 Engels, 'Socialism: Utopian and Scientific,' in Lewis S. Feuer (ed.) *Marx and Engels: Basic Writings on Politics and Philosophy* (Garden City, NY, Doubleday, 1959), p. 91.

83 The feminist liberation theologian Maria Bingemer couples the social, cultural, and political concerns Ruether rightly raises with an interesting account of theological production related to women's work in the church. See Ivone Gebara and Maria Clara Bingemer, *Mary: Mother of God, Mother of the Poor* (Maryknoll, NY, Orbis, 1996). Mary McClintock Fulkerson also does this in her work *Changing the Subject: Women's Discourses and Feminist Theology* (Minneapolis, MN, Fortress Press, 1994).

84 Ruether, *Women and Redemption*, pp. 51–62.

85 Gutiérrez, *The Truth Shall Make You Free* (Maryknoll, NY, Orbis, 1990), p. 13.

86 Gutiérrez, *Power of the Poor in History* (Maryknoll, NY, Orbis, 1983), p. 178, n. 27 and *The Truth Shall Make You Free*, p. 108. In the latter work, he also notes that *Libertatis Conscientia* 'honestly acknowledges the errors of judgment and serious omissions for which Christians have been responsible in the course of the centuries' (ibid., p. 109).

87 For instance, Novak argues that liberal society 'does not make ultimate sense apart from biblical perceptions.' Gutiérrez does argue also that modern freedoms were eventually accepted by the church because 'it came to be realized that many claims of modernity had a Christian source' (*The Truth Shall Make You Free*, p. 108). I am unclear how this statement fits with the one quoted above. Gutiérrez's argument is quite similar to Bernard Dempsey's that

modern economics was distorted because of the loss of Catholic institutions. His argument will be examined in Part III (the residual tradition).

88 'Only, this time those who attempt to vindicate the rights of this world's oppressed stand accused of threatening the very "modern liberties" the popes rejected' (Gutiérrez, *The Power of the Poor in History*, p. 215, n. 27).

89 Ibid., p. 179.

90 Ibid., p. 203.

91 For further accounts of Barth's work by Gutiérrez, see *God of Life*, pp. 26 and 116.

92 Gutiérrez, *A Theology of Liberation*, pp. 43–6.

93 Most of Sobrino's work is on Christology, and all of his work assumes this Christological center. He admits that this work originated because of 'certain suspicions against traditional Christologies' and 'classic treatments of Christology.' What he finds suspicious about these traditional treatments is that they 'ignore or even contradict fundamental principles and values that were preached and acted upon by Jesus of Nazareth' (*Christology at the Crossroads*, Maryknoll, NY, Orbis, 1978, pp. xi and xv). The result is that Christ becomes a 'sublime abstraction' and he is separated from the 'concrete history of Jesus' with no 'dialectical thrust.' Jesus is then turned into a 'pacifist' whose blessings are separated from his maledictions (ibid., p. xvi).

94 Sobrino, *Jesus the Liberator*, p. 91.

95 Ibid., p. 127.

96 Ibid., p. 186.

97 Sobrino, *The True Church and the Poor* (Maryknoll, NY, Orbis, 1984), p. 279.

98 Robert Gilpin, *The Political Economy of International Relations* (Princeton, NJ, Princeton University Press, 1987), pp. 61, 87 and 271.

99 See Gilpin, pp. 87 and 284, and Lenin, *Imperialism* (New York, International Publishers, 1993 [1939]), pp. 65–7.

100 Gilpin argues that dependency theory has demonstrated only individual cases of exploitation, but has failed to give a compelling case for systematic exploitation. The difficulty with dependency theory is that it tries to 'explain three distinct phenomena' – underdevelopment, marginalization, and dependent development. The charge of underdevelopment he finds warranted; he attributes it, however, not to the exploitation of the periphery by the core but to the inefficient economic institutions in the periphery which, because of poor political leadership, refused to open markets. As for dependent development, Gilpin seems to find therein instances of exploitation, which are sometimes necessary for development to occur. He argues that 'all development is in varying degrees dependent development' (*The Political Economy of International Relations*, pp. 288–94). Gilpin's 'realism' assumes that some political hegemony is necessary for the functioning of the international economy.

101 In *The Emergence of Liberation Theology* (Chicago, University of Chicago Press, 1991), Christian Smith has argued that liberation theology becomes unintelligible without dependency theory.

102 Sobrino, *The True Church and the Poor*, p. 19.

103 Ibid., pp. 15 and 20. What 'European theology' represents in Sobrino's work is unclear. He criticizes European theologians, such as Kasper and Pannenberg, but he often uses Moltmann to do so. Thus he states that Pannenberg's Christology 'ignores [the Kingdom's] dialectical and conflictual dimension and the agonistic nature of human existence stemming precisely from the fact that human beings have to choose between the Kingdom and the anti-Kingdom.' But he also suggests that 'a fundamental contribution made by Moltmann is his retrieval of the dialectical and conflictual dimension of reality, and, specifically, stressing its aspect of negativity' (*Jesus the Liberator*, pp. 116–17).

104 We find here some gross theological generalizations. For instance, Sobrino asserts that 'theological reflection on the cross of Jesus is very infrequent,' especially among European theologians (*Christology at the Crossroads*, p. 179). He also asserts that 'In European theology the "following of Jesus" is a subject usually relegated to spiritual theology.' He then notes certain exceptions – the theology of Bonhoeffer, von Balthasar, and Moltmann. But don't these three theologians offer a rather major exception to his argument? They are not on the margins of 'European theology.' Are these categories finally helpful? What makes theology European?

105 Cone, *Black Theology and Black Power* (Maryknoll, NY, Orbis, , 1983 [1969]), p. xiii.

106 Cone, *A Black Theology of Liberation* (Maryknoll, NY, Orbis, 1986 [1970]), p. xv.

107 Cone, *Black Theology and Black Power* (1983), p. xiv.

108 Cone, *A Black Theology of Liberation* (1970), p. v.

109 Ibid., p. 9.

110 Ibid., p. 39.

## 8 The subordination of theology to metaphysics

1 Ruether, *Liberation Theology*, p. 12.

2 Ruether, *God and Gaia*, p. 142.

3 See Ruether, *Disputed Questions: On Being a Christian* (Maryknoll, New York, Orbis, 1989), p. 23, where she identifies her own development as a 'flight into critical freedom.'

4 Ruether, 1982, *Disputed Questions*, p. 67.

5 Ibid.

6 I originally included the term 'Gaia' in this list. But here I had misread Ruether. She specifically notes that the term *Gaia* in *Gaia and God* is not a term for God.

7 'Philosophy deals with the structure of being in itself; theology deals with the meaning of being for us' (Tillich, *Systematic Theology*, Chicago, University of Chicago Press, 1951, vol. I, p. 22).

8 Paul Tillich, ibid., vol. I, p. 64; vol. III (1963), pp. 289 and 291.

9 Ibid., vol. I, p. 136.

10 It leads also to a defense of the Cold War. Tillich argued that war was necessary for the 'creation of higher imperial unities.' Thus, it is simply part of the 'compulsory element of power from history.... One can never start an atomic war with the claim that it is a just war, because it cannot serve the unity which belongs to the Kingdom of God. But one must be ready to answer in kind even with atomic weapons, if the other side uses them first' (ibid., vol. III, pp. 387–8).

11 Ibid., vol. I, p. 12.

12 Tillich's theology presupposes something such as Duns Scotus' doctrine of the univocity of being; in fact, as we will see, Tillich draws upon Scotus as someone who, along with the nominalists and Luther, prepares the way for a more 'dynamic' understanding of God. And by dynamic Tillich seems to mean this dialectical struggle of Being with Being. God actualizes himself only in conflict. God does this by 'resisting' the threat of non-being and demanding a sacrifice of the historical to the 'infinite ground of courage.' This is surely why Tillich argues that Jesus is the 'final revelation': he 'sacrifices himself completely to Jesus as the Christ.' Tillich's use of Scotus and his understanding of being seems to lend support to the connection of Scotus' univocity of being and Ockham's nominalism with modernity and capitalism that has been well traced by a number of contemporary theologians. Such a critique of Scotus is contro-

versial, in large part because of its implications for Protestantism. Nevertheless, that Tillich can trace his own work back to Scotus shows the soundness of these narratives, at least in their critique of this particular trajectory of modern theology. See for instance Hans Urs von Balthasar, *The Glory of the Lord*, vol. V: *The Realm of Metaphysics in the Modern Age* (San Francisco, Ignatius Press, 1989); John Milbank, *Theology and Social Theory: Beyond Secular Reason* (Oxford, Blackwell, 1990); pp. 1–48, Catherine Pickstock, *After Writing: On the Liturgical Consummation of Philosophy* (Oxford, Blackwell, 1998), pp. 120–66; Gerard Loughlin, 'The Basis and Authority of Doctrine,' in Colin Gunton (ed.) *The Cambridge Companion to Christian Doctrine* (Cambridge, Cambridge University Press, 1997), pp. 41–65; Eric Alliez, *Capital Times* (Minneapolis, MN, University of Minnesota Press, 1996), pp. 196–239; and John C. Cort, *Christian Socialism* (Maryknoll, NY, Orbis, 1988), pp. 53–61.

13  Ruether, *Disputed Questions*, p. 26.

14  Von Balthasar, *Theo-Drama: Theological Dramatic Theory*, vol. III: *Dramatis Personae: Persons in Christ* (San Francisco, Ignatius Press, 1988), p. 425.

15  Ruether, *The Radical Kingdom*, p. 2.

16  Ibid., p. 3.

17  Ibid., p. 17.

18  Ruether, in *The Radical Kingdom*, writes:

> The apocalyptic view of redemption is basically social and outer-directed.... Apocalypticism is the social relation of oppressed peoples, not oppressed into unconsciousness, but conscious of their oppression and without the power to alter their situation under present circumstances.... Every movement that preaches the irreformability of the present system and its total corruption, that believes that the only solution is radical overthrow and reconstitution of the world on an entirely new and different basis, is apocalyptic in structure, even if it uses social-scientific rather than religious language.
>
> (p. 9)

19  Ibid., pp. 10–13.

20  Ibid., p. 17.

21  Ibid., p. 16.

22  Ibid., p. 17.

23  Ibid., pp. 25 and 43–4. This story line seems to have been slightly modified in her *Women and Redemption* where patriarchy is associated more with a future eschatology rather than an already realized eschatology that fundamentally transforms social relationships in the temporal order. But it remains basically the same because the future eschatology associated with patriarchy is one that exists atemporally.

24  Ruether, *The Radical Kingdom*, pp. 75–6.

25  Ruether 1972, p. 175.

26  Ibid., p. 172. There seem to be similarities between Ruether's flight and Deleuze's notion of flight in 'Micropolitics and Segmentarity,' in *A Thousand Plateaus: Capitalism and Schizophrenia* (Minneapolis, MN, University of Minnesota Press, 1988), pp. 208–32.

27  Some critics seem to find fault with liberation theology primarily for its Catholicism. See for instance Alistair Kee's *Marx and the Failure of Liberation Theology* (London, SCM Press; Philadelphia, Trinity Press International, 1990).

28  Karl Rahner, *Theological Investigations* (New York, Crossroad Publishing, 1982), vol. I, pp. 312–15.

29  Karl Rahner, *Foundations of Christian Faith* (New York, Crossroad, 1987), pp. 52–3.

30 Karl Rahner, *Spirit in the World* (New York, Herder & Herder, 1968), p. liii.
31 Ibid., pp. 52–3 and 143.
32 Elizabeth Johnson, *She Who Is* (New York, Crossroad, 1996), p. 110.
33 Gutiérrez, *A Theology of Liberation*, pp. 43–6.
34 Milbank, *Theology and Social Theory*, p. 223.
35 Gutiérrez, *The Truth Shall Make You Free*, p. 58.
36 Ibid., p. 37.
37 For a description of how this occurred, see Simon Clarke's *Marx, Marginalism and Modern Sociology: From Adam Smith to Max Weber*.
38 Gutiérrez, *The Truth Shall Make You Free*, p. 57.
39 Gutiérrez, *The Power of the Poor in History*, p. 202.
40 Ibid., p. 93.
41 Ibid., p. 228.
42 Milbank does note that

> the political and liberation theologians are aware, as de Lubac, Congar and von Balthasar are not, that ecclesial history is not insulated from political and social history. Therefore, they realize that to uphold ecclesial (rather than political or private) practice as the site of salvation involves also subscribing to a particular theological interpretation of history and society (an enterprise which they take to be rendered impossible by the Enlightenment and its aftermath). For the Church was only constituted, historically, by a particular theoretical perspective upon history: a certain history, culminating at a certain point, and continued in the practice of the Church, interprets and 'locates' all other history. It 'reads' all other history as most fundamentally anticipation, or sinful refusal of salvation. If one takes one's salvation from the Church, if one identifies oneself primarily as a member of the body of Christ, then inevitably one offers the most 'ultimate' explanations of socio-historical processes in terms of the embracing or refusal of the specifically Christian virtues. Not to embrace such a 'metanarrative', or to ascribe to it a merely partial interpretative power, would undo the logic of incarnation.
>
> (*Theology and Social Theory*, p. 46)

43 Gutiérrez, *Power of the Poor in History*, p. 211.
44 Gutiérrez wrote: 'The effort at clarification has given me an opportunity to reaffirm my communion with the magisterium and my will and desire to place my theological thinking at the service of the church's work of evangelization' (*The Truth Shall Make You Free*, p. 52, n.1). He also stated: 'Revealed truth must be made known to every human being; this is the starting point of every discourse on the faith. In the light of that truth it becomes possible to discern the Christian legitimacy of a particular praxis' (ibid., p. 87).
45 Gutiérrez, *The Power of the Poor in History*, pp. 210, 220 and 230. He also states that

> persons are saved if they open themselves to God and to others, even if they are not clearly aware that they are doing so. This is valid for Christians and non-Christians alike – for all people. To speak about the presence of grace – whether accepted or rejected – in all people implies on the other hand, to value from a Christian standpoint the very roots of human activity. We can no longer speak properly of a profane world.
>
> (Gutiérrez, *A Theology of Liberation*, p. 84)

46 For an excellent discussion of the relationship between liberation theology and Maritain, see William Cavanaugh's *Torture and Eucharist*, Oxford, Blackwell, 1998, p. 181. Cavanaugh's point is that Gutiérrez does not move beyond Maritain's New Christendom and the distinction of planes because the 'New

Christendom model found in Catholic Action and Maritain is unable to envision the church as anything like a "culture," that is a set of specific social practices' (p. 181). Cavanaugh argues that Gutiérrez does not move us sufficiently beyond this inability of Maritain. See also Dan Bell's 1998 dissertation, 'The Refusal to Cease Suffering,' Duke University.

47  Rahner, *Theological Investigations*, vol. 1.
48  Gutiérrez, *A Theology of Liberation*, p. 44.
49  Ibid., p. 46.
50  Von Balthasar suggests that

> metaphysics in itself defies completion, and in the event that it nevertheless wants to attain completion, must make the different levels of the Ontological Difference identical.... The confusion is complete if in the end the negations of Negative Theology, the inner-divine mystery of self-outpouring (as basis for the following two aspects), the 'noughting' of the communicated fullness of Being in its non-subsistence, and ultimately the kenosis of Christ are partially or wholly equated; thereby the ultimate theolougomenon is totally shorn of its theological character and cannot therefore be fruitful for metaphysics either.
>
> (*Glory of the Lord*, vol. V, pp. 628–9)

For von Balthasar the attempt by metaphysics to complete itself inevitably ends in an embrace of nothingness, in nihilism, and in the theological equation of this nothingness with God.

51  Gutiérrez, *A Theology of Liberation*, p. 14.
52  Ibid., p. 29.
53  Ibid., p. 30.
54  Ibid., p. 31.
55  Ibid.
56  So Gutiérrez suggests: 'The direct immediate relationship between faith and political action ... encourages one to seek from faith norms and criteria for particular political options. To be really effective, these options ought to be based on rational analyses of reality,' and this should respect the 'autonomy of the political arena' (*A Theology of Liberation*, p. 138).
57  For Sobrino (*Archbishop Romero*, p. 85), this emphasis on the Kingdom arises not from liberal Protestant theology, but from four principles from Medellín:
1   'The church is not the same thing as the Kingdom of God; it is the servant of the Kingdom.'
2   'The poor are those for whom the Kingdom is primarily intended.'
3   'As the servant of the Kingdom, the church ought also to promote the values of the members of the Kingdom, both while the new society is being built up and when it is at length achieved.'
4   'For the church in any way to impede or thwart either the Kingdom of God or the members of the Kingdom is sinful.'
Sobrino's understanding of the significance of Jesus' life bears a resemblance to Harnack's essence of Christianity. For Sobrino Jesus' life is 'organized around three fundamental and historically established data: his relationship to the Kingdom of God, his relationship with God the Father and his death on the cross' (*Jesus the Liberator*, p. 63).
58  Albert Schweitzer, *The Quest of the Historical Jesus: A Critical Study of its Progress from Reimarus to Wrede* (Baltimore, MD, Johns Hopkins University Press, 1998), pp. 398, 401–3; and Walter Rauschenbusch, *Christianizing the Social Order* (New York, MacMillan, 1912), p. 7.
59  *Jesus the Liberator*, pp. 106–7.
60  Sobrino, *The True Church and the Poor*, p. 202.

61 So, Sobrino asserts: 'We usually find a sizeable part of the hierarchy ignorant of theology's (including First World theology) rediscovery of the priority of the Kingdom over the Church' (Sobrino, *The True Church and the Poor*, p. 216).

62 Sobrino, *Archbishop Romero*, pp. 152–5.

63 Oscar Romero, *Voice of the Voiceless* (Maryknoll, New York, Orbis Books, 1994), pp. 58, 70, and 77. Likewise in his third episcopal letter Romero argued that the church 'can and must pass judgment on the general intention and the particular methods of political parties and organizations' (ibid., p. 97).

64 Ibid., p. 146.

65 Sobrino, *True Church and the Poor*, p. 201.

66 Ibid., p. 316.

67 Ibid., pp. 84, 93, and 95.

68 Ibid., pp. 135–7.

69 Ibid., p. 97.

70 Sobrino, *Christology at the Crossroads*, p. 209.

71 Sobrino, *Jesus the Liberator*, p. 174.

72 This is further discussed in Part III.

73 Sobrino, in good Thomistic fashion, likewise recognizes a central place for the Sermon on the Mount in his political theology. Sobrino argues that the Sermon on the Mount is 'catechesis on the radical way to behave as a Christian.' It contains 'abundant prescriptions on how to behave toward one's neighbor and minimal indications of duties of a religious nature.' Happiness, according to Jesus, is to be 'found in the beatitudes, not riches,' which indicates that 'there is always some injustice at the root of all fortunes' (Sobrino, *Jesus the Liberator*, pp. 166–73).

74 Sobrino, *The True Church and the Poor*, Chapter 2.

75 Ibid., pp. 60 and 63.

76 Ibid., pp. 70 and 73.

77 In *The Graced Horizon: Nature and Grace in Modern Catholic Thought* (Collegeville, MN, Liturgical Press, 1992), Duffy writes: 'Borne, too, on the swelling tide of this renewed theology of nature and grace would be the new liberation theologies of the century's last decades' (p. 9). And again:

> Grace now finds humanity more easily in its dependence on the human community in quest of life and good. God is found in nature not by reason of consciousness of immediate dependence upon its process, but by awareness of dependence on one's neighbors in the mastery of it. This is an insight that had much to do with the development of the liberation theologies pursuant to the mid-century nature-grace development that we have been examining.
>
> (Ibid., p. 41)

For a negative evaluation of this see John Milbank's 'Founding the Supernatural,' in *Theology and Social Theory*.

78 Rahner, *Foundations: An Introduction to the Idea of Christianity* (New York, Crossroad, 1987), p. 52.

79 R. R. Reno, *The Ordinary Transformed: Karl Rahner and the Christian Vision of Transcendence* (Grand Rapids, MI, W. B. Eerdmans, 1995), p. 110.

80 See Kerr, *Theology After Wittgenstein* (Oxford, Blackwell, 1986), pp. 10–13. For a different reading of Rahner by Kerr that takes into account Reno's criticism, see *Immortal Longings: Versions of Transcending Humanity* (Notre Dame, IN, University of Notre Dame Press, 1997), pp. 176–84.

81 See von Balthasar's 'Metaphysics of Spirit,' in *The Glory of the Lord*, vol. V; and for his accusation that this is the stream within which Rahner stands, see *The Moment of Christian Witness* (San Francisco, Ignatius Press, 1994), pp. 83 and 100–14.

82 Duffy, *The Graced Horizon*, pp. 210–12.
83 Sobrino, *The Principle of Mercy* (Maryknoll, NY, Orbis, 1994), p. 2.
84 Ibid., p. 34.
85 This can be seen also in Sobrino's interpretation of Jesus. Rather than a distinctive politics, a social ethic, the possibility of a new power to live into the life of God, and the creation of a new community to challenge the pagan polis, Jesus gives us 'values.' We discover that 'on the basis of Jesus' own history we can say that the first principle governing the concretion of moral values is the situation itself.' Jesus himself is political only in his desire to change things (*Christology at the Crossroads*, p. 123). Again:

> This does not mean to say that we should look to Jesus for theories of society and its transformation, still less in the modern sense of the term 'praxis' as transforming social activity guided by an ideology and carried out by the organized people as privileged subject, but it does mean to say that Jesus, objectively, faced up to the subject of society as a whole – including its structural dimension – and sought to change it.
>
> (Sobrino, *Jesus the Liberator*, p. 161)

## 9   Scarcity, orthodoxy, and heresy

1 Baumol and Blinder, 'Scarcity and Choice: THE Economic Problem,' *Economics, Principles and Policy*, p. 49. Of course this is the standard economic claim that can be found in any basic economics textbook.
2 Derrida, *The Gift of Death* (Chicago, University of Chicago Press, 1995), p. 60.
3 Ibid., p. 61.
4 Ibid., p. 66.
5 Ibid., p. 71.
6 It comes as no surprise that in *Of Grammatology* Derrida's description of what the 'trader' does to language seems so closely to approximate his own understanding of language. 'The trader invents a system of graphic signs which in its principle is no longer attached to a particular language.... It is a system of signifiers where the signifieds are signifiers: phonemes' (*Of Grammatology*, Baltimore, MD, Johns Hopkins University Press, 1976, pp. 299–300).
7 'The eschatological God is that transcendent otherness that comes in judgment upon such closed ontological or historical systems and restores us to freedom without a divine ground and before an undetermined future' (Ruether, *Radical Kingdom*, p. 151).
8 Ibid., p. 58.
9 Ibid., p. 162. 'If the church is human society considered from the point of view of God's renewing activity in history, then it is basically a secular reality.'
10 Ibid., p. 159.
11 Balthasar, *The Glory of the Lord*, vol. I, p. 214.
12 Ibid., p. 212.
13 Ruether, *Sexism and God-Talk*, pp. 125–6.
14 Ibid., p. 114.
15 Ruether, *Liberation Theology*, p. 10.
16 Ruether, *Disputed Questions*, pp. 56–7.
17 Ruether seems to have qualified this claim in her *Women and Redemption*, where she herself speaks of Jesus as establishing the 'new family' and 'new community of Israel' (pp. 18–19).
18 Ruether, *Disputed Questions*, p. 73.
19 Ruether, *Liberation Theology*, p. 183.
20 Ruether (*Liberation Theology*, p. 92) writes:

Gentile attitudes toward Jews are unalterably fixed by the totalistic univer-salism of a Christian fulfilled messianism. Such a Christian theological stance demands, in some form, the drawing of a mental ghetto of negation around those who reject this fundamental Christian self-affirmation. But should Christians really believe in their messianism in this form, or hasn't this very history demonstrated its false ideological character? This de-mands nothing less than a fundamental rethinking of the meaning of the basic proposition of Christian faith that 'Jesus is the Christ.'

21 Ibid.
22 Ruether, *Sexism and God-Talk*, p. 11.
23 Ruether, *Liberation Theology*, pp. 124–5.
24 Ruether, *Gaia and God*, p. 263. Compare Ruether's claim to Malthus' that a cataclysmic famine was inevitable unless 'epidemics, pestilence and plague advance in terrific array and sweep off their thousands and ten thousands.' Neither Ruether nor Malthus think such evil is something good, but both seem to suggest that creation is structured such that 'nature' or 'providence' will do this to us if we do not control population first.
25 Christine Kiealy (*The Great Irish Famine*, ed. Cathal Póirtéir, Chester Springs, PA, Dufour Editions, 1995, p. 104) argues:

> The belief that Ireland suffered from over-population was given weight and intellectual respectability by influential economists such as Thomas Malthus and Nassau Senior. Ireland's poverty was seen as a threat to Brit-ain's prosperity unless a solution was found. This debate on Irish poverty was concurrent with concern in England regarding the mounting costs and demoralising effects of the so-called 'old' Poor Law.
>
> (Ibid., p. 93)

26 Ruether describes the 'four horseman of destruction' as human population explosion, environmental damage, misery of growing masses of the poor, and global militarization. She does, however, state: 'Yet our task is not to indulge in apocalyptic despair, but to continue the struggle to reconcile justice in human relations with a sustainable life community on earth' (*God and Gaia*, p. 111).
27 Ibid., p. 253.
28 Ibid., pp. 49 and 53.
29 Ibid., pp. 29–30.
30 Gutiérrez, *A Theology of Liberation*, p. 9.
31 Gutiérrez, *The Power of the Poor in History*, p. 37.
32 Ibid., p. 56.
33 Ibid., pp. 56–7.
34 Ibid., p. 69.
35 Lindbeck, *Nature of Doctrine*, p. 31.
36 Gutiérrez, *A Theology of Liberation*, p. 113.
37 'Encounter with Christ in the poor person constitutes an authentic spiritual experience. It is a life in the Spirit, the bond of love between Father and Son, between God and human being, and between human being and human being' (Gutiérrez, *Power of the Poor in History*, p. 53). 'The reason for believing is the free and gratuitousness of divine love; ... the gratuitousness of divine love – not retribution – is the hinge on which the world turns' (Gutiérrez, *On Job: God-Talk and the Suffering of the Innocent*, Maryknoll, NY, Orbis Books, 1987, p. 71). '[The] cross is the result of the resistance of those who refuse to accept the unmerited and demanding gift of God's love' (ibid., p. 97). 'Liberating praxis, which is, in the final analysis, a praxis of love, is thus based, without reduc-tionism of any kind, on the gratuitousness of God's love' (*The Truth Shall Make You Free*, p. 100).

38 'Christ, the Word of the Father, is the center of all theology, of all talk about God' (*The Truth Shall Make You Free*, p. 4).

39 Gutiérrez asks (*On Job*, pp. 102–3) 'How are we to do theology while Ayacucho lasts?'

40 Gutiérrez, *A Theology of Liberation*, p. 97. Only the Beatitudes and Matthew 25 play an equivalent role in his work.

41 This vision is much more central than is the Exodus to Gutiérrez's work. Concerning the Exodus, Gutiérrez has stated that the importance attributed to it for liberation theology is overrated. It is 'not a major theme in our theology of liberation' (*The Truth Shall Make You Free*, p. 29).

42 Gutiérrez, *A Theology of Liberation*, p. 116.

43 Quoted in Hans Urs von Balthasar's *The Theology of Karl Barth* (San Francisco, Ignatius Press, 1992), p. 54.

44 Ibid.

45 For instance, note the contradiction in the *Catechism of the Catholic Church* (paragraphs 2262–6) where it is first established that Jesus told us 'not to kill' and refused the sword in the garden. 'He did not defend himself and told Peter to leave his sword in his sheath.' But then, without any explanation of the obvious contradiction implied, the Catechism goes on to suggest that 'legitimate defense' is not only a right, but a 'grave duty.' This is based on the natural law of the 'preservation of the common good.' The obvious implication is that Jesus, the king of creation, violated the natural law by refusing to bear arms in favor of the oppressed in the garden. This kind of argument lets us know that there is still some truth in Barth's worry about the '*analogia entis*.' A philosophy of being or nature seems to create an architectonic within which Catholic moral theology proceeds.

46 Sobrino, *The True Church and the Poor*, p. 296.

47 Ibid., pp. 166, 208 and 209.

48 Sobrino, *Jesus the Liberator*, pp. 245 and 261.

49 'The crucified people are those who fill up in their flesh what is lacking in Christ's passion, as Paul says about himself' (ibid., p. 255). In this sense, Sobrino's work would find an ally in Milbank, whose work lays emphasis on the continuation of the atonement. But this recognition also takes issue with Milbank's characterization of liberation theology in his *The Word Made Strange: Theology, Language, Culture* (Oxford, Blackwell, 1997), where he states (p. 269):

> Since free human practice and the logic of history will 'of their nature' deliver the liberated future, imaginings of future ideal space are relatively inappropriate. Utopianism and specifically Christian social prescriptions are both ruled out by a single gesture which entrusts emancipation to a negative casting-off of mystifying shackles, and the formalism of a truly self-legislating humanity.

50 Sobrino, *The True Church and the Poor*, p. 166.

51 Sobrino (*Jesus the Liberator*, pp. 249–51) writes:

> If God can be known in the presence of the cross, the principal motor of that knowing is not wonder but suffering. Only through suffering can there be a *sumpatia*, a connaturality with the object one seeks to know.... To stand at the foot of Jesus' cross and to stand at the foot of historical crosses is absolutely necessary if we want to know the crucified God.

52 Ibid., p. 210.

53 Cone, *The God of the Oppressed*, p. 36.

54 Ibid., pp. 78–9.

55 Paul Tillich, *The Dynamics of Faith* (New York, Harper Torchbooks, 1957), p. 60.

56 So Cone writes: 'Any advice from whites to blacks on how to deal with white oppression is automatically under suspicion as a clever device to further enslavement' (*Black Theology and Black Power*, p. 20).

57 The significance of survival is a constant, if not a central theme, in Cone's theology: 'Black theology is a theology of survival because it seeks to interpret the theological significance of the being of a community whose existence is threatened by the power of nonbeing' (*A Black Theology of Liberation*, p. 16).

58 Cone, *The God of the Oppressed*, p. 34.

59 Cone, *Black Theology and Black Power*, p. 16.

60 Cone does not suffer the pathos of humility when he makes claims for the Church: 'the authentic Christian gospel as expressed in the New Testament is found more in the pre-Civil War black church than in its white counterpart' (*A Black Theology of Liberation*, p. 34).Who could deny the truthfulness of his statement?

61 Ibid. He also states: 'By becoming the religion of the Roman state, replacing the public state sacrifices, Christianity became the opposite of what Jesus intended' (*The God of the Oppressed*, p. 182).

62 Cone, *A Black Theology of Liberation*, pp. 134–5.

63 Delores Williams, 'James Cone's Liberation: Twenty Years Later,' in ibid., pp. 193–4.

64 Alasdair MacIntyre, *After Virtue* (Notre Dame, IN, University of Notre Dame Press, 1984), p. 220.

65 Cone, *The God of the Oppressed*, pp. 75–6.

66 Ibid., p. 104.

67 Cone writes:

> The dialectic of Scripture and tradition in relation to our contemporary social context forces us to affirm that there is no knowledge of Jesus Christ today that contradicts who he was yesterday, i.e. his historical appearance in first-century Palestine.... If we do not take the historical Jesus seriously as the key to locating the meaning of Christ's presence today, there is no way to avoid the charge of subjectivism, the identification of Christ today with a momentary political persuasion.
>
> (Ibid., p. 106)

68 Ibid., p. 27.

69 Cone, *A Black Theology of Liberation*, p. 20.

70 Cone, *A Black Theology and Black Power*, p. xii.

71 So he asserts: 'Theology cannot be indifferent to the importance of blackness by making some kind of existential leap beyond blackness to an undefined universalism' (*A Black Theology of Liberation*, p. 36).

72 And that scope is limited precisely because blackness functions more as a symbol than as a history. For instance, in describing the role of blackness in black theology Cone refers to Tillich's *The Dynamics of Faith* and then argues that 'blackness is an ontological symbol and a visible reality which best describes what oppression means in America.' Likewise 'whiteness is the symbol of the Anti-Christ' (*A Black Theology of Liberation*, pp. 7–8).

73 Ibid., p. 41.

74 Preface to the 1989 edition of *Black Theology and Black Power*, p. ix.

75 Ibid., pp. 84–5.

76 Preface to the 1986 edition of *A Black Theology of Liberation*, p. ix.

77 Preface to the 1989 edition of *Black Theology and Black Power*, p. xi.

78 Karl Barth, *Church Dogmatics*, vol. I, Book 1: The Doctrine of the Word of God (Edinburgh, T. & T. Clark, 1975), pp. 144–5.

79 *Black Theology and Black Power*, p. 7.
80 Tillich, *Courage to Be* (New Haven, CT, Yale University Press, 1963), p. 27.
81 That Tillich intends to use a method of analogy can be seen in his *Courage to Be*, p. 25, and in his *Systematic Theology*, vol. I, p. 179.
82 Ibid., p. 49.
83 Tillich, *The Dynamics of Faith*, p. 41.
84 Tillich, *Systematic Theology*, vol. I, p. 12.
85 Tillich, *The Dynamics of Faith*, p. 125.
86 For an account of the influence of Scotus on Tillich see his *Systematic Theology*, vol. 1, pp. 167–8. Tillich notes:

> In Duns Scotus and all ontology and theology influenced by him … an element of ultimate indeterminacy is seen in the ground of being. God's *potestas absoluta* is a perennial threat to any given structure of things. It undercuts any absolute apriorism, but it does not remove ontology and the relatively a priori structures with which ontology is concerned.

For a helpful discussion of Scotus' position, see David Burrel's *Analogy and Philosophical Language* (New Haven, CT, Yale University Press, 1973), pp. 102–4.
87 For a helpful discussion of the distinction between Thomas' 'real distinction' between God and creatures as against Scotus' 'formal distinction' based on the 'univocity of being,' see Catherine Pickstock, 'Can My Eating Slake Your Hunger,' in her *After Writing: On the Liturgical Consummation of Philosophy* (Oxford, Blackwell, 1998), pp. 120–66.
88 Tillich, *Courage to Be*, pp. 113–15 and 141.
89 Cone, *Black Theology and Black Power*, p. 9.
90 *A Black Theology of Liberation*, p. 75.
91 Tillich, *Dynamics of Faith*, p. 16.
92 Ibid., p. 35.
93 McCabe, *God Matters* (London, Templegate Publishers, 1987), pp. 226–34.
94 *Black Theology and Black Power*, p. 54.
95 *A Black Theology of Liberation*, p. 26. It was after all Luther who first put forth the idea of using violence 'by whatever means you can' for the sake of the neighbor's liberty, as an alien work of charity. See 'On Secular Authority,' in *Martin Luther: Selections from His Writings* (ed. Dillenberger, Garden City, NY, Doubleday, 1961), p. 373.
96 *Black Theology and Black Power*, p. 6.
97 *A Black Theology of Liberation*, pp. 10 and 37.
98 'God in Christ has freed us. The battle was fought and won on Good Friday and the triumph was revealed to men at Easter' (*Black Theology and Black Power*, p. 40).
99 Ibid., p. 107.

## 10 Conclusion to Part II

1 Unfortunately this also leads Roman Catholicism to deny the ordination of women because the highest vocation of the Christian life, the life of holiness, is already open to both women and men. But I don't see how that is a necessary feature of this important distinction.

## 11 Introduction to Part III

1 Raymond Williams, *Marxism and Literature* (Oxford, Oxford University Press, 1977), p. 122.

2 Milbank argues that nihilism does not oppose the kind of foundational epistemology one finds, for example, in Stackhouse's work. Milbank suggests that 'nihilism is not scepticism, nor relativism.... Nihilism is the purest objectivity, since it is possible objectively to conclude that there is only nothing.' See John Milbank, Catherine Pickstock, and Graham Ward (eds) *Radical Orthodoxy* (London, Routledge, 1998), p. 32.
3 Milbank, *The Word Made Strange: Theology, Language, Culture*, p. 285.
4 The transcendental predicates of being were viewed as the one, the true, the good, and the beautiful.
5 Alasdair MacIntyre, *After Virtue* (Notre Dame, IN, University of Notre Dame Press, 1984), p. 219.
6 Ibid., pp. 62–7.

## 12 A true economic order

1 See ST Ia IIae Q 94, art. 5. See also Pamela Hall's *Narrative and the Natural Law: An Interpretation of Thomistic Ethics* (Notre Dame, IN, University of Notre Dame Press, 1994).
2 Waterman, 'The Intellectual Context of *Rerum Novarum,' Review of Social Economy*, 1991 (winter), pp. 475–6.
3 Waterman, *Revolution, Economics and Religion* (Cambridge, Cambridge University Press, 1991), p. 110.
4 Ibid., p. 165.
5 Ibid., p. 121.
6 As Paley put it: 'These points being assured to us by natural theology [i.e. the existence and character of the Deity], we may well leave to revelation the disclosure of many particulars which our research cannot reach ...' (*Natural Theology, Selections*, The Library of Liberal Arts, Bobbs-Merrill Co., 1963, p. 86).
7 Paul Misner, *Social Catholicism in Europe: From the Onset of Industrialization to the First World War* (New York, Crossroad, 1991), p. 85.
8 See Waterman in note 2, p. 472.
9 Quoted in Paul Misner, *Social Catholicism in Europe*, p. 51.
10 Ibid., p. 71.
11 John Paul II's *Veritatis Splendor* is an exception here because it recognized that freedom should be related to the true and the good, and that the latter was preeminently found in Jesus.
12 *Rerum Novarum*, in Walsh and Davies (eds), *Proclaiming Justice and Peace: Papal Documents from* Rerum Novarum *through* Centesimus Annus (Mystic, CT, Twenty-Third Publications, 1991), paragraph 23.
13 This distinction between internal and external goods is developed in Chapter 8, in relation to Alasdair MacIntyre's work.
14 Such an obvious implication of Leo's teaching seems to resonate well with Milbank's priority of ecclesiology over Christology, which is examined in Chapter 9.
15 *Rerum Novarum*, paragraph 2.
16 Marx wrote (*Capital*, New York: International Publishers, 1973):

> The exchange of commodities of itself implies no other relations of dependence than those which result from its own nature. On this assumption, labour-power can appear upon the market as a commodity, only if, and so far as, its possessor, the individual whose labor it is, offers it for sale, or sells it, as a commodity. In order that he may be able to do this, he must have it at his disposal, must be the untrammeled owner of his capacity for labour, of his person.

> (Vol. I, p. 168)

Marx goes on to critique the so-called freedom of the Benthamites that makes it possible for labor to be reduced to a mere commodity because it is assumed that this is the only property certain people have to sell (ibid., p. 176). Compare Marx's critique with that of *Rerum Novarum* (paragraphs 44–5), when Leo XIII writes:

> It is argued that given that the scale of wages is decided by free agreement, it would appear that the employer fulfills the contract by paying the wage agreed upon, that nothing further is due from him and that injustice will be done only if the employer does not pay the full price or the worker does not perform the whole of his task. In these cases and not otherwise it would be right for the political authority to intervene and require each party to give to the other his due. This is an argument which a balanced judgment can neither entirely agree with nor easily accept. It does not take every consideration into account; and there is one consideration of the greatest importance which is omitted altogether. This is that to work is to exert oneself to obtain those things which are necessary for the various requirements of life and most of all for life itself.... Thus, human work has stamped upon it by nature, as it were, two marks peculiar to it. First, it is personal, because the force acting adheres to the person acting; and therefore it belongs entirely to the worker and is intended for his advantage. Second it is necessary because man needs the results of his work to maintain himself in accordance with a command of nature itself which he must take particular care to obey.... Let worker and employer, therefore, make any bargains they like, and in particular agree freely about wages; nevertheless, there underlies a requirement of natural justice higher and older than any bargain voluntarily struck: the wage ought not to be in any way insufficient for the bodily needs of a temperate and well-behaved worker. If, having no alternative and fearing a worse evil, a workman is forced to accept harder conditions imposed by an employer or contractor, he is the victim of violence against which justice cries out.

17  Jeremy Bentham, Letter XIII, 'Defence of Usury,' in *Jeremy Bentham's Economic Writings* (W. Stark, London, Blackfriars, 1952), p. 163.

18  Notice that John Paul II, in *Veritatis Splendor* (paragraph 80), repeats that 'subhuman living conditions' and 'degrading conditions of work which treat labourers as mere instruments of profit and not as free responsible persons' are both examples of 'intrinsically evil acts.' And he is quoting from the Second Vatican Council's document, *Gaudium et Spes*. *Veritatis Splendor*, in John Wilkins (ed.) *Considering Veritatis Splendor* (Cleveland, OH, Pilgrim Press, 1994).

19  For instance, in *Mater et Magistra* (Walsh and Davies (eds) *Proclaiming Justice and Peace*, paragraph 109), John XXIII argues that 'the exercise of freedom finds its guarantee and incentive in the right of ownership.' He follows Pius XII in arguing that the defense of individual dignity also requires a defense of private property ownership. The solution to poverty, for John XXIII, is to 'extend dominion over nature' for the sake of development. John XXIII was the pope most open, by far, to modern capitalist ideology. For a good discussion of this see Donal Dorr's *Option for the Poor: A Hundred Years of Vatican Social Teaching* (Maryknoll, NY, Orbis Books), Chapter 3.

20  As Waterman (see note 2) has noted, the Roman Catholic account of liberty in *Rerum Novarum*, and throughout the encyclical tradition, is 'extremely difficult if not impossible to reconcile with the methodological individualism of economic theory,' and thus Leo 'destroyed the intellectual foundation of economic liberalism.'

21 Leo writes

> It follows that when socialists endeavor to transfer privately owned goods into common ownership they worsen the condition of all wage-earners. By taking away from them freedom to dispose of their wages they rob them of all hope and opportunity of increasing their possessions and bettering their condition.
>
> > (*Rerum Novarum*, paragraph 4)

Marx and Leo XIII agreed that the capitalist order was destroying the family, but Marx thought the conflict between the market and the family would result in a stronger and better form of family relations, because

> modern industry, in overturning the economic foundation on which was based the traditional family, and the family labour corresponding to it, had also unloosened all traditional family ties.... It was not however, the misuse of parental authority that created the capitalistic exploitation, whether direct or indirect, of children's labour; but, on the contrary, it was the capitalistic mode of exploitation which, by sweeping away the economic basis of parental authority, made its exercise degenerate into a mischievous misuse of power. However terrible and disgusting the dissolution, under the capitalist system, of the old family ties may appear, nevertheless, modern industry, by assigning as it does an important part in the process of production, outside the domestic sphere, to women, to young persons and to children of both sexes, creates a new economic foundation for a higher form of the family and of the relations between the sexes. It is, of course, just as absurd to hold the Teutonic-Christian form of the family to be absolute and final as it would be to apply that character to the ancient Roman, the ancient Greek or the Eastern forms which, moreover, taken together form a series in historical development. Moreover, it is obvious that the fact of the collective working group being composed of individuals of both sexes and all ages, must necessarily, under suitable conditions, become a source of humane development.
>
> > (*Capital*, vol. I, p. 490)

22 The financiers – that is, super-efficient accountants like John Pierpont Morgan – are the wielders of power in the 1890s. This power is not based on birth, nobility, or any traditional hierarchical ordering. It stems solely from 'free' competition. Even publicly elected officials become dependent for power on these financiers. In the panic of 1893, then-president Grover Cleveland has to call upon Morgan to get the United States out of trouble when a run on gold threatens the economic viability of the nation. See H. W. Brands, *The Reckless Decade* (New York, St Martin's Press, 1995).

23 As can be clearly seen from his *Theory of Moral Sentiments* (Indianapolis, IN, Liberty Fund 1982, p. 36), Smith's free-market system contained an explicit theology:

> The ancient stoics were of opinion, that as the world was governed by the all-ruling providence of a wise, powerful and good God, every single event ought to be regarded, as making a necessary part of the plan of the universe, and as tending to promote the general order and happiness of the whole: that the vices and follies of mankind, therefore, made as necessary a part of this plan as their wisdom or their virtue; and by that eternal art which educes good from ill, were made to tend equally to the prosperity and perfection of the great system of nature.

To argue that Smith freed the market from theological interference is incorrect. He freed it from *church* interference, but the free market still serves the interests of a Stoic theology.

24  Adam Smith, *The Wealth of Nations*, p. 66.
25  Laborers, suggested Smith,

> have always recourse to the loudest clamour, and sometimes to the most shocking violence and outrage. They are desperate, and act with the folly and extravagance of desperate men, who must either starve, or frighten their masters into an immediate compliance with their demands. The masters upon these occasions are just as clamorous upon the other side, and never cease to call aloud for the assistance of the civil magistrate, and the rigorous execution of those laws which have been enacted with so much severity against the combinations of servants, labourers and journeymen. The workmen, accordingly, very seldom derive any advantage from the violence of those tumultuous combinations ...
>
> (Ibid., p.67)

This conflict is accepted as inevitable and built into the system. The papal teachings conflict with both the free-market system and Marxism on this point. They consistently argue, beginning with *Rerum Novarum*, that the relationships within the economy should be based on cooperation, peace and harmony, and not on conflict and antagonism. They do not, however, always recognize that the source of conflict in modern economic arrangements arises originally from the free-market system.

26  As previously noted, Malthus with his population principle and Ricardo with his rent-differential theory revealed the limitations to Smith's argument at this point.
27  Smith, *Wealth of Nations*, p. 71.
28  Ibid., p. 754.
29  Smith (ibid.) writes:

> In the ancient philosophy the perfection of virtue was represented as necessarily productive, to the person who possessed it, of the most perfect happiness in this life. In the modern philosophy it was frequently represented as generally, or rather as almost always, inconsistent with any degree of happiness in this life; and heaven was to be earned only by penance and mortification, by the austerities and abasement of a monk; not by the liberal, generous, and spirited conduct of a man. Casuistry and an ascetic morality made up, in most cases, the greater part of the moral philosophies of the schools. By far the most important of all the different branches of philosophy, became in this manner by far the most corrupted.... The alterations which the universities of Europe thus introduced into the ancient course of philosophy, were all meant for the education of ecclesiastics, and to render it a more proper introduction to the study of theology. But the additional quantity of subtlety and sophistry; the casuistry and the ascetic morality which those alterations introduced into it, certainly did not render it more proper for the education of gentlemen or men of the world, or more likely either to improve the understanding, or to mend the heart.... The greater part of what is taught in schools and universities, however, does not seem to be the most proper preparation for the real business of the world.

30  Ibid., pp. 135–6.
31  See John Milbank, *Theology and Social Theory*, pp. 34–7.
32  Smith wrote:

The obstruction which corporation laws give to the free circulation of labour is common, I believe, to every part of Europe. That which is given to it by the poor laws is, so far as I know, peculiar to England. It consists in the difficulty which a poor man finds in obtaining a settlement, or even in being allowed to exercise his industry in any parish but that to which he belongs. The difficulty of obtaining settlement obstructs even that of common labour.

> (*The Wealth of Nations*, p. 135)

33 Malthus, *An Essay on the Principle of Population* (Cambridge, Cambridge University Press, 1992), pp. 41–3.
34 Ricardo, *On the Principles of Political Economy and Taxation*, pp. 106–9.
35 Mill, *Autobiography* (London, Penguin Books, 1989), p. 26.
36 If this analysis is correct, and if this is the world we have inherited, then Catholic families are placed in a bind. They live within a church that teaches them to be open to children and that the economy should provide the means by which life can be received. And they live in an economy that seeks to discipline us against children by habituating 'prudence' into us as consisting in late marriage, few children and sexual restraint (if sexual restraint is burdensome, then at least be 'prudent' in practicing non-procreative sexual intercourse). Given this bind, it seems to me, Catholics are tempted to turn against the teaching of the church, think themselves free, and not recognize that our sexuality can serve the interest of the economy by adopting the sexual practices perpetuated by the market's discipline.
37 The family is one social institution that remains somewhat impervious to the detrimental effects of Adam Smith's cultural logic. Few of us who are parents make decisions about our children's health care, nourishment or education based on the anticipated marginal return of our investment. Even though Smith's free-market system has greatly impacted the size of our families, and we often perpetuate the moral condemnation of large poor families, we still recognize the family as a place where relations should not be based on the logic of commodities.

Without a doubt there is, in the Papal letters, an idealization of the family. I admit that many families do not promote the internal good of togetherness. Too many families embody the opposite tendency, as Sartre pointed out when he called the family the 'hell-hole of togetherness.' But I don't find this to be a decisive critique of Leo XIII. The fact that many families do not embody the ideal provides greater need of an ideal against which the abuse of the family should be checked. Certainly the papal teachings can be used to thoroughly privatize the family. This can result in an unchecked form of violence and abuse where the family becomes the domain of the father, his castle, and he rules as a tyrant. Unfortunately, the history of the family also includes this narrative. This is found in our everyday speech. The expression 'rule of thumb' came from English common law and related to a husband's innocence of abuse for beating his wife unless he used a stick larger than his thumb. Also, the famous nursery rhyme

> Peter, Peter, pumpkin eater
> Had a wife and couldn't keep her,
> So he put her in a shell
> And there he kept her very well

is a story about keeping one's wife pregnant and in the kitchen so that she can deliver the goods the husband enjoys. If the household is to serve as an economic alternative it cannot be merely the patriarchal family that serves the interest of the father alone. And this is accomplished when the role of the father is not only that of breadwinner but also of breadmaker.

Nor should the family be turned into a salvific institution. Only the church, and not the family, offers salvation. To ask the family to save is to destroy its internal good by placing upon it a burden it cannot and should not bear. Nevertheless, the family remains one place where virtue can be cultivated. But this requires that the social institution of the family should be free as an internal good, and that commodities should serve the interest of the family. This cannot happen when commodities are kept free and the family is forced to serve their interest.

38 *Review of Social Economy* (winter 1991), pp. 543–6.
39 Dempsey seemed to be attracted to Schumpeter's work because of his sympathetic portrayal of the scholastics. This portrayal can be found in Schumpeter's 1954 publication, *History of Economic Analysis* (New York, Oxford University Press), pp. 73–141.
40 Joseph Schumpeter, 'Introduction' to Bernard Dempsey's *Interest and Usury* (Washington, DC, American Council on Public Affairs, 1943), p. vii.
41 Adam Smith, *Wealth of Nations*, p. 52.
42 Ibid., p. 339.
43 Bentham, Letter XIII, 'Defence of Usury,' in *Jeremy Bentham's Economic Writings*, W. Stark, London, Blackfriars, 1952.
44 The Austrian school originated in Vienna with the work of Carl Menger (1840–1921). His contribution to economics was the development of the marginal theory of utility which viewed exchange in terms of subjective preferences that could be ordered hierarchically. This led the Austrian school to depart from the classical liberal emphasis on production and to emphasize consumption instead. Menger's work was developed by Friedrich von Weiser (1851–1926), who developed the idea of opportunity costs, and then by Eugene Böhm-Bawerk (1851–1941), Ludwig von Mises (1881–1973) and Friedrich von Hayek (1899–1995).
45 This first volume is now published in the three-volume set known as *Capital and Interest* (trans. George D. Huncke and Hans F. Sennholz, South Holland, IL, Libertarian, 1959), pp. 16–36.
46 Ibid., pp. 9–17.
47 Ludwig von Mises, *The Theory of Money and Credit* (Indianapolis, IN, Liberty Fund, 1980), p. 84.
48 Joseph Schumpeter, *Theory of Economic Development* (Cambridge, MA, Harvard University Press, 1949), p. 178.
49 Dempsey, *The Functional Economy* (Englewood Cliffs, NJ, Prentice-Hall, 1958), p. 14.
50 H. Somerville, 'Interest and Usury in a New Light,' *Economic Journal* 41 (1931), p. 647.
51 Ibid., p. 648.
52 Ibid., p. 649.
53 Somerville, *Economic Journal* 42 (1932), p. 126.
54 Ibid., p. 128.
55 Ibid., p. 132.
56 Keynes, *General Theory of Employment, Interest and Money* (San Diego, CA, Harcourt Brace, 1964), pp. 351–2.
57 In fact, he was not truly interested in avoiding usury. He once stated: 'Avarice and usury and precaution must be our foods for a little longer still. For only they can lead us out of the tunnel of economic necessity into the daylight' (Robert Skidelsky, *John Maynard Keynes: The Economist as Saviour, 1920–1937*, London, Penguin, 1994, p. 237).
58 Ibid., p. 369.
59 Schumpeter's disagreement with Keynes can be found in Schumpeter's *Capitalism, Socialism and Democracy* (New York, Harper Torchbooks, 1976,

p. 396), where he notes that 'decisions to save depend upon and presuppose decisions to invest.' Schumpeter denied Keynes' distinction between savings and investment.

60 Dempsey, *Interest and Usury*, p. 220.
61 Ibid.
62 John T. Noonan, Jr, *The Scholastic Analysis of Usury* (Cambridge, MA, Harvard University Press, 1957), p. 1.
63 Ibid., p. 403.
64 He justified the possibility of the comparison on the basis of the natural law. Because the scholastics' theological economics was fundamentally based on observations of the natural law and not of the divine law alone, a congruence can be assumed between their work and modern economists. See Chapter 1, 'Terms of a Comparison,' *Interest and Usury*, pp. 1–6.
65 Ibid., p. 228.
66 Ibid., p. 207.
67 Ibid., p. 26.
68 Wicksell, *Interest and Prices* (New York, Sentry, 1965), p. xxv.
69 Ibid., p. 3.
70 Ibid., p. 19.
71 Ibid., p. 135. The use of the distinction between uncontrolled and contractual rates of interest at this point in Wicksell's argument is confusing. However, I take it that the former is similar to the natural or normal rate and the latter is the market rate which is determined by the banking system.
72 Dempsey, *Interest and Usury*, p. 207.
73 Ludwig von Mises, *The Theory of Money and Credit*, p. 308.
74 Ibid., p. 297.
75 Ibid., p. 340.
76 Ibid., p. 341.
77 Dempsey, *Interest and Usury*, p. 212.
78 'Only within community can man make any decent progress in fulfilling his basic urge to the perfection of his powers' (Dempsey, *The Functional Economy*, p. 273).
79 Dempsey suggested, following Walter Lippman, that business corporations are nothing but 'creatures of the state.' They bear no resemblance to the medieval guild organization (ibid., p. 294).
80 An 'impersonal moral argument' is an expression used by Alasdair MacIntyre to explain a moral theory that does not depend upon any particular social roles for its intelligibility. Thus it is putatively open and accessible to any individual. The moral position requires no particular formation (*After Virtue*, pp. 8–9). MacIntyre argues that incommensurable and impersonal moral arguments characterize modern moral debates. Thus these debates contain an inherent contradiction. The debates themselves are irresolvable subject to 'resolution' by force and assertion of will, yet the positions advocated are warranted by supposedly impersonal arguments.
81 This expression 'semi-autonomous' is not mine. I have no idea what it means although one regularly finds theologians appeal to it to describe the position of economics to theology.
82 John Courtney Murray, *We Hold These Truths: Catholic Reflections on the American Proposition* (New York, Sheed & Ward, 1960), p. 109. Although this strategy appeals to Thomas for an ethic based on the natural law alone, it loses what is most interesting about his work. Thomas denied the independent character of distinct autonomous forms of reasoning and placed them all within an order of charity that moves toward God. For this reason, any adequately articulated Thomism will be in irremediable conflict with the autonomous disciplinary divisions that reduce the modern academy to (borrowing a phrase

from George Grant) a 'multi-versity'. It is not natural law that makes possible the integration of knowledge. It is, for Thomas, only the *lex nova*. For an excellent critique of Murray's argument, see Michael Baxter's 1996 'Writing History in a World Without Ends,' in *Pro Ecclesia*, vol. V, no. 4.

83  See for instance, William E. May's *Introduction to Moral Theology* (Huntingdon, IN, Our Sunday Visitor, 1994). This methodology may have been reinforced by the natural law strategy dominant in the twentieth century among Catholic moral theologians, but it is also surely a residual element of the two-tiered system of scholasticism.

84  Dempsey, *The Functional Economy* (Englewood Cliffs, NJ, Prentice-Hall, 1958), p. 65.

85  Dempsey writes: 'Both the businessman and the labor leader who regard class conflict as normal and inevitable, by that very attitude, sharpen, extend, and aggravate whatever conflicts there may be' (ibid., p. 135).

86  Ibid., pp. 150–63.

87  Ibid., p. 162.

88  Ibid., p. 311.

89  Ibid., p. 84.

90  Ibid., p. 103.

91  Ibid., p. 106.

92  Dempsey, *Interest and Usury*, p. 116.

93  Dempsey, *The Functional Economy*, p. 81.

94  Ibid., pp. 182 and 164.

95  Ibid., p. 167.

96  This term first appears in Catholic social teaching in Pius XI's encyclical, *Quadragesimo Anno*.

97  Dempsey, *The Functional Economy*, pp. 164–83 and 392–411, particularly 405.

98  ST Ia IIae Q 98, art. 5, resp.: *lex vetus manifestabat pracepta legis naturae et superaddebat quaedam propria praecepta.*

99  ST Ia IIae Q 100, art. 6.

100  ST Ia IIae Q 98, art. 6.

101  ST Ia IIae Q 99, art. 2, rep. obj. 1. Thomas goes on to note that although the precepts of the natural law '*non poterat errare in universali: sed tamen, propter consuetudinem peccandi, obscurabatur in particularibus agendis.*'

102  Ibid.

103  ST Ia IIae Q 98, art. 1. As Thomas stated: 'Complete goodness is to be found in that which is sufficient of itself to attain the end.'

104  ST Ia IIae Q 108, art. 3.

105  My interpretation of Thomas has been influenced by Hans Urs von Balthasar's theological aesthetics as expounded in *The Glory of the Lord: A Theological Aesthetics*, vol. I: *Seeing the Form* (San Francisco, Ignatius Press, 1982). He notes:

> The supernatural is not there in order to supply that part of our natural capacities we have failed to develop. *Gratiam perficit naturam, non supplet.* God's incarnation perfects the whole ontology and aesthetics of created Being.... [Jesus] is what he expresses – namely God – but he is not whom he expresses – namely, the Father. This incomparable paradox stands at the fountainhead of the Christian aesthetic, and therefore of all aesthetics.... How greatly therefore the power of sight is demanded.... Christ becomes for us the image that reveals the invisible God.
>
> (pp. 29–32)

106  The most exact definition of the *lex nova* is *est gratia Spiritus sancti, quae datur per fidem Christi*. Although the grace of the Holy Spirit is the primary definition of the New law, Thomas also mentions *quaedam sicut dispositiva ad gra-*

*tiam Spiritus sancti, et ad usum hujus gratiae pertinentia, quae sunt quasi se-cundaria in lege nova; de quibus opportuit instui fideles Christi et verbis et scrip-tis, tam circa credenda quam circa agenda.* These things which are, as it were, secondary to the grace of the Holy Spirit are transmitted both orally and in writing. It is obvious that the Sermon on the Mount has a central role in the secondary written things of the New law.

107 It must be admitted that when it comes to the sixth commandment, 'Thou shalt not kill,' Thomas lost his own insight about the relationship between the internal and the external. In Q 108, art. 4 he wrote:

> What the Lord says in Matthew 5 and Luke 6 about true love for enemies is necessary for salvation, if it is taken to refer to inward readiness of mind; in the sense that one should be ready to do good to enemies and so on when necessity demands. And so these matters are put among the precepts. But that someone should readily put this into effect to enemies, when no special necessity arises, belongs to the particular counsels.

Here Thomas has rendered asunder the relationship between the internal and the external that he sought to maintain throughout his discussion of the rela-tionship between the old law and the New law. Replacing Jesus' prohibition of violence with the prohibition of adultery reveals the scandalous nature of his argument. 'What the Lord says about [adultery] and the like is necessary for salvation, if it is taken to refer to inward readiness of mind; in the sense that one should be ready [not to commit adultery] and so on when necessity de-mands.'

**13 Theology and the good**

1 While this may not be a fair criticism of much of liberation theology it is certainly the case that the early power of liberation theology occurred precisely because these theologians figured out how to influence the newly formed na-tional conferences of Catholic bishops. For a discussion of this see Christian Smith's *The Emergence of Liberation Theology: Radical Religion and Social Movement Theory* (Chicago, University of Chicago Press, 1991), particularly p. 235, where Smith concludes his sympathetic social analysis of the emergence of liberation theology by suggesting that

> the liberation theology movement should be understood as one of many elite-initiated revitalization movements that aim to force drastic redirec-tions in the strategies and resources of established institutions.... [A] small cadre of young, aggressive, radicalized theologians outraged by Latin America's poverty and dependency gained access to positions of influence in the Latin American Catholic Church. They did so at a critical time when, because of a growing organizational crisis and an increased ideo-logical openness, the Church was searching for a new organizational strat-egy that would strengthen its ability to achieve its mission in society.

2 Walter M. Miller, *A Canticle For Leibowitz* (New York, Bantam Books, 1976), p. 62.
3 Alasdair MacIntyre, *After Virtue*, p. 5.
4 Ronald Thiemann, *Religion in Public Life: A Dilemma for Democracy* (Washington, DC, Georgetown University Press, 1996), p. 36.
5 MacIntyre, *After Virtue*, p. 6 (emphasis added).
6 Ibid., p. 23.
7 Ibid., p. 109.
8 Ibid.

9 This is why Nietzsche becomes an option to advance moral rationality beyond Weber. Nietzsche reveals that behind this vague notion of utility is a political act of will that now is no longer recognized as such because morality first 'anaesthetizes' its adherents. In 'Our Virtues' Nietzsche wrote:

> I hope to be forgiven for discovering that all moral philosophy hitherto has been tedious and has belonged to the soporofic appliances – and that 'virtue,' in my opinion, has been more injured by the tediousness of its advocates than by anything else; at the same time, however, I would not wish to overlook their general usefulness. It is desirable that as few people as possible should reflect upon morals, and consequently it is very desirable that morals should not some day become interesting.... Observe, for example, the indefatigable, inevitable, English utilitarians: how ponderously and respectably they stalk on, stalk along.... In the end they all want English morality to be recognised as authoritative, inasmuch as mankind, or the 'general utility,' or 'the happiness of the greatest number,' – no! the happiness of England – will be best served thereby.
> (*Beyond Good and Evil* (New York, Modern Library, 1927), pp. 532–3)

10 Keynes once wrote that 'economics is essentially a moral and not a natural science' (cited in Robert Skidelsky, *John Maynard Keynes: Economist as Saviour, 1920–1937*, New York, Penguin Books, 1992, p. 619).
11 Ibid., pp. 170, 379.
12 Edwin Mansfield, *Principles of Macroeconomics* (New York, Norton, 1977), pp. 15–16.
13 MacIntyre, *After Virtue*, p. 59.
14 Alasdair MacIntyre, *Marxism and Christianity* (Notre Dame, IN, University of Notre Dame Press, 1995), p. viii.
15 Ibid., p. x. MacIntyre's appeal to a 'justice of desert' has prompted John Milbank to question whether he has offered a sufficiently radical challenge to capitalism. In *Theology and Social Theory* (pp. 352–3) Milbank states:

> If virtue is still heroic honour, then virtue as such is linked to a competition for scarce resources, albeit not a modern, naked, economic competition but a competition in the exercise of excellence and patronage, and for the educative and political means to do so. (Even MacIntyre himself suggests that excellence should be *rewarded*, rather than merely provided with the resources necessary for its exercise – an idea that is certainly not socialist and perhaps not fully Christian either.)

16 MacIntyre, *Marxism and Christianity*, p. 124.
17 MacIntyre argues that for both Marxism and Christianity 'knowledge of nature and society is the principal determinant of action' (ibid., p. 124). MacIntyre also states that 'Marx's original criticisms of alienation and of class society rely upon a notion of unalienated man which provides a standard by which the present is judged and found wanting' (ibid., p. 129).
18 This was the English title of Pius XI's encyclical *Quadragesimo Anno*.
19 Robert A. Sirico, 'The Bishops' Big Economic Tent,' *Wall Street Journal* (December 10, 1996), p. 22.
20 MacIntyre, *Marxism and Christianity*, p. viii.
21 MacIntyre, 'How Can We Learn What *Veritatis Splendor* Has To Teach Us?', *The Thomist* (1994), pp. 171–95.
22 Ibid., p. 172.
23 Ibid., pp. 174–5.
24 *Catechism of the Catholic Church* (New York, Paulist Press, 1994), paragraph 2434: 'A just wage is the legitimate fruit of work. To refuse or withhold it can be a grave injustice' (cf. Lev. 19:13; Deut. 24:14–15; James 5:4). In determining

fair pay both the needs and the contributions of each person must be taken into account:

> Remuneration for work should guarantee man the opportunity to provide a dignified livelihood for himself and his family on the material, social, cultural, and spiritual level, taking into account the role and productivity of each, the state of the business and the common good.... Agreement between the parties is not sufficient to justify morally the amount to be received in wages.
>
> (Ibid.)

25 *Rerum Novarum*, in Walsh and Davies (eds), *Proclaiming Justice and Peace*, paragraph 45.
26 ST IIa IIae Q 57, art. 1: *ius est objectum iustitae*.
27 ST IIa IIae Q 58, art. 11, rep. obj. 3.
28 ST IIa IIae Q 59, art. 4, resp.
29 John Ryan, *Distributive Justice* (New York, Arno Press, 1978), pp. 360–2.
30 *Catechism of the Catholic Church*, paragraph 2401.
31 Milbank critiques MacIntyre for this assumption because it insufficiently integrates the theological virtues with the natural virtues. It assumes a self-possession.
32 MacIntyre defines a virtue as 'an acquired human quality the possession and exercise of which tends to enable us to achieve those goods which are internal to practices and the lack of which effectively prevents us from achieving any such goods' (*After Virtue*, p. 191). MacIntyre also states that this account of virtue 'requires for its application the acceptance for some prior account of certain features of social and moral life in terms of which it has to be defined and explained' (ibid., p. 186).
33 This draws on MacIntyre's account of a 'practice' (ibid., p. 187).
34 Ibid., p. 190.
35 Ibid., p. 222. MacIntyre also states (p. 223):

> The virtues find their point and purpose not only in sustaining those relationships necessary if the variety of goods internal to practices are to be achieved and not only in sustaining the form of an individual life in which that individual may seek out his or her good as the good of his or her whole life, but also in sustaining those traditions which provide both practices and individual lives with their necessary historical context.

36 See Schumpeter's discussion of 'creative destruction' in *Capitalism, Socialism and Democracy*, or its contemporary manifestation in Romer's 'new growth theory' where new and original ideas are viewed as the sources of wealth production. Of course, what actually produces wealth remains a mystery to economists; perhaps it must remain such a mystery since it is viewed as non-historical.
37 See MacIntyre, *Three Rival Versions: Encyclopedia, Genealogy, and Tradition* (Notre Dame, IN, University of Notre Dame Press, 1990), pp. 212–18. MacIntyre writes:

> What I am suggesting, then, is that the genealogist faces grave difficulties in constructing a narrative of his or her past which would allow any acknowledgment in that past of a failure, let alone a guilty failure, which is also the failure of the same still-present self ...
>
> (Ibid., p. 213)

Notice the similarity between MacIntyre's claim here against the genealogists and their loss of identity and the 'individualist' identity of liberalism which also disavows the phenomenon of embeddedness by denying 'any responsibility for

the effects of slavery upon black Americans, saying "I never owned slaves" '
(*After Virtue*, p. 220). In fact, both positions seem to fall under the category of
the damnable, as MacIntyre (drawing on Aquinas) explains it: 'hell is persistence in defection from the integrity both of a self and of its communities'
(*Three Rival Versions*, p. 144).

38 ST Ia IIae Q 108, art. 3.
39 For a discussion of how Christian tradition 'challenges the primacy of the
   political,' see Jean Bethke Elshtain, *Private Man, Public Woman* (Princeton,
   NJ, Princeton University Press, 1981).
40 ST IIa IIae Q 57, art. 1: *aliquid opus adequatum alteri secundem aliquem
   aequalitatis modum*.
41 MacIntyre, *Three Rival Versions*, pp. 137–8.
42 Ibid., p. 140.
43 Ibid., p. 139. See also *After Virtue*, p. 119.
44 This point has also been made persuasively by Servais Pinckaers in *Sources of
   Christian Ethics* (Washington, DC, Catholic University of America Press,
   1995), where he challenges the ethics of obligation that has come to characterize Catholic moral theology. It is also found in John Paul II's reading of
   Jesus' encounter with the rich young ruler, in Part I of *Veritatis Splendor*.
45 ST IIa IIae Q 24, art. 3.
46 IIa IIae Q 23, art 2. What constitutes these 'superadditions' will be discussed in
   Chapter 9 in relation to the work of John Milbank.
47 IIa IIae Q 24, art. 3.
48 Ia IIae Q 65: 'all the infused moral virtues also depend on charity.' He states
   this in the context of a discussion of 'infused prudence' where he argues that
   even the moral virtue of prudence requires the grace of the Holy Spirit for its
   completion. Thus, even the acquired virtues require 'infusion' if they are to be
   properly ordered to our ultimate end.
49 ST IIa IIae Q 59, art. 1.
50 IIa IIae Q 62, arts 1–4.
51 Thus the first three commandments direct us to God, reminding us to have no
   strange gods, to not take the name of God in vain, and to remember to keep
   holy the Lord's Day. Only when the virtue of faith and hope is established by
   directing our lives toward God can we then embody the virtue of charity where
   we love God and our neighbor. This leads us to the second table of the decalogue.
52 ST IIa IIae Q 66, art. 7.
53 See *Veritatis Splendor*, paragraph 80.
54 IIa IIae Q 78, art. 1, rep. obj. 5.
55 Quoted in Jonsen and Toulmin, *The Abuse of Casuistry* (Berkeley, University
   of California Press, 1988), p. 183.
56 IIa IIae Q 78, art. 1.
57 Tertullian, 'On Idolatry,' in *The Ante-Nicene Fathers*, vol. III: *Latin Christianity: Its Founder Tertullian* (Edinburgh, T. & T. Clark, 1989).
58 IIa IIae Q 77, art. 4.

## 14 The beauty of theology

1 Von Balthasar's trilogy is first his theological aesthetics *The Glory of the Lord*;
   second his *TheoDrama*; and third his *TheoLogic*.
2 Hans Urs von Balthasar, *The Glory of the Lord: A Theological Aesthetics*, vol.
   I: *Seeing the Form*, p. 18.
3 John Milbank, 'The Body By Love Possessed,' *Modern Theology*, vol. 3, no. 1
   (1986), p. 61.
4 See Milbank's 'Can Morality be Christian?' in *The Word Made Strange*.

5 Ibid., p. 229.

6 'Despite scarcity, despite our submission to the law which it imposes, we must act as if there were plenitude, and no death, since to believe is to believe that this is what really pertains, despite the fall' (*The Word Made Strange*, p. 229). Milbank worries that the language of virtue still assumes scarcity. Thus he places 'virtue' in scare-quotes, and suggests that other designations would be preferable to an 'ethic of virtue.' He writes that 'it is better to speak of a "charismatic ethic" or an "ethic of gift" than a Christian "ethic of virtue" – although one might also define this gift-ethic as an *anarchic* virtue-ethic' (ibid., p. 227).

7 *Theology and Social Theory*, pp. 326–30.

8 Milbank thus wonders whether the term 'virtue' can be appropriately applied to the Christian moral life. He refers to this account of virtue as 'non-heroic virtue' (ibid., p. 331), and as 'anarchic virtue' (*The Word Made Strange* p. 227). This is precisely because virtue here is gift rather than possession.

9 *Theology and Social Theory*, p. 423.

10 Ibid., p. 424.

11 See Milbank, 'Only Theology Overcomes Metaphysics,' in *The Word Made Strange*, particularly p. 44.

12 *Theology and Social Theory*, p. 208.

13 Ibid., p. 177.

14 My earlier discussion of Gutiérrez and Sobrino was an effort to show the extent to which I think this criticism is sound and unsound. In so far as they do use the language of the social sciences to present a natural social reality, the criticism is sound. However, in so far as they fail to carry out this incorporation of sociology into theology, which as I argued they fortunately have not accomplished, the criticism loses its power.

15 Ibid., p. 228.

16 Milbank, *The Word Made Strange,* p. 11.

17 Ibid., p. 3.

18 Karl Barth, 'Kant,' in *Protestant Thought: From Rousseau to Ritschl* (Salem, NH, Ayer & Co. Publishers, Inc., 1971), p. 167.

19 Milbank, Pickstock, and Ward (eds), *Radical Orthodoxy*, p. 33.

20 Barth, *Protestant Thought: From Rousseau to Ritschl*, pp. 150–87.

21 Milbank, *Theology and Social Theory*, p. 221. Milbank refuses to separate creation from redemption. Both re-present the same gracious event. This has prompted Nicholas Lash to suggest that 'Milbank is so (admirably) concerned to keep the "graciousness" of creation centre stage that he risks effacing those further distinctions between creation and election, for example, and between creation and incarnation, without which Christian narratives crumble into incoherence' ('Not Exactly Politics or Power?', *Modern Theology*, vol. 8, no. 4 (1992), p. 353). Barth's own position, that creation is the external basis of redemption and redemption the internal basis of creation, would indeed point in the direction of Milbank, although it would not lead to Milbank's conclusion.

22 Milbank, *Theology and Social Theory*, p. 223.

23 Milbank, *The Word Made Strange*, p. 32.

24 Ibid, pp. 14–15.

25 Milbank, *Theology and Social Theory*, p. 425.

26 Hans Urs von Balthasar, *Glaubhaft ist nur Liebe* (Einsiedeln, Johannes Verlag, 1963), p. 6.

27 Hans Urs von Balthasar, *The Glory of the Lord: A Theological Aesthetics*, vol. I: *Seeing the Form*, p. 9. The first two transcendentals are the true and the good.

28 Ibid., p. 80.

29 Ibid., p. 67.

30  As Edward T. Oakes notes in his analysis of von Balthasar's work: 'One of the key methodological presuppositions of Balthasar's theology is that content and form can in fact never be neatly separated out from each other' (*Pattern of Redemption: The Theology of Hans Urs von Balthasar*, New York, Continuum, 1997, p. 108).
31  Hans Urs von Balthasar, *The Glory of the Lord*, vol. I, p. 180.
32  *The Word Made Strange*, p. 123.
33  Ibid., p. 130.
34  Milbank states:

> I am implying here that an approach to Christology from the context of ecclesiology actually allows a full retrieval of the Chalcedonian position.... I do not wish to disguise the fact that I am transposing Chalcedonian orthodoxy into a new idiom which only perfects it by dissolving 'substantial' notions of subjectivity which it did not always fully overcome.
>
> (Ibid., pp. 156–7)

This is what I mean by suggesting that he eviscerates Jesus of 'substantial' content. See also his 'Postmodern Critical Augustinianism: A Short Summa in Forty-Two Responses to Unasked Questions,' in Graham Ward (ed.) *The Postmodern God* (Oxford, Blackwell, 1998), pp. 265–79.

35  Milbank, *The Word Made Strange*, p. 150.
36  Mark MacIntosh and David Cunningham were of immense help to me in understanding Milbank on this point.
37  Ibid., p. 146.
38  Ibid., pp. 150–2.
39  This Christology bears some striking resemblance to Sobrino's, although Sobrino still seeks the historical Jesus behind the tradition's practice.
40  Op. cit., p. 150.
41  Milbank writes:

> The words of Jesus are thus 'strongly poetic' in that they establish a new possibility of truth and cannot be abandoned. While Jesus's whole being seems to be directed towards the production of such verbal works as opening up the situation of man in relation to God, it is equally the case that he aims to recover from his more concrete works a plenitude of significance. Here he seems to learn from his own works his own nature, in so far as they are works the Father has given him to do. Yet above and beyond all this, he seems at times to be saying, particularly in St. John's Gospel, that he himself is the message.
>
> (Ibid., p. 135)

42  Ibid., p. 164.
43  Ibid., pp. 154–5.
44  Milbank considers the Son 'as Logos meaning an infinite aesthetic plenitude of expression, which yet does not pre-determine in "totalizing" fashion, a freedom of interpretation' (ibid., p. 187).
45  Ibid., p. 285.
46  Ibid., pp. 220–1.
47  Ibid., p. 228.
48  Ibid., p. 262.
49  Ibid., p. 269.
50  Ibid., p. 285.
51  Milbank himself is accused of a kind of crypto-fascism or colonization of the other, rendering him or her to nothing; see Rom Coles, 'Storied Others and Possibilities of Caritas: Milbank and Neo-Nietzschean Ethics,' *Modern Theology*, vol. 8, no. 4 (1992), pp. 331–51. In this essay Coles argued that

Milbank's meta-narrative colonizes the other because Milbank argued that his Christian meta-narrative needed no reference to 'external supplementation.' For Coles, the result is that we cannot learn from others and thus it renders their narratives empty. In contrast, a 'more heterogeneous space' is necessary. Coles seems to read Milbank with suspicion because he thinks Christianity is false. His position does precisely what he accuses Milbank of doing: it seeks to convert us away from Christianity to a different world described by Nietzsche. Curiously enough, Milbank's refusal of 'external supplementation' is not a refusal to hear or listen to those outside the Christian narrative. It is a refusal of the necessity of supplementing a particular narrative with 'some universal, and so foundationalist, principle of "suspicion".' It is precisely in his refusal of an antagonistic structure in favor of the Christian narrative that Milbank can produce a non-antagonist posture toward others. See *Theology and Social Theory*, p. 389.

52 *The Word Made Strange*, p. 276.
53 Milbank contends that

> the legacy of traditionalism has led Catholics again and again to assume that a 'natural' social order must still in some fashion be in place ('surely providence cannot have abandoned us?' seems to be the unspoken thought). Thereby one runs into the contradiction of thinking both that liberal capitalism subverts the natural order, and yet that it in some sense still discloses it. Catholic social teaching becomes in consequence a grotesque hybrid: liberal Lockean understandings of property rights, and Smithian construals of the supposed 'contribution' of capital to production are freely incorporated, and yet upon them is superimposed an organicist, patriarchal vision of society. Capital and labour are here constantly conceived as belonging to a *natural* hierarchy, such that they should ideally be united in corporate harmony: this is of course to disguise the initially rawly coercive and quite unpatriarchal origins of the specifically modern power structure. Once one has combined modern formal emptiness and de facto rule of coercive power with paternalist sentiment, then what one has is kitsch, and a doctrine that in the end will only give a sentimental colouring to, and also emotionally reinforce, a culture of violence.
>
> (Ibid., p. 283)

54 Ibid., p. 284.
55 Ibid., p. 277.
56 So Milbank argues that

> a workable and authentic socialism cannot replace the operation of the market with exhaustive central planning. Instead it must discover a way of ensuring that market exchanges are also democratically or freely assented-to transactions – the outcomes of processes of free and equal negotiation – which repeatedly seek to preserve or extend a distribution of resources held to be 'just'.
>
> (Ibid., p. 271)

This is not the market socialism advocated by John Paul II for two reasons: First, Milbank's proposal 'accords no place to pure market forces of supply and demand regarded as essentially indifferent to the pursuit of justice and the presence of collective democratic and individual unconstrained agreement' (ibid., p. 271). Second, this 'rules out the exploitation of scarcity and necessity for profit and the automatic legitimacy of any expressed "need", while not at all trying to inhibit the free proliferation of needs that can be judged legitimate and beneficial' (ibid.).

57 *Theology and Social Theory*, p. 14.

58  Ibid., p. 15.
59  Milbank, 'Socialism of the Gift, Socialism by Grace,' *New Black Friars*, vol. 77, no. 9 (1996), p. 545.
60  Milbank, 'Midwinter Sacrifice,' *Studies in Christian Ethics*, vol. 10, no. 2 (1997), p. 13.
61  Milbank, 'Can a Gift Be Given?', *Modern Theology*, vol. 11, no. 1 (1995), p. 136.
62  Milbank, 'Socialism of the Gift, Socialism by Grace,' p. 544.

## 15 Conclusion

1  This does not imply that such infallibility should be understood through a mere assertion of power similar to the function of the *polis*. In fact, it implies the opposite.
2  Maria Bingemer, 'Women in the Future of the Theology of Liberation,' *Expanding the View: Gustavo Gutiérrez and the Future of Liberation Theology* (Maryknoll, New York, Orbis Books, 1988), p. 188 and 'A Post-Christian and Postmodern Christianism,' *Liberation Theologies, Postmodernity and the Americas* (London, Routledge, 1997), pp. 89–90.
3  See Novak's 'Toward a Theology of the Corporation,' where he applies Isaiah 53:2–3 'to the modern corporation, a much despised incarnation of God's presence in the world' in Max Stackhouse (ed.) *On Moral Business* (Grand Rapids, MI, W. B. Eerdmans, 1995), p. 775.

# Index